Wisdom of the Daoist Masters

Léon Wieger

WISDOM OF THE DAOIST MASTERS
Lao Zi, Lie Zi and Zhuang Zhou

LÉON WIEGER

WISDOM OF THE DAOIST MASTERS
© and translation 2022 by Daniel Bernardo

ANTIQUA SAPIENTIA

Translated from:

LES PÈRES DU SYSTÈME TAOISTE

Léon Wieger

ISBN: 978-1-989586-82-2

Table of Contents

Preface...   1

Dao De Jing
(Treatise of the Principle and its Action)

Book I...   5

Chapter 1 (text)...   5

Chapter 2 (text)...   6

Chapter 3 (text)...   7

Chapter 4 (text)...   7

Chapter 5 (text)...   8

Chapter 6 (text)...   9

Chapter 7 (text)...   9

Chapter 8 (text)...   10

Chapter 9 (text)...   11

Chapter 10 (text).   11

Chapter 11 (text).   12

Chapter 12 (text).   12

Chapter 13 (text).   13

Chapter 14 (text).   13

Chapter 15 (text).   14

Chapter 16 (text).   15

Chapter 17 (text).   15

Chapter 18 (text).   16

Chapter 19 (text).   16

Chapter 20 (text).   17

Chapter 21 (text).   17

Chapter 22 (text).   18

Chapter 23 (text).   18

Chapter 24 (text).   19

Chapter 25 (text).   19

Chapter 26 (text).   20

Chapter 27 (text).   20

Chapter 28 (text).   20

Chapter 29 (text).   21

Chapter 30 (text).   21

Chapter 31 (text).   22

Chapter 32 (text).   22

Chapter 33 (text).   23

Chapter 34 (text).   23

Chapter 35 (text).   23

Chapter 36 (text).   24

Chapter 37 (text).   24

Book II   25

Chapter 38 (text).   25

Chapter 39 (text).   25

Chapter 40 (text).   26

Chapter 41 (text).   26

Chapter 42 (text).   27

Chapter 43 (text).   27

Chapter 44 (text).   27

Chapter 45 (text).   27

Chapter 46 (text).   28

Chapter 47 (text).   28

Chapter 48 (text).   28

Chapter 49 (text).   28

Chapter 50 (text).   28

Chapter 51 (text). 29

Chapter 52 (text). 29

Chapter 53 (text). 30

Chapter 54 (text). 30

Chapter 55 (text). 30

Chapter 56 (text). 31

Chapter 57 (text). 31

Chapter 58 (text). 31

Chapter 59 (text). 32

Chapter 60 (text). 32

Chapter 61 (text). 32

Chapter 62 (text). 33

Chapter 63 (text). 33

Chapter 64 (text). 33

Chapter 65 (text). 34

Chapter 66 (text). 34

Chapter 67 (text). 34

Chapter 68 (text). 35

Chapter 69 (text). 35

Chapter 70 (text). 35

Chapter 71 (text). 36

Chapter 72 (text). 36

Chapter 73 (text). 36

Chapter 74 (text). 37

Chapter 75 (text). 37

Chapter 76 (text). 37

Chapter 77 (text). 38

Chapter 78 (text). 38

Chapter 79 (text). 38

Chapter 80 (text). 39

Chapter 81 (text). 39

Chongxu Zhenjing
(Treatise on perfect emptiness)

Chapter 1 - Genesis and Transformation 41

Chapter 2 - Natural Simplicity.. 49

Chapter 3 - Psychical States...   60

Chapter 4 - Extinction and Union   66

Chapter 5 - The Cosmic Continuum   74

Chapter 6 - Fate   85

Chapter 7 - Yang Zhu.   91

Chapter 8 - Anecdotes   99

Zhuangzi
(The Treatise of the Transcendent Master from *Nan Hua*)

Chapter 1 - Towards the Ideal...   111

Chapter 2 - Universal Harmony   114

Chapter 3 - Maintenance of the Vital Principle..   120

Chapter 4 - The World of Men..   121

Chapter 5 - Perfect Action.   126

Chapter 6 - The Principle, First Master   130

Chapter 7 - The Government of Princes   137

Chapter 8 - Webbed Feet   140

Chapter 9 - Trained Horses   142

Chapter 10 - Thieves, Small and Great   143

Chapter 11 - True and False Politics   146

Chapter 12 - Heaven and Earth   152

Chapter 13 - The Influence of Heaven.   160

Chapter 14 - Natural Evolution   165

Chapter 15 - Wisdom and Stultification..   170

Chapter 16 - Nature and Convention   172

Chapter 17 - The Autumn Flood..   174

Chapter 18 - Perfect Joy.   180

Chapter 19 - The Meaning of Life   184

Chapter 20 - Voluntary Obscurity   191

Chapter 21 - Transcendent Action...   196

Chapter 22 - Knowledge of the Principle   202

Chapter 23 - Return to Nature..   210

Chapter 24 - Simplicity..   216

Chapter 25 - Truth..   224

Chapter 26 - Fate   230

Chapter 27 - Speech and Words   235

Chapter 28 - Independence 238

Chapter 29 - Politicians 245

Chapter 30 - Swordsmen 251

Chapter 31 - The Old Fisherman.. 253

Chapter 32 - Wisdom. 257

Chapter 33 - Various Schools 261

Subject Index 269

The Principle 269

The Virtue of the Principle 269

The Great Whole. 270

Nature... 270

Artificial, conventional 270

Against nature 270

The Sage 270

Psychical states 271

Single anecdotes.. 272

Repeated anecdotes 272

Index of Names 273

Preface

This volume contains what has come down to our times of the work of three Chinese thinkers, *Lao Zi*, *Lie Zi* and *Zhuang Zhou*, who lived between the sixth and fourth centuries BC.

Lao Zi, the Old Master, was a contemporary of Confucius, about twenty years his senior. His life probably spanned the period 570-490 BC (Confucius' dates are 552-479 BC). Nothing about this man is historically certain. According to Daoist tradition he was a librarian at the court of *Zhou* and saw Confucius once, around 501 BC. Tired of the disorder of the empire, he left it and never returned. As he was about to cross the western pass, he composed for his friend, the keeper of the pass, *Yin Xi*, the famous writing translated in this volume. This too is a Daoist tradition. In the very brief and insignificant note dedicated to him around 100 BC, *Sima Qian* says that, according to some, the Old Master's surname was *Li*, his common name *Er*, his noble name *Baiyang*, and his posthumous name *Dan* (hence the posthumous appellation *Lao Dan*). But, adds the famous historian, who was, like his father, more than half a Daoist, "others say otherwise, and of the Old Master we can only ascertain this, that having loved obscurity above all else, this man deliberately erased the trace of his life." (*Shi Ji*, ch. 63). - I will not explain here the legend of *Lao Zi*, since this volume is historical.

It is said that *Lie Zi*, the master *Lie*, whose name was *Lie Yukou*, lived, obscure and poor, in the principality of *Zheng*, for forty years. He was driven out by famine in 398 BC. It is said that his disciples wrote down the gist of his teaching at that time. These data, which are based solely on the Daoist tradition, have been attacked, often and strongly. But the critics of the bibliographical index *Sikucuan Shu*, judged that the writing should be maintained.

Master *Zhuang*, whose name is *Zhuang Zhou*, is hardly known to us. He must have been in the twilight of his life, around 330 BC. *Sima Qian* says that he was very learned (*Shi Ji*, appendix), spent his life in obscurity and poverty, fighting briskly against the theories and abuses of his time.

It is, then, between 500-330 BC that we must place the elaboration of the ideas contained in this volume. I say ideas, not writings; here is the reason:

Of *Lao Zi*, tradition formally asserts that he wrote. A close examination of his work seems to prove the tradition right. It is, in effect, a tirade, all at once, taken up from the beginning when the author has strayed; a string of points and maxims, rather than a continuous essay; a statement by a man who clarifies and completes his thought, not obscure but very profound, by repeating, retouching, insisting. At first, there was no division into books and chapters. The division was made later, rather clumsily.

As for *Lie Zi* and *Zhuang Zhou*, an examination of the two treatises bearing their names shows clearly that these two men did not write. The treatises consist of a collection of notes, of index cards, collected by listeners often with variants and errors, then collated, scrambled and reclassified by copyists, interpolated by tendentious non-Daoist hands, so that, in the present text, there are some pieces diametrically contrary to the certain doctrine of the authors. The chapters are the work of those who collated the parts. They were constructed by putting together what was more or less the same. Many of them were thrown into disarray by the accident that marred so many ancient Chinese writings, the breaking of the joint of a bundle of tablets and mixing them up. — It should be noted that these Daoist treatises were not included in the destruction of books in 213 BC.

The doctrine of these three authors is one. *Lie Zi* and *Zhuang Zhou* develop *Lao Zi*, and claim that his ideas go back to Emperor *Huang Di*, founder of the Chinese empire. These ideas are, more or less, those of India in contemporary times, that of the *Upanishads*. A realistic pantheism, not idealistic.

In the beginning there was only one being, not intelligent but a fatal law, not spiritual but material, imperceptible by dint of tenuousness, at first motionless, *Dao* the Principle, for everything derived from it. One day this Principle began to emit *De*, its Virtue, which acting in two alternative modes *yin* and *yang*, produced as if by condensation the heaven, the earth and the air between them, unintelligent agents of the production of all sentient beings. These sentient beings come and go in a circular evolution, birth, growth, decay, death, rebirth, etc. The High Sovereign (Heavenly Sovereign) of the Annals and the Odes is not expressly denied, but is degraded, annulled, so that it is indirectly denied. Man has no other origin than the multitude of beings. He is more successful than others, that's all. And that, just this once. After his death, he enters a new existence of some kind, not necessarily human, not even necessarily animal or vegetable. Transformism, in the broadest sense of the word. The sage makes his life last, through temperance, tranquility, abstention from everything that causes fatigue or wear. That is why he remains in seclusion and darkness. If he is removed by force, he governs and manages according to the same principles, without getting tired or worn out, doing as little as possible, if possible doing nothing, so as not to hinder the rotation of the cosmic wheel, universal evolution. Apathy for abstraction. Seeing everything from such a height, from such a distance, so that everything seems to merge into one, without details, or individuals; consequently there is no interest, no passion. Above all, there is no system, no rule, no art, no morality. There is nothing good or bad, there is no penalties. Follow the instincts of your nature. Let the world go on day by day. Evolve with the great whole.

For the correct understanding of the content of this volume, it remains to point out the following points.

Many of the characters used by the ancient Daoists are taken in their primitive etymological sense, a sense that has since fallen out of use or become rare. Hence a special language, typical of these authors. Thus, *Dao De Jing* does not mean "Treatise on the Way and its Virtue" (meanings derived from *Dao* and *De*), but "Treatise on the Principle and its Action" (older meaning).

None of the facts alleged by *Lie Zi* and especially by *Zhuang Zhou* have historical value. The men they mention are no more real than the personified abstractions they represent. They are oratorical devices, nothing more. One must be especially wary of taking Confucius' statements, all invented at will, as true. Some ill-informed authors have fallen into this error in the past, and have in good faith imputed to the Sage defects lent to him by his enemy *Zhuang Zhou*, in order to ridicule him.

Confucius, the target of *Zhuang Zhou*, presents himself in three positions. — First, as the author of conventionalism and the destroyer of naturalism; therefore as the sworn enemy of Daoism. This is the real note. All these texts are authentic. — Second, as a preacher, as a convert, of Daoism more or less pure, to his own disciples. Fiction sometimes very cleverly conducted, to show, from the Master's own speeches, the inadequacy of Confucianism and the advantages of Daoism. Authentic texts, but not to be imputed to Confucius. — Thirds, some few texts, purely Confucian, are interpolations. I will take note of all of them.

Similarly, the paragons of the Confucian system, *Huang Di* (the Yellow Emperor), *Yao*, *Shun*, the great *Yu* and others, are presented in three positions. — First, abhorred as authors or instigators of artificial civilization. This is the real note. Authentic texts. — Second, praised for a particular point, common to Confucians and Daoists. Authentic texts. — Third, praised in general, without restriction. Some Confucian interpolations, which I will note. — I also believe that, in the text, more than one *Yao*, or *Shun*, are copyists' errors, who have written one character for another.

The date when *Lao Zi*'s work was called *Dao De Jing* is unknown. The name appears in *Huai Nan Zi*, in the 2nd century BC. — In 742, the Emperor *Huan Zhong* of the *Tang* dynasty gave *Lie Zi*'s treatise the title *Chongxu Zhenjing*, "Treatise on Perfect Emptiness"; and to *Zhuang Zhou*'s treatise the title *Nan Hua Chen Jing*, "Treatise of the Transcendent Master of *Nan Hua*" (the name of a place where *Zhuang Zhou* is said to have stayed), both authors having received the title of *Zhen*

Ren, Transcendent Men. The *Dao De Jing* is also often called *Dao De Zeng Jing*, since the same time.

Notes clarify difficult passages, either in the text itself or at the foot of the page. — For all proper names, consult the table of names at the end of the volume.

I have tried to make my translation as easy to read as possible, without detracting from the accuracy of the interpretation. For my aim is to make available to all readers these ancient thoughts, which have since been rethought so many times by others, and taken by them as new.

Xian Xian (He Jian Fu) April 2, 1913

Dao De Jing[1]
(Treatise of the Principle and its Action)
LAO ZI

BOOK I

CHAPTER 1 (TEXT)

A. The principle that can be enunciated is not the principle that has always been. The being that can be named is not the being that has always been. Before time, there was an ineffable, unnamable being.

B. When it was still unnamable, it conceived heaven and earth. After it became namable, he gave birth to all beings.

C. These two acts are one, with two different names. The one generating act is the mystery of origin. Mystery of mysteries. The door through which all the wonders that fill the stage of the universe were opened.

D. Man's knowledge of the universal principle depends upon his state of mind. The mind habitually free from passions, knows its mysterious essence. The habitually passionate mind will know only its effects.

Summary of commentaries

Before time, and from all times, there was a being existing by itself, eternal, infinite, complete, omnipresent. It is impossible to name it, to speak of it, because human terms apply only to sentient beings. Now, the primordial being was primitively, and still is, essentially non-sentient. Outside of this being, before the origin, there was nothing. It

---

1   The *Dao De Jing*, previously transliterated as "Tao Te Ching" (according to Wade-Giles romanization, now in disuse), is attributed to *Lao Zi*, also known as *Lao Tse* (Wade-Giles) (Translator Note).

is called wu, *formless,* huan, *mystery, or* dao, *the Principle. The time when there was no sentient being, when the essence of the beginning existed alone, is called* xian tian, *before Heaven. This essence possessed two immanent properties, the concentration of* yin *and the expansion of* yang, *which were externalized one day, in the sentient forms of heaven (*yang*) and earth (*yin*). That day was the beginning of time. From that moment on, the beginning could be called by the double term heaven-earth. The binomial heaven-earth gave rise to all existing sentient beings. We call you, sentient being, this heaven-earth binomial which produces through* de, *the virtue of the Principle, all its products which fill the world. The times after the externalization of heaven-earth are called* hou tian, *after heaven. The* yin *state of concentration and repose, of imperceptibility, which was that of the Principle before time, is its own state. The* yang *state of expansion and action, of manifestation in sentient beings, is its state in time, in a certain improper way. These two states of the Principle correspond in man's faculty of knowledge to rest and activity, that is, to emptiness and fullness. When the human mind produces ideas, is full of images, is moved by the passions, then it is only capable of knowing the effects of the Principle, the various sensible beings. When the human mind, absolutely arrested, is completely empty and calm, it is a pure and clear mirror, capable of reflecting the ineffable and unnamable essence of the Principle itself. — Compare with chapter 32.*

CHAPTER 2 (TEXT)

A. All men have the notion of the beautiful, and by it (by opposition) that of the non beautiful (the ugly). All men have the notion of the good, and by it (by contrast) that of the not good (the bad). Thus, being and nothingness, the difficult and the easy, the long and the short, the high and the low, the sound and the tone, the before and the after, are correlative notions; the one being known, the other is revealed.

B. Being thus, the Sage serves without acting, teaches without speaking.

C. He allows all beings to come into being without frustrating them, to live without monopolizing them, to act without exploiting them.

D. He does not attribute to himself the effects produced and, consequently, these effects remain.

Summary of commentaries

The correlatives, opposites, contraries like yes and no, have all entered this world through the common door, have all come out of the One Principle (Ch. 1 C). They are not subjective illusions of the human mind, but objective states, responding to the two alternate states of the Principle, yin and yang, concentration and expansion. The deep reality, the Principle, remains always the same, essentially; but the alternation of its rest and its movement creates the play of causes and effects, an incessant coming and going. The Sage gives free rein to this play. He refrains from intervening, either with physical actions or with moral pressure. He refrains from putting his finger in the gear of causes, in the perpetual movement of natural evolution, for fear of distorting this complicated and delicate mechanism. All he does, when he does something, is to let his example be seen. He leaves to each his place under the sun, his freedom, his works. He does not attribute to himself the general effect produced (good government), which belongs to all causes. Consequently, this effect (good order), not being subject to the jealousy or ambition of others, is likely to last.

CHAPTER 3 (TEXT)

A. If skill were not emphasized, no one would try harder. If rare objects were not rewarded, no one would steal more. If nothing tempting were shown, hearts would rest.

B. Therefore, the policy of the Sages is to empty men's minds and fill their bellies, to weaken their initiative and strengthen their bones. Their constant care is to keep the people in ignorance and apathy.

C. To make the intelligent dare not act. For there is nothing that cannot be improved by the practice of non-action.

Summary of commentaries.

All emotion, all disorder, all perversion of the mind, comes from the fact that the mind has been brought into communication, through the senses, with attractive and seductive external objects. The sight of the pomp of the rich makes men ambitious. The sight of precious objects piled up, makes men thieves. Suppress all objects capable of tempting, or at least the knowledge of them, and the world will enjoy perfect peace. Make men productive and docile beasts of labor; see to it that they are well fed and do not think; hinder all initiative, suppress all enterprise. Knowing nothing, men will have no envy, will require no supervision, and will be profitable to the State.

CHAPTER 4 (TEXT)

A. The Principle abounds and produces, but without filling.

B. Empty abyss, it seems to be (is) the ancestor (origin) of all beings.

C. It is peaceful, simple, modest, friendly.

D. Spreading in waves, it seems to go on (remain) always the same.

E. I don't know whose son it is (where it comes from). He seems to have been (it was) before the Sovereign.

Summary of commentaries

This important chapter is devoted to the description of the Principle. Because of the abstraction of the subject, and perhaps also out of prudence, since his conclusions clash with ancient Chinese traditions, Lao Zi uses the attenuated term "seem" three times, instead of the categorical term "to be". — He does not declare himself on the origin of the Principle, but makes it prior to the High Sovereign of the Annals and the Odes. This Sovereign cannot therefore be, for Lao Zi, a God creator of the universe. Nor is he a God who rules the universe, for Lao Zi will never give him a place in his system as such. Therefore, the statement that he is subsequent to the Principle is practically tantamount to his negation. — The Principle, in itself, is like an immense abyss, like an infinite source. All sentient beings are produced by its externalization, by its virtue "de", which operates in the heaven-earth binomial. But sentient beings, terminations of the Principle, do not add to the Principle, they do not increase it, they do not fill it, as the text says. As they do not go out of it, they do not diminish it, nor do they empty it, and the Principle remains always the same. — Four qualities are attributed to it, which will later often be proposed in imitation of the Sage (e.g., in chapter 56). These qualities are rather ill-defined by the positive terms peaceful, simple, modest, and kind. The terms of Lao Zi *text are more complex: Soft, without point or edge; not tangled or complicated; it is not dazzling, but shines with a tempered, rather dull light; it willingly shares the dust, the baseness of the vulgar.*

CHAPTER 5 (TEXT)

A. Heaven and earth are not kind to the beings they produce, but treat them like straw dogs.

B. Like heaven and earth, the Sage is not kind to the people he governs, but treats them like straw dogs.

C. The intermediate of heaven and earth, the seat of the Principle, the place from which its virtue acts, is like a bellows, like the bag of a bellows of which heaven and earth would be the two boards, which empties itself without exhausting itself, which moves outwardly without ceasing.

D. This is all that we can understand of the Principle and its productive action. To attempt to detail it in words and numbers would be a waste of time. Let us remain with this global notion.

Summary of commentaries

There are two kinds of goodness: First, the goodness of the higher order, which loves the whole, and loves the constituent parts of this whole, only in so far as they are constituent parts, not for themselves, nor for their own sake; second, the goodness of the lower order, which loves individuals, in themselves and for their particular good. Heaven and earth, which produce all beings by the virtue of the Principle, produce them unconsciously, and are not good to them, says the text. They are good to them, with superior goodness, not with inferior goodness, says the commentary. That is, they treat them with cold opportunism, considering only the universal good, not their particular good; making them flourish if they are useful, suppressing them when they are useless. This cold opportunism is expressed by the term straw dog. In ancient times, at the head of funeral processions were carried figures of straw dogs, which were supposed to catch all evil influences in their wake. Before the funerals, they were carefully prepared and well cared for, because they would soon be useful. After the funeral, they were destroyed, because they had become harmful, filled as they were with noxious influences, as Zhuang Zhou teaches us in chapter 14 D. — In government, the Sage should act as heaven and earth. He should love the State, not individuals. He should favor useful matters and suppress useless, troublesome or harmful ones, according to expediency, without any other consideration. Chinese history is full of applications of this principle. A minister, long pampered, is suddenly executed because the political orientation has changed and he would be a nuisance from now on, whatever his previous merits may have been; his time has come; in the universal revolution, the straw dog is eliminated. It is not necessary to show that these ideas are diametrically opposed to the Christian notions of Providence, of God's love for each of his creatures, of grace, of blessing, etc. That is goodness of a lower order, say the Daoist sages, with a scornful smile. — This is followed by the famous comparison of the universal bellows, to which Daoist authors often refer. It will be developed in the next chapter. — In conclusion, this is all that is known about the Principle and its action. It produces the universe made of beings; but it cares only for the universe, not for any being. If the term "cares" can be applied to a producer who performs his work without knowing it. The Brahma of the Hindus at least has some complacency in the soap bubbles it blows; the Principle of the Daoists does not.

CHAPTER 6 (TEXT)

A. The transcendent expansive power that resides in the middle space, the virtue of the Principle, does not die. It is ever the same, and acts the same, without diminution or cessation.

B. It is the mysterious mother of all beings.

C. The door of this mysterious mother is the root of heaven and earth, the Principle.

D. Proliferating, it is not spent. Acting, it does not tire.

Summary of commentaries

It should not be forgotten that the work of Lao Zi was not originally divided into chapters, and that the division, made later, is often arbitrary, sometimes awkward. This chapter continues and completes sections C and D of chapter 5. It deals with the genesis of beings, by virtue of the Principle, which resides in the middle space, in the bag of the universal bellows, from which everything emanates. Sections A and B refer to the virtue of the Principle; sections C and D to the Principle itself. The term gate, the idea of two swinging doors, signifies the alternative movement, the play of yin and yang, the first modification of the Principle. This play was the root, i.e., it produced heaven and earth... In other words, it was through the Principle that heaven and earth, the two boards of the bellows, were externalized. From the Principle emanates the universal producing virtue, which operates through heaven and earth, between heaven and earth, in the intervening space, producing all sentient beings without exhaustion and without fatigue.

CHAPTER 7 (TEXT)

A. If heaven and earth last forever, it is because they do not live for themselves.

B. Following this example, the wise man, by withdrawing, advances; by neglecting himself, he preserves himself. Since he does not seek his own benefit, everything turns in his favor.

Summary of commentaries

If heaven and earth last forever and are not destroyed by jealousy, envy and enemies, it is because they live for all beings, doing good to all. If they were to seek their own interest, says Wang Bi, *they would come into conflict with all beings, for a particular interest is always the enemy of the general interest. But, as they are perfectly selfless, all beings come to them. — Likewise, if the Sage were to seek his own interest, he would have nothing but trouble, and would not succeed in anything. If he is selfless as heaven and earth, he will have only friends and succeed in everything. — To endure successfully, one must forget oneself, says* Jiang Hong Yang. *Heaven and earth do not think of themselves, so nothing is more enduring. If the Sage has no self-love, his person will endure and his enterprises will succeed. If not, it will be very different. —* Wu Deng *reminds us, and rightly so, that by heaven and earth we should understand the Principle that acts through heaven and earth. It is, then, the unselfishness of Principle that is proposed as an example to the Sage in this chapter.*

CHAPTER 8 (TEXT)

A. Transcendent goodness is like water.

B. Water likes to do good to all beings; it does not strive for any definite form or position, but places itself in the low places that no one wants.

In so doing, it is the image of the Principle.

C. Following his example, those who imitate the Principle, lower themselves, go deeper; they are beneficent, sincere, regulated, efficient, and adjust themselves to the times. They do not fight for their own interests, but yield. Therefore, they feel no contradiction.

Summary of commentaries

This chapter is a continuation of the previous one. After the altruism of heaven and earth, the altruism of water is proposed as an example. Ge Zhanggeng *summarizes it thus: Shunning the heights, water seeks the depths. It is not idle, day or night. Above it forms rain and dew, below it rivers. Everywhere it waters, it purifies. It does good and is useful to all. It always obeys and never resists. If you block it, it stops; if you open a floodgate, it flows. Moreover, it adapts itself to any vessel, round, square or otherwise. — The inclination of men is just the opposite. Naturally, they love their profit. They must imitate water. He who bends down to serve others will be loved by all and will have no adversaries.*

Chapter 9 (text)

A. It is impossible to keep a vessel full without anything coming out of it; it would have been better not to fill it. To keep a razor extremely sharp, without its edge dulling, is impossible; it would have been better not to sharpen it so much. To keep a room full of gold and precious stones, without anything being stolen, is impossible; it would have been better not to amass this treasure.

No extreme can be maintained for long. Every apogee is necessarily followed by decadence. It is the same with man…

B. He who, having become rich and powerful, is proud of himself, is preparing his own ruin.

C. To retire, at the height of merit and fame, is the way to heaven.

Summary of commentaries

A vessel absolutely full, overflows at the slightest movement or loses its contents by evaporation. An extremely sharp blade loses its edge due to the effect of atmospheric agents. A treasure will inevitably be stolen or confiscated. When the sun is at its zenith, it sets; when it is full, the moon begins to wane. In a revolving wheel, the point that has risen to the top, immediately falls again. He who has understood this universal and inescapable law of decrease which necessarily follows increase, resigns himself, withdraws, as soon as he realizes that his fortune is at its height. He does so, not out of fear of humiliation, but out of concern for his own preservation, and above all to unite himself perfectly with the intention of destiny… When he feels that the time has come, says a commentator, the Sage cuts his bonds, escapes from his cage, leaves the world of vulgarities. As the Mutations say, he no longer serves a prince, because his heart is higher. So did many Daoists, who withdrew into private life, at the apex of their fortune, and ended up in voluntary obscurity.

Chapter 10 (text)

A. Keep your body, and your spermatic soul closely united, not separated.

B. Make the inspired air, turned into an aerial soul, animate this compound and keep it intact as the child that has just been born.

C. Abstain from too deep considerations, so as not to wear yourself out.

D. As for love for the people and concern for the State, simply do not act.

E. Let the gates of heaven open and close, without wanting to do anything, without interfering.

F. Know everything, be informed of everything, and yet remain indifferent as if you knew nothing.

G. Produce, breed, without taking credit for what you have produced, without demanding retribution for your action, without imposing yourself on your governed.

This is the formula of transcendent action.

Summary of commentaries

Man has two souls, a double life principle. First, pai, *the soul derived from the paternal sperm, the principle of genesis and development of the fetus in the mother's womb. The closer this soul is to the body, the healthier and stronger the new being will be. After birth, the absorption and condensation of air produces a second soul, the air soul, the principle of further development and especially of survival. Flexibility here means life, as opposed to the rigidity of a corpse. The newborn child is, for Daoists, the ideal perfection of nature still absolutely intact and without any admixture. Later, this child will be interpreted as a transcendent inner being, the principle of survival. Sickness, excesses, weaken the union of the spermatic soul with the body, thus bringing sickness. Study, preoccupations, wear out the aerial soul, thus hastening death. The maintenance of the bodily compound and the aerial soul, by good hygiene, rest and aerotherapy; this is the program of the Daoist's life. — For G, compare chapter 2 C D.*

CHAPTER 11 (TEXT)

A. A wheel is made up of thirty perceptible spokes, but it is thanks to the central void, not perceptible, of the hub, that it turns.

B. Vessels are made of perceptible clay, but it is their non-perceptible hollow that serves.

C. The non-perceptible holes of the door and the windows are the essence of a house.

D. It is from the non-perceptible that the effectiveness, the result, comes from.

Summary of commentaries

This is related to sections A and B of the previous chapter. Man does not live from his perceptible body, but from his two non-perceptible, spermatic and aerial souls. Therefore, the Daoist takes special care of these two invisible entities. Whereas the common man does not believe in them, or does not pay attention to them, because they are invisible. What concerns him is the material, the perceptible. Now, in many perceptible beings, says the text, what is useful, what is effective, is what is not perceptible, their hollowness, their emptiness, a hole. The commentators generalize and say: all efficacy comes from emptiness; a being is only efficacious insofar as it is empty. — It seems that the ancient wheels had thirty spokes, because the month has thirty days.

CHAPTER 12 (TEXT)

A. The vision of colors blinds man's eyes. Hearing sounds blinds his hearing. The tasting of flavors wears out his taste. Running and hunting, by unleashing wild passions in him, make his heart overflow. The love of rare and hard-to-obtain objects drives him to efforts that are detrimental to him.

B. Therefore, the wise man cares for his stomach, not for his senses.

C. He renounces this, to embrace that (He renounces that which wears him out, to embrace that which preserves him).

Summary of commentaries

This chapter is related to the previous one. The stomach is the hollow, the void, and therefore the essential and effective part of man. It is the stomach that maintains the human compound and all its parts, through digestion and assimilation. It is therefore the object of the judicious care of the Daoist sage. It is easy to understand why bellies are so prized in China, and why great Daoist figures are very often depicted with pot-bellies. On the contrary, the Sage carefully abstains from the application of the senses, the exercise of the mind, curiosity, all activity and all passion that wear out the two souls and the composite.

CHAPTER 13 (TEXT)

A. The favor that can be lost is a source of anxiety. Greatness that can be ruined is a source of shame. What do these two phrases mean?

B. The first means that both the dedication to maintain the favors received and the fear of losing them fill the mind with anxiety.

C. The second warns that ruin often comes from too great a concern for self-aggrandizement. He who has no personal ambition need not fear ruin.

D. He who is concerned only with the greatness of the empire (and not with his own), he who desires only the good of the empire (and not his own), let the empire be entrusted to him (and it will be in good hands).

Summary of commentaries

Continuation of the previous chapter. Other causes of wear and tear, other precautions to be taken to avoid it. For those who are favored, who occupy positions, the preoccupation to maintain themselves wears out the soul and the body. Because deep down they are attached to their favors, to their position. Many Daoist sages were honored with the favor of the great, occupied high positions, without any inconvenience to them, detached as they were from all affection for their situation; desiring, not to maintain themselves, but to see their resignation accepted. Men of this class can be princes, emperors or ministers, without injury to themselves, and without injury to the empire, which they govern with the highest and entire disinterestedness. — The text of this chapter is defective in many modern editions.

CHAPTER 14 (TEXT)

A. Looking, it is not seen, because it is not visible. Listening, it is not heard, because it is silent. Touching, we do not feel it, because it is not palpable. These three attributes are not to be distinguished, for they designate the same being.

B. This being, the Principle, is not luminous above and dark below, like the opaque material bodies, so tenuous is it. It unfolds (continuous existence and action). It has no name of its own. It goes back to the time when there were no beings but itself. Superlatively devoid of form and shape, it is indeterminate. It has no parts; from the front it has no head, from the back it has no hindquarters.

C. It is this primordial Principle, which governs all beings, even the present ones. All that is, from the ancient origin, is the unfolding of the Principle.

Summary of commentaries

The first thirteen chapters form a series. Here the author starts from the beginning. A new description of the Principle, so dim that it is not perceptible; the nothingness of form; the indefinite infinite being; that it was before everything; that it was the cause of all. Picturesque description of de, its continuous and varied productive action, by the metaphor ji, unwinding a spool of thread. The meaning is clear: the various products of the Principle are the manifestations of its virtue; the infinite chain of these manifestations of the Principle's virtue may be called the winding of the Principle. — This important chapter presents no difficulty.

CHAPTER 15 (TEXT)

A. The sages of antiquity were subtle, abstract and profound to a degree that words cannot express. Therefore, I will use pictorial comparisons to make myself understood.

B. They were circumspect as one who crosses a frozen river; prudent as one who knows that his neighbors' eyes are upon him; reserved as a guest before his host. They were indifferent like melting ice (which is ice or water, which is neither ice nor water). They were rustic as a tree trunk (whose rough bark hides the excellent heartwood). They were empty like the valley (in comparison with the mountains that form it). They were accommodating as muddy water (they, the clear water, do not repel the mud, they do not refuse to live in contact with the vulgar, they are not selfish).

C. (To seek purity and peace in separation from the world is an exaggeration. They can be obtained in the world). Purity is obtained in the disturbance (of this world), through (inner) calm, provided one does not grieve over the impurity of the world. Peace is obtained in the movement (of this world), by him who knows how to take his part in this movement, and who does not become irritated by wishing it to stop.

D. He who keeps this rule of not consuming himself in fruitless desires of a chimerical state, will willingly live in darkness, and will not pretend to renew the world.

Summary of commentaries

Zhang Hongyang explains the last paragraph D, rather obscure because of its extreme conciseness, as follows: He will remain faithful to the teachings of the ancients and will not be seduced by new doctrines. This explanation seems difficult to support.

Chapter 16 (text)

A. He who has attained the peak of emptiness (indifference) will be firmly fixed in rest.

B. The innumerable beings come out (of non-being), and I see them return to it. They swarm, then all return to their roots.

C. To return to the root is to enter the state of rest. From this rest they come out, to a new destination. And so on, continuously, endlessly.

D. To recognize the law of this immutable continuity (of the two states of life and death) is wisdom. To ignore it is to insanely provoke misfortune (by its untimely interference).

E. He who knows that this law weighs upon beings is just (he treats all beings according to their nature, with equity), as a king should do, as heaven does, as the Principle does. And therefore he endures, and lives to the end of his days, without having made enemies.

Summary of commentaries

Immutability is an attribute proper to the Principle. Beings participate in it, in proportion to their acquired resemblance to the Principle. The absolutely indifferent Daoist sage, being the one who most resembles the Principle, is the most immutable in consequence. — Except for the Principle, all beings are subject to the continuous alternation of the two states of life and death. Commentators call this alternation the coming and going of the shuttle in the cosmic loom. Zhang Hongyang compares it to breathing, the active inhalation responding to life, the passive exhalation responding to death, the end of one being the beginning of the other. The man himself uses the lunar revolution as a term of comparison, the full moon is life, the new moon is death, with two intervening periods of growth and decay. All this is classical, and is repeated in all Daoist authors.

Chapter 17 (text)

A. In the early times (when everything was still in accordance with the action of the Principle in human things), the subjects hardly knew that they had a prince (so discreet was his action).

B. Later the people loved and flattered the prince (because of his benefits). Later they feared him (because of his laws), and despised him (because of his injustices). They became disloyal, because they were treated unjustly, and lost confidence, receiving only promises, which were never fulfilled.

C. How delicate was the touch of the ancient rulers. While everything prospered through their administration, their people imagined that they had done their own will in everything.

Summary of commentaries

The meaning is oblique, and the commentators are all in agreement. This utopia of imperceptible rule, without punishment and without reward, still haunted the brains of Chinese scholars not so long ago.

Chapter 18 (text)

A. When action in accordance with the Principle withered away (when men ceased to act spontaneously with goodness and equity), artificial principles of goodness and equity are invented; and those of prudence and wisdom, which soon degenerated into politics.

B. When parents no longer lived in the old natural harmony, an attempt was made to make up for this deficit by inventing artificial principles of filial piety and parental affection.

C. When the States fell into disorder, the type of faithful minister was invented.

Summary of commentaries

Principles and precepts, in a word conventional morality, useless in the age of spontaneous good, were invented when the world fell into decadence, as a remedy for that decadence. The invention was rather unfortunate. The only real remedy would have been to return to the primitive Principle. — This is Lao Zi's declaration of war against Confucius. All Daoist authors, Zhuang Zhou in particular, have declared themselves against artificial goodness and equity, the watchword of Confucianism.

Chapter 19 (text)

A. Reject wisdom and prudence (artificial, conventional, political, to return to primitive natural righteousness), and the people will be a hundred times happier.

B. Reject goodness and equity (artificial and conventional filial and paternal piety), and the people will return (for their sake, to natural goodness and equity) to spontaneous filial and paternal piety.

C. Reject art and profit, and evildoers will disappear (with primordial simplicity, they will return to primordial honesty).

D. Renounce these three artificial categories, for the artificial is good for nothing.

E. This is what you should strive for: to be simple, to be natural, to have few special interests and few desires.

Summary of commentaries

This chapter is a continuation of the previous one. It is perfectly clear. The commentators agree. Theme developed extensively by Zhuang Zhou.

CHAPTER 20 (TEXT)

A. Renounce all science and you will be free from all worry. What is the difference between "perhaps" and "no doubt" (about which the rhetoricians have so much to say). What is the difference between good and evil (about which the critics disagree) (These are trivialities, which prevent one from having a free mind. However, freedom of mind is necessary to enter into relation with the Principle).

B. No doubt, among the things that vulgar men fear, there are some things that are also to be feared; but not as they do, with disturbance of the mind, to the point of losing mental equilibrium.

C. Neither should we allow ourselves to be unbalanced by pleasure, as happens to them, when they have eaten a good meal, when they have contemplated the landscape from the top of a tower in springtime (with the accompaniment of wine, etc.).

D. I (the Sage) am as colorless and indefinite; as neutral as a child who has not yet experienced his first emotion; as without purpose and without goal.

E. The vulgar abound (in diverse knowledge), while I am poor (having rid myself of all uselessness), and seem ignorant, so much have I purified myself. They seem to be full of light, I seem to be dark. They search and scrutinize, I remain focused on myself. I float, indeterminate, like the vastness of the waters. They are full of talents, while I seem stubborn and uneducated.

F. I thus differ from the vulgar, because I revere and imitate the universal nourishing mother, the Principle.

Summary of commentaries

The text of this chapter varies in different editions; it must have been mutilated or retouched. The commentaries also differ widely. The obscurity comes, I think, from the fact that Lao Zi, *speaking of himself and proposing himself as a model for the disciples of the Principle, did not want to speak more clearly. It seems to me that* Zhang Hongyang *has interpreted his thought better.*

CHAPTER 21 (TEXT)

A. All beings who play a part in the great manifestation in the cosmic theater are derived from the Principle, by their virtue (their unfoldment).

B. The Principle it is indistinct and indeterminate. Oh, how indistinct and indeterminate! — In this indistinctness and indeterminacy there are types. Oh, how indistinct and indeterminate it is! — In this indistinctness and indeterminacy, there are beings in potency. Oh, how mysterious and obscure it is! — In this mystery, in this darkness, there is an essence, which is reality. — This is the kind of being which is the Principle.

C. From ancient times until now, its name (its being) remains the same, from it all beings have arisen.

D. How do I know that it was the origin of all beings? By this (by objective observation of the universe, which reveals that contingent beings must have come from the absolute).

Summary of commentaries

This lofty chapter is not obscure, and the commentators agree. All these notions are already known to us. This is the third chapter devoted to the definition of the Principle and its Virtue; clearer than the previous ones; as if Lao Zi, *by returning to it, had clarified his ideas.*

CHAPTER 22 (TEXT)

A. The ancients said: the incomplete will be completed, the curved will be straightened, the hollow will be filled, the worn out will be renewed; simplicity triumphs, multiplicity misleads.

B. Therefore, the Sage who holds fast to unity is the model of the empire (of the world, the ideal man). He shines, because he does not presume. He imposes himself, because he does not pretend to be right. We find merit in him, because he does not boast. He grows constantly, because he does not put pressure on himself. Because he opposes no one, no one opposes him.

C. Are not the axioms of the ancients quoted above full of meaning? Yes, everything flows spontaneously toward the one who is perfect (which does nothing to attract them).

Summary of commentaries

The meaning is clear. To cling to unity is, says Zhang Hongyang, *to forget oneself and all things, to concentrate on the contemplation of the original unity.*

CHAPTER 23 (TEXT)

A. To speak little and act only without effort, that is the formula.

B. An impetuous wind is not sustained for a morning, a torrential rain does not last a day. And yet these effects are produced by the sky and the earth (the most powerful of all agents. But they are forced effects, exaggerated, so they cannot be sustained). If heaven and earth cannot sustain a forced action, how much less can man.

C. He who conforms to the Principle, conforms his principles to that Principle, his action to the action of that Principle, his non-action to the inaction of that Principle. Thus, his principles, his actions, his inactions (speculations, interventions, abstentions), will always give him the pleasure of success (for, whatever happens or does not happen, the Principle evolves, therefore he is content).

D. (This doctrine of the abnegation of one's own opinions and actions is to the taste of few). Many believe in it only a little, others do not believe in it at all.

Summary of commentaries

The meaning is clear, and the commentators are in agreement. The text of this chapter is very incorrect in modern editions, having been edited unintelligently.

CHAPTER 24 (TEXT)

A. If you stand on tiptoe, you lose your balance. If you try to take steps that are too long, you do not advance. If you show off, you lose your reputation. If you assert yourself, you lose your influence. If you boast, you lose your reputation. If you push yourself, you stop growing.

B. In the light of the Principle, all these ways of acting are hateful, disgusting. For they are excess, superfluity; what indigestion is to the stomach, what a tumor is to the body. He who is principled (according to the Principle), does not act like this.

Summary of commentaries

This chapter is a continuation of the previous two. The meaning is clear. The commentators agree. Excess destroys natural simplicity.

CHAPTER 25 (TEXT)

A. It is a being of unknown origin, who existed before heaven and earth, imperceptible and indefinite, unique and immutable, omnipresent and unchanging, mother of everything that is.

B. I do not know an appropriate name for it. I call it Principle. If it had to be named, it could be called the Great, great going forth, great distance, great return (the beginning of the immense cyclic evolution of the cosmos, of the becoming and the end of all beings).

C. The name Great is appropriate (proportionally) for four (superimposed) beings: the emperor, the earth, heaven (classical Chinese triad) and the Principle. The emperor owes his greatness to the earth (his theater), the earth owes its greatness to heaven (which fertilizes it), heaven owes its greatness to the Principle (of which it is the principal agent). (Borrowed greatness, as we can see. Whereas) the Principle owes its essential greatness to its essentiality.

Summary of commentaries

Famous chapter; compare with chapter 1. Serious commentators agree, verbose ones babble. The Principle is called the mother of all that is, as the source of the being of all that is. It cannot be named, since it is formless nothingness, which is devoid of any accident to which a qualifier can be assigned. Indefinite Being, or Universal Principle, are the only terms properly applicable to it.

CHAPTER 26 (TEXT)

A. The heavy is the basis (root) of the light, repose is the support (prince) of motion (These things must always be united in a just temperament).

B. That is why a wise prince, when he travels (in his light chariot), never separates himself from the heavy chariots that carry his baggage. Through the beautiful landscapes he traverses, he lodges only in quiet places.

C. Alas, how could an emperor have given the empire the spectacle of mad conduct, losing by dint of frivolity all authority, and by dint of licentiousness all repose?

Summary of commentaries

Historical allusion to the emperor You Wang, *or to another, we do not know exactly. Commentators are of the opinion that this chapter is only an exhortation to regulated conduct.*

CHAPTER 27 (TEXT)

A. The good walker leaves no footprints, the good speaker offends no one, the good reckoner does not need to write anything down, the expert in locks makes locks that no one can open, the expert in knots, makes them in such a way that no one can untie them. (All specialists thus have their specialty, which is their glory, from which they profit).

B. Similarly, the Sage (Confucian politician), the professional savior of men and things, has his own procedures. He considers himself the born master of other men, whom he considers the material of his profession.

C. But this is to blind oneself (to veil the light, the Daoist principles). Not to want to rule, not to appropriate others, even if wise, seeming to be foolish (to persist in living in seclusion), this is the essential truth.

Summary of commentaries

Translated according to Zhang Hongyang, *who rightly points out that almost all commentators have erred in their interpretation of this chapter. Clear opposition of the Confucian and the Daoist. The former only dreams of a function which gives him authority over men. The latter avoids as best he can such positions.*

CHAPTER 28 (TEXT)

A. To be conscious of one's virile potency (to know oneself to be a cock), and yet to keep oneself voluntarily in the inferior state of the female (of the hen); to keep oneself voluntarily in the lowest point of the empire... To behave in this way is to show that one preserves the primordial virtue (absolute disinterestedness, participation of the Principle).

B. To know oneself to be enlightened and to pass voluntarily for ignorant; to be voluntarily the footstool of all... To behave in this way is to demonstrate that in oneself the primordial virtue has not weakened, that one is still united to the first Principle.

C. To know oneself worthy of glory, and to remain voluntarily in darkness; to be voluntarily the valley (the lowest point) of the empire… To behave thus is to demonstrate that one still possesses intact the original abnegation, that one is still in the state of natural simplicity.

D. (The Sage, therefore, will refuse the office of ruler. If he is forced to accept it, he should remember that) from the primordial unity arose the manifold beings by dispersion. (Let him never concern himself with these diverse beings), but rule as the chief (prime mover), applied only to the general government, without concern for details.

Summary of commentaries

This chapter is related to paragraph C, the end of the previous chapter. It describes well the Olympian government, as understood by Daoists. Chapter 29 continues to develop this theme.

CHAPTER 29 (TEXT)

A. For the one who has the empire, to want to manipulate it (to act positively, to rule actively), in my opinion, is to want failure. The empire is an extremely delicate mechanism. You have to leave it by itself. You must not touch it. If you touch it, it goes crazy. Whoever wants to appropriate it, will lose it.

B. When he rules, the Sage lets all beings (and the empire which is their sum) act, according to their diverse natures; the agile and the slow; the apathetic and the ardent; the strong and the weak; the lasting and the ephemeral.

C. It is limited to repressing the forms of excess that would be harmful to all beings, such as power, wealth and ambition.

Summary of commentaries

Zhang Hongyang calls this repression of excesses, the only intervention permitted to the Daoist, action in non-action.

CHAPTER 30 (TEXT)

(Of all excesses, the most harmful, the most condemnable, is that of weapons, war).

A. Let those who help a prince with their counsels, beware of attempting to make a country feel the force of arms. (For such action calls for revenge, it always pays dearly.) Where troops remain, lands abandoned by husbandmen, produce only thorns. Where great armies have passed, years of misfortune (famine and banditry) follow.

B. Therefore, the good general contents himself with doing what is necessary (as little as possible; moral rather than material repression), and stops immediately, taking care not to exploit his forces to the maximum. He does just what is necessary (to restore peace), not for his own glory and advantage, but out of necessity and reluctantly, with no intention of increasing his power.

C. For the peak of all power is always followed by decadence. To become powerful, therefore, is contrary to the Principle, (the source of duration). He who fails the Principle at this point, soon perishes.

Literal commentaries. No controversy.

CHAPTER 31 (TEXT)

A. The best-made weapons are evil instruments, which all beings abhor. Therefore, those who conform to the Principle, do not use them.

B. In time of peace, the prince places on his left (the place of honor) the civil minister whom he honors; but even in time of war, he places the military commander on his right (not the place of honor, even while in the exercise of his functions).

Weapons are evil instruments, which a wise prince uses only reluctantly and out of necessity, always preferring a modest peace to a glorious victory.

It is not fitting that a victory should be considered a good. He who does so shows that he has the heart of a murderer. It would not be appropriate for such a man to rule the empire.

C. According to the rites, we put on the left the good beings, and on the right the nefarious ones. (Now when the emperor receives the two generals together), the substitute general (who only acts in the absence of the incumbent and is therefore less harmful) is placed on the left, while the commanding general is placed on the right, that is, in the first place according to the funeral rites (the place of the mourner, the chief mourner). For to who has killed many men, it is incumbent upon him to mourn them, with tears and lamentations. The only place that really belongs to a victorious general is that of chief mourner, (leading the mourning of those whose death he has caused).

Literal commentaries. No controversy.

CHAPTER 32 (TEXT)

A. The Principle has no proper name. It is nature. This nature, so unmanifest, is more powerful than anything else. If the princes and the emperor comply with it, all beings will spontaneously become its collaborators; heaven and earth acting in perfect harmony, will spread a sweet dew (the most splendid possible sign); the people will be regulated, without being forced.

B. When, in the beginning, in this visible world, the Principle by its transmission produced the beings that have (sensible) names, it did not transmitted infinitely, nor in such a way as to be exhausted (but only as by tenuous extensions, its mass remaining intact). This is the case of the Principle in relation to the various beings that fill the world, like that of the mass of the great rivers and seas in relation to the streams and brooks.

Summary of commentaries

Each being exists through an extension of the Principle within it. These extensions are not detached from the Principle, which therefore does not diminish by transmitting itself. The extension of the Principle in a being is the nature of that being. The Principle is the universal nature, being the sum of all individual natures, its extensions.

Chapter 33 (text)

A. To know others is wisdom; but to know oneself is a higher wisdom (one's own nature is the deepest and most hidden). — To impose one's will on others is force; but to impose it on oneself is a superior force (one's passions are the most difficult to tame). To be satisfied (to be content with what destiny has given) is true wealth; to master oneself (to bend to what destiny has arranged) is true character.

B. To remain in one's place (natural, that which destiny has given), makes one last long. After death, not ceasing to be, is true longevity (which is shared by those who have lived in accordance with nature and destiny).

Summary of commentaries

Death and life, two ways of being. In B, it is about conscious survival after death.

Chapter 34 (text)

A. The great Principle extends in all directions. It lends itself complacently to the genesis of all beings (its participants). When a work has come into being, he does not attribute it to itself. It benevolently nourishes all beings, without imposing himself upon them as master (for having nourished them; leaving them free; not demanding from them any degrading return). Because of his constant unselfishness, it might be thought that it would diminish. But it is not so; all beings towards whom he is so liberal, flock to him. Thus it magnifies itself (by this universal trust).

B. The Sage imitates this conduct. He too becomes small (by his unselfishness and delicate reserve), and thus acquires true greatness.

No more in the commentaries.

Chapter 35 (text)

A. Because he resembles the great prototype (the Principle, by his selfless devotion), everything flock to the Sage. He welcomes them all, does them good, gives them rest, peace and happiness.

B. Music and good food retain a passing guest only for one night (sensual pleasures are fleeting and nothing remains). Whereas the exposition of the great principle of unselfish devotion, simple and unadorned, which charms neither the eyes nor the ears, pleases, is recorded and is inexhaustibly fruitful in practical applications.

No more in the commentaries.

Chapter 36 (text)

A. The onset of contraction necessarily follows the climax of expansion. Weakening follows strength, decadence follows prosperity, destitution follows opulence. This is the subtle light (which many do not want to see). All previous power and superiority are atoned for by subsequent weakness and inferiority. More leads to less, excess brings deficit.

B. A fish should not come out of the depths (where it lives ignored but safe, to show itself on the surface where it will be harpooned). A state should not show its resources (if it does not want the whole world to turn against it and crush it).

Summary of commentaries

Remain small, humble, hidden; do not attract attention; this is the secret of living well and long.

Chapter 37 (text)

A. The principle is always non-acting (does not actively act) and yet everything is done by it (without seeming to participate).

B. If the prince and the lords could rule in this way (without intervening), all beings would become spontaneously perfect (by return to nature).

C. Then it would only be necessary to suppress any inclination they might have to get out of this state (by acting, calling them each time to the innate nature of the primordial simplicity of the Principle). In this state of innate nature, there are no desires. When there are no desires all is at peace, and the state governs itself.

The commentaries add nothing. Compare with chapter 3.

BOOK II

Chapter 38 (text)

A. Whatever is superior to the Virtue of the Principle (the Principle itself considered in its essence), does not act, but preserves in itself the Virtue in a state of immanence. All that is inferior to the Virtue of the Principle (artificial rules of conduct), is only a palliative for the loss of the Virtue; a palliative that has nothing in common with it.

B. That which is superior to Virtue (the Principle), does not act in detail. That which is inferior to Virtue (the artificial rules), exists only for action in detail.

C. What is above goodness (artificial Confucian, over which is the Principle), does not act in detail. That which is above equity (artificial, goodness is above it) acts in detail. That which is above rites (equity) struggles with the inclinations of different beings, hence rites and laws.

In other words, after the oblivion of nature with its natural good instincts, came the artificial palliative principles of this deficit; which are, in descending order, goodness, equity, rites and laws.

Rites are but a poor expedient to cover up the loss of original righteousness and directness. They are a source of disorder (etiquette, rubrics) rather than order.

Finally, the last term of this downward evolution, political wisdom, was the beginning of all abuses.

D. The true man abides by natural rectitude and common sense, despising artificial principles. Using discernment, he rejects this (the false), to embrace that (the true).

Summary of commentaries

This chapter is directed against Confucianism. The general natural common sense is unity. Artificial moral precepts are multiplicity. The next chapter will show that multiplicity ruins, unity saves.

Chapter 39 (text)

A. These are the beings that partake of primitive simplicity. Heaven, which owes its luminosity to this simplicity. The earth, which owes its stability to it. The universal generative action, which owes its activity to it. The intermediate space, which owes its fecundity to it. The common life of all beings. The power of the emperor and princes (Life and power are emanations of the Principle).

B. What makes them such is the (primitive) simplicity of which they partake. If heaven were to lose it, it would fall. If the earth were to lose it, it would totter. If the generating action were to lose it, it would cease. If the intervening space were to lose it, it would be exhausted. If life lost it, all beings would disappear. If the emperor and the princes lost it, their dignity would also be lost.

C. All elevation, all nobility, is based on abasement and simplicity (the very characteristics of the Principle). Therefore, it is with reason that the emperor and princes, the most exalted of men, designate themselves by the terms, alone, unique, incapable, without degrading themselves by this.

D. (Applying the same principle of simplicity in their government), that they reduce the multitudes of their subjects to unity, considering them as an undivided mass with serene impartiality, without esteeming some as precious as jade and others as vile stones.

Summary of commentaries

This chapter offers a global perspective, as if from an infinite distance, neither individuals nor details being visible, and completes the previous one.

CHAPTER 40 (TEXT)

A. Backward movement (toward the Principle), is the characteristic form of movement of those who conform to the Principle. Attenuation is the effect produced in them by their conformity to the Principle.

B. Considering that all that is, is born of simple being, and that being is born of formless non-being, they tend, constantly diminishing themselves, to return to primordial simplicity.

The commentaries add nothing to the meaning, which is clear.

CHAPTER 41 (TEXT)

A. When a scholar of the higher order has heard of the return to the Principle, he applies himself to it with zeal. If he is a middle-level scholar, he applies to it with hesitation. If he is a lower level scholar, he does not care. And it is a mark of the truth of this doctrine that such people do not care. The fact that they do not understand it, shows its transcendence.

B. It is said, as in the proverb: those who have grasped the Principle, seem blinded; those who tend toward it, seem misguided; those who have attained it, seem vulgar. This is because great virtue hollows itself out like a valley, great light voluntarily veils itself in darkness, vast virtue makes believe that it is defective, solid virtue appears to be incapable, and the Sage hides his qualities under rather unpleasant appearances.

C. He who believes in these appearances would be greatly deceived. Like a square so large that its corners are invisible (infinite), like a great vessel never finished, like a great meaning in a faint sound, like a great model, but ungraspable! The Sage resembles the Principle. — Now the Principle is latent and nameless, but by its gentle transmission everything is produced. It is the same, in proportion, to the Sage.

No more in the commentaries.

Chapter 42 (text)

A. When the Principle emitted its unique virtue, it began to evolve in two alternating modalities. This evolution produced (or condensed) the intermediate air (the tenuous matter). From the tenuous matter, under the influence of the two modes *yin* and *yang*, all sentient beings were produced. Coming out of *yin* (power), they pass to *yang* (act), through the influence of the two modalities on matter.

B. What men do not like is to be alone, to be unique, incapable (obscurity and abasement), and yet emperors and princes refer to themselves by these terms (humility that does not debase them). Beings diminish themselves by wanting to increase themselves, and increase themselves by diminishing themselves.

C. Speaking thus, I repeat the traditional teaching. Strong and arrogant men do not die willingly. I make this axiom the basis of my teaching.

No more in the commentaries.

In A, there is no mention of the Trinity. Compare A and B with chapter 39 C.

Chapter 43 (text)

A. Everywhere and always, it is the soft that wears away the hard (water wears away stone). Non-being penetrates even where there are no cracks (the most homogeneous bodies, such as metal and stone). From this I deduce that non-action is supremely effective.

B. Silence and inaction! Few men can understand its efficacy.

No more in the commentaries.

Chapter 44 (text)

A. Is not the body more important than fame? Is not life more important than wealth? Is it wise to expose oneself to great loss for a small advantage?

B. He who loves much, uses much (his heart). He who gathers much, goes to great ruin (plunder or confiscation). While the modest person does not incur disgrace, the moderate person does not perish but endures.

No more in the commentaries.

Chapter 45 (text)

A. Fulfilled, under imperfect appearances, and giving without wearing out. Full, without seeming so, and pouring without wearing out. Very upright, under a stooped countenance; very skillful, under awkward appearances; very cunning, with the outward appearance of an embarrassed man; this is the Sage.

B. Movement triumphs over cold (warms), repose reduces heat (cools). The withdrawn life of the Sage, rectifies the whole empire (overcomes its depravity).

Remarks: Intense influence, under the guise of inaction.

CHAPTER 46 (TEXT)

A. When the Principle reigns (peace is perfect), the war horses work in the fields. When the Principle is forgotten, (war is the order of the day), war horses are bred even in the suburbs of cities.

B. Giving in to one's lusts (and the mania of war is one of them), is the worst of crimes. Not knowing how to limit oneself is the worst of evils. The worst defect is to want to acquire more and more. Those who know how to say "enough" are always happy.

Nothing more in the commentaries.

CHAPTER 47 (TEXT)

A. Without going out of the door, one can know the whole world; without looking out of the window, one can realize the ways of heaven (principles that govern all things). — The more one advances, the less one learns.

B. The Sage arrives at the goal without having taken a step to reach it. He knows, before he has seen, by the higher principles. He completes, without having acted, by his transcendent influence.

Commentaries: Superior global knowledge is that of the Sage.
Knowledge of details is unworthy of him.

CHAPTER 48 (TEXT)

A. By study, one multiplies every day (the particular useless and harmful notions in one's memory); by concentration on the Principle, one diminishes them every day. Carried to the end, this diminution leads to non-action (as a result of the absence of particular notions).

B. Now there is nothing that non-action (letting go) does not overcome. It is by not acting that one gains the empire. From acting to gain it, one does not gain it.

Nothing else in the commentaries.

CHAPTER 49 (TEXT)

A. The Sage has no fixed will; he accommodates himself to the will of the people. He treats equally the good and the bad, which is true practical kindness. He also trusts the sincere and the insincere; which is true practical trust.

B. In this mixed world, the Sage has no emotions, and has the same feelings for all. All men fix their eyes and ears on him. He treats them all as children, (Daoist benevolence, somewhat contemptuous).

No more in the commentaries.

CHAPTER 50 (TEXT)

A. Men go out to life and return to death.

B. Out of ten men, three prolong their life (by hygiene), three hasten their death (by their excesses), three compromise their life by their attachment to it, (only one out of ten preserves his life to the end, because he detaches himself from it).

C. He who is detached from his life does not turn aside to avoid an encounter with a rhinoceros or a tiger; he throws himself into the fray without armor and without weapons, and that without experiencing any harm, for he is proof against the horn of the rhinoceros, the claws of the tiger and the weapons of the combatants. Why? Because, externalized by his indifference, he does not surrender to death.

Summary of commentaries

When the soul is transported out of the body by ecstasy, the body cannot be struck. The idea seems to be that, to be mortal, a blow must reach the union of body and soul. This union ceases temporarily, in ecstasy.

Chapter 51 (text)

A. The Principle gives life to beings; then their Virtue nourishes them, until their nature is complete, until their faculties are perfect. Therefore, all beings revere the Principle and its Virtue.

B. The eminence of the Principle and its Virtue, has not been conferred by anyone; they have it from everlasting, naturally.

C. The Principle gives life; its Virtue grows, protects, perfects, matures, maintains, covers (all beings). When they are born, it does not monopolize them; it lets them act freely, without exploiting them; it lets them grow, without tyrannizing them. This is the transcendent Virtue.

The commentaries add nothing.

Chapter 52 (text)

A. That which was before the world became the mother of the world. He who has attained the mother (the matter, the body), knows through her her son (the vital spirit enclosed in him). He who knows the son (the vital spirit, enclosed in the body) and preserves the mother (his body), will reach the end of his days without accidents.

B. If he keeps his mouth closed and his nostrils closed (to avoid the evaporation of the vital principle), he will reach the end of his days without having experienced decadence. On the other hand, if he talks too much and worries too much, he will wear himself out and shorten his life.

C. Limiting considerations to small matters, and worries to matters of little importance, makes the mind clear and the body strong. To concentrate your intellectual rays on your mind, and not to let mental application harm your body, is to watch (your mind) to make (your life) lasting.

Summary of commentaries

Obscure text, but the commentators agree. It is the basis of Daoist breathing therapy.

Chapter 53 (text)

A. Whoever has some wisdom, should stick to the great Principle, avoiding above all pompous boasting. But instead of this broad way, narrow paths are preferred. (Few are the men who walk the path of obscure unselfishness. They prefer the ways of their vanity, their advantage. So do the princes of this age).

B. When palaces are too well kept, lands are uncultivated and granaries are empty (for the husbandmen are requisitioned for heavy labor).

C. To dress magnificently, to wear a sharp sword at one's waist, to gorge oneself with food and drink, to amass such wealth that one does not know what to do with it (as the princes of this time do), is to resemble a brigand (who ostentatiously enjoys his spoils). This conduct is opposed to the Principle.

The commentaries add nothing.

Chapter 54 (text)

A. The work of the one who builds on selflessness, shall not be destroyed. He who preserves with unselfishness, will not lose what he has. His children and grandchildren will make offerings to him without interruption (that is, they will succeed him and enjoy the fruit of his works).

B. First of all, one must have perfectly conformed to the Principle; then this conformity will spontaneously extend from oneself to one's family, to one's district, to one's principality, to one's empire; (central focus; ever-widening radius).

C. By one's own nature, one knows the nature of other individuals, and of all collections of individuals, families, districts, principalities, empire.

D. How can one know the nature of a whole empire? By this (by its very nature), as stated above).

The commentaries add nothing.

Chapter 55 (text)

A. He who holds in himself perfect Virtue (without lust or anger), is like a little child, whom the scorpion does not sting, whom the tiger does not devour, whom the vulture does not ravish, whom everyone respects.

B. The child's bones are weak, his sinews are weak, but he grasps objects tightly (as his soul and body grasp tightly). He has no idea yet of the act of generation and therefore retains his full seminal virtue. He moans all day long, without his throat becoming hoarse, so perfect is his peace.

C. Peace is lasting; he who understands this is enlightened. Whereas all excitation, especially lust and anger, wear out, Therefore manhood (which man abuses) is followed by decay. Intense life is contrary to the Principle, and therefore prematurely fatal.

Summary of commentaries

This chapter condemns lust and anger as the most destructive causes of all.

CHAPTER 56 (TEXT)

A. He who speaks (much, shows thereby that) he does not know (the Principle).

B. He who knows (the Principle), does not speak. He closes his mouth, holds his breath, dulls his activity, frees himself from all complication, tempers his light, merges with the vulgar. This is the mysterious union (with the Principle).

C. No one can attract such a man (with favors), nor can he repel him (with ill-treatment). He is insensible to gain and loss, to exaltation and humiliation. As such, it is the noblest thing in the world.

Summary of commentaries

Superior to all that seems, he converses with the author of beings, the Principle. Zhang Hongyang.

CHAPTER 57 (TEXT)

A. With righteousness one can rule, with skill one can wage war, but it is non-action that wins and maintains the empire.

B. How do I know this to be so? What I am about to say explains it: The more regulations there are, the less people get richer. The more sources of income there are, the less order there is. The more ingenious inventions there are, the fewer serious and useful objects there are. The more detailed the code, the more thieves abound. Multiplication ruins everything.

C. The program of the Sage is therefore the opposite. Do not act, and the people will reform. Be silent, and the people will rectify themselves. Do nothing, and the people will become richer. If you want nothing, the people will return to their natural spontaneity.

The commentaries add nothing.

CHAPTER 58 (TEXT)

A. When government is simple, the people abound in virtue. When government is political, the people lack virtue.

B. Evil and good, they succeed each other, they alternate. Who will discern the climaxes? (of this circular movement of evil and good). It is very delicate, an excess or a defect that changes the moral entity). Many lack the right measure. In some, exaggerated righteousness degenerates into mania, in others exaggerated goodness becomes extravagance. (Opinions vary accordingly.) Men have been very mad for a long time.

C. (The Sage takes them as they are.) Admonishing them, he is not blunt. Straight, he is not harsh. Enlightened, he does not humiliate.

The commentaries add nothing.

CHAPTER 59 (TEXT)

A. To cooperate with heaven in the government of men, the essential thing is to temper one's action.

B. This moderation must be the first concern. It provides perfect efficiency, which succeeds in everything, even in the government of the empire.

C. He who possesses this mother of empire (wise moderation), will last long. It is what has been called the primary root, the solid trunk. It is the principle of perpetuity.

The commentaries add nothing.

CHAPTER 60 (TEXT)

A. To govern a great State, it is necessary to do it as one who cooks a very small fish (with great delicacy, otherwise it will fall apart).

B. When a State is governed according to the Principle, ghosts do not appear there to harm the people, because the Sage who governs does not harm the people,

C. The merit of this double tranquility (on the part of the dead and the living), therefore, belongs to the Sage.

Summary of commentaries

The ghosts are not the souls of the dead. They are, in moral harmony, what a vortex is in the physical atmosphere at rest. This disorder is produced by the movement of passions, hatreds and similar feelings. It does not occur when minds are calm.

CHAPTER 61 (TEXT)

A. If a great state lowers itself, like those hollows into which the waters flow, the whole world will flock to it. It will be like the universal female (chapters 8 and 28).

B. In her apparent passivity and inferiority, woman is superior to man (for it is she who gives birth). — On condition that it knows how to lower itself, the great State will win over the small States, which, lowering themselves, will seek its suzerainty. Once it has lowered itself, it will win the other states. Basically, the large state wishes to protect the others, the small states only want to recognize its protectorate.

C. For this common desire to be fulfilled, only one thing is needed (to lower itself), but it is essential (If it is proud and hard, there is no hope).

Nothing else in the commentaries.

CHAPTER 62 (TEXT)

A. The Principle is the safeguard of all beings. It is the treasure of the good (that for which it is good), and the salvation of the bad (that which keeps them from perishing).

B. It is to be thanked for the loving words and noble conduct of the good. It is for his sake that the wicked are not to be rejected.

C. It is for this purpose (for the preservation and development of that part of the Principle which is in beings), that the emperor and the great ministers are instituted. Not that they should delight in their scepter and chariot. But that they should meditate on the Principle (advance in their knowledge and develop it in others).

D. Why did the ancients pay so much attention to the Principle? Was it not because it is the source of all good and the remedy for all evils? The noblest thing in the world!

The commentaries add nothing.

CHAPTER 63 (TEXT)

A. To act without acting; to be busy without being busy; to savor without tasting; to see in the same way the great, the small, the many, the few; to give equal heed to reproaches and thanks; this is how the Sage does it.

B. He undertakes difficult complications only in their simple details, and applies himself to great problems only in their feeble beginnings.

C. The Sage never undertakes anything great, therefore he does great things. He who promises much cannot keep his word. He who worries about too many things, even if they are easy, achieves nothing.

D. The Wise One avoids difficulties, so he never has difficulties.

The commentaries add nothing.

CHAPTER 64 (TEXT)

A. What is peaceful is easy to contain; what has not yet appeared is easy to prevent; what is weak is easy to break; what is small is easy to disperse. Action must be taken before anything happens, and order must be protected before disorder has broken out.

B. A tree that two arms can barely embrace was born from a root as thin as a hair; a nine-story tower rises from a heap of earth; a journey of a thousand furlongs began with a single step.

C. Those who overdo, spoil their business. Those who over-tighten, end up loosening. The Sage who does not act, spoils no business. As he cares for nothing, nothing escapes him.

D. When the commoner makes a deal, he usually fails just when he is about to succeed (the intoxication of his initial success makes him lose his temper and make mistakes). It is necessary, in order to succeed, that the circumspection of the beginning, lasts until the completion.

E. The wise man is not passionate about anything. He takes no object, because it is rare. He adheres to no system, but learns from the defects of others. To cooperate in the universal evolution, he does not act, but lets himself go.

The commentaries add nothing.

Chapter 65 (text)

A. In ancient times, those who conformed to the Principle did not seek to make the people intelligent, but sought to keep them simple.

B. When people are difficult to govern, it is because they know too much. He who pretends to do good by spreading education, errs and ruins the country. Keeping the people in ignorance, achieves the salvation of a country.

C. This is the formula of a mysterious, far-reaching and transcendental action. It is not to the liking of the people (the curious); but, thanks to it, everything comes to fruition peacefully.

Compare with chapter 3 B. Nothing else in the commentaries.

Chapter 66 (text)

A. Why rivers and oceans are the kings of all valleys (receiving in tribute all streams). Because they are voluntarily the inferior of all valleys (with respect to level). Therefore all waters flow into them.

B. Following this example, the Sage who wants to become superior to the common people, places himself below them with his words (he speaks very humbly of himself), if he wants to become the first, he places himself in the last place (and continues to do so, after having been exalted). Then he can be elevated to the top, without the people feeling oppressed by him; he can be the first, without the people complaining about him. The whole empire will serve him with joy, without tiring. For since he opposes no one, no one will oppose him.

Compare with chapter 8. The commentaries do not add anything.

Chapter 67 (text)

A. The whole empire says that the Sage is noble, despite his vulgar air; an air he gives himself, precisely because he is noble (to veil his nobility and not attract envy). Everyone knows, on the contrary, that those who pretend to be noble are men of little value.

B. The wise man takes three things and clings to them: charity, simplicity and humility. Being charitable, he will be courageous (within proper limits, without cruelty). Being simple, he will be liberal (within proper limits, without profligacy). Being humble, he will rule men without tyranny.

C. The men of today forget charity, simplicity and humility. They devote themselves to war, to pomp, to ambition. This is wanting to perish. This is wanting to be unsuccessful.

D. The charitable aggressor is the one who wins the battle (not the barbarous aggressor); the charitable defender is the one who is impregnable (not the ruthless fighter). Those whom heaven wishes well, it makes charitable.

Summary of commentaries

Simplicity and humility are discussed elsewhere in chapters 75, 77 and 78.

CHAPTER 68 (TEXT)

A. Let not the one in command think that tactics, courage and effort bring victory.

B. It is by putting oneself at the service of men that men are tamed. This is the true process, which is sometimes formulated as follows: the art of not fighting (of accommodating oneself, of winning by becoming all things to all men); the power to manage men; action in conformity with that of heaven. All these formulas designate the same thing, which is the greatness of the Ancients.

The commentaries add nothing.

CHAPTER 69 (TEXT)

A. Rather defensive than offensive, rather retreat a foot than advance an inch, are common principles in the military art. To yield is better than to triumph. To prevent by diplomacy is still better.

B. This is the meaning of certain abstruse formulas of military art, such as: advance without marching; defend without waving arms; maintain the status quo without fighting; conserve without arms, and others.

C. There is no greater scourge than a war begun lightly (deliberately sought, pushed beyond what is necessary). He who does this exposes his property to loss, and causes much grief.

Continuation of the previous chapter. The commentaries add nothing.

CHAPTER 70 (TEXT)

A. What I teach (*Lao Zi* speaks), is easy to understand and practice, and yet the world does not want to understand and practice it.

B. My precepts and procedures are derived from a higher principle and procedure, the Principle and its virtue.

C. The world does not recognize the Principle that directs me, therefore it does not know me. Very few understand me. This is my glory. It happens to me as to the Sage, who is not known by the common of mortals because of his coarse clothing, although he has a chest full of precious stones.

The commentaries add nothing.

Chapter 71 (text)

A. To know everything and to believe that one knows nothing is true knowledge (higher science). Knowing nothing and believing that one knows everything is the common human evil.

B. To see this evil as an evil, preserves one. The Sage is free from fatuity, because he fears fatuity. This fear preserves him from it.

Summary of commentaries

Non-knowledge is part of non-action, because knowing is an act, say the Daoists, who reject theories, generalizations and classifications, admitting only the objective apprehension of particular cases.

Chapter 72 (text)

A. Those who do not fear, when they should fear, are lost (who expose themselves to danger, out of curiosity, love of gain, ambition).

B. Do not find your native home too narrow, do not be displeased with the condition in which you were born (Remain what you are and stay where you are. The effort to look for something better may lead you to get lost). One does not become disgusted, as long as one does not want to become disgusted (Disgust is always voluntary, since it comes from the fact that one has compared his situation with that of another, and has preferred the latter).

C. The Sage knows his value, but does not show it (he does not feel the need to show his value). He loves himself, but does not seek to be esteemed. He discerns, adopting this and rejecting that (according to the lights of his wisdom).

The commentaries add nothing.

Chapter 73 (text)

A. Active courage (warlike courage) brings death. Passive courage (patience, endurance) preserves life. Therefore, there are two kinds of courage, one harmful and the other helpful.

B. (Patience and suffering are always better than incisive action, even in government, in politics). If heaven harms a man or a nation, to what is it due? Who knows? — So the wise man always feels ashamed (hesitating, deciding with difficulty about forceful intervention).

C. For the way of heaven (his constant conduct) is not to intervene positively. It conquers without fighting. It makes itself obeyed without giving orders. It makes people come without calling them. It brings everything to a conclusion, even though it seems to neglect everything.

D. The net of heaven encloses everything. Its meshes are wide, but no one escapes them.

Summary of commentaries

In D, if the Sage has let a culprit escape from the net of human law out of kindness, the heavenly net will seize him. The Sage, therefore, trusts heaven and acts less rather than more, so as not to act against heaven's intentions or encroach upon its rights.

CHAPTER 74 (TEXT)

A. If people do not fear death, what is the use of trying to restrain them with the fear of death? If they feared death, then taking and killing those who cause trouble, would succeed in keeping others from doing the same.

B. (The Legists, who lavish the death penalty, and believe that everything will work out that way, then are mistaken). He who is in charge of death (heaven), kills (Let him do it. Let us not do his work. He alone is capable of doing it).

C. To the man who wants to kill, it will happen as to the one who plays with the carpenter's chisel. Rare are those who do not cut their fingers in this game.

Summary of commentaries

To get something from men, it is better to treat them benignly. — Against the school of the Legists of Fa Jia, *who know only of torments. It is a fact of experience, say the commentators, that people fear death less than hard labor, for example; and that, after they get carried away, they lose all fear.*

CHAPTER 75 (TEXT)

A. If the people are hungry, it is because the prince devours excessive sums (that he extorts from them).

B. If the people are restless, it is because the prince acts too much, (indisposing them with his innovations).

C. If the people expose themselves lightly to death (in risky enterprises), it is because they love life too much (love of well-being, of enjoyment, of glory).

D. He who does nothing to live is wiser than he who strives to live.

Summary of commentaries

Let the prince and the people cultivate simplicity, and all will be well. This chapter continues chapter 67. The meaning of D is: He who cares not for wealth and glory is wiser than he who tires and endangers himself for wealth and glory.

CHAPTER 76 (TEXT)

A. When a man is just born, he is soft and weak (but full of life); when he has become strong and powerful, then he dies.

B. So it is with plants, they are delicate (herbaceous) when they are born, woody when they die.

C. He who is strong and powerful is marked for death; he who is supple and weak is marked for life.

D. The great army will be defeated. The great tree shall be cut down.

E. Everything that is strong and great is in a worse situation. The soft and weak always have the advantage.

Like "The Oak and the Reed", by La Fontaine.

CHAPTER 77 (TEXT)

A. Heaven acts (with respect to men), like the archer who, bending his bow, depresses the convexities and makes the concavities (which his bow presented in a state of repose) bulge, diminishing what is excessive and increasing what is lacking (lowering what is raised, and raising what is lowered). He takes away from those who have in abundance and adds to those who have little.

B. Whereas men (wicked princes who defraud the people), do the contrary, taking from those who have little (the people), and adding to those who have plenty (their favorites)… Whereas all that is superfluous must return to the empire (the people)… But only he who possesses the Principle is able to do this.

C. The Sage conforms to the Principle. He influences, without attributing to himself the result. He fulfills, without appropriating his work to himself. He does not claim the title of Sage, (but remains voluntarily in obscurity).

Note: the Chinese bow reverses its shape when drawn, which produces exactly the effect described in A.

CHAPTER 78 (TEXT)

A. In this world, nothing is so soft and weak as water; yet no being, however strong and powerful, resists its action (corrosion, wear and tear, shock of waves); and no being can do without it (to drink, to grow, etc.).

B. Is it sufficiently clear that weakness is better than strength, that flexibility is better than rigidity? Everyone agrees; but no one puts it into practice.

C. The Sages say: He who is repelled neither by moral filth nor by political unhappiness is capable of being the ruler of the land and the ruler of the empire (He who is flexible enough to accommodate all this; not the rigid and systematic man).

D. This is a very true statement, though it offends the ears of many.

This chapter and the preceding one are related to chapter 67.

CHAPTER 79 (TEXT)

A. After the main part of a dispute has been settled, there always remain incidental grievances, and things do not return to the state they were in before (resentments).

B. (That is why the Sage never disputes, in spite of his right). Although he has his written contract, he does not demand the execution (of what is written).

C. He who knows how to conduct himself according to the Virtue of the Principle, lets his written contract sleep. He who does not know how to behave in this way, demands what is due to him.

D. Heaven is impartial. (If it were capable of any partiality,) it would favor good people (those who do what is said in C. It would fulfill them, because they ask for nothing).

The commentaries do not add anything.

Chapter 80 (text)

A. If I were king of a small state, of a small town, I would be careful not to use (put in charge) the few dozen able-bodied men in that state.

B. I would prevent my subjects from traveling, making them fear death by possible accident, so much so that they would not dare to board a ship or a chariot.

C. I would forbid the use of arms.

D. It would force them to return to knotted ropes, for writing and sciences.

E. Then they would find their food tasty, their clothes beautiful, their houses quiet, their habits and customs pleasant.

F. (I would impede curiosity and communication, to the point that,) if my subjects heard from their houses the cries of the roosters and dogs of the neighboring State, they would die of old age before they had crossed the frontier and had intercourse with those of the neighboring State.

The mouse in its cheese, Daoist ideal.

Chapter 81 (text)

A. (I have finished. It is possible that my speech is somewhat crude, not very subtle, hardly learned). And it is that native frankness wears no clothing, natural rectitude has no qualms, common sense needs no artificial erudition.

B. The wise man does not accumulate, but gives. The more he acts for men, the more he can do; the more he gives to them, the more he has. Heaven does good to all, does evil to none. The wise man imitates him, acting for the good of all and opposing none.

The commentaries do not add anything.

Chongxu Zhenjing[1]
(Treatise on perfect emptiness)
LIE ZI

CHAPTER 1 - GENESIS AND TRANSFORMATION

A. *Lie Zi* lived in a cottage in the principality of *Zheng*, for forty years, unnoticed by anyone, included the prince, his ministers and officials, who saw in him anything more than an ordinary man. When famine came to the country, he prepared to emigrate to *Wei*. Then his disciples said to him:

"Master, you are going away, and it is not clear if and when you will return. Please teach us, before you leave, what you have learned from your master *Lin* of *Hu Zi*."

Lie Zi smiled and said:

"What have I learned from my master? When he was teaching *Bo Hun Wu Ren*[2], I picked up something, which I will try to relate to you. He said that there is a non-produced producer, a transformer that has not been transformed. This non-produced producer, has produced all beings, this non-transformed transforms all beings. From the beginning of production, the producer cannot stop producing; from the beginning of transformations, the transformer cannot stop transforming. Therefore, the chain of productions and transformations is uninterrupted, with the producer and the transformer constantly producing and transforming. The producer is the *Yin-yang* (the Principle in its double alternation mode); the transformer is the cycle of the four seasons (revolution of the heaven-earth

---

1   *Chongxu Zhenjing* is attributed to *Lie Zi*, or *Lieh-tzu* (according to Wade-Giles romanization, now in disuse) (Translator Note).

2   A fellow student. Ritual humility. One should not make oneself known as a disciple of an illustrious man, lest one embarrass him.

binomial). The producer is immobile, the transformer comes and goes. And the mobile, and the immobile, will last forever."

B. In the writings of *Huang Di* (The Yellow Emperor), it is said[3]: The transcendent expansive power that resides in the middle space (the virtue of the Principle) does not die. It is the mysterious mother (of all beings). Its gate is the root of heaven and earth (the Principle). Proliferating, it does not pass away. It acts without tiring... That is to say, the producer does not produce, the transformer does not transform. The producer-transformer produces and transforms himself, becomes sensitive, takes figures, attains intelligence, acquires energies, acts and sleeps, remaining always himself (unicity of the cosmos, without real distinction). To say that distinct beings are produced and transformed, become sentient, take figures, attain intelligence, acquire energies, act and sleep, is to err.

C. *Lie Zi* said:

"Analyzing the production of the cosmos by the Principle under its double modality *Yin* and *yang*, the hatching of the sensible from the non-sensible, the germ of the peaceful generative action of heaven and earth, the ancient Sages distinguished the following stages in it: great mutation, great origin, great beginning, great flux[4]. The great mutation is the stage before the appearance of tenuous matter (turning of the two modes, into indefinite being, into the nothingness of form, into the Principle, out of its absolute immobility). The great origin is the stage of tenuous matter. The great beginning is the stage of palpable matter. The great flow is the stage of plastic matter, of corporeal substances, of real material beings. — The primitive state, when matter was still imperceptible, is also called *Hun Lun*, which means that, at that time, all beings to come in the future were contained as in a confused, indiscernible, unknowable swell. Its ordinary name is *Yi*, mutation, because from it everything comes out by way of transformation. — From the non-sentient, undifferentiated state, beginning with one, the progression through seven, passes to nine[5]; the regression brings everything back to unity. — Unity was the starting point of the genesis of sentient beings. It happened thus: the purest and lightest matter, having ascended, became heaven; the less pure and heavier matter, having descended, became earth; from the better tempered matter, remaining in the middle void, men arose. The essence of all beings was first part of heaven and earth, from which all beings arose successively through transformation."

---

3   Verbatim, chapter 6 of *Lao Zi*.

4   More correctly, "great unfolding." The regular course of things, such as they are, in the world as it is.

5   Seven may indicate an allusion to the genesis of the seven heavenly bodies, the seven rulers of Chinese philosophy. Nine, is the last of the simple numbers, after which there are infinite multiples.

D. *Lie Zi* said:

"Taken in isolation, heaven and earth do not have all capacities, a Sage does not have all talents, a being does not have all properties. Heaven gives life and covers, earth provides matter and supports, the Sage teaches and corrects, the beings each have their own limited qualities. Heaven and earth have their respective deficits which they compensate reciprocally, the Sage has his defects which oblige him to resort to others, all beings must help each other. Heaven cannot replace earth, earth cannot replace the Sage, the Sage cannot change the nature of beings, specific beings cannot go beyond their level. The action of heaven and earth consists in the alternation of *yin* and *yang*, the influence of the Sage consists in instilling goodness and fairness, the nature of beings is either active or passive; all this is natural and immutable. — Because there are products, there is a producer of these products. There is an author, bodily forms, sounds, colors, tastes. The products are mortal, their producer is not. The author of bodily forms is not corporeal, the author of sounds is not perceptible to the ear, the author of colors is not visible to the eye, the author of tastes is not perceived by the taste. Except for its infinity and immortality, the producer, the author (the Principle), is indeterminate, capable of becoming, in beings, *yin* or *yang*, active or passive; contracted or extended, round or square, agent of life or death, hot or cold, light or heavy, noble or vile, visible or invisible, black or yellow, sweet or bitter, stinking or fragrant. Devoid of all intellectual knowledge and intentional power, it knows all and can all (for it is immanent to all that it knows and can, which is, says the commentary, supreme knowledge and power)."

E. When *Lie Zi*, who was on his way to the principality of *Wei*, was eating at the side of the road, one of those who accompanied him, seeing an old skull lying there, picked it up and showed it to him. *Lie Zi* looked at it and then said to his disciple *Bai Feng*:

"He and I know that the distinction between life and death is only imaginary, he by experience, I by reasoning. He and I know that clinging to life and fearing death is unreasonable, for life and death are only two fatally successive phases. Everything passes, according to time or circumstance, through successive states, without essentially changing. Thus, frogs become quails and quails become frogs, according to whether the environment is wet or dry. The same germ will become a clump of duckweed in a pond, or a carpet of moss on a hill. When fertilized, the moss becomes the *Wu zu* plant, whose roots become worms and whose leaves become butterflies. These butterflies produce a kind of larva, which lodges under the stokes, and is called *Qu tuo*. After a thousand days, this *Qu tuo* becomes the bird *Qian yu gu*, whose saliva gives rise to the insect *Si mi*. The latter becomes *Shi xi*, *Mu rui*, *Fu kuan* (all successive forms of the same being, says the commentary). Sheep's liver becomes *Di gao*. The blood of horses becomes the will of magicians. Human blood becomes goblins. The kestrel becomes a hawk, then a vulture and the cycle begins again. The swallow becomes a shell, then a swallow again. The field mouse becomes a quail, then a field mouse again. The pumpkin, when rotting, produces fish. Old leeks become hares. Old goats become monkeys. From the spawn of fish spawn grasshoppers in times of drought. The quadruped *lei* of the mountains *Tan Yüan* is self-fertilized. The bird *Yi* becomes fertile by looking at the water. Insects *Da yao* are all female and reproduce without the intervention of a male; wasps *Zhi fong* are all male and reproduce without the intervention of a female. *Hou ji* was born from the footprint of a large foot, *Yi yin* from a hollow mulberry tree. The insect *Kui zhao* is born from water, and *Xi ji* from wine. The plants *Yang xi* and *Bu sun*, are two alternate forms. From the old bamboos arises the insect *Qing ning*, which becomes a leopard, then a horse, then a man. Man enters the loom (i.e., for him, the coming and going of the shuttle, the series of transformations begins anew). All beings leave the great cosmic loom, to return to it[6]."

F. In the writings of *Huang Di* it is said: the substance that is projected, does not produce a new substance, but a shadow; the sound that resounds, does not produce a new sound, but an echo; when the formless nothingness moves, it does not produce a new nothingness, but a sentient being. Every substance will have an end. Heaven and earth, being substances, will come to their end as I do; if, however, that which is only a change of state may be called an end. For the Principle, from which all things emanate, will have no end, since it had no beginning, and is not subject to the laws of duration. Beings pass successively through the states of being living and non-living, of being material and non-material. The state of non-life is not produced by non-life, but follows the state of life (as its shadow, as mentioned above). The state of immateriality is not produced by immateriality, but follows the state of materiality (like its echo, as mentioned above). This successive alternation is fatal, inevitable. Every living being will necessarily cease to live, and then it will necessarily cease to be non-living, it will necessarily return to life. Therefore, to want life to last and to escape death is to want the impossible. — In the human compound, the vital spirit is the contribution of heaven, the body is the contribution of earth. Man begins by the aggregation of his vital spirit with the gross earthly elements, and ends by the union of the same spirit with the pure heavenly elements. When the vital spirit leaves matter, each of the two components returns to its origin. Hence the pronunciation of the words for "dead" and *returned* is the same: *gui*. In effect, they have returned to their own abode (the cosmos). *Huang Di* said: the vital spirit returns through its gate (in the Principle, see *Lao Zi*, ch. 6 C and elsewhere), the body returns to its origin (matter), and the personality ends.

G. The life of a man, from birth to death, comprises four great periods, the time of infancy, the time of robust youth, the years of old age and death. During infancy,

---

6   Of this passage, which seems to summarize certain exotic legends, the commentary says very well: apparent disorder, but in reality, all forms of transformation are traversed; parthenogenesis, alternate generation, transformation in the same class (plants), transformation in two or more classes (plants, animals, etc.), transformation of inanimate beings into living ones, transformation with or without intermediate death.

all energies being concentrated, the harmony of the complex is perfect, nothing can harm it because its functioning is precise. During robust youth, blood and spirits boil, imagination and lusts proliferate, the harmony of the complex is no longer perfect, external influences make its functioning defective. During the years of old age, as the imagination and lust subside, the body quiets down and external beings cease to have influence upon it; although there is no return to the perfection of childhood, yet there is progress over the period of youth. Finally, through the end of existence, through death, man comes to rest, returns to his peak (to his integral perfection, to union with the cosmos).

H. Confucius, on his way to visit Mount *Tai Shan*, met a certain *Rong Qi* on the plain of *Cheng*, dressed in a deerskin, girded with a rope, playing the zither and singing.

"Master," he asked him, "what is it that makes you happy?"

"I have," said *Rong Qi*, "much to rejoice about. Of all beings, man is the noblest; and I have had a man's body for my fortune; that is my first reason for joy. The male sex is nobler than the female, and I have had a male body as my prize; this is my second reason for joy. How many men, after their conception, die before they see the light, or die in swaddling clothes before their reason awakens; but nothing of the kind has happened to me; I have lived ninety years; that is my third reason for joy… And why should I be sad. Because my poverty? That is the ordinary lot of the wise. That is the end of all life."

Confucius said to his disciples:

"This man knows how to console himself."

I. A certain *Lin Lei*, more than a hundred years old, still dressed in a skin at the time of the wheat harvest (for he had no other clothes for this warm season), was gleaning ears of corn while singing. Confucius, who was on his way to *Wei*, having met him in the field, said to his disciples:

"Try to converse with this old man, perhaps he will teach us something."

Therefore, *Zi Gong* went to *Lin Lei*, greeted him and said with compassion:

"Master, don't you regret anything, that you sing like this, doing this beggar's work?"

Lin Lei went on gleaning and humming, paying no attention to *Zi Gong*. But the latter continued to insist; finally *Lin Lei* looked at him and said:

"What should I regret?"

"You should repent," said *Zi Gong*, "for not having applied yourself more diligently in your youth and in your mature age, to attain some fortune; for having remained unmarried, thus reaching old age without wife or children; for having to die early, without help and without offerings. Having created such a condition for yourself, how can you sing, doing this work of a beggar?"

"Because," said *Lin Lei*, laughing "I have put my happiness in things which are within the reach of all and which all hate (poverty, obscurity, etc.). Yes, I have not been diligent or resourceful; this has kept me from wasting away, and I have lived to the age I am. Yes, I have remained a bachelor, and so the prospect of death does not sadden me, nor the widow and orphans I will not leave."

"But," said *Zi Gong*, "every man loves life and fears death, how can you thus despise life and love death?"

"Because," said *Lin Lei*, "death is to life what the return journey is to the outward journey. When I die here, shall I not be reborn elsewhere? And if I am born again, will it not be under different circumstances? Since I have only to gain from the exchange, whatever it may be, would it not be foolish of me to fear death, by which I shall get more than I have?"

Zi Gong, who did not quite understand the meaning of these words, communicated them to Confucius.

"I was right in thinking," said Confucius, "that we could learn something from this man. He knows something, but not everything (for he stops in the succession of existences, without passing to the union with the Principle, which is the end)."

J. *Zi Gong*, bored with studying, said to Confucius:

"Please give me some rest!"

"There is no place of rest among the living," said Confucius.

"Then," said *Zi Gong*, "give some rest without place."

"You will find," said Confucius, "rest without place in death."

"Then," said *Zi Gong*, "long live death, the rest of the Sage, whom fools fear so wrongly!"

"You have been initiated," said Confucius. "Yes, the common people speak of the joys of life, the honors of old age, the pains of death. The reality is that life is bitter, that old age is decay, that death is rest."

K. *Yen Zi* said:

"The ancients have best understood what death is, the rest desired by the good, the fate feared by the wicked. Death is the return. That is why we call the dead, the returned. Logically, we should call the living, the returned. — To walk without knowing where one is going is an act of those who have gone astray, the ones we laugh at. Unfortunately, now most men are lost, not knowing where they are going in death, and no one laughs at them. If a man neglects his affairs and wanders aimlessly, he will be called a fool. The same I say of those who, forgetting the Hereafter, immerse themselves in riches and honors; though, to these, the world judges them wise. No, they are mistaken. Only the wise know where they are going."

L. Someone asked *Lie Zi*:

"Why do you value emptiness so much?"

"Emptiness," said *Lie Zi*, "cannot be esteemed for its own sake. It is estimable by the peace found in it. Peace in emptiness is an indefinable state. One gets to settle there. It is neither taken nor given. In the past, we used to strive for it. Now the exercise of kindness and fairness is preferred, which does not give the same result."

M. *Yu Xiong* used to say:

"The transport of deceased beings, under the action of heaven and earth, is imperceptible. The being that perishes here is reborn elsewhere; the being that is added here is subtracted elsewhere. Decay and prosperity, becoming and ending, comings and goings follow one another, without the thread of this sequence being grasped. So imperceptible is the arrival of those who come and the departure of those who go that the universe always presents the same aspect. Just as the changes in a human organism, in the face, skin, and hair, from birth to death, are daily, but cannot be seen from one day to the next."

N. In the land of *Qi*, a man was tormented by the fear that the sky would fall on his head and the earth would collapse beneath his feet. The fear of this great cataclysm haunted him to the point of making him lose sleep and appetite.

A friend was moved by his condition and undertook to cheer him up.

"The sky," he said, "is not solid. Up there there are only vapors coming and going, expanding and contracting, forming the cosmic breath. It cannot fall."

"So be it," said the trembling one, "but the sun, the moon, the stars…"

"These celestial bodies," said the friend, "are also made only of luminous gases. If they were to fall, they would not have enough mass to make even a wound."

"What if the earth were to collapse?" asked the trembling one.

"The earth is too great a lump," said the friend, "for the footsteps of men to wear it away; and it is too well suspended in space for their shaking to agitate it."

Reassured, the trembling man laughed; and the friend, pleased that he had succeeded in reassuring him, laughed also.

However, *Chang Lu Zi*, hearing this story, criticized both the worrier and his friend, saying:

"That the sky and the heavenly bodies are made of light vapors, and that the all-bearing earth is made of solid matter, it is true. But these vapors and this matter are compounds. Who can guarantee that these compounds will never decompose? Given this uncertainty, speculating about the possibility of the ruin of heaven and earth is reasonable. But to live in continual expectation of that ruin is unreasonable. Let us leave the lamentations about the great collapse to those who will be his contemporaries."

Lie Zi, after hearing this solution, said:

"To assert that heaven and earth will be ruined, would be going too far; to assert that they will not be ruined, would also be going too far. It is impossible to know with certainty what will happen, whether it will happen or whether it will not happen. I conclude this with an analogy. The living know nothing of their future state of death, the dead know nothing of their future state of new life. Those who are coming (the living) know not how their departure (death) will be, and those who have gone (the dead) know not how they will return (alive). Unable to realize the phases of their own evolution, how could men realize the crises of heaven and earth?"

O. *Shun* asked *Zheng*:

"Can one possess the Principle?"

"You do not even possess your body," said *Zheng*; "then how could you possess the Principle?"

"If I do not possess my body," said *Shun* in surprise, "then to whom does it belong?"

"To heaven and earth, of which it is a part," replied *Zheng*. "Your life is an atom of cosmic harmony. Your nature and its destiny are an atom of the universal accord. Your children and grandchildren are not yours, but of the great whole of which they are children. You walk without knowing what pushes you, you stand without knowing what fixes you, you eat without knowing how you assimilate. All that you are is an effect of the irresistible cosmic emanation. And what do you have?"

P. In the country of *Qi*, a certain *Guo* was very rich. In the country of the *Song*, a certain *Xiang* was very poor. The poor man went to ask the rich man how he had become rich.

"By stealing," said the rich man. "When I began to steal, after one year I had what I needed, after two years I had plenty, after three years I had reached affluence, and then I became a great man."

Misunderstanding the term "steal," *Xiang* did not ask him any more questions. At the height of joy, he took his leave and immediately went to work, climbing or drilling the walls, grabbing whatever was convenient. Soon he was arrested, had to give up his loot, and even lost what little he had before, but he was happy to get off without further trouble. Convinced that *Guo* had cheated him, he went to reproach him bitterly.

"How did you do it?" *Guo* asked him, astonished.

When *Xiang* told him of his methods, *Guo* said: "Ah, but it was not by that kind of robbery that I became rich. I, according to times and circumstances, stole the riches of heaven and earth, from the rain, the mountains and the plains. I have appropriated what they have made to grow and ripen, the wild animals of the prairies, the fish and the turtles of the waters. All that I have I stole from nature, but before it belonged to anyone; while you stole what heaven had already given to other men."

Xiang went away dissatisfied, convinced that *Guo* was still deceiving him. He met with the master of the eastern suburb and told him his case.

"Yes," said the latter, "all appropriation is theft. Even being, life, is a theft of a part of the harmony of *yin* and *yang*; how much more any appropriation of a material being is theft from nature. But we must distinguish between theft and robbery. Theft from nature is the common theft that everyone commits and which is not punished. Theft from others is the private theft that thieves commit and which is punished. All men live by stealing from heaven and earth, without being thieves."

CHAPTER 2 - NATURAL SIMPLICITY

A. *Huang Di* had reigned for fifteen years, enjoying his popularity, worrying about his health, indulging his senses, to the point of being emaciated. When he had reigned for thirty years, making continuous intellectual and physical efforts to organize the empire and improve the lot of the people, he found himself even thinner and more tired. Then he said to himself with a sigh: I must have exaggerated. If I am not able to do good to myself, how will I be able to do good to all beings?

With that, *Huang Di* abandoned the concerns of government, left the palace, got rid of his entourage, deprived himself of all music, reduced himself to a frugal diet, and confined himself to an isolated apartment, where for three months he devoted himself solely to regulating his thoughts and restraining his body. During this seclusion, one day, during naptime, he dreamed that he was walking in the country of *Hua Xu*.

This country is to the west of *Yen Zhou*, to the north of *Tai Zhou*, I don't know how far from this country of *Qi*. One cannot go there, neither by boat nor in a carriage; only the flight of the soul reaches it. In this country there is no leader; everything works spontaneously. People have no desires or lust, but only their natural instinct. No one loves life, no one fears death; everyone lives to the end. There are no friendships or hatreds. There are no gains and no losses. No interests and no fears. Water does not drown them, fire does not burn them. No weapon can hurt them, no hand can harm them. They rise in the air as if climbing steps, and lie down in the void as in a bed. Clouds and mists do not intercept their sight, the sound of thunder does not affect their hearing, no beauty, no ugliness stirs their heart, no height, no depth impedes their course. The flight of the soul carries them everywhere.

When he awoke, a light of peace illumined the emperor's mind. He called his chief ministers, *Tian Lao, Li Mu* and *Tai Shan Ji*, and said to them:

"For three months of retreat, I regulated my mind and tamed my body, thinking how I could rule without tiring myself. In the waking state I did not find the solution; it came to me in my dream. Now I know that the Supreme Principle is not attained by positive efforts (but by abstraction and inaction). The light is made in my mind, but I cannot explain the matter better."

After this dream, *Huang Di* reigned for another twenty-eight years, (applying the method of letting all things pass). Thus, the empire became very prosperous, almost as prosperous as the land of *Hua Xu*. Then the emperor ascended to the heights. Two centuries later, the people (who missed him) still remembered him.

B. Mount *Gu ye* is situated on the island of *He Zhou*. It is inhabited by transcendent men, who use no food, but breathe the air and drink the dew. Their minds are as clear as spring water, their complexion as fresh as that of a young girl. Some are endowed with extraordinary faculties, others are only very wise, without love, without fear, living quietly, simply, modestly, having what they need without needing to obtain it. Among them, *yin* and *yang* are constantly in harmony, the sun and moon shine without interruption, the four seasons are regular, the wind and rain come at the right time, the reproduction of animals and the ripening of crops are punctual. There are no deadly miasmas, no evil beasts, no ghosts that cause illness or death, no apparitions or extraordinary noises (phenomena that always indicate a defect in the cosmic balance).

C. *Lie Zi* learned from his master *Lao Shang*, and from his friend *Bo Gao Zi*, the art of riding on the wind (ecstatic rides). When *Yin Sheng* learned of this, he went to stay with him, intending to learn this art from him, and attended his ecstasies, which deprived him of all sense for a considerable time. Several times he asked for the prescription, but was refused on every occasion. Dissatisfied, he asked for his discharge. *Lie Zi* did not answer him. *Yin Sheng* left. But, still driven by the same desire, after a few months he returned to *Lie Zi*. The latter asked him:

"Why did you leave, and why did you come back?"

Yin Sheng replied:

"You refused all my requests; you displeased me and I left; now that my resentment has been extinguished, I have returned."

Lie Zi said:

"I thought you had a better soul than this; can it be that you have become so vile? I will tell you how I was trained by my master. I entered his house with a friend. I spent three whole years in his house, busy curbing my heart and mouth, without him honoring me with a single glance. As I went along, after five years he smiled at me for the first time. As I went along, after seven years he made me sit on his mat. After nine years of effort, I finally lost all notion of yes and no, of advantage and disadvantage, of my master's superiority and my partner's friendship. Then the specific use of my various senses was replaced by a general sense; my mind became condensed, while my body became rarefied; my bones and flesh liquefied (etherized); I lost the feeling that I was heavy on my seat, that I was supported by my feet (levitation); finally, I went, at the whim of the wind, eastward, westward, in all directions, like a dead leaf blown away, without realizing whether it was the wind that carried me, or whether it was I who rode the wind. This is what I had to go through to reach ecstasy. And you, who have just entered the house of a master, who are still so imperfect that you become impatient and angry; you, who push the air and have a coarse and heavy body that the earth must support, do you intend to rise above the wind in the void?"

Yin Sheng withdrew in confusion, not daring to answer anything.

D. *Lie Zi* asked *Guan Yin Zi*:

"The superior man passes through where there is no opening, passes through fire without being burned, rises very high without experiencing vertigo; tell me, please, how does he achieve it?"

"By preserving," said *Guan Yin Zi*, "his perfectly pure nature; not by any scholarly or ingenious process. I will explain. All that has form, shape, figure, sound and color, all these are beings. Why should these beings be opposed to each other? Why should there be any other order among them than priority in time? Why should their evolution cease with the deposition of their present form? To understand this thoroughly is true science. He who has understood this, having a firm foundation, will embrace the whole chain of beings, unify his powers, strengthen his body, retract his energies and communicate with the universal evolution. His nature will retain its perfect integrity, his spirit will retain its complete freedom, nothing external will have control over him. If this man, in a state of drunkenness, should fall from a carriage, he will not be mortally injured. Although his bones and joints are like those of other men, the same traumatism will not have the same effect on him; for his mind, being whole, protects his body. Unconsciousness acts as a protective sheath. Nothing can take hold of the body when the mind is not moving. No being can harm the Sage, enveloped in the integrity of his nature, protected by the freedom of his mind."

E. *Lie Zi* drew the bow in the presence of *Bo Hun Wu Ren*, with a cup of water tied to his left elbow. He drew the bow to the maximum, with his right hand, made the shot, placed another arrow, and shot again; and thus, with the impassivity of a statue, without the water in the cup wavering.

Bo Hun Wu Ren said to him:

"Your shooting is the shooting of an archer fully occupied with his shooting (artificial shooting), not the shooting of an archer indifferent to his shooting (natural shooting). Come with me to some high mountain, on the edge of a cliff, and we will see if you still have that presence of mind."

The two men did so. *Bo Hun Wu Ren* camped on the edge of the cliff, his back to the chasm, with his heels sticking out into the void (note that the archer must lean back in order to shoot), then saluted *Lie Zi* according to the rites, before beginning to shoot. But *Lie Zi*, dizzy, was already lying on the ground, sweat pouring down to his heels. *Bo Hun Wu Ren* said to him:

"The superior man sinks his gaze into the depths of the sky, into the abysses of the earth, into the remoteness of the horizon, without his mind being moved. It seems to me that your eyes are haggard, and that, if you were to shoot, you would not reach the goal."

F. A member of the *Fan* clan, named *Zi Hua*, very greedy for popularity, had become closely linked with the people of the *Jin* principality. The prince of *Jin* had made him his favorite, and listened to him more willingly than to his ministers, doling out honors and rebukes at his instigation. Beggars also queued at *Zi Hua*'s door, and he amused himself by making them display their wits before him, and even made them fight, not bothering in the least about the accidents that occurred in these jousts. The public morale of *Jin*'s principality was affected by these excesses.

One day *He Sheng* and *Zi Bo*, returning from visiting the *Fan* family, spent the night, a day's journey away from the city, at an inn run by a certain *Shang Qiu Kai* (a Daoist). They commented on what they had just seen. This *Zi Hua*, they said, is all-powerful; he saves or destroys whom he wills; he enriches or ruins as he pleases.

Shang Qiu Kai, who could not sleep for hunger and cold, overheard this conversation across the threshold. The next day, carrying some provisions, he went to the city and presented himself at the gate of *Zi Hua*. Those who besieged this gate were all people of good position, richly dressed and riding in carriages, conceited and arrogant. When they saw this old man, sallow-faced, ill-dressed and ill-coiffed, they all looked down on him, then belittled him, and finally mocked him in every way. Whatever they said, *Shang Qiu Kai* remained impassive, smiling lending himself to their game with a smile.

Meanwhile, *Zi Hua*, having led the whole band to a high terrace, said:

"I promise a hundred ounces of gold to anyone who jumps down."

Those who were laughing before were afraid. *Shang Qiu Kai* jumped at once, descended gently like a flying bird and landed on the ground without breaking any bones.

"This is an effect of chance," said the gang.

Then *Zi Hua* led them all to the river bank, to a bend that produced a deep whirlpool.

"In this place," he said, "at the very bottom, there is a rare pearl; whoever pulls it out, he can keep it!"

Shang Qiu Kai immediately dived down and pulled out the rare pearl from the bottom of the abyss. Then the group began to suspect that he was an extraordinary being.

Zi Hua made him get dressed and they sat down together at the table. Suddenly, a fire broke out in a tent belonging to the *Fan* family.

"I'll give," said *Zi Hua*, "everything he can get back, to whoever enters this hell."

Without his face altering, *Shang Qiu Kai* immediately entered the fire and came out without being burned or scorched.

Convinced at last that this man possessed transcendental endowments, the gang apologized to him.

"We didn't know," they said, "that's why we disrespected you. You paid no more attention to us than a deaf man or a blind man, confirming with this stoicism your transcendence. Please tell us your formula."

"I have no formula," said *Shang Qiu Kai*. "I go as my natural instinct leads me, without knowing why or how. I came to see you, because two of my hosts told me about you, the distance is not great. I perfectly believed everything you told me, and I wanted to do it, without any ulterior motive connected with myself. Therefore, I acted under the impulse of my complete and indivisible natural instinct. No being opposes one who acts thus (this action being in the direction of the cosmic movement). If you had not told me this, I would never have suspected that you were making fun of me. Now that I know, I am somewhat moved. In this state, I would not dare to confront water and fire as before, for I would not do so with impunity."

After this lesson, the customers of the *Fan* family no longer insult anyone. They get out of their carts to greet even beggars and veterinaries on the road.

Zai Wo related this whole story to Confucius.

"There is no doubt about it," said the latter, "Don't you know that a man who is absolutely simple bends all beings by this simplicity, touches heaven and earth, and propitiates the spirits, so that in the six regions of space nothing opposes him, nothing is hostile to him, and fire and water do him no harm? If his unenlightened simplicity protected *Shang Qiu Kai*, how much more will my wise righteousness protect me? Remember this! (Revelation of the head of the school)."

G. The administrator of the grazing lands of the emperor *Xuan* of the *Zhou* dynasty, had in his service an employee named *Liang Yang*, endowed with extraordinary power over wild animals. When he entered his enclosure to feed them, the most rebellious ones, tigers, wolves and ospreys, obediently submitted to his voice. He could confront them with impunity in the most critical situations, during the rutting or nursing period, or when there were enemy species. When the emperor learned of this, he believed he was using some amulet, and ordered the official *Mao Qiu Yuan* to investigate. *Liang Yang* said:

"I, a small clerk, how could I possess an amulet? If I possessed one, how could I dare to hide it from the emperor? In short, this is my secret: All beings who have blood in their veins experience attractions and repulsions. These passions are not kindled spontaneously, but by the presence of their object. It is on this principle that I base my dealings with ferocious beasts. I never give my tigers a live prey, lest I should arouse their passion for killing; nor a whole prey, lest I should excite their appetite for tearing. I judge what their dispositions should be, according to the degree of hunger or satiety. The tiger has this in common with man, who loves those who feed and caress him, and only kills those who provoke him. Therefore, I try never to irritate my tigers, and strive, on the contrary, to please them. This is difficult for men of unstable temperament. My mood is always the same. Happy with me, my animals look at me as one of their own. They forget, in my zoo, their deep forests, their vast swamps, their mountains and valleys. It is the simple effect of rational treatment."

H. *Yen Hui* said to Confucius:

"One day when I was crossing the rapids of *Shang*, I admired the extraordinary skill of the boatman, and asked him: can this art be learned? — 'Yes', he said. 'Anyone who can swim can learn it. A good swimmer learns it quickly. A good diver knows it without having learned it.' I did not dare to tell the boatman that I did not understand his answer. Please explain it to me."

"Ah," said Confucius, "I have explained that to you many times in other words, and you still don't understand. Listen and remember this time! Anyone who can swim can learn it, because he has no fear of water. A good swimmer learns it quickly, because he doesn't even think about the water. A good diver knows it without having learned it, because water, having developed into his element, does not cause him the slightest emotion. Nothing hinders the exercise of the faculties of one whose interior is free from all disturbance... When the stake is a shard of pottery, the gamblers are ready. When it's money, they get nervous. When it is gold, they lose their heads. The acquired skill being the same, they are more or less unable to deploy it, the affection of an external object distracting them more or less. Any attention paid to an external thing, disturbs or troubles the interior."

I. One day when Confucius was admiring the waterfall of *Lu Liang*, a waterfall of two hundred and forty feet, which produces a torrent that bubbles along thirty stades, so fast that neither the alligator nor the turtle nor the fish can go up it, he saw a man swimming among the whirlpools. Believing him to be a desperate man seeking death, he asked his disciples to skirt the shore, so that if he came within reach, they might pull him out. Now, a few hundred paces downstream, this same man emerged from the water, untied his hair to dry it, and began to follow the bank, at the foot of the dam, humming. Confucius joined him and said:

"When I saw you swimming in this stream, I thought you wanted to end your life. Then, seeing the ease with which you came out of the water, I took you for a transcendent being. But no, you are a man, flesh and blood. Tell me, please, how to play like that in the water."

"I don't know the way," said the man. "When I started, I applied myself; in time, the thing came easy to me; finally I did it naturally, unconsciously. I let myself be sucked into the central funnel of the whirlpool and then I was thrown into the peripheral whirlpool. I follow the movement of the water, without making any movement. That is all I can tell you about it."

J. Confucius was on his way to the kingdom of *Chu*. In a clearing he saw a hunchback knocking down flying cicadas, as if catching them with his hands.

You are very clever," he said, "tell me your secret."

"This is my secret," said the hunchback. "I practiced for five or six months, balancing balls on a stick. When I managed to balance two of them, only a few cicadas escaped me. When I managed to balance three balls, I only missed one cicada out of ten times. When I managed to balance five balls, I caught the cicadas on the fly, with my stick, as surely as with my hand. Neither my body nor my arm feels any spontaneous nervous tremors anymore. My attention is no longer distracted by anything. In this immense universe filled with so many beings, I only see the cicada I am aiming at, so I never lose it."

Confucius looked at his disciples and said:

"The concentration of the will on a single object produces a perfect cooperation of the body with the mind."

The hunchback, in turn, asked Confucius:

"But you, scholar, for what purpose have you asked me this? Why do you ask about things that are none of your business? Have you no malicious intention?"

A young man who lived by the sea was very fond of seagulls. Every morning he would go to the seashore to greet them, and the seagulls would come down by the hundreds to play with him. One day the young man's father said to him:

"Since the seagulls are so familiar with you, take some and bring them to me, so that I too can play with them".

The next day, the young man went to the beach as usual, but with the secret intention of obeying his father. His exterior betrayed his interior. The seagulls were wary. They played in the air above his head, but none came down.

The best use of speech is silence. The best action is not to act. To want to embrace all that is knowable produces only a superficial science.

K. At the head of a march of a hundred thousand people, *Zhao Xiang Zi* was hunting in the mountains of *Zhung Shan*. To drive the wild beasts from their dens, he set fire to the undergrowth. The glow of the fire was visible a hundred stades away. In the midst of this fire, a man was seen emerging from a rock, flitting through the flames, playing with the smoke. All onlookers judged that he could only be a transcendent being.

When the fire passed, the man approached them, as if nothing had happened. Surprised, *Zhao Xiang Zi* held him back and examined him calmly. He was a man constituted like any other. *Zhao Xiang Zi* asked him about his secret for penetrating the rocks and remaining in the fire, this man said:

"What is a rock, what is fire?"

Zhao Xiang Zi answered him:

"That from which you came out is a rock; what you went through was fire."

"Ah," said the man, "I didn't know anything about that."

Marquis *Wen* of *Wei*, having heard this story, asked *Zi Xia* what he thought of this man.

"I have heard my master (Confucius) say," said *Zi Xia*, "that he who has attained perfect union with the cosmos is no longer harmed by any being; that he penetrates metal and stone at will; that he walks at will on water and fire."

"Do you possess," asked the marquis, "such a gift?"

"No," said *Zi Xia*, "for I have not yet succeeded in ridding myself of my intelligence and my will; I am still only a disciple."

"And your master Confucius, does he possess this gift?"

"Yes," said *Zi Xia*, "but he does not show it."

Marquis *Wen* felt edified.

L. A very transcendent soothsayer, named *Ji Xian*, originally from the principality of *Qi*, settled in that of *Zheng*, and always predicted misfortunes and death, to the exact day, infallibly. So the inhabitants of *Zheng*, who did not want to know so much, fled as soon as they saw him approaching.

Lie Zi went to see him and was amazed at what he saw and heard. When he returned, he said to his master *Hu Zi*:

"Until now I have regarded your doctrine as the most perfect, but now I have found a superior one."

Hu Zi said:

"It is that you do not know all my doctrine, having received from me only the exoteric teaching, and not the esoteric. Your knowledge is like eggs laid by hens without a rooster; the essential (the germ) is missing. And then, when one argues, one must have firm faith in one's opinion, otherwise, if one wavers, the opponent will notice one's weakness. This is what must have happened to you. You must have betrayed yourself, and mistaken the natural gift of *Ji Xian* for transcendental divination. Bring this man to me, and see how the experiment goes."

The next day, *Lie Zi* took the fortune-teller to *Hu Zi's* house, under the pretext of a medical consultation. When he came out, the soothsayer said to *Lie Zi*:

"Alas, your master is a dead man. His life will be over in a few days. When I examined him I had a strange vision, like wet ashes, an omen of death."

When he dismissed the soothsayer, *Lie Zi* returned weeping and informed *Hu Zi* of what he had just been told. *Hu Zi* said:

"It is that I manifested myself to him under the figure of an inert and sterile earth, with all my energies arrested (an aspect which the vulgar present only in the vicinity of death, but which the contemplative presents at will). That blocked him. Bring him back another time and see what happens."

The next day, *Lie Zi* brought back the soothsayer. When he came out, he said to *Lie Zi*:

"It is fortunate that your master came to me; there is already an improvement; the ashes are reviving; I have seen signs of vital energy."

Lie Zi reported these words to *Hu Zi*, who said:

"It is that I manifested myself to him under the aspect of an earth fertilized by heaven, the energy arising from the depths under the influx from above. He saw well, but interpreted wrongly, (taking as natural the result of his contemplation). Bring him back, so that we can continue the experiment."

The next day, *Lie Zi* brought back the soothsayer. Having made his examination, he said to him:

"Today I found your lord looking vague and indeterminate, from which I cannot draw any prognosis; when his condition becomes more clearly defined, I will be able to tell you what it is."

Lie Zi reported these words to *Hu Zi*, who said:

"It is that I manifested myself to him in the figure of the great chaos not yet differentiated, with all my powers in a state of neutral equilibrium. In fact, he could not get anything clear from this figure. A whirlpool in the water may be caused equally by the frolic of a sea monster, by a reef, the force of the current, a spring, a waterfall, the union of two streams, a dam, a detour, or by the breaking of a dam; identical effect of nine different causes (it is therefore impossible to infer directly from the whirlpool the nature of its cause; it is necessary for further examination to determine this). Bring it once more and see what happens."

The next day, the soothsayer returned, stopped only a moment in front of *Hu Zi*, understood nothing, lost his temper and fled.

"Run after him," said *Hu Zi*.

Lie Zi obeyed, but could not catch up with him.

"He won't come back," said *Hu Zi*. "It is because I manifested myself as arising from the primordial principle before time, a movement in the void without apparent form, a seething of inert power. This was too much for him, so he fled."

Seeing that he still understood nothing of his master's esoteric doctrine, *Lie Zi* secluded himself in his house for three consecutive years. He cooked for his wife, served the pigs as if they were men (to destroy the human prejudices inside him). He lost interest in everything. He abandoned everything in him of artificial culture, returning to primitive natural simplicity. He became as coarse as a clod of earth, oblivious to all events and accidents, and thus remained concentrated on unity until the end of his days.

M. When Master *Lie Zi* was on his way to *Qi*, he suddenly retraced his steps. *Bo Hun Wu Ren*, whom he knew, asked him:

"Why do you return in this way?"

"Because I am afraid," said *Lie Zi*.

"Afraid of what?" asked *Bo Hun Wu Ren*.

"I have been to ten restaurants," said *Lie Zi*, "and five times I have been served first. My inner perfection must have been perceptible to those people, for them to serve customers richer or older than me after me. Therefore I feared that if I reached the capital of *Qi*, knowing also my merit, the prince would unload on my shoulders the government that burdens him so much."

"This is well thought out," said *Bo Hun Wu Ren*. "You have escaped from a princely patron; but I fear you will soon have masters at home."

Some time later, *Bo Hun Wu Ren* went to visit *Lie Zi* and saw several shoes in front of his door (an indication of the presence of many visitors). Stopping in the courtyard, he thought for a long time, with his chin resting on the end of his cane, and then left without a word. However, the doorman had warned *Lie Zi*. The latter quickly grabbed his sandals and, without taking the time to put them on, ran after his friend. When he caught up with him at the outer gate, he said:

"Why are you leaving like this, without leaving me any useful advice?"

"What good would it do now?" said *Bo Hun Wu Ren*. "Didn't I tell you? Now you have masters at home. You certainly did not attract them, but you did not know how to repel them either. What influence will you have over them now? You can only influence someone if you keep your distance. You can't say anything to those who have conquered you. Those with whom you are connected, you cannot reject. The words of vulgar people are poisonous to the perfect man. What is the use of conversing with people who neither hear nor understand?"

N. *Yang Zhu* was going to *Pei* and *Lao Zi* was going to *Qin*. The two met at *Liang*. Seeing *Yang Zhu*, *Lao Zi* raised his eyes to the sky and said with a sigh:

"I was hoping to instruct you, but I see that there is no way."

Yang Zhu did not answer anything. When the two travelers arrived at the inn where they were to spend the night, *Yang Zhu* first brought all the necessary toiletries. Then, when *Lao Zi* was settled in his room, having left his shoes at the door, *Yang Zhu* walked in on his knees and said to *Lao Zi*:

"I didn't understand what you said about me, looking at the sky and sighing. Since I didn't want to delay your journey, I didn't ask you for explanations then. But now that you are free, please explain to me the meaning of your words."

"You have," said *Lao Zi*, "a haughty air that repels; while the Sage seems confused, however blameless he may be, and considers himself inadequate, however perfect he may be."

"Your lesson will serve me well," said *Yang Zhu*, "much mortified."

That very night *Yang Zhu* humbled himself so much that the staff of the inn, who had treated him with respect in the evening when he arrived, no longer respected him in the morning when he left (in China, the respect of the servants is proportional to the haughtiness of the traveler).

O. *Yang Zhu*, passing through the principality of *Song*, received hospitality in an inn. The innkeeper had two women, one beautiful and one ugly. The ugly one was loved, the beautiful one was hated.

"Why?" Asked *Yang Zhu* to a little servant.

"Because," said the boy, "the beautiful woman always exhibits her beauty, which makes her displeasing to us; while the ugly woman knows that she is ugly, which makes us forget her ugliness."

"Remember this, disciples!" said *Yang Zhu* "Be wise, but do not pretend to be wise; that is the secret of being loved everywhere."

P. There are, in this world, only two ways; that of subordination, deference; and that of insubordination, arrogance. Its adherents have been defined by the ancients in this way: the arrogant only feel sympathy for those who are smaller than themselves, the deferential also love those who are superior to them. Arrogance is dangerous, because it attracts enemies; deference is safe, because it only gets friends. Everything is successful for the deferent, both in private and public life; while the arrogant only obtains failures. Therefore *Yu Zi* said that power must always be tempered by condescension; for it is condescension that makes power enduring; and that this rule makes it possible to predict with certainty whether a particular individual or State will prosper or fail. Strength is not solid, while nothing equals the solidity of gentleness. That is why *Lao Dan* said, "The power of a state brings it to ruin, as the greatness of a tree calls for the axe. Weakness brings life, strength brings death."

Q. The wise man allies himself with those who have the same inner feelings as himself, the vulgar man allies himself with those who please him on the outside. Now, in a human body may be hidden a beast's heart; a beast's body may contain a human heart. In both cases, judging by the exterior will be misleading.

Fu Xi, Nü Gua, Shen Nong, Yu the Great, had a human head on a serpent's body, or an ox's head, or a tiger's snout; but, under these animal forms, they were great Sages. While *Jie* the last of the *Xias, Zhou* the last of the *Yin,* Duke *Huan* of *Lu*, and Duke *Mu* of *Chu*, were beasts in human form. — When *Huang Di* fought against

Yen Di on the plain of *Fan Quan*, ferocious beasts formed his battle front and birds of prey were his light infantry. He had attached these animals to himself by his ancestry. — When *Yao* put *Kui* in charge of the music, the animals came running and dancing, enchanted by the musical tones.

Can it be said, after this, that there is any essential difference between animals and men? No doubt their ways and languages differ from those of men, but is there no way to get along with them in spite of this? The aforementioned Sages, who knew everything and extended their concern to all, also knew how to win over animals. There is much in common between the instincts of animals and the habits of men. They too live in pairs, parents love their children. They also look for safe places to live. They also prefer temperate regions to cold ones. They also gather in groups, they walk in order, the small ones in the center, the big ones around. They also point out to each other suitable places to drink or graze. — In early times, animals and men lived and traveled together. When men were given emperors and kings, distrust arose and that caused separation. Later, fear drove animals further and further away from man. Even now, however, the distance is not unbridgeable. In the East, among the *Jie* people still understand their language, at least of domestic animals. The ancient Sages understood the language and penetrated the feelings of all beings, and communicated with all as with their human people, both with the *Kui, Shen, Li*, and *Mei* (transcendent beings), and with birds, quadrupeds, and insects. On the principle that the feelings of beings having the same blood and breathing the same air cannot differ much, they treated animals like humans, with success.

A monkey breeder in the principality of *Song* had managed to understand monkeys and be understood by them. He treated them better than his family members, denying them nothing. However, he fell on hard times. Forced to ration his monkeys, he came up with the following way to make them accept rationing.

"From now on," he told them, "you shall each have three taro roots in the morning and four in the afternoon; is that all right?"

All the monkeys stood up, very angry. Then he said to them:

"From now on, each of you shall have four taro roots in the morning and three in the afternoon; is that all right with you?"

Satisfied that their dissatisfaction had been taken into account, all the monkeys went back to bed, very happy… This is how one wins over the animals. The Sage defeats foolish humans in the same way. It does not matter whether the means used are real or apparent; as long as it succeeds in satisfying, not irritating[7].

Another example of the close analogy between animals and men: *Ji Xing Zi* trained a fighting cock for Emperor *Xuan* of the *Zhou*. At the end of ten days, when asked about him, he said:

"He is not yet fit to fight; he is still vain and stubborn".

Ten days later, when questioned again, he replied:

---

7   Compare chapter 2 C of *Zhuang Zhou*, a somewhat different application of the same theme.

"Not yet; he still responds to the crowing of other roosters."
Ten days later he said:
"Not yet; he is still nervous and passionate."
Ten days later he said:
"Now he is ready; he no longer pays attention to the crowing of his companions; he is not moved, at the sight of them any more than if he were made of wood. All his energies are unified. No other rooster will be able to face him."

R. When *Hui Ang*, a relative of *Hui Shu*, and a sophist like him, appeared before King *Kang* of *Song*, the latter stumbled and coughed impatiently at the sight of him, and said volubly.

"I love strength and bravery; kindness and fairness are subjects which tell me nothing; you are warned; now tell me what you have to tell me."

"One of my favorite subjects is to explain why the blows of the brave and the strong are sometimes left without effect," said *Hui Ang*; "would you like to hear this speech?"

"I will gladly listen to it," said the king.

"They are without effect," said the sophist, "when they are not executed. And why are they not executed? Either because they don't dare or because they don't want to. This is another of my favorite topics… Let's say it's because they don't want to. Why don't they want to do it? Because there won't be any benefit. That's another one of my favorite topics… Now suppose there were a way to get all the advantages, to win the hearts of all the men and women in the empire, to be safe from all the trouble, wouldn't you like to know what that way is?"

"Oh, yes!" said the king.

"Well," said the sophist, "it is the doctrine of Confucius and *Mo Zi*, of which you did not want to hear before. Confucius and *Mo Zi*, those two princes without land, those nobles without titles, are the joy and pride of the men and women of the whole empire. If you, prince, who have lands and titles, embrace the doctrine of these two men, all will give themselves to you, and you will become more famous than they, having also power[8]."

The King of the *Song* did not know how to answer him. *Hui Ang* left in triumph. He was already far away, when the King of the *Song* said to his courtiers:

"But say something! This man has left me speechless!"

CHAPTER 3[9] - PSYCHICAL STATES

A. In the time of Emperor *Mu* of the *Zhou*, there came to the court of this emperor a magician from a country in the far west. This man entered with impunity into

---

8   *Hui Ang* was not a disciple of Confucius. But the triumph of the sophists consisted in putting his adversary at a point where it is impossible to defend his own thesis. Having declared beforehand, the King of the *Song*, that he disliked Confucianism, *Hui Ang* proves to him, without believing it himself, that it is the best of doctrines.

9   Reality, memory, imagination, dream, ecstasy, madness, etc.

water and fire, passed through metal and stone, caused streams to return to their source, changed the location of city walls, held himself in the air without falling, penetrated solids without resistance, took all forms at will, maintained his human intelligence in the form of an inanimate object, etc. The emperor *Mu* worshipped him as a genie, served him as his master, and gave him the best of his wealth in lodging, food, and women. However, the magician found the imperial palace uninhabitable, the imperial kitchen inedible, and the harem women unworthy of his affection. So the emperor had a special palace built for him. The materials and workmanship were exquisite. The costs drained the imperial treasury. The finished building rose to a height of eight thousand feet. When the emperor dedicated it, he called it the Tower Touching Heaven. He populated it with chosen young people, called from the principalities of *Zheng* and *Wei*. He installed baths and a harem there. He filled it with precious objects, fine fabrics, cosmetics, perfumes and trinkets. He had the most famous symphonies performed there. Each month he offered a supply of magnificent clothes, each day a profusion of exquisite food… None of this had any effect. The magician found nothing to his taste, lived in his new house without enjoying it and was frequently absent.

One day, during a feast, the magician said to the emperor:

"Come with me."

The emperor grabbed the sleeve of the magician, who immediately lifted him into space, to the palace of transcendent men, located in the middle of heaven. This palace was made of gold and silver, adorned with pearls and jade, higher than the region of the rainy nimbus, without apparent foundations, floating in space like a cloud. In this supra-terrestrial world, the sights, the harmonies, the smells, the tastes, nothing was like in the world of men. The emperor understood that he was in the city of the Heavenly Sovereign. Seen from above, his earthly palace looked to him like a tiny heap of clods and twigs. He would have stayed there for years, without remembering his empire; but the magician invited him to follow him higher… This time he took him still higher, beyond the sun and the moon, out of sight of land and sea, into a blinding light, a deafening harmony. Gripped by terror and vertigo, the emperor asked to descend. The descent was made with the speed of an aerolite falling into the void.

When he came to, the emperor found himself sitting in his chair, surrounded by his courtiers, his cup half-filled and his stew half-eaten.

"What has happened to me?" he asked his entourage.

"You seem to have withdrawn into yourself for a moment," said his people.

The emperor felt that he had been away for at least three months.

"What was this?" he asked the magician.

"Oh, nothing could be simpler," said the latter. "I raised your spirit. Your body did not move. Or rather, I did not even move your spirit. All distinctions, of place and time, are illusory. The mental representation of all possibilities is realized without movement and abstracted from time."

It is from this episode, that dates the displeasure of the emperor *Mu* for the government of his empire, for the pleasures of his court, and his taste for walks. It was then that, with his eight famous horses, all of different coats, with *Zao Fu* as his chariot driver, *Qi He* serving as his squire, *Shen Bai* driving the wagon with *Ben Rong* as his attendant, he set out on his famous journey across the western frontiers. After traveling a thousand stades, he arrived at the tribe of the *Ju Sou*, who offered him swan's blood to drink and washed his feet with *kumis* (two fortifiers). The next night was spent on the banks of the red stream. At dawn, the emperor climbed the *Kun Lun* mountain, visited the ancient palace of *Huang Di* and erected a cairn in memory of his passage. He then visited *Xi Wang Mu*[10], and was entertained by him (or her) near the green lake. They exchanged toasts, and the emperor made no secret that it pained him to have to return. After contemplating the place where the sun sets at the end of his daytime journey of ten thousand stades, he headed back toward the empire. Ultimately, he returned disappointed, having found nothing resembling his vision.

"Posterity will say of me that I have sacrificed duty to pleasure."

And indeed, having sought only present happiness, he was not a good emperor, nor did he achieved spiritual perfection, but only managed to live a long life, and died at the age of one hundred.

B. *Lao Cheng Zi* entered the school of master *Yin Wen* (*Guan Yin Zi*), to learn from him the secret of universal phantasmagoria. For three whole years his master taught him nothing. *Lao Cheng Zi* attributed this coldness to the fact that his master judged him not capable and offered him to withdraw. Master *Yin Wen*, after greeting him (a sign of extraordinary esteem), led him to his room, and there, without witnesses (to secretly divulge esoteric knowledge), said to him.

"Once, when *Lao Dan* went to the West[11], he summed up his doctrine to me in these words, 'The vital spirit, and the material body, are phantasmagoria. The terms life and death designate the initial genesis of a being by the action of generative virtue, and its final transformation by the influence of natural agents. The succession of these genesis, of these transformations, when the number is full, under the influence of the universal motor, is phantasmagoria. The first Principle of beings is too mysterious, too profound, to be deciphered. We can only study the becoming and the cessation of the body, which are visible and manifest. To understand that cosmic evolution consists practically in the succession of the two states of life and death is the key to the intelligence of phantasmagoria. We are subject to this vicissitude, you and I, and we can see its effects on ourselves.'"

After receiving this instruction, *Lao Cheng Zi* returned home, meditated on it for three months and found the secret of the mystery, so that he became master of life and death, could change the seasons at will, produce storms in winter and ice in summer, transform birds into quadrupeds and vice versa. He taught no one the formula, which nobody has found since, Besides, says *Lie Zi*, for those who possess the science of transformations, it would be better to keep it secret, it is better not

---

10   Probably a king, of whom legend has made a woman. Perhaps towards the Pamir.

11   If authentic, it is the oldest text that speaks of this departure.

to use it. The ancient rulers did not owe their fame to extraordinary displays of science or courage. They were thanked for having acted for the good of mankind without ostentation.

C. The application of the mind has eight effects, namely: deliberation, action, success, failure, sadness, joy, life and death; all of them related to the body. The abstraction of the mind has six causes, namely, will, aversion, intense thought, sleep, rapture, and terror; all of which are of the mind[12]. Those who do not know the natural origin of emotions, worry about their cause, when they have experienced one. Those who know that the origin of emotions is natural, do not worry about it, since they know the cause. Everything in the body of a being, fullness and emptiness, expenditure and increase, everything is in harmony, in balance, with the state of heaven and earth, with all beings inhabiting the cosmos. A predominance of *yin*, makes one dream of wading in the water, with a feeling of freshness. A predominance of *yang* makes one dream of crossing fire, with a sensation of burning. A simultaneous excess of *yin* and *yang* makes one dream of dangers and risks, of hope and fear. In the state of satiety, one dreams of giving; in the state of fasting, one dreams of taking. Light spirits dream of rising in the air, solemn spirits dream of sinking in the water. Going to bed girded with a belt makes one dream of snakes; the sight of birds with hair makes one dream of flying. Before a duel, one dreams of fire; before an illness, one dreams of eating. After drinking too much, one has sad dreams; after dancing too much, one cries in one's sleep.

Lie Zi said:

"The dream is an encounter realized by the mind; reality (objective perception) is a contact with the body. Daytime thoughts and nighttime dreams are also impressions. Therefore, those who are of sound mind, think and dream little, and give little importance to their thoughts and dreams. They know that both thought and dream do not have the reality they appear to have, but are reflections of cosmic phantasmagoria. The ancient sages thought little when awake, dreamed little when asleep, and spoke of neither their thoughts nor their dreams, for they believed as little in the one as in the other. In the southwest corner of the square earth there is a country whose frontiers I do not know. It is called *Gu Mang*. The alternations of *yin* and *yang* are not felt there, so it has no seasons; the sun and moon do not illuminate it, so it has no days and nights. Its inhabitants neither eat nor dress. They sleep almost continuously and wake up only once every fifty days. They take as reality what they have experienced during sleep, and as illusion what they have experienced in the waking state. — In the center of the earth and the four seas is the central kingdom (China), seated on the Yellow River, extending from the country of *Yue* to Mount *Tai Shan*, with an east-west breadth of more than ten thousand stades. The alternation of *yin* and *yang* produces cold and hot seasons, the alternation of light and darkness produces days and nights. Among its inhabitants, there are wise men and fools. Its natural and industrial products

---

12   Compare with *Rituel des Tcheou*, book 24.

are numerous and varied. It has its princes and officials, its rites and laws. There is much talk and much action. Men watch and sleep there by turns, taking as real what they have experienced in the waking state, and as vain what they have experienced in the sleeping state. In the northeast corner of the square earth is the country of *Fu Lao*, whose soil is constantly scorched by the sun's rays and produces no grain. They feed on roots and fruits which they eat raw. They are brutal and value strength more than justice. They are almost constantly on the move, rarely resting. They are awake most of the time and sleep little. They take as real what they have experienced in the waking state.

D. A certain *Yin*, an official of the *Zhou*, lived luxuriously. His servants had no rest from dawn to dusk. One old servant, battered and sick, was no less ill-treated than the others. Now, after working hard all day, every night this man dreamed that he was a prince, sitting on a throne, ruling a country, enjoying all the pleasures. When he woke up, he found that he was a servant, and worked like one all day long. When his friends pitied him, he would say to them:

"I am not so pitiable. Men's lives are equally divided into day and night. During the day I am a servant and work; but at night I am a prince and enjoy myself very much. I have a good time half the day; why should I complain?"

However, this servant's master, after a day of pleasure, dreamed every night that he was a servant, overworked, scolded and punished. He told this to a friend. The latter said to him:

"It must be that you exceed, during the day, the amount of pleasures that fate has assigned you; fate compensates for this with the suffering of your nights."

The officer believed his friend, moderated his luxury, treated his people better and came out well (As a result, the old valet also lost his nightly pleasure, which fate had assigned him in compensation for the excess of his daytime fatigue).

E. A woodcutter from *Zheng* who was gathering firewood, came across a stray deer, which he killed and hid in a ditch under some branches, intending to return and carry it away secretly. When he could not find the place, he thought he had been dreaming, and told the story. One of his listeners, following his instructions, found the deer and took it home. — "This woodcutter's dream was real," he said to the people at home. "Real to you," they replied, "since you were the one who got the deer."

However, the next night, the woodcutter had a revelation in his dream that his deer had been found by a certain person, who had hidden it in his house. When he went there early in the morning, he discovered the deer and accused so-and-so before the village chief. The latter said to the woodcutter:

"If you killed this deer while awake, why did you say you killed it in a dream? If you kill a deer in a dream, it cannot be the real deer. But, since he does not dispute that you killed the animal, I cannot adjudicate it. On the other hand, since your adversary found it from the indications of your dream, and you found it as a result of another dream, share it between the two of you."

The village chief's judgment was brought to the attention of the prince of *Zheng*, who referred it to his minister for examination. The minister said:

"Only *Huang Di* and Confucius are qualified to decide what is a dream and what is not, and what is the law in the matter of dreams. As at present we have neither of them to decide this dispute, I think we must accept the arbitration award of the village headman."

F. In *Yang Li*, in the principality of *Song*, a certain *Hua Zi* of middle age suffered from an illness which completely took away his memory. He could no longer remember at night whether he had made such and such a purchase in the morning; the next day he did not know whether he had made this or that expenditure the day before. Outside his house, he would forget to walk; at home, he would not think of sitting down. All memory of the past gradually faded for him.

A scholar from the principality of *Lu* offered to treat this case of amnesia. The family of *Hua Zi* promised him half of his fortune if he succeeded. The scholar said:

"Against this disease, incantations, prayers, medicines and acupuncture, have no effect. He will only be cured if I can reform his mind."

After experimentally observing that the patient kept asking for clothes when he was naked, food when he was hungry and light when it was dark, he told the family:

"There is hope of recovery. But my procedure is secret; I will communicate it to no one."

He then locked himself up alone with the patient, who, after seven days, was cured of this amnesia of many years. But, oh surprise! As soon as he regained his memory, *Hua Zi* became very angry, made bloody reproaches to his family, took a spear and put the scholar to flight.

They seized him and asked him the reason for that fury.

"Ah!" he said, "I was so happy, when I didn't even know if there is a heaven and an earth! Now I will have to register in my memory the successes and failures, the joys and sorrows, the good and the bad of the past, and worry about them for the future. Who will restore to me, even for a moment, the happiness of unconsciousness?"

When *Zi Gong* heard this story, he was very surprised and asked Confucius for an explanation.

"You are not capable of understanding this (you have an overly practical mind)," said Confucius; "*Yen Hui* (the abstract contemplative) will understand it better."

G. A certain *Pang* of the principality of *Qin* had a son. When he was very young, this child seemed intelligent. But when he grew up, his mentality became very strange. Singing made him cry, white seemed black to him, perfumes seemed stinky to him, sugar bitter, evil good. In a word, in thoughts and things, in each and everything, he was the opposite of other men.

A certain *Yang* said to his father:

"This case is quite extraordinary, but the scholars of *Lu* are very learned; ask their advice."

So the father of the unbalanced man went to *Lu*. Passing by *Chen*, he met *Lao Dan* and told him about his son's case. *Lao Dan* replied to him:

"Is this why you think he is crazy? But the men of this age are all like that. They all take evil for good, holding their profit as the standard of morality. Your son's disease is the common disease; there is no one who does not suffer from it. One madman per family, one family of madmen per village, one village of madmen per principality, one principality of madmen in the empire, this would be tolerable, at best. But now the whole empire is mad, of the same madness as your son; or rather, the one who is mad is you, who thinks differently from everyone else. Who is going to define the rule of feelings, sounds, colors, smells, tastes, good and evil? I don't know if I am wise, but I certainly know that the *Lu* literati (who claim to define these things), are the worst sowers of insanity. And it is them you will ask to cure your child! Believe me, save yourself the expense of a useless journey and return home by the shortest way."

H. A boy born in the principality of *Yen* (in the far north) was transferred to and brought up in the kingdom of *Chu* (in the far south of the empire), where he spent his whole life. When he reached old age, he returned to his native country. Halfway there, as he approached the main city of *Jin*, his fellow travelers said to him, mockingly:

"This is the main city of *Yen*, your homeland."

Our man believed them, turned pale and became sad. Then, showing him a mound of the genie of the earth, they said to him:

"This is the mound of your hometown".

The man sighed painfully. Then they showed him a house and said:

"This is the home of your ancestors."

The man burst into tears. Then they showed him some graves and said:

"And these are their graves."

At these words, our man burst out crying. Then his companions, laughing at him, discovered his deception.

"We have deceived you," they said. "This is *Jin*; this is not *Yen*."

Our man was very confused, and henceforth restrained his feelings. Therefore, when he came to *Yen*, and actually saw its main town, the mound of his village, the home of his ancestors and their tombs, he felt hardly any emotion[13].

Chapter 4 - Extinction and Union

A. Confucius was meditating in his retreat. *Zi Gong* came in to serve him and found him sad. As he dared not ask him what afflicted him, he went out and told *Yen Hui* (the favorite disciple). The latter took his zither and began to sing. Confucius heard him, called him over and asked:

---

13   For the Daoists, feeling is a mistake, emotion is a fault.

"Why are you so happy?"

"And why are you sad?" asked *Yen Hui*.

"First tell me why you are happy," said Confucius.

Yen Hui said:

"You taught me before, that pleasing heaven and submitting to fate, drove away all sadness. I do this. Hence my joy."

Confucius, looking gloomy, meditated for a moment and then said:

"It is true that I have said these words, but you have misunderstood them. I myself have had to change my interpretation of them since then. You have taken them in the limited sense of the work of self-improvement, of patience in poverty and vicissitudes, of resting your mind in all situations. Having achieved them, you feel joy... I myself have understood them in a broader sense. I wanted, cooperating with heaven and destiny, to amend with my doctrines the principality of *Lu*, the whole empire, the present time and the ages to come. But the princes did not help me. My doctrines were not accepted. Having failed in the present, applying them to a single principality, what hope can I have of succeeding in the future, applying them to the empire? At first I was grieved at this failure of my doctrines, judging it contrary to the opinions of heaven and the decrees of destiny. But since then I have seen it more clearly. I understood that I had misinterpreted the ancient texts, taking them literally. The intention of heaven, the decrees of destiny, are all forms of expression, figures of speech. That being so, there is nothing worth loving, desiring, regretting or doing. I no longer care about the success or failure of my doctrines."

Yen Hui greeted Confucius and said:

"Master, I think like you."

Then, going out, he told everything to *Zi Gong*, who almost lost his head. He left Confucius, returned home, meditated for seven days and seven nights without sleep or food, and became as thin as a skeleton. However, *Yen Hui* went to talk to him and shook his faith in the literal meaning of the ancient texts, but without getting him to achieve Daoist indifference. *Zi Gong* returned to Confucius, and repeated the Odes and Annals without believing them for the rest of his life.

B. An officer of *Chen* on a mission in the principality of *Lu*, saw in particular a certain *Shu Sun*, who said to him:

"We have a sage here."

"Is he not *Kong Qiu* (Confucius)?" asked the officer.

"It's him," said *Shu Sun*.

"How do you know he is really a sage?"

"Because," said *Shu Sun*, "I heard from his disciple *Yen Hui*, that *Kong Qiu* thinks with his body."

"Then," said the officer, "we also have a sage, *Geng Sang Zi*, disciple of *Lao Dan*, who sees with his ears and hears with his eyes."

This statement of *Chen*'s official was communicated to the prince of *Lu*, who was greatly intrigued and sent a senior minister to bring *Geng Sang Zi* rich gifts and invite him to his court. *Geng Sang Zi* accepted the invitation. The prince received him with the greatest respect. At once *Geng Sang Sang Zi* said to him:

"You have been misinformed, about my seeing with my ears and hearing with my eyes; one organ cannot serve in place of another."

"That does not matter," said the prince; "I want to know your doctrine."

"My body is intimately united with my mind; my body and mind are intimately united with cosmic matter and force, which are intimately united with the primordial nothingness of form, with the indefinite infinite being, with the Principle. As a result of this intimate union, any dissonance or consonance occurring in the universal harmony, whether at infinite or near distance, is perceived by me, but without my being able to say by what organ I perceive it. I know it, without knowing how I knew it[14]!"

This explanation pleased the Prince of *Lu* very much, who communicated it to Confucius the next day. The latter smiled without saying anything[15].

C. The minister of *Song* met Confucius and asked him:

"Are you really a Sage?"

"If I were," replied Confucius, "I would not say that I am. So I will only say that I have studied and learned much."

"Were the first three emperors wise?"

"They ruled well, were prudent and brave; I don't know if they were wise," replied Confucius.

"And the five emperors who succeeded them?"

"Those," said Confucius, "also ruled well; they were good and just; I don't know if they were Wise."

"And the three emperors who followed?"

"Those," said Confucius, "also ruled well, according to the times and circumstances; I do not know whether they were Wise."

"But then," said the minister with great astonishment, "whom do you consider wise?"

Confucius looked very serious, thought a moment, and then said:

"Among the men of the West[16], there are some who are said to keep the peace without ruling, who inspire confidence without speaking, who make everything work without interfering, so imperceptibly, so impersonally, that people do not even know them by name. I think these are the Wise Ones, if there are any, as they say."

The *Song* minister did not ask for more. After thinking about it, he said:

"*Kong Qiu* lectured me."

---

14   Perfect Daoist knowledge; consonance of two instruments tuned to the same pitch, the cosmos and the individual, perceived by the intimate sense, the global sense.

15   Smile of approval. He, too, turned Daoist, had nothing to say, says the commentary.

16   Fiction, says the commentary. Confucius lectures the minister, by praising imaginary Sages, to do the opposite of what he did. This text has no geographical or historical significance.

D. *Zi Xia* asked Confucius:

"Is *Yen Hui* worthwhile?"

"In kindness," said Confucius, "he surpasses me."

"And *Zi Gong*?" asked *Zi Xia*.

"In discernment," said Confucius, "*Zi Gong* is better than me."

"And *Zi Lu*?" asked *Zi Xia*.

"As for bravery," said Confucius, "*Zi Lu* surpasses me."

"And *Zi Zhang*?" asked *Zi Xia*.

"As for tenacity," said Confucius, "*Zi Zhang* surpasses me."

Zi Xia was astonished, he stood up and asked:

"But then, why are these four men still in your school?"

"This is the reason," said Confucius. "*Yen Hui*, so good, cannot resist. *Zi Gong*, so far-sighted, cannot give in. *Zi Lu*, so brave, lacks prudence. *Zi Zhang*, so dignified, has no interpersonal skills. If each one surpasses me in some quality, they are all inferior to me because of some defect. It is because of this defect that they remain in my school, and that I agree to treat them as disciples."

E. Becoming a master in his own right, *Lie Zi*, disciple of master *Lin* of *Hu Qiu*, friend of *Bo Hun Wu Ren*, lived in the southern suburb (where also lived the famous Daoist, whose name is known only as *Nan Guo Zi*, master of the southern suburb). *Lie Zi* argued every day with anyone who came along, without even bothering to know who he was dealing with. As for *Nan Guo Zi*, he was his neighbor for twenty years without visiting him, and often met him on the street without looking at him.

The disciples concluded that the two masters were enemies. A newcomer from *Chu* naively asked *Lie Zi* why. *Lie Zi* told him:

"There is no enmity between *Nan Guo Zi* and me. This man hides the perfection of emptiness under a corporeal appearance. His ears no longer hear, his eyes no longer see, his mouth no longer speaks, his mind no longer thinks. He is no longer capable of any interest; therefore, it is useless to try to have any relationship with him. If you wish, we will try it."

Followed by about forty disciples, *Lie Zi* went to *Nan Guo Zi*. The latter was in fact so lost in abstraction that it was impossible to establish any conversation with him. He cast a vague glance at *Lie Zi*, without addressing a word to him; then, turning to the last of the disciples, he said.

"I congratulate you on your courageous pursuit of the truth."

That was all. The disciples came back very surprised. *Lie Zi* said to them:

"Why are you surprised? He who has obtained what he sought, speaks no more. It is the same with the Sage, who keeps silent when he has found the truth. The silence of *Nan Guo Zi* is more significant than any words. His apathetic air covers the perfection of science. This man no longer speaks or thinks, because he knows everything. Why are you surprised?"

F. Once, when *Lie Zi* was a disciple, it took him three years to unlearn to judge and qualify with words; then his master *Leo Shang* honored him for the first time by looking at him. After five years, he no longer judged nor qualified, even mentally; then *Leo Shang* smiled at him for the first time. After seven years, when he had forgotten the distinction between yes and no, between advantage and disadvantage, his master made him sit on his mat for the first time. At the end of nine years, when he had lost all notion of right and wrong, of good and evil, for himself and for others; when he had become absolutely indifferent to everything, then he achieved a perfect communication between the outer world and his own inner self. He ceased to use his senses, (but knew everything by universal and abstract higher science). His mind solidified as his body dissolved; his bones and flesh liquefied (became etherized); he lost all sense of the seat on which he sat, of the ground on which his feet rested; he lost all intelligence of ideas formulated, of words uttered; he reached that state in which the mind is no longer altered by anything.

G. When he was a young disciple, *Lie Zi* liked going for walks. His master *Hu Zi*, asked him:

"What do you like about walking?"

Lie Zi said:

"In general, it is a restorative rest; many seek in it the pleasure of contemplating the scenery; I find in it the pleasure of meditating; there are walkers and walkers; I differ from the common people."

"Not so much as you think," said *Hu Zi*; "for, like others, you enjoy yourself. They amuse themselves visually, you amuse yourself mentally. There is a great difference between outer meditation and inner contemplation. The meditator gets pleasure from beings, the contemplator gets it from himself. To take it from oneself is the perfect way; to take it from beings is the imperfect way."

After this instruction, *Lie Zi* thought he was doing the right thing by stopping walking altogether.

"That is not how I understand it," said *Hu Qiu*tzeu; "walk, but perfectly. The perfect walker walks without knowing where he is going, looks without realizing what he sees. To go everywhere and look at everything in this mental disposition (total abstraction, global vision, nothing in detail), that is the perfect walk and contemplation. I have not forbidden you to go for a walk; I have advised you to walk in perfection."

H. *Long Shu* said to Doctor *Wen Zhi*:

"You are a skillful diagnostician. I am sick, can you cure me?"

"If fate permits, I can," said *Wen Zhi*. "Tell me what you are suffering from."

"I suffer," said *Long Shu*, "from a strange malady. Praise leaves me cold, contempt does not affect me; gain does not delight me, loss does not sadden me; I look with equal indifference on death and life, wealth and poverty. I care no more for men than for swine, nor for myself than for others. I feel as strange in my home as in an inn, and in my native district as in a barbarous country. No distinction attracts me, no torment frightens me; fortune or misfortune, advantage or disadvantage, joy or sorrow, all is the same to me. This being so, I dare not serve my prince, deal with my kith and kin, live with my wife and children, take care of my servants. What is this disease? With what remedy can it be cured?"

Wen Zhi asked *Long Shu* to uncover his torso. Then, having placed him so that the sun shone on his bare back, he stood in front of his chest, to examine his viscera, for transparency.

"Ah," he said suddenly, "I see your heart as a small empty object, about the size of a thumb. Six orifices are already perfectly open, the seventh will open. You suffer from the wisdom of the Wise. What can my poor remedies do against such a disease?"[17]

I. Having had no cause and living forever is a way, (that of the Principle alone)[18]. To be born of a living being, not to cease to be after a long time, is a permanence (that of geniuses). After life, to cease to be, would be the great misfortune. — Having had a cause, to be always dead, would be the other way. Having died a death, to cease to be soon, would be the other permanence (that of nothingness). After death, to live again, is the great happiness. — Not to act, and to live, is a way. To live long is the permanence. — To act and die is the other way. To get thereby to be no more, is the other permanence. — When *Ji Liang* died, *Yang Zhu* went home and sang (because *Ji Liang* had lived happily to the end of his days). When *Sui Wu* died, *Yang Zhu* caressed his corpse and cried (as if to comfort him, because after a hard life, *Sui Wu* had died prematurely). It hurts in both cases, that everything changes after death. About lives and deaths, the vulgar sing or cry, without knowing why, mistakenly and without reason. — To last long, nothing must be done, nothing must be carried to the extreme. It is a fact of experience that, shortly before it is extinguished, the sight sharpens for a time, which wears it out. Hearing the flight of mosquitoes is a sign that one is going deaf (same reason). The same is true of taste and smell. Excessive agitation precedes and brings paralysis. Excessive penetration precedes and introduces insanity. Every climax demands ruin.

J. In the principality of *Zheng*, in *Bu Ze* there were many thinkers (theoreticians), in *Dong Li* there were many men of talent (practitioners). A certain *Bai Feng Zi* of *Bu Ze* (theoretician) passing through *Dong Li* with his disciples, met *Deng Xi* (practitioner) with his. The latter said to his disciples:

"How about having fun with them?"

"Let's do it!" said the disciples.

Addressing *Bai Feng Zi*, *Deng Xi* said to him:

"About breeding… dogs and pigs are bred for your use. For what purpose are you breeding your disciples?"

---

17   *Long Shu* is an almost perfect indifferent Daoist. It only remains for him to get rid of the illusion of mistaking his wisdom for a disease and wanting to cure it.

18   Some parts of this paragraph, inserted only for the sake of parallelism, are nonsense. The general meaning is that there are two states, that of life and that of death; that inaction makes life last, that action is suicide. We know that.

One of the disciples accompanying *Bai Feng Zi* immediately replied:

"In the countries of *Qi* and *Lu*, man with talent, from your school, abound. There are artists of clay, wood, metal, leather; musicians, writers, mathematicians; tacticians, ceremonialists and many more. The only thing missing are the thinkers to lead this people. This is what we are destined for. Without theoreticians, practitioners are useless."

Deng Xi found nothing to answer. With his eyes he signaled his disciples to be quiet, and timidly withdrew.

K. *Gong Yi* was famous for his strength. A great lord, *Tang Xi*, praised him before Emperor *Xuan* of the *Zhou*. The emperor invited him to come to his court. *Gong Yi* had to obey. But he looked rather puny. The emperor was surprised and said to him:

"What are you capable of doing?"

Gong Yi said:

"I can break the leg of a grasshopper, and tear the wing of a cicada."

The emperor was not pleased.

"I," he said, "call a man strong if he can tear the skin of a buffalo, or hold nine oxen by pulling them by the tail. If you are only capable of the feats you have just mentioned, why do they praise your strength?"

"It is a wise question," said Gong Yi, sighing and stepping back modestly, "so I will answer you frankly. I was a disciple of *Shang Qiu Zi* (a Daoist), who had no equal in strength in the empire, but who was ignored even by his family, because he never displayed it. I assisted my master in his death. He left me this instruction: 'Those who seek fame, obtain it only by extraordinary actions. By doing only ordinary things, one does not even become famous in his family. Yet this is the course of action which I have judged to be the best, and I advise you to imitate me...' Now, if a great lord has been able to boast of my strength before your Majesty, it is because, in failing to comply with the supreme recommendations of my dying lord, I have given a token of it. The fact that I have betrayed myself proves that I have no strength. For he who knows how to conceal his strength is stronger than he who knows how to exercise it."

L. Prince *Mou* of *Zhung Shan* was the strong man of *Wei*. He liked to talk to intelligent people, cared little for administration, and had an avowed affection for *Gong Sun Long*, the sophist of *Zhao*. This weakness made the music master *Zi Yu* laugh. *Mou* asked him:

"Why do you laugh at my affection for *Gong Sun Long*?"

Zi Yu said:

"That man recognizes no master, is a friend to no one, rejects all received principles, fights all existing schools, loves only singular ideas, and speaks only strange words. The only thing he sets out to do is to confuse people and embarrass them. Just like *Han Tan* (an unknown sophist) and his ilk in the past."

Disgusted, Prince *Mou* said:

"Don't you exaggerate? Keep within the bounds of truth."

Zi Yu replied:

"Judge for yourself. This is what *Gong Sun Long* said to *Kong Chuan*:"

"A good archer," he said to him, "must be able to shoot arrow after arrow, so fast and so accurate, that the tip of each successive arrow sinks into the tail of the previous one, the arrows, strung together, will form a line from the bowstring to the target." — Seeing that *Kong Chuan* was astonished, *Gong Sun Long* went on to say:

"*Hong Chao*, *Peng Meng*'s pupil, has done better than this. Wanting to frighten his wife, who had made him angry, he drew his best bow and shot his best arrow so accurately that it shaved her pupils without flinching, and fell to the ground without kicking up dust. Are these the words of a reasonable man?"

Prince *Mou* said:

"Sometimes the words of the Wise, are not understood by fools. All that you have just quoted can be reasonably explained."

"You were *Gong Sun Long*'s pupil," said *Zi Yu*, "so you think you should praise him. I, who do not have your reasons, will continue to denigrate him. Here are some samples of the paradoxes he developed in the presence of the king of *Wei*:"

"One can think without intention; one can touch without reaching; what is, cannot end; a shadow cannot move; a hair can support thirty thousand pounds; a horse is not a horse; an orphan calf can have a mother; and other claptrap."

Prince *Mou* said:

"Perhaps it is you who do not understand these profound words[19]. To think without intention, may be understood as the concentration of the mind united to the Principle; to touch without reaching, is understood as pre-existent universal contact; that what is cannot end, to say that a shadow cannot move, serves to introduce the discussion of the notions of change and motion; to say that a hair supports thirty thousand pounds, serves to introduce the question of what is continuous and what is gravity; to say that a white horse is not a horse, calls for the discussion of the identity or difference of substance and accidents; an orphan calf can have a mother, if it is not an orphan; etc."

"You have," said *Zi Yu*, "learned to whistle the one note of *Gong Sun Long*. Others will have to teach you how to use the other holes of your intellectual flute."

At first, the prince was silent at this impertinence. When he recovered, he dismissed *Zi Yu*, saying to him:

"Wait until I invite you to appear before me again."

M. After fifty years of reign, *Yao* wanted to know whether his rule had had happy effects and whether the people were satisfied with it. So he questioned his ordinary advisors, those in the capital and those outside, but none could give him a positive answer. So *Yao* disguised himself and went to wander the streets. There he heard a child humming this refrain:

---

19   Compare *Zhuang Zhou*, chapter 33 G.

"In the village crowd, there are no villains anymore, everything is at its best. Without being told, without realizing it, everyone conforms to the emperor's laws."

Full of joy, *Yao* asked the boy who had taught him that refrain.

"My master," he said.

Yao asked the master who had composed this refrain.

"It comes from the elders," said the master.

(Happy that his reign had preserved the old status quo, that his rule had been so inactive that the ruled had not even noticed it), *Yao* hastened to abdicate and hand over his throne to *Shun* (so that his glory would not be tarnished before his death).

N. *Guan Yin Xi (Guan Yin Zi)* said:

"To him who abides in nothingness (of inner form, indeterminate state), all beings manifest. He is sensitive to their impression like still water; he reflects it like a mirror; he repeats it like an echo. United with the Principle, he is in harmony through it, with all beings, he knows everything by the higher general reasons, and consequently no longer uses his various senses to know in particular and in detail. The true reason of things is invisible, ungraspable, indefinable, indeterminable. Only the mind, restored to a state of perfect natural simplicity, can glimpse it confusedly in deep contemplation. After this revelation, to want nothing more and to do nothing more is the true science and the true talent. What more would he want, what more would he do, who has been revealed the nothingness of all will and all action. If he would limit himself to picking up a clod of earth, if he would limit himself to heaping up dust, even though this is not really doing nothing, he would still be lacking in his principles, for he would have acted."

Chapter 5 - The Cosmic Continuum

A. Emperor *Tang* of the *Yin* dynasty asked *Xia Ji*:

"Where there beings in the past, in the beginning?"

Xia Ji said:

"If there were not, how could they exist now? If we doubt that there were in the past, men in the future might doubt that there are any now (our present would have to be their past one day), which would be absurd."

"Then," said *Tang*, "is there division or continuity in time? What determines anteriority and posteriority?"

Xia Ji said:

"We speak, from the beginning, of ends and beginnings of beings. In the end, is there really beginning and end, or a successive and continuous transition, who can know? Being external to other beings, and prior to my own future states, how can I know (whether the ends, the deaths, are cessations or transformations)?"

"In any case," said *Tang*, "you say that time is infinite; what do you think of space, is it also infinite?"

"I don't know," said *Xia Ji*.

At *Tang's* insistence, *Xia Ji* said:

"Emptiness is infinite, for emptiness cannot have emptiness added to it; but as for existing beings, other beings can be added to them, whether the cosmos is finite or infinite, I don't know."

Tang continued:

"Is there anything beyond the four seas (of known terrestrial space)?"

Xia Ji said:

"I headed east, to *Ying*, and asked what lies beyond. I was told that what lies beyond is the same. Then I headed west, to *Pinn*, and asked, beyond here what is there? I was told that what lies beyond is the same... From this experience I concluded that the terms, four seas, four regions, four poles, may not be absolute. Because, in the end, always adding up, we arrive at an infinite value. If our cosmos (heaven-earth) is finite, does it not continue endlessly with other neighboring cosmoses (heaven-earth)? Who knows if our world (heaven-earth) is more than a unity in infinity? Once *Nü Gua* closed with stones of the five colors the gap left on the horizon between the edge of the celestial cap and the terrestrial plateau (thus delimiting this world). He immobilized the turtle (which carries the earth), cutting off its four legs, thus fixing the position of the four poles (cardinal points). Thus, everything in this world was in stable equilibrium. But later, in his fight against the emperor *Zhuan Xu*, *Gong Gong* broke the celestial column (from the northwest), and broke the ties of the earth (with the southeast firmament). As a result, the sky tilted to the northwest and the earth tilted to the southeast. Since then, the sun, the moon, the constellations, everything slides westward (its setting); all the rivers (of China) flow eastward."

B. *Tang* asked again:

"Are beings naturally large or small, long or short, similar or different?"

But, continuing his development, *Xia Ji* said:

"Far to the east (southeast) of the China Sea, (where the sky rises from the earth), there is an immense bottomless abyss, which is called the universal confluence, where all the waters of the earth, and those of the Milky Way (the collecting river of celestial waters), flow without ever increasing or decreasing in content. Between this abyss and China, there are (were) five great islands, *DaiYu, Yüan Jiao, Fang Hu, Jing Zhou* and *Peng Lai*[20]. — At their base, these islands each measure thirty thousand stades in circumference. Their flat summits have a circumference of nine thousand stades. They are all seventy thousand stades apart. The buildings that cover these islands are all of gold and jade; the animals do not fear man; the vegetation is marvelous; the flowers are fragrant; the fruits that are eaten preserve men from old age and death. The inhabitants of these islands are all geniuses, wise men. Every day they visit each other, flying through the air. Originally the islands were not fixed to the bottom, but floated on the sea, rising and falling with the tide, wavering at the shock of the feet. Annoyed by their instability, the genies and wise men complained to the Sovereign. Fearing that one day they would run aground

---

20   This is probably the oldest text, about the isles of the Genies.

in the western lands, the Sovereign ordered the Genie of the North Sea to remedy this danger. The latter commissioned monstrous turtles to hold the five islands on their backs, three per island. They were to be replaced every sixty thousand years. So the islands no longer wobbled. But one day one of the giants from the country of *Long Bai* (in the north), came to these regions by air, and cast his line. He took six of the fifteen turtles, put them on his back, returned as he had come, and prepared their shells for divination. As a result, the two islands, *Dai Yu* and *Yüan Jiao* (held by these six turtles), sank into the ocean, (and the islands of the Genie were reduced to the three of the legend). The Sovereign was very irritated by this adventure. He reduced the size of the country of *Long Bai* and the gigantic stature of its inhabitants. However, at the time of *Fu Xi* and *Shen Nong*, they were still several tens of standard stature high. — Four hundred thousand stades east of China, in the country of *Jiao Yao*, men are one foot five inches tall. — In the northeast corner of the earth, the *Zheng Ren* are only nine inches tall. — These are standard measurements.

C. Let us now speak of duration. In southern China grows the tree *Ming Ling*, whose foliation period (spring and summer) is five centuries, and whose bare period (autumn and winter) is also five centuries, (thus the cycle lasts a thousand years). In ancient times, the great tree *Chun* had a cycle of sixteen thousand years. On the dunghill grows a mushroom which, born in the morning, dies in the evening. In summer, mayflies are born during the rain and die as soon as the sun appears. In the far north, in the black waters of the celestial lake, there is a fish thousands of stades wide, and long in proportion, which is called *Kun*; and a bird called *Peng*, whose outstretched wings darken the sky like clouds, its other dimensions being proportional. We know these animals from the great *Yu*, who saw them, from *Bo Yi* who named them, and from *Yi Jian* who classified them... At the edge of the waters are born the *Jiao Ming*, so small that many can perch on the antennae of a mosquito, unnoticed by it; invisible even to the eyes of *Li Zu* and *Zi Yu*. But *Huang Di*, after his three months' fast on Mount *Kong Tong* in the company of *Rong Chen Zi*, when his mind was as if extinguished and his body as if dead, saw them with his transcendent gaze as clearly as Mount *Song*, heard them with his innermost ear as clearly as thunder. In the countries of *Wu* and *Chu* (in the south), there grows a large tree, the *Yu Bi*, which in winter produces sour-tasting red fruit; transplanted north of the *Huai*, it becomes a thorny, barren thicket (*Citrus spinosa*). The thrush does not cross the *Ji* river, the badger can no longer live south of the *Wen*. Since the nature of the places seems to be the same, the life of some is adapted to them, while that of others is not, without one being able to discover why. If we cannot realize these concrete things, what do you want me to tell you about abstract things, such as the big and the small, the long and the short, the similarities and the differences?" (A return to the question posed in B)

D. The massif of the *Tai Xing* and *Wang Wu* mountains was seven hundred stades square and eighty thousand feet high[21]. A nonagenarian of *Bei Shan* disliked it, because it intercepted communications between the South and the North. Having summoned the people of his household, he said to them:

"Let's get to work! Let's level this height! Let's put the North in communication with the Han valley!"

"Let's get to work," they said in chorus…

But the old woman of the nonagenarian objected: "Where will you put the earth and stones of these mountains?"

"We will throw them into the sea," they said in chorus…

And so the work began. Under the direction of the old man, his son and grandsons, able to carry anything, attacked the rocks, dug up the earth and carried the debris basket by basket to the sea. Their enthusiasm spread throughout the neighborhood. Even the son of an official's widow, a teething toddler, ran with the workers when it was not too hot or too cold.

However, a man from *He Qiu* who considered himself wise, tried to stop the nonagenarian by telling him.

"What you are doing here is unreasonable. With the strength you have left, you will not be able to overcome these mountains…"

The nonagenarian said:

"It is you who are unreasonable; whereas the widow's child is less so. I will die soon, it is true; but my son will follow, then my grandchildren will come, then my grandchildren's children, and so on. They will multiply endlessly, while nothing will ever be added to the finite mass of this mountain. So eventually they will flatten it."

The constancy of the nonagenarian frightened the genie of the serpents, who begged the Sovereign to prevent his proteges from being expropriated by this obstinate old man. The latter ordered the two giants, sons of *Kua Er*, to separate the two mountains *Tai Xing* and *Wang Wu*. Thus was produced the gap which unites the northern plains with the basin of the *Han* (the moral of the history is that one must count on the effect of time).

E. Once the father of the two giants mentioned, pretending to run a race with the sun, ran into the valley of the *Yu*. Altered, he drank the river and then swallowed the *Wei*. This was not enough, so he ran toward the great lake, but could not reach it, dying of thirst on the way. His corpse and his staff became the *Deng* forest, which stretches for several thousand stades.

F. The great *Yu* said:

"In the six regions, among the four seas, illuminated by the sun and moon, regulated by the course of the stars, ordered by the succession of the seasons, governed by the duodenal cycle of Jupiter, beings live in an order which the Sage can penetrate."

---

21   That is, in the Chinese way, the distance one had to travel to reach the top.

Xia Ji said:

"Other beings live in other conditions of which the Sage has not the key. For example, when the great *Yu* was channeling the waters to dry up the land, he turned aside, skirted the northern sea, and came, far away, in the very north, to a country without wind or rain, without animals or plants of any kind, a high plateau bordered by steep cliffs, with a conical mountain in the center. From a bottomless hole at the top of the cone springs a water of pungent odor and vinous taste, which flows in four streams to the bottom of the mountain and irrigates the whole country. The region is very healthy, its inhabitants are friendly and simple. They all live together, without distinction of age or sex, without chiefs, without families. They do not cultivate the land, nor do they dress themselves. Very numerous, these men know neither the joys of youth, nor the sadness of old age. They love music and sing together all day long. They appease their hunger by drinking the water of the marvelous geyser, and repair their strength by bathing in the same waters. In this way, they all live exactly one hundred years and die without ever having been ill. Once, on his journey northward, Emperor *Mu* of the *Zhou* visited this country and stayed there for three years. When he returned, the memory he retained made him find his empire, his palace, his feasts, his women and everything else insipid. After a few months, he left everything to return. *Guan Zhong*, being a minister of Duke *Huan* of *Qi*, had almost decided to conquer that country. But *Xi Peng* reproached the duke for leaving *Qi*, so vast, so populous, so civilized, so beautiful, so rich, to expose his soldiers to death and his feudatories to the temptation to desert, and all this on the whim of an old man, Duke *Huan* gave up the enterprise, and told *Guan Zhong* the words of *Xi Peng*. *Guan Zhong* said: 'Xi Peng's ideas are different from mine, he is so absorbed with *Qi* that he sees nothing beyond.'"

Southern men cut their hair and go naked; northern men wrap their heads and bodies with furs; Chinese men have their own style of hairstyle and clothes. In each country, according to its particular circumstances and natural conditions, the inhabitants have devised the best in terms of culture, trade, fishing, clothing, means of communication, etc.

No doubt there are irrational or barbarous practices in some peoples; but these are artificial; we should try to reform them, but not be scandalized by them.

Thus, east of *Yue*, the *Che Mu* devour all the first-born, for the sake, they say, of the children who will come after. When their grandfather has died, they expel the grandmother because, they say, being the wife of a dead man, she would bring them misfortune.

In southern *Chu*, the *Yen Ren* scrape the flesh of their dead relatives and throw it away, and then devoutly bury their bones. Any of them who did not do so would not be considered a pious son.

West of *Qin*, among the *Yi Chu*, in the country of *Wen Kang*, dead relatives are burned so that they ascend to heaven with the smoke. Anyone who did not do so would be considered impious.

G. Let us be reserved in our judgments, for even the Sage is ignorant of many things, even those which are seen every day... Confucius, traveling in the east, saw two boys arguing, and asked them the reason for their quarrel. The first said:

"I maintain that when the sun rises it is nearer, and that at noon it is farther away."

The second said:

"I say that when the sun rises, it is farther away, and at noon it is nearer."

The first said:

"When the sun rises, it seems large; at noon, it seems small; that is why it is nearer in the morning, and farther away at noon; because distance makes objects smaller."

The second says:

"At sunrise, the sun is cool; at noon, it is hot; that is why it is farther away in the morning, and nearer at noon; for distance from a focus diminishes its heat."

Confucius found nothing to say to decide this question, which he had never thought of. The two boys laughed at him and said:

"Then why do they say of you that you are a scholar?"

H. The continuum (continuity) is the greatest law in the world. It is different from cohesion, from contact. Let's take a hair. We hang weights on it. It breaks. What breaks is the hair, not the continuum. The continuum cannot break. Some people don't believe it. I will show them, with examples, that the continuum is independent of contact.

Zhan He fished with a line made of a single strand of natural silk[22], a curved needle served him as a hook, a reed stick and half a grain of wheat as bait. With this rudimentary device, he drew huge fish from a deep abyss, without his line breaking, without his hook being deformed, without his rod being bent. When the king of *Chu* heard this, he asked him for an explanation. *Zhan He* told him: "In the past the famous archer *Pu Ju Zi*, with a very weak bow and an arrow shot with a simple thread, reached the gray cranes in the clouds, thanks to his mental application that established the continuity of his hand towards the object. I have been trying to achieve the same result in rod-fishing for five years. When I cast the hook, my mind, completely void of any other thought, goes directly to the fish, through my hand and my tackle, establishing a continuity, and the fish is caught without challenge or resistance. And if you, O king, were to apply the same procedure to the government of your kingdom, the result would be the same..."

"Thank you," said the king of *Chu*... *So the will establishes continuity, between the mind and its object.*

I. *The heart creates continuity, between man and his family.*

Gong Hu of *Lu*, and *Qi Ying* of *Zhao*, being ill, asked *Pian Qiao*, the famous physician, to cure them. He did so, and then said to them:

---

22   Like those produced by the silkworm; several of these filaments must be joined together to make a thread.

"This was only a temporary crisis; the constitutional predisposition remains, exposing you to certain relapses; it would take more than medicines, to eliminate this one."

"What is needed?" asked the two men.

"You," said *Pian Qiao* to *Gong Hu*, "have a strong heart and a weak body, and consequently exhaust yourself in impracticable projects. You, *Qi Ying*, have a weak heart and a strong body, and consequently exhaust yourself in thoughtless endeavors. If I were to exchange the hearts of both of you, your bodies would be in good condition."

"Do it!" said the two men.

Pian Qiao, after making them drink wine containing a drug that deprived them of all knowledge for three days, opened both their chests, extracted both their hearts, exchanged them and closed the two incisions with his famous ointment. When they awoke, both men were perfectly healthy.

But when they took their leave, *Gong Hu* went straight to *Qi Ying*'s house and settled in with his wife and children, who did not recognize him. *Qi Ying* also went directly to *Gong Hu*'s house and settled down with his wife and children, who also did not recognize him. The two families were on the verge of coming to a quarrel. But when *Pian Qiao* explained the mystery to them, they calmed down.

J. *Music creates continuity between man and the whole of nature.*

When *Pao Ba* played his zither, the birds danced and the fish jumped. Wishing to acquire the same talent, *Shi Wen* (later to become chief musician of *Zheng*) left his family to join *Shi Xiang*. At first he spent three whole years practicing fingering and playing, without playing any tunes. Judging that he was not very capable, *Shi Xiang* finally said to him:

"You could go back home..."

Putting down his zither, *Shi Wen* said with a sigh:

"No, I am not without ability; but I have a goal, a higher ideal than ordinary classical musical performance; I do not yet have what it takes to communicate the influence of my heart to external beings; that is why I dare not sound my zither; it would not yet make the sounds I intend. As I must go, I will go; but it will only be a temporary absence; we shall soon meet again."

In fact, not long after, *Shi Wen* returned to *Shi Xiang*.

"How are you doing with your zither?"

"I have reached my ideal," said *Shi Wen*, "you will see..."

It was then the middle of spring. *Shi Wen* played the chord *Shang*, which corresponds to the pipe *Nan*[23] and the autumn season; immediately a cool wind blew and the fruit ripened. When, in autumn, he played the chord *Jiao*, which answers to the bell *Jia* and the spring season, a warm wind blew and the plants blossomed. When, in summer, he rang the chord *You*, which answers to the bell

---

23   The ancient flutes of the Chinese were made from 12 bamboo pipes, one for each pitch (Translator Note).

Huang and the winter season, snow began to fall and the rivers froze. When, in winter, he played the chord *Zheng*, which answers to the pipe *Rui Pin*, and the summer season, lightning flashed and the ice melted. Finally, when he played all four chords simultaneously, a gentle breeze blew, graceful clouds floated in the air, sweet dew fell from the sky, and vinous springs flowed from the earth…

Beating his chest and jumping (marks of regret), *Shi Xiang* said:

"What a great execution! It equals or surpasses in potency that of *Shi Kuang* and *Zi Yen*. In your presence, these masters should put down the zither and take up the flageolet, to accompany you."

K. *Another example of the mysterious correspondence established by music.* When *Xue Tan* was learning to sing with *Qin Qing*, he became discouraged and told his teacher that he was leaving. *Qin Qing* did not ask him to stay; but, at the customary farewell tea, he sang such a touching lament that *Xue Tan*, repenting, apologized for his inconstancy and asked to be allowed to stay.

Then *Qin Qing* told his friend the following story:

"Once *Er Han*, going to *Qi* and having exhausted his food, sang at an inn in *Yong Men* to earn his food. After his departure, the beams of the rafters of the inn where he had sung kept repeating his song for three whole days, so that people came running, believing that he had not left, not wanting to believe the innkeeper who sent them away… When *Er Han* sang a lament, young and old became so distressed that they did not eat for three days. Then *Er Han* sang them a merry refrain, and at one point in the round, young and old, forgetting their grief, danced for joy and showered the singer with their gifts. Even today, the inhabitants of *Yong Men* express their joy or grief in a particularly elegant way. They learned it from *Er Han*."

L. *Another example of the mystic continuum.* When *Bo Ya* played his zither, *Zhong Zi Qi* perceived the intention he had in playing. Thus, once *Bo Ya* tried to express the idea of a high mountain with his chords:

"Well, well," said *Zhong Zi Qi Qi*; "it rises, like Mount *Tai Shan*…"

On another occasion, while *Bo Ya* was trying to represent the flow of water:

"Well, well," said *Zhong Zi Qi Qi*; "it flows like *Jiang* or the River…"

Whatever idea *Bo Ya* formed within him, *Zhong Zi Qi* perceived it by listening to his zither. One day, as the two friends were passing north of Mount *Tai Shan*, they were caught in a downpour and took shelter under a rock. To ease the discomfort of waiting, *Bo Ya* played his zither and tried to depict, first, the effect of a downpour and, then, the collapse of a rock. *Zhong Zi Qi* immediately guessed these two successive intentions… Then *Bo Ya* put down his zither, sighed and said:

"Your hearing is wonderful. Everything I think in my heart translates into an image in your mind. Where shall I go when I want to keep a secret?"

M. *Another example of continuity by intention.*

Emperor *Mu* of the *Zhou* went west to hunt, crossed the *Kun Lun* mountains, went as far as Mount *Yen* and then returned to China. On his return, he was introduced to an inventor named *Yen Shi.*

"What can you do?" the emperor asked him.

"I will show you if your majesty allows me," said the inventor.

"I will give you one day," said the emperor.

When the day came, *Yen Shi* appeared before the emperor with an escort.

"Who are these?" asked the emperor.

"They are my creatures," said *Yen Shi;* "they know how to act."

The emperor looked at them in amazement. The automatons of *Yen Shi* walked, raised and lowered their heads and moved like real men. When touched on the chin, they sang, and very correctly. When their hands were held, they danced to the rhythm. They did everything you could imagine.

The emperor decided to make a spectacle of them before his harem. But now, as they performed, the automatons winked at the ladies. Furious, the emperor was about to have *Yen Shi* killed, believing he had fraudulently introduced real men. Then *Yen Shi* opened his automatons and showed the emperor that they were made of leather and painted and varnished wood. However, all the viscera were formed, and *Yen Shi* taught the emperor that (according to Chinese physiology), when an automaton had its heart removed, its mouth became mute; when its liver was removed, its eyes could no longer see; when its kidneys were removed, its feet could no longer move[24].

"It is marvelous," said the emperor calmly; "you are almost as skillful as the Principle, the author of all things."

And he ordered the automatons to be loaded into a wagon and taken to his capital.

Since then, nothing similar has been seen. The disciples of *Ban Shu*, the inventor of the famous approach tower used in sieges, and of *Mo Zi*, the philosopher who invented the automatic falcon, vainly urged these two masters to repeat what *Yen Shi* had done. But they did not even dare to try (lacking the willpower to produce effective continuity).

N. *Another example of continuity by intention.*

When *Gan Ying*, the famous archer, drew his bow, beasts and birds came to him without waiting for his arrow. His disciple was *Fei Wei*, who surpassed him. *Fei Wei* took *Ji Chang* as his disciple, and began by saying to him:

"First learn not to blink, then I'll teach you how to draw the bow."

Ji Chang thought of the following way. When his wife was weaving, he would lie on his back under the loom, watching the threads intertwine and the shuttle pass back and forth. After two years of this exercise, his eyes became so fixed that an

---

24   The automatons were moved by the will of *Yen Shi*, by mental continuity. Therefore, it was he who made the winks. His demonstration of the viscera was a deception, to save his life.

awl could touch them without making them blink. Then *Ji Chang* went to *Fei Wei* and told him he was ready.

"Not yet," said *Fei Wei*. "You still have to learn to fix on a point. When you see it magnified (by the force of your intention) to the point where you cannot miss, then come back and I will teach you how to draw the bow."

Ji Chang hung from his window a long yak hair, on which he made a louse climb, and then practiced watching the louse, when the sun, passing behind the object, made it glow. Day by day, the louse seemed larger. After three years of practice, he saw it huge and distinguished its heart. When he succeeded in piercing the louse's heart without the arrow cutting the hair, he turned to *Fei Wei*.

"Now," said *Fei Wei*, "you know how to draw the bow; I have nothing more to teach you."

Ji Chang, however, said to himself that he had no rival in the world but his master, and resolved to get rid of him (in one of those combats of skill, such as archers waged in those days).

Meeting on a plain, the two men took up their positions and shot at each other simultaneously, determining the number of arrows. At each shot, the two arrows collided halfway and fell dead, raising no dust. But *Ji Chang* had put one more arrow in his quiver, which he shot last, intending to pierce his unarmed master. *Fei Wei* parried the arrow with a thorny branch (which he had time to pick up, and did not suspect perfidy).

Then, after putting down their bows, the two men greeted each other on the field, weeping with emotion and promising to be to each other as father and son. They also swore to each other, with the shedding of their blood, not to reveal to anyone the secret of their art (mental continuity).

O. *Another example of the efficacy of the will.* Zao Fu learned from *Tai Dou* the art of driving a chariot. When he entered his master's house as a disciple, he began by serving him very humbly. For three years, *Tai Dou* did not speak to him. *Zao Fu* redoubled his submission. Finally *Tai Dou* said to him:

"According to an ancient adage, the apprentice archer should be as supple as a wicker, and the apprentice smelter as supple as a skin. Now you have more or less what you need. Look at what I'm going to show you. When you know how to do the same, you will be able to hold the reins of a six-horse chariot."

"Good," said *Zao Fu*.

Then *Tai Dou*, having placed a pole in a horizontal position, just wide enough to rest his foot on it, began to walk step by step, calmly, from one end of the pole to the other, going from one side to the other without taking a single false step.

Three days later, *Zao Fu* did the same. Surprised, *Tai Dou* said to him:

"How clever you are, how quickly you have succeeded! You now possess the secret of driving a chariot. The concentration of your inner faculties on the movement of your feet has enabled you to walk on the pole as safely as you do. Concentrate your faculties equally intensely on the reins of your chariot. Let your mind act upon the bits of your horses, and your will upon theirs, through your hand. Then you will be able to describe perfect circumferences and draw perfect right angles, to run your chariot without exhausting them. Again, let your mind be one with the reins and the bits; that is the secret. Once this is done, you won't need to use your eyes or the whip. As the carriage is entirely in your power, the twenty-four hoofs of your six horses will land in cadence, and their movements will be mathematically precise; you will pass safely, where the road is only as wide as the distance between your wheels, where the road is barely wide enough for the hoofs of your horses. I have nothing more to teach you; you already know as much as I do[25]."

P. *Hei Luan* of *Wei* treacherously murdered *Qiu Bingzhang*; the latter's son, *Lai Dan*, tried to avenge his father's death. *Lai Dan* was brave but stupid. *Hei Luan* was a colossus, who feared *Lai Dan* no more than a chick.

Shen Tuo, a friend of *Lai Dan*, said to him:

"You resent *Hei Luan*; but he is so superior to you; what can you do about it?"

"Advise me," said *Lai Dan*, bursting into tears.

"I have heard," said *Shen Tuo*, "that in the principality of *Wei*, in the *Kong Zhou* family, there are three wonderful swords which belonged to the last emperor of the *Yin*, and with which a child could stop an army. Borrow them."

Lai Dan, having gone to *Wei*, went to *Kong Zhou*, offered himself to him as a slave with his wife and children, and then told him what he expected in return.

"I will lend you a sword," said *Kong Zhou*, "which of the three do you want? The first one throws lightning. The second is invisible. The third cuts through everything. For thirteen generations these three swords have remained unused in the possession of my family. Which one do you want?"

"The third one," said *Lai Dan*.

So *Kong Zhou* accepted *Lai Dan* as a client of his clan. At the end of seven days, having given a banquet in his honor, he gave him the desired sword, which *Lai Dan* received prostrate. Armed with this weapon, *Lai Dan* sought out *Hei Luan*. After finding him sleeping drunk, he stabbed him three times, from shoulder to waist, without waking him. When he came out, he met *Hei Luan*'s son, and also stabbed him three times. All his blows passed through the bodies, experiencing no more resistance than in the air; but the cuts closed after the passage of the blade.

Seeing that his marvelous sword did not kill, *Lai Dan* fled in anguish. However, *Hei Luan*, after waking up, scolded his wife for not covering him better during sleep.

"I have a cold," he said, "and my neck and back feel numb."

Meanwhile, his son came in and said:

---

25   Commentary: Any hesitation, an absence, a vertigo, comes from the fact that the mind is not master of the acting member or instrument. There is a defect of continuity. The intentional fluid does not pass.

"*Lai Dan* must also have passed this way. He gave me three blows outside, which produced precisely the same effect on me[26]."

Q. During their journey to the West, the *Rong*, a tribe of those regions, offered the emperor *Mu* of the *Zhou*, an extraordinary sword and some asbestos cloth. The eighteen-inch long sword cut through jade like mud. When the cloth was dirty, after putting into the fire, came out white as snow. Attempts have been made to cast doubt on these facts, but they are true.

CHAPTER 6 - FATE

A. Energy said to Fate:

"You are not worth as much as I am."

"Why not?" asked Fate.

"Because," said Energy, "I am the one who gives longevity, success, nobility and wealth to men."

"Ah," said Fate, "if that were so, would you really have reason to boast of it? *Peng Zu* lived for eight centuries, far longer than *Yao* and *Shun*, having no more merit than they. *Yen Yuan*, so wise, died at the age of thirty-two, while many fools reach an advanced age. *Zhong Ni*, who was worth as much as the princes of his time, suffered great misfortune in *Chen* and *Cai*. The emperor *Zhou* of the *Yin* was no match for the three paragons *Wei Zi, Ji Zi* and *Bi Gan*, and yet he occupied a throne, while they were disgraced. *Ji Zha* of *Wu*, who would have deserved the highest honors, obtained none; while *Tian Heng*, utterly unworthy, obtained the reign of *Qi*. *Bo Yi* and *Shu Qi*, so noble, died of starvation in *Shou Yang*, while *Ji Shi* grew rich in *Zhan Qin*. If it was you who made these apportionments, why did you make them as if you were blind."

"If it wasn't me," said Energy, "then it was you, Fate, who made them, and the blame falls on you."

"Pardon," said Fate; "I do nothing. I push (spin the wheel) and then let go. Fatally one lives long and the other does not, fatally one succeeds and the other does not, fatally one becomes famous and the other does not, fatally one is rich and the other poor. I don't do any of this; I don't even know anything about it; it's a natural thing."

B. *Bei Gong Zi* said to *Xi Men Zi*:

"I was born at the same time and of the same stock as you; in face, speech and gait, there is hardly any difference between the two of us; and yet you succeed, you are honored, you are loved, you are beloved, you are cherished, you are praised, while the opposite is true of me. We have used the same means to try our fortune; you have succeeded in everything, and I in nothing. I am ill-clad, ill-fed, ill-housed, and go everywhere on foot; while you live in luxury and plenty, and go out only in a

---

26   The marvelous property of this sword was that it went through matter, dividing neither cohesion nor continuity.

chariot. Both in private life and in public life you are so superior to me, that I dare not compare myself with you."

"I suppose," said *Xi Men Zi*, "that the difference in our conditions is due to the difference in our conduct. You must have behaved worse than I did."

Greatly humiliated, *Bei Gong Zi* did not know what to reply and left in bewilderment. On the street he met the lord of the eastern suburb, who asked him:

"Where are you going, at that pace and with that look?"

Bei Gong Zi told him of his discomfort:

"Let us go back together," said the Master; "I will correct this affront."

When they arrived at *Xi Men Zi*'s house, the Master asked him:

"What wrong did you do to *Bei Gong Zi*?"

"I told him," said *Xi Men Zi*, "that I considered that the difference in our conditions should come from the difference in our conduct."

"It is not like that," said the Master. "This is how it should be explained. *Bei Gong Zi* is well endowed and has a bad destiny. You, *Xi Men Zi*, are poorly endowed, but you have a good destiny. Your success is not due to your qualities; his failures are not due to his inability. It is not you who have become what you are; it is fate that has made you what you are. Therefore, if you, the fortunate one, have humiliated him; if he, the well-endowed one, has been ashamed of it, it is because both of you are unaware what's going on with you."

"Say no more, master," said *Xi Men Zi*; "I will not do it again."

When *Bei Gong Zi* returned home, he found that his coarse cloth robe was warmer than fox or badger fur; his coarse food seemed delicious to him; his hut seemed like a palace, and his curtain like a chariot. Inwardly enlightened, he paid no more attention to social distinctions until he died.

The master of the eastern suburb, hearing of this, said:

"After a very long sleep (ignorance), one word was enough to awaken this man, and change him in a lasting way."

C. *Guan Zhong* and *Bao Shu Ya*, both from *Qi*, were close friends. *Guan Zhong* followed Prince *Jiu*, *Bao Shu Ya* followed Prince *Xiao Bo*. As a consequence of the preference given by Duke *Xi* of *Qi* to *Wu Zhi*, son of a favorite concubine, a revolution broke out when the succession of the deceased duke had to be arranged. *Guan Zhong* and *Shao Hu* fled to *Lu* with prince *Jiu*, while *Bao Shu Ya* fled to *Ju* with prince *Xiao Bo*. Then these two princes, having become competitors for the throne, declared war on each other, *Guan Zhong* fought on *Jiu*'s side when the latter marched on *Ju*, and shot an arrow at *Xiao Bo* which would have killed him, had it not stuck in his belt buckle. After he conquered, *Xiao Bo*, demanded that *Lu*'s people put his rival *Jiu* to death, which they obligingly did. *Shao Hu* perished and *Guan Zhong* was imprisoned.

Then *Bao Shu Ya* said to his protege *Xiao Bo*, who became Duke *Huan*:

"*Guan Zhong* is an extremely clever politician."

"I know that well," said the duke, "but I hate that man who almost killed me."

Bao Shu Ya continued:

"A wise prince should know how to suppress his personal resentments. Inferiors must continually do this with respect to their superiors; a superior must sometimes do it with one of his inferiors. If you intend to become the supreme ruler, *Guan Zhong* is the only man who can make your plan succeed. You must give him amnesty."

So the duke summoned *Guan Zhong*, supposedly to put him to death. He was sent from *Lu* in bonds. *Bao Shu Ya* went out to meet him in the suburb and removed his bonds. Duke *Huan* invested him with the dignity of prime minister. *Bao Shu Ya* became his subordinate. The duke treated *Guan ZHong* like a son and he called him his father. *Guan Zhong* made the duke the supreme ruler. He often said with a sigh:

"When, in my youth, I traded with *Bao Shu Ya*, and took the good part, *Bao Shu Ya* excused me, because of my poverty. When, later, in politics, he triumphed and I surpassed him, *Bao Shu Ya* thought that my time had not yet come and did not doubt me. When I fled when Prince *Jiu* was defeated, *Bao Shu Ya* did not judge me cowardly, but excused me on the grounds that I still had my old mother, for whom I should preserve myself. When I was imprisoned, *Bao Shu Ya* maintained his esteem for me, knowing that for me there is only one dishonor, that of remaining idle without working for the good of the State. Ah, if I owe my life to my parents, I owe more to *Bao Shu Ya* who understood my soul."

Since then, it is customary to admire *Bao Shu Ya*'s selfless friendship for *Guan Zhong* and to praise Duke *Huan* for his magnanimity and discernment of men. Actually, in this matter, there is neither friendship nor discernment to speak of. The truth is that there was neither intervention of the actors, nor change of fortune. It was all a game of blind fate. If *Shao Hu* perished, it was because he had to perish. If *Bao Shu Ya* condescended to *Guan Zhong*, it was because he had to. If Duke *Huan* forgave *Guan Zhong*, it was because he had to forgive him. Fatal necessity, and nothing more.

The same thing happened at the end of *Guan Zhong*'s career. When *Guan Zhong* was confined to bed, the duke went to visit him and said:

"Father *Zhong*, you are very ill; I must allude to that which is not named (death); if your illness worsens (to the point of taking you), whom shall I take as minister in your stead?"

"Whom you will," said the dying man.

"Would *Bao Shu Ya* be suitable?" asked the Duke.

"No," said *Guan Zhong*; "his ideal is too high; he despises those who fall short of it, and he never forgets a fault committed. If you were to take him for a minister, both you and the people would come off badly. You will not be able to bear it for long."

"Then whom shall I take?" said the duke.

"If I must answer you," said *Guan Zhong*, "take *Xi Peng*, he will be all right. He is equally pliant with superiors and inferiors. He is absorbed by the fanciful desire to equal *Huang Di*'s virtue. Transcendent gaze is the characteristic of first-rank Sages, practical vision is the characteristic of second-rank Sages. To make men feel one's own wisdom indisposes them, to make them forget it makes them love. *Xi Peng* is not a Sage of the first order; he has, as a Sage of the second rank, the art of self-examination. Moreover, both his person and his family are unknown. That is why I consider him fit for the office of Prime Minister." — What can we say about this? *Guan Zhong* did not recommend *Bao Shu Ya*, because he should not be recommended; he sponsored *Xi Peng*, because he should sponsor him. Fortune first and misfortune afterwards, misfortune first and fortune afterwards, in all the vicissitudes of fate, nothing is of man (willed, made by him); all is blind fatality.

D. *Deng Xi* knew how to discuss the pros and cons of an issue in endless words. Having drawn up a new code for *Zheng* principality, *Zi Chan* was criticized by many and *Deng Xi* mocked him. *Zi Chan* rebuked his critics and had *Deng Xi* killed. In this he did not act, but served fate. *Deng Xi* had to die like this. *Deng Xi* was to mock *Zi Chan*, and thus bring about his death. To be born and die in its time, these two things are happiness. Not to be born and not to die in due time, these two things are misfortunes. These different fates happen to one and the other, not by their own action, but because of fatality. They are unpredictable. That is why, in speaking of them, we use the expressions, mystery without rule, way of heaven that knows only itself, inscrutable darkness, law of heaven that moves by itself, and other analogous ones. This means that heaven and earth, that the science of the Wise, that the manes and the goblins, can do nothing against fatality. According to its whim, it destroys or builds, crushes or caresses, delays or impedes.

E. *Ji Liang*, a friend of *Yang Zhu*, seven days after falling ill, found himself at the end of his life. His son, in tears, ran to see all the doctors in the vicinity. The sick man said to *Yang Zhu*:

"Try to bring my foolish son to his senses."

Yang Zhu then recited the verse to his son:

"What heaven does not know (the future), how can men guess? It is not true that heaven blesses, nor that anyone is cursed. You and I know that fate is blind and inescapable. What can doctors and magicians do?"

But the son did not give up and brought three doctors, a certain *Jiao*, a *Yu* and a *Lu*. The three examined the patient, one after the other. The *Jiao* said:

"In your case, cold and heat are unbalanced, emptiness and fullness are disproportionate; you have eaten too much, enjoyed too much, thought too much, tired too much; your illness is natural and not the effect of some evil influence; although it is serious, it is curable."

"This one is reciting the books; let him be dismissed without further ado!" said *Ji Liang*.

The *Yu* said to the patient:

"Here is your case. You came out of your mother's womb with defective vitality, and then sucked more milk than you could digest. The origin of your disease goes back to that time. As it is inveterate, it can hardly be completely cured."

"This one speaks well," said *Ji Liang*, "We should invite him over for dinner!"

The *Lu* said to the patient:

"Neither heaven, nor a man, nor a specter, are the cause of your illness. Born with a composite body, you are subject to the law of dissolution, and you must understand that the time is drawing near; no medicine will do anything."

"You have spirit," said *Ji Liang*; "may you be paid handsomely."

Ji Liang took no medicine and recovered perfectly (fate).

Care for life does not lengthen it, lack of care does not shorten it. Appreciation of the body does not improve it, contempt does not deteriorate it. The consequences, in this matter, do not correspond to the actions performed. They even often seem diametrically opposed, without really being so. Because destiny has no opposite. We live or die, because we had to live or die. Care or neglect of life, of the body, does nothing to change this, neither in one direction nor the other. That is why *You Xiong* said to King *Wen*: "Man can neither add to nor subtract from his stature; all his calculations can do nothing about it."

In the same vein, *Lao Dan* said to *Guan Yin Zi*:

"It is better to be silent than to try to find out the intentions of heaven, to guess the splendor and evil (vain calculations, everything is governed by a blind, unpredictable, ineluctable fatality)."

F. *Yang Bu*, the younger brother of *Yang Zhu*, said to his elder brother:

"There are men who are completely equal in age, in exterior, in all natural gifts, but who differ absolutely, in length of life, in fortune and in success. I cannot explain this mystery."

Yang Zhu answered him:

"You have again forgotten the saying of the ancients that I have repeated to you so many times: 'the mystery that cannot be explained is fate. It is composed of impenetrable obscurities, of inextricable complications, of actions and omissions that add up day by day. Those who are convinced of the existence of this destiny no longer believe in the possibility of achieving, with effort, to prolong their lives, to succeed in their enterprises, to avoid misfortune. They no longer trust in anything, knowing that they are the playthings of a blind destiny. They are upright and honest, no longer tending in any direction; no longer grieving or rejoicing over anything; no longer acting, but letting everything pass them by.'"

The following sentences of *Huang Di* sum up well the conduct that the enlightened man should follow: "Let the superior man remain inert as a corpse, and move only passively, because he is being moved. Let him not reason about his inertia, about his movements. Let him never concern himself with the opinions of men, and let him never change his feelings according to theirs. Let him follow the way, his personal way. For no one can harm him" (fate is the only one who disposes of him).

G. Four men lived together all their lives without regard for each other's feelings. Four others spent their lives without communicating any purpose to each other. Four others, without showing anything to others. Four others, without ever speaking. Four others, without even looking at each other... All marched on as befits men governed by fate[27]. — What seemed favorable, finally proved to be disastrous. What seemed fatal, is later found to have been favorable. How many men spend their lives in foolish efforts to discern confused appearances, to penetrate mysterious obscurities. Would it not be better not to fear misfortune, not to desire happiness, to move or stand still according to necessity, with the profound conviction that reason has no understanding and that the will can do nothing about it? He who has well understood this, must apply it to others as to himself. If he governs men according to different principles, he will be a blind and obstinately deaf man, who will throw himself with them into a ditch.

Let us recapitulate: Life and death, fortune and misfortune, depend on destiny, on the horoscope. Whoever complains of having to die young, of being poor or afflicted, shows that he ignores the law. He who looks death in the face without fear and endures misery without complaining, shows that he knows the law. The conjectures of the so-called wise men, about plus and minus, about fullness and emptiness, about luck and bad luck, never give any certainty; after all their calculations, the result will be positive or negative, without knowing why. Whether it is calculated or not, the same thing will happen. Salvation and ruin do not depend on prior knowledge. One is saved because he had to be saved, another perishes because he had to perish.

H. Duke *Jing* of *Qi* had gone for a walk north of Mount *Ni Shan* and was returning to his capital. When he saw it from afar, moved to tears, he cried out:

"Oh, my beautiful city, so well populated! Why is the time gradually approaching when I must leave it? Ah, if men did not have to die!"

Shi Kong and *Liang Qiu Ju*, members of the duke's escort, also wept, to please him, and said:

"If for us, who are only squires, men of very modest condition, the thought of death is painful, how much more must it be for you, Lord!"

The scholar *Yen Zi*, who also accompanied the duke, burst out laughing. The duke saw him. Wiping away his tears, he stared at *Yen Zi* and asked:

"When I am crying, and these two men are crying with me, what can you laugh at?"

"I believe," said *Yen Zi*, "that if, according to your wish, men did not die, the wise dukes *Tai* and *Huan*, the brave dukes *Zhuang* and *Ling*, your ancestors, would still be alive. If they were still alive, the eldest would occupy the throne, and you, his distant descendant, would no doubt be engaged in guarding some farm. Do you not owe the throne to the fact that, having died, your ancestors are no longer here? By their successive disappearance, the throne has come to you. Is there not in your sorrow for the death of men some ingratitude to those who have done you the service of dying, and are not the two squires who have wept with you to please you foolish flatterers? It was these thoughts that made me laugh."

---

27   Absurd introduction; an exercise in parallel sentences.

Embarrassed by his outburst of irrational sentimentality, the duke drank a full horn of wine as penance, and then forced his two squires to drink two horns of wine each.

I. In *Wei*, a certain *Dong Men Wu*, having lost his son, did not mourn him. Someone who lived with him said to him:

"Yet you loved your son; how is it that, now that he is dead, you do not mourn him?"

Dong Men Wu said:

"Once, for many years before he was born, I lived without this son, without mourning. Now that he is dead, I look back and think that I never had him, and I no longer grieve. Besides, what's the point? Farmers worry about their crops, merchants about their trade, artisans about their craft, civil servants about their work. But all this depends on circumstances beyond their control. The farmer needs rain, the merchant needs luck, the craftsman needs work, the official needs an opportunity to distinguish himself. But it is only on fate that circumstances and opportunities depend."

CHAPTER 7 - YANG ZHU[28]

A. *Yang Zhu*, traveling in the country of *Lu*, stayed with the *Meng* family. Master *Meng* asked him:

"Is it not enough to be a man (the noblest of creatures)?"

"Renown," said *Yang Zhu*, "calls for fortune."

"And then?"

"Then comes nobility."

"And then?"

"Then comes death."

"So it is only to die that we fret?" said *Meng*.

"No," said *Yang Zhu*, "it is to pass on our reputation, after our death, to our descendants."

"Is it certain that they will inherit it?" said Master *Meng*. "Is it not the case that those who have worked and suffered to become famous, pass nothing on to their descendants; while those whose life has been mediocre or bad, succeed in bringing up their family? Thus, *Guan Zhong*, minister to the Duke of *Qi*, who served his lord with the greatest servility, to the point of making his vices his own, left nothing to his family. While *Tieng Heng*, another minister of *Qi*, who always took the opposite view to that of his master, managed to bequeath to his descendants the dukedom he had usurped. In these two parallel cases, *Guan Zhong's* deserved reputation brought his descendants nothing but poverty, while *Tieng Heng's* undeserved reputation made his family's fortune."

---

28   We owe to *Lie Zi* and *Zhuang Zhou* what we know of this selfish epicurean philosopher, whom Mencius criticized greatly; supposing there is some truth in what they tell of him.

"Too often, fame is coupled with a false assumption, a false pretense. They glorify *Yao* and *Shun* for having abdicated in favor of *Xu You* and *Shan Guan*. In reality their abdication was a vain pretense. They enjoyed the advantages of imperial dignity until their death. Their glory is a false glory. — Whereas *Bo Yi* and *Shu Qi*, who really renounced their paternal fief and starved to death on Mount *Shou Yang* because of their loyalty, are pitied by some, mocked by others, and glorified by none. Who shall distinguish, in this matter, the true from the false?"

B. *Yang Zhu* said:

"Out of a thousand men, not even one lives a hundred years. But let us say that out of every thousand, there is one centenarian. A great part of his life will have passed between the helplessness of early childhood and the decrepitude of extreme old age. A large part will have been consumed in the sleep of the night or the distractions of the day. A large part will have been sterilized by sadness or fear. A relatively small fraction is left for action and enjoyment. — But what will make you decide to act? What will make you enjoy? Will it be the beauty of shapes and sounds? These things either tire or do not last… Will it be the law, with its rewards and punishments, its distinctions and its scourgings? These motives are too weak. Is a reprimand so fearful? Is a posthumous title so enviable? Is there any reason, for so little, to give up the pleasure of the eyes and ears, to apply the moral restraint to your exterior and interior? Is spending life in this way, with privations and restrictions, less hard than spending it in prison and in fetters? No, it is not. Thus, the ancients, who knew that life and death are two alternative and transitory phases, let their instincts manifest themselves freely, without restraining their natural appetites, without depriving their bodies of their pleasures. They did not care whether they were praised or blamed in life or after death. They gave their nature its satisfactions, and let others have theirs.

C. *Yang Zhu* said:

"Beings differ in life, but not in death. In life, some are wise and others foolish, some noble and others base; in death, all are the same, a mass of putrid carrion. These differences in life, this equality in death, are the work of destiny. Wisdom and folly, nobility and vulgarity, are not to be considered as real entities, but as modes distributed at random over the mass of men. Whatever the duration and form of life, it ends with death. The good and the wise, the wicked and the foolish, all die alike. At the death of the emperors *Yao* and *Shun*, of the tyrants *Jie* and *Zhou*, only putrefied corpses remained, impossible to distinguish. Therefore, live the present life, without worrying about what will follow death."

D. *Yang Zhu* said:

"It was by excess of loyalty, that *Bo Yi* let himself starve to death; it was by excess of continence, that *Zhan Qin* extinguished his lineage. This is where ignorance of true principles leads to the best people."

Yang Zhu said:

"*Yen Xian* was poor in *Lu*, *Zi Gong* was rich in *Wei*. The poverty of *Yen Xian* shortened his life, the wealth of *Zi Gong* exhausted him with worries. But then, if poverty and wealth are equally harmful, what should we do? Here it is: live happily, treat your body well, that's what you should do. To the cheerful, even poverty cannot harm him (because he does not grieve). To the one who treats his body well, wealth will not harm him either (because he will not be worn out by worries)."

Yang Zhu quoted:

"'To help oneself during life, to cease in death'; I like this saying of the ancients. By help, I mean provide the comforts of life, food and heating, all the necessities of life. By cessation in death I do not mean the suppression of the usual lamentations, but the suppression of such refuse as pearls or jade placed in the mouth of the corpse, rich clothes, immolated victims, objects offered to the dead."

E. *Yen Pingzhong*, a disciple of *Mo Zi*, asked *Guan Zhong*, a politician inclined to Daoism, how the living should be treated:

"We should favor natural inclinations, we should not hinder them."

"Please go into details," said *Yen Pingzhong*.

"You must allow complete freedom to hear, to look, to smell, and to taste," said *Guan Zhong*; "every license for the ease of the body and the rest of the mind. Any restriction imposed on any of these faculties, afflicts nature, is tyranny. To be free from all restraint, to be able to satisfy all instincts, from day to day, until death, that is what I call living. To be constrained, to be mortified, to be in constant pain, in my opinion, is not living. And now that I have told you how to treat the living, please tell me how to treat the dead."

"No matter how the dead are treated," said *Yen Pingzhong* "(the body is only a worn-out garment). Whether they are burned, immersed, buried, exposed, tied with straw and thrown into the river, or richly dressed and placed in a sarcophagus or coffin, it is all the same."

Looking at his friends who had attended this talk, *Guan Zhong* said:

"He and I understand what the matter of life and death is."

F. *Zi Chan*, being a minister of the *Zheng* principality, made innovations for three years, which were beneficial to the people, but which greatly displeased the aristocracy. *Zi Chan* had two brothers, the elder named *Chao*, and the younger named *Mu*. *Chao* was a drunkard, *Mu* was a libertine. People could smell the wine and dregs a hundred paces from *Chao*'s door, whose habitual drunkenness had caused him to lose all sense of modesty and prudence. *Mu*'s harem occupied an entire neighborhood, which its owner populated by all means, and which he seldom left. *Zi Chan* was much mortified by the misconduct of his two brothers, which made him the object of the ridicule of his enemies, and he secretly consulted *Deng Xi*.

"I fear," he said to him, "that it may be said of me that, since I cannot reform my brothers, I have not what is necessary to govern the State. I beg you to advise me."

"You should have intervened earlier," said *Deng Xi*. "Make them understand the price of life, the importance of decorum and morality."

So *Zi Chan* delivered a speech to his two brothers on the following three points: that what distinguishes man from animals are reason, rites and morals; that indulgence in bestial passions wastes life and ruins reputation; that if they were rehabilitated, they could receive a position.

Far from being moved by these arguments, *Chao* and *Mu* retorted:

"We have known all this for a long time; we have also long since decided to disregard it. Since death is the inevitable end of everything, the important thing, in our opinion, is to enjoy life. We are not at all willing to turn life into an anticipated death through ritual, moral and other restrictions. Satisfying instincts, exhausting all pleasures, that is really living. We only regret that the capacity of our bellies is less than our appetite, and that the strength of our bodies is no match for our lust. What do we care, that men speak ill of us, and that our lives wear out. Don't think we are men who can be intimidated or convinced. We have tastes very different from yours. You regulate the outward, making men suffer, whose inward inclinations are thus compressed. Let all instincts run free, which makes men happy. You can succeed in imposing your system by force on a principality. Our system is spontaneously accepted by the princes and subjects of the whole empire. Thank you for your advice. We are glad that you gave us the opportunity to express our opinion."

Zi Chan was completely bewildered and found nothing to reply. He consulted *Deng Xi* again, who said:

"You are wrong not to understand that your brothers see more clearly than you. How can there be men who admire you? What good can you do for *Zheng's* principality?"

G. *Duan Mushu* of *Wei*, a wealthy contemporary of *Zi Gong*, used the great fortune amassed by his ancestors to please himself and others. His buildings, gardens, food, costumes, music, and harem eclipsed the princes of *Qi* and *Chu*. He satisfied, for himself and his guests, all the desires of the heart, ears, eyes and mouth, bringing for this purpose the rarest objects from the farthest countries. He traveled in the same luxury and comfort. Guests flocked to him by the hundreds, the fire never went out in his kitchens, the music never ceased to resound in his salons. He distributed the surplus of his wealth among his relatives, his fellow citizens and his country. He sustained this lifestyle for sixty years. Then, feeling his strength failing him and death approaching, in one year he distributed all his possessions as gifts, giving nothing to his children. He dispossessed himself so well, that in his last illness he lacked the necessary medicines, and after his death he lacked the money for his funeral. Those who had benefited from his generosity then contributed, buried him and provided an income for his descendants... What should we think of this man's conduct? *Qin Gu Li* judged that he behaved like a madman and dishonored his ancestors. *Duan Gan Sheng* judged that he behaved like a superior man, and that he was much wiser than his thrifty ancestors. He acted contrary to the vulgar sense, but in accordance with the superior sense. This spendthrift was wiser than all the princes of *Wei* who mortified themselves (So judges the epicurean *Yang Zhu*).

H. *Men Sun Yang* asked *Yang Zhu*:

"Can a man who watches over his life and cares for his body succeed in never dying?"

"You will surely manage to live longer," said *Yang Zhu*. "But is it worth going to so much trouble and effort to live longer? The world has always been, and always will be, full of passions, dangers, evils and vicissitudes. One hears and sees the same things over and over again; even changes lead to nothing new. After a hundred years of existence, those who have not died of pain die of boredom."

"Then," said *Men Sun Yang*, "in your opinion, would the ideal be suicide?"

"Not at all," said *Yang Zhu*. "You must endure life while it lasts, striving for every possible satisfaction. You must accept death when it comes, consoling yourself with the thought that it will all end. One cannot prolong one's life, but neither should one hasten one's death."

I. *Yang Zhu* said:

"*Bo Cheng Zi Gao* would not have sacrificed one of his hairs for love of anyone. He left the capital and became a farmer in an unknown corner. The great *Yu*, on the other hand, spent and wore himself out for others. — The ancients did not give the State a single hair, and would not have accepted that one should devote himself to them in the name of the State. It was in those days, when individuals did nothing for the State, and the State did nothing for individuals; that the State was doing well."

"And you," asked *Qin Gu Li* to *Yang Zhu* "would you sacrifice one hair of your body for the sake of the State?"

"One hair," said *Yang Zhu*, "it would hardly benefit it."

"But if it did benefit it, would you sacrifice it?" *Qin Gu Li* insisted.

Yang Zhu did not reply[29]. — *Qin Gu Li* went out and informed *Men Sun Yang* of the conversation he had just had with *Yang Zhu*. "Perhaps you have not grasped the extent of his thinking," said *Meng Sun Yang*. "If you were offered a large sum for a piece of your skin, would you give it?" "Yes," said *Qin Gu Li*.

"And if you were offered a princedom for one of your limbs, would you give it?" *Qin Gu Li* hesitated to answer, then *Meng Sun Yang* said:

"A hair is less than a piece of skin; a piece of skin is less than a limb. But, added together, many hairs would be worth a piece of skin, many pieces of skin would be worth a limb. A hair is a part of the body and, therefore, something precious."

Qin Gu Li said:

---

29   Hence the reputation for egoism of *Yang Zhu*. His egoism is only a particular point of his general epicureanism.

"Master I am not strong enough in dialectics, to be able to answer your argument; but I feel that, if I were to put our propositions to them, *Lao Dan* and *Guan Yin Zi* would approve of yours (and *Yang Zhu's*), the great *Yu* and *Mo Zi* would approve of mine."

Men Sun Yang changed the subject.

J. *Yang Zhu* said:

"Only the good of *Shun, Yu, Zhou Gong* and Confucius are told; and only the bad of *Jie* (the last emperor of the *Xia*) and *Zhou* (the last emperor of the *Yin*). *Shun* was a laborer in *He Yang*, a potter in *Lie Zhai*, wasting his strength (a Daoist sin), depriving his stomach, worrying his parents, displeasing his brothers and sisters. At the age of thirty he married, without permission. When *Yao* handed over the empire to him, he was old and soft. Then, his son *Shang Jun* being unable, he had to cede the empire to *Yu*, and ended his life in a dreary old age; all that men who live according to nature avoid. — Unable to make the waters flow, *Kun*, was put to death in *Yu Shan*. His son *Yu* served under the one who had so treated his father, so much so that he did not return home to see and name his newborn son. He toiled and toiled, so much so that his body was worn out, so that his hands and feet were covered with calluses. Finally, when *Shun* ceded the empire to him, he shone little, and ended in a morose old age, which men who live according to nature avoid. — After the death of Emperor *Wu*, during the youth of Emperor *Cheng*, *Zhou* (the Duke of *Zhou*, brother of the deceased, uncle of the successor), who was in charge of the regency, did not get along well with the Duke of *Shao*, was strongly criticized, had to disappear for three years, put to death two of his brothers, had difficulty in preserving his own life, and ended in a gloomy old age, which men who live according to nature avoid. — Confucius devoted himself to the task of illustrating the teachings of the ancient emperors and making them acceptable to the princes of his time. As a reward for his efforts, the tree under which he took refuge was cut down in *Song*, he was forced to flee from *Wei*, was persecuted in *Shang* and in the state of *Zhou*, and was blocked between *Chen* and *Cai*. He was offended by *Ji Shi*, outraged by *Yang Hu*, and finally died in a morose old age, from which those who live according to nature escape. — These four sages did not have a single day of true contentment during their lives. After their death, their reputation grew from age to age. Is this vain posthumous renown a compensation for the real pleasures of which they were deprived during their lifetime? Now they are praised and offerings are made to them, without their knowing anything about it more than a beam or a clod of earth. — Whereas *Jie*, rich, powerful, cultured and feared, enjoyed all pleasures, satisfied all his appetites, was glorious until his death, had everything desired by men who live according to nature. — *Zhou* also mocked the rites, and enjoyed until his death, a fate preferred by men who live according to nature. — These two men had, during their lifetime, everything they wanted. Now, no doubt, they are called fools, wicked, tyrants; but what do they care, they know nothing of that, any more than a beam or a clod of earth. — The four Wise Men suffered all evils, died sadly, and have for all compensation only their vain fame.

The two Tyrants enjoyed all good things until death, and their bad reputation does not make them suffer now. (The Epicureanism of *Yang Zhu*.)

K. *Yang Zhu* was received by the king of *Liang*. He told the king that, with his prescription, ruling the empire would be as easy as turning his hand. The king of *Liang* said to him:

"Master, you have a wife and a concubine, two people whom you cannot shut up; you have three acres of garden which you do not know how to cultivate; and you dare to tell me that, with your recipe, ruling the empire would be as easy as turning your hand. Do you want to make fun of me?"

Yang Zhu said:

"Have you ever seen a shepherd leading a flock of a hundred sheep, walking behind quietly with his whip, and letting the sheep go where they will? (This is my system, leaving each one to his own instinct.) Whereas (with your system of artificial coercion) *Yao* pulling and *Shun* pushing, the two of them would not succeed in making a single sheep walk. And as for my domestic affairs (wife and garden) to which you just alluded, I will only say this. Fish as big as a boat are not to be found in ravines; swans of powerful flight do not frequent ponds. The fundamental bell and the greater pipe are not used to make music. Those who are fit to govern great things do not like to occupy themselves with trifles. I think you must have understood me."

L. *Yang Zhu* said:

"The things of the highest antiquity have disappeared so completely, that no one will be able to tell anything about them any more. The affairs of the three August Ones are more or less forgotten. Those of the five sovereigns are confused like a dream. Of those of the three emperors, we know the hundredth part. Of the contemporary affairs, we know the ten-thousandth part. Of what one has seen oneself, one knows the thousandth part. High antiquity is so far from us! *Fu Xi* reigned more than three hundred thousand years ago, and since then, in the world, there have been wise and foolish men, beautiful and ugly things, successes and failures, good and evil. All this happens in a continuous chain, sometimes slower, sometimes faster. Is it worth tiring one's mind and body to obtain a posthumous reputation as a good prince, which will last a few centuries, and of which one will not even be aware? It costs the pleasure of a lifetime, and does not refresh the bones after death."

M. *Yang Zhu* said:

"Man takes from heaven and earth. There is something of the five elements in him. He is the most transcendent of all living beings. He has no claws or teeth to defend himself, no impenetrable skin, no nimble feet to flee, no hair or feathers to protect himself from the elements. It obtains its sustenance from other beings, which it dominates not by its strength but by its intelligence. It is his intelligence that makes man noble and his superiority over beings that are inferior to him, even if they are much stronger than he is. Strictly speaking, his body is not his (it is not an absolute dominion); the fact that he cannot preserve its integrity proves it. Nor are beings his (in the same sense); the fact that he cannot preserve himself from those who are harmful to him proves it. Man depends on his body to live, and on the other beings to maintain life. It is impossible for man to give himself life, and for beings to give themselves being. He who enslaves men and beings for his personal mastery or enjoyment is not a Sage. He who fraternizes with men and beings, seeking and letting each one seek his natural good, is a superior man, the highest of all men."

N. *Yang Zhu* said:

"Four desires agitate men, to the point of not letting them rest; namely, the desire for longevity, the desire for reputation, the desire for dignity, and the desire for wealth. Those who have obtained these things, fearing that they may be taken from them, are afraid of the dead, of the living, of princes, and of torments. They always tremble, wondering whether they will die or live, because they have understood nothing of destiny, and believe that external things have power over them. There are, on the contrary, men who, trusting in destiny, care nothing for the length of life; who disdain reputation, dignities, riches. These are the ones who are always satisfied and enjoy an incomparable peace, because they have understood that, as everything is governed by destiny, nothing has power over them."

The Daoist ideal is the practice of agriculture in obscurity, producing what is necessary to live, no more. The ancients said it well: love causes half of man's problems, and the desire for well-being the rest. Also very true is the adage of the *Zhou* that farmers are, in their condition, the happiest of men. They work from dawn to night, proud of their endurance. They find nothing tastier than their coarse vegetables. Their hardened bodies feel no fatigue. If they were forced to spend a single day in the luxury and good food of the townspeople, they would fall ill; whereas a nobleman or a prince would perish if they had to live a day like a peasant. The barbarians, on the other hand, discover that nothing in the empire is worth what they possess and love. Nature is satisfied when needs are met; all needs beyond that are superfluous, an artificial civilization.

Once, in the principality of *Song*, a peasant, utterly ignorant of city things, had spent the winter in rags barely able to protect him from the frost. When spring came, he took them off to warm himself naked in the sun. The warmth seemed so good to him that he said to his wife, "Perhaps they forgot to propose this to our prince; if we did, we could get a good reward." A rich man from the countryside then said to him, "Once a peasant offered watercress to a prince. The prince ate them and was very upset. The poor peasant was mocked by some and reprimanded by others. Beware lest a similar misfortune befall you if you teach the prince to warm himself naked in the sun."

O. *Yang Zhu* said:

"A luxurious dwelling, fine clothes, good food, beautiful women, when one has all this, what more would one desire, who would pretend to more, would be insatiable. But the insatiable wear out their lives like wood or paper eaten by worms. They are not loyal to their princes, nor good to beings, for they are selfish and ill-intentioned. Or if they seem otherwise, it is only in appearance, for the sake of a vain reputation of loyalty or goodness. — The teaching handed down by the elders is peace between superiors and inferiors, and the mutual granting of congruent advantages by all. — *Yu Zi* said: suppress the love of reputation, and there will be no more sorrows. *Lao Zi* said: Reputation is not worth what truth is worth, and yet one runs after it more than after truth. Reputation is neither to be sought nor avoided. For the efforts made to acquire it wear us down, but its peaceful possession comforts. Disgrace also wears us down, because of the sorrow it engenders. Therefore, do not seek, do not avoid. What is to be avoided is to injure ourselves, acquiring a false reputation, losing true glory. No doubt, the ideal would be to be equally insensible to honor and dishonor; but few attain this ideal.

CHAPTER 8 - ANECDOTES

A. When *Lie Zi* was a disciple Master *Lin* of *Hu Qiu*, the latter said to him one day.

"When you have understood what is behind you, I will teach you to understand yourself."

"And what is behind me?" asked *Lie Zi*.

"Your shadow," said the master, "examine it."

Then *Lie Zi* examined his shadow. He noticed that when his body bent, the shadow became curved; when his body rose, the shadow became straight. It was said that the shadow was neither curved nor straight, but depended entirely on the shape of the body. And from this consideration he drew the consequence that man must adapt himself in everything, since nothing depends on him. This is the meaning of the formula "after having grasped what is behind, stand still in front."

Guan Yin Zi said to *Lie Zi*:

"According as the sound is beautiful or ugly, the echo is beautiful or ugly; when the object grows, its shadow grows; when the object diminishes, its shadow diminishes. Reputation is the echo of man, conduct is the shadow of man. The saying goes, 'watch your words and your conduct, for your words will be repeated and your conduct will be imitated.' The wise man judges from the inside by the outside; this is his way of prognosticating. He imputes to a man what he has noticed in his manners. — Each one loves whom he loves, and hates whom he hates. The emperors *Tang* and *Wu* reigned because, having loved the people of the empire, the latter repaid them. The tyrants *Jie* and *Zhou* perished because, having hated the people of the empire, the empire repaid them. This is the great law, the summary of history. Since *Shen Nong*, *Shun*, and the three dynasties, all fortunes, all misfortunes, have had these two reasons.

Yen Hui said:

"What is the point of so many theories? I think it is enough to seize the opportunities."

Lie Zi said:

"I don't accept your opinion. If one has more than the opportunity, if one has the thing, one loses it by disorderly conduct, as happened to *Jie* and *Zhou*. Those who indulge in gluttony are no better than chickens and dogs. Those who only know how to fight are animals. No one respects these men, who are not men. Their dishonor is their downfall."

B. *Lie Zi*, wishing to learn to draw the bow, approached *Guan Yin Zi* and asked him to teach him. The latter asked him:

"Do you know the aim of archery?"

"No," said *Lie Zi*.

"Then go and learn it," said *Guan Yin Zi*, "and then come back."

Three years later, *Lie Zi* returned.

"Do you know what the purpose is?" asked *Guan Yin Zi*.

"Yes," said *Lie Zi*.

"Well," said *Guan Yin Zi*; "keep it well in your memory; beware of forgetting it. This is the rule of all progress, that before you undertake anything you must know why. The Sage does not calculate whether he will succeed or fail, the odds for and against. He sets the goal and then strives to achieve it."

C. The arrogant and the violent would be told of the Principle in vain; they have not what is necessary to understand it; their vices prevent them from being taught and helped. To be teachable, one must believe that one does not know everything. This is the indispensable condition. Age is not an obstacle, intelligence is not always a means, submission of the mind is the essential.

An artist from *Song* took three years to carve a jade mulberry leaf for his prince. When *Lie Zi* heard about it, he said:

"If nature took the same time, there would be very few leaves on the trees. Similarly, for doctrinal propaganda, the Sage relies on the power inherent in truth, not on artificial art."

D. *Lie Zi* was extremely poor. The sufferings of hunger could be seen on his haggard face. A foreigner who came to visit the minister *Zi Yang*, said to him:

"*Lie Zi* is a Sage; if you leave him in this misery, it will be said that you do not value the Sages."

Zi Yang ordered an official to take grain to *Lie Zi*. The latter came out of his house, saw the officer, saluted, thanked him, and refused. The officer returned, taking his grain with him.

When *Lie Zi* returned home, his wife looked at him sadly, beat her chest in grief and said.

"I thought the wife and children of a Sage, had some right to live happily. Now we are worn out by misery. The prince has been indifferent for a long time, but now he has remembered you, and you have refused his gifts. Shall we have to starve?"

"No," said *Lie Zi*, laughing, "the prince has not remembered me. He granted me this gift at the request of others; just as he would have sent me to his henchmen if anyone had spoken ill of me. I do not accept a gift given for that reason." (*Lie Zi* did not want to owe *Zi Yang* anything. The latter was massacred by *Zheng*'s people soon after).

E. A certain *Shi* of *Lu* had two sons, one learned and the other brave. The learned one went to offer himself to the Marquis of *Qi*, who accepted him and appointed him guardian of his sons. The brave one went to offer himself to the king of *Chu*, pleased him and was made a general by him, enriched and ennobled.

A neighbor of *Shi*, named *Meng*, also had two sons, one learned and the other brave. As he was very poor, the fortune of the *Shi* family tempted him with envy, and he asked how they had done it. *Shi* simply told him.

Immediately the learned *Meng* went to offer himself to the king of *Qin*. The latter said:

"In this time of wars, I need only soldiers; this scholar who teaches kindness and fairness will harm my kingdom... and ordered him to be castrated, then dismissed him."

The brave *Meng* offered himself to the Marquis of *Wei*. The latter said:

"My principality, small and weak, has great and formidable neighbors, whom I must beware of displeasing. I must keep my peace. Any appearance of warlike inclination might cost me the marquisate. I cannot employ this able man without risk. On the other hand, if I dismiss him without crippling him, he will go and offer himself to another prince and ruin me..."

So he ordered to cut one of the foot of the man and dismissed him.

When old *Meng* saw his two mutilated sons returning, beating his chest in pain, he went to reproach father *Shi*. The latter said to him:

"In the hour of fortune, one succeeds; in the hour of misfortune, only misfortune occurs. Your children and mine took exactly the same steps. The result was absolutely different. This is only due to fate (the bad hour), and not to the procedures employed. Fortune and misfortune are not governed by mathematical rules. What succeeded yesterday will fail today. What failed today may succeed tomorrow. Success comes from doing it at the right time, but there are no rules to determine that time. The wisest sometimes get it wrong. Even *Kong Qiu*, and *Lü Shang*, knew failure."

When they received these explanations, *Meng* and her children calmed down and said:

"Thank you! Say no more, we have understood."

F. When Duke *Wen* of *Jin* decided to attack *Wei*, his son, Prince *Chu* burst out laughing.

"What are you laughing at?" asked the duke.

"I laugh," answered the prince, "at the misfortune that has befallen one of my neighbors. This man was going to the city to accuse his wife of infidelity. On the way he met a woman who pleased him, who accepted his proposals. A moment later, he realized that he had done the same thing as his wife, and realized that there were some witnesses. He repaid his wife with the same coin. Isn't this story laughable?"

The duke understood that his son was warning him that he would be attacked while he was attacking *Wei*. He abandoned his expedition, and had his army return suddenly. He had not yet returned to his capital when he learned that an enemy had already invaded his northern border.

Thieves abounded in the principality of *Jin*. A certain *Xi Yong*, endowed with a special gift of second sight, recognized thieves by their faces. The marquis asked him to discover the thieves on his behalf, and indeed *Xi Yong* had hundreds of them captured. The marquis was very satisfied and said to *Zhao Wen Zi*:

"A single man has almost cleansed my principality of the thieves who infested it…"

"Believe me," replied *Zhao Wen Zi*, "that before he has completed his cleansing, this man will be killed…"

And indeed, exasperated, the remaining robbers said to each other:

"We will all perish, if we do not get rid of this *Xi Yong*…"

So they all got together and slaughtered *Xi Yong*. When the marquis heard about this, he became very nervous, called *Zhao Wen Zi* and said to him.

"What you have predicted, has happened; *Xi Yong* has been killed; how will I do now, to catch the rest of the robbers?"

Zhao Wen Zi said:

"Remember the proverb of the *Zhou*, 'Wanting to see the fish at the bottom of the water is harmful, wanting to know the hidden things brings misfortune.' One should never look too closely. To get rid of thieves, it will be enough if you put good officials in charge, who administer well and instill good morals in the people…"

The marquis laughed, and soon, having become an object of public reprobation, all the thieves left in his estates fled to the country of *Qin*.

G. When returning from *Wei* to *Lu*, Confucius stopped to contemplate the waterfall of *He Liang*[30], which falling from two hundred and forty feet high, produces a torrent bubbling for ninety stades, so strong that no fish or reptile can inhabit it. Now, before the eyes of Confucius, a man crossed these tumultuous waters. Confucius had his disciples congratulate him, and then said to him himself:

"You are very skillful; do you have a formula that allows you to entrust yourself to these waters in this way?"

"Before I enter the water," said the man, "I examine whether my heart is absolutely upright and loyal, and then I let myself go. My uprightness unites my body with the waves. As I am one with them, they cannot harm me."

"Remember this," said Confucius to his disciples. "Righteousness conquers even water, how much more men."

---

30   Compare chapter 2 I.

H. The crown prince *Jian*, son of King *Ping* of *Chu*, having been slandered by *Fei Wuji*, had fled to *Zheng*, where he was killed. His son *Bai Gong* planned to avenge him. He asked Confucius:

"Is there any chance that a plot will not be discovered?"

Confucius sensed his intention and did not answer. *Bai Gong* continued:

"Can a stone thrown into the water be discovered?"

"Yes," said Confucius, "by a diver from the country of *Wu*."

"And water mixed with water, can be discovered?"

"Yes," said Confucius. "*Yi Ya* discerned that there was, in a mixture, water from the river *Zi*, and water from the river *Sheng*."

"Then, in your opinion," said *Bai Gong*, "a conspiracy cannot go unnoticed?"

"It will not be perceived," said Confucius, "if it is not spoken of. To succeed in fishing and hunting, one must be silent. The most effective speech is that which is not heard; the most intense action is that which is not seen. Carelessness and agitation produce no good. You betray your plans with your speeches and your attitude."

Bai Gong did not heed this warning, and provoked a riot in which he perished.

I. After *Zhao Xiang Zi* commissioned *Mu Zi*, the master of his hounds, to attack the *Di* (a nomadic people), *Mu Zi* won a victory and conquered two of their encampments in one day. *Mu Zi* sent the news to *Zhao Xian Zi*. The latter, upon hearing the news, during his meal, became sad.

"What is your concern?" asked those present. "Two camps taken in one day, that's good news. What is it that distresses you?"

"I think," said *Zhao Xiang Zi*, "that river floods only last three days, that storms only last a fraction of a day. My house is at the height of its fortune. Perhaps its ruin may come[31]."

Confucius, having learned this saying, said:

"The prince of *Zhao* will prosper."

Indeed, it is sadness (with the prudence derived from it) that prospers, while (imprudent) joy ruins. To gain a victory is easy enough, but to preserve its fruits is difficult, and only a wise ruler achieves it. *Qi*, *Chu*, *Wu* and *Yue*, won many victories, without retaining any of the advantage gained. Only a prince imbued with wise doctrines will keep what he has conquered. It is wisdom that exalts, not force… Confucius was so strong that he could single-handedly remove the huge bar that closed the gate of the capital of *Lu*, but he never showed his strength. *Mo Zi*, who was well versed in the construction of defensive and offensive war machines, never displayed this talent. The best way to preserve what has been acquired is to step aside.

J. A certain *Song* man practiced humanity and justice. So has his family continued to do for three generations.

---

31   Compare chapter 9 of *Lao Zi*.

One day, without being able to discover the cause, his black cow gave birth to a white calf. Our man sent to ask Confucius what this phenomenon portended.

"This is a great thing," said Confucius, "this calf must be sacrificed to the Heavenly Sovereign."

After a year, for no known cause, the father of the family became blind. Soon after, his black cow gave birth to a second white calf. The father again sent his son to ask Confucius what this meant to him. The son said:

"After the previous consultation, you lost your sight; what's the use of starting over again?"

"Go," said the father. "The words of the Sages sometimes seem wrong, but they are verified by time. Let us believe that the time has not yet come. Go!"

So the son asked Confucius, who again said:

"This is something great, offer it back to the Heavenly Sovereign..."

The son reported the answer to the father, who ordered him to obey it.

A year later, the son also became blind. Suddenly, the *Chus* invaded the *Song* country and laid siege to its capital. The famine became so great that families exchanged their children to eat them and crushed the bones of the dead to make a kind of food. All able-bodied men had to defend the wall. More than half of them died. At this end, the two blind men, being unable to render any service, were exempted from any charge. When the siege was lifted, they suddenly regained their sight. Fate had made them blind, to their salvation.

K. In *Song*, an adventurer asked Prince *Yuan* to let him show him his skills. Once permission was obtained, he began to walk on two stilts taller than his body, juggling seven swords, five of which flew in the air, while his hands received or threw the other two. Filled with admiration for his skill, Prince *Yuan* ordered him to be rewarded handsomely. — When another adventurer heard of this, he also presented himself to the prince. The latter took offense at his request. "This man only came because I treated the previous one well," he said... "and held him captive and ill-treated for a month[32]."

L. Duke *Mu* of *Qin* said to *Bo Luo*, his horse-supplier:

"You are getting old, do you have a son or other relative who can replace you in your business?"

Bo Luo replied:

"A good horse can be recognized by examination of the bones and sinews, and my children would be capable of it. But to recognize a horse worthy of the prince is more difficult, and my sons would not be able to do it. But among my grooms there is one *Gao* of *Jiu Fang*, who knows as much as I do. Try him."

Duke *Mu* sent for the stable boy and asked him to find a prince's horse for him. *Gao* returned after three months, announcing that a horse had been found in *Sha Qiu*.

---

32   Compare with previous paragraph E. Same talent, not the same time.

"What horse is this?" asked the duke.

"It is a chestnut mare," said *Gao*.

The duke ordered the animal to be brought to him, which turned out to be a bay stallion. Duke *Mu* was not pleased. Having sent for *Bo Luo*, he said to him:

"Something is wrong. The one I sent on your recommendation cannot even distinguish the sex and coat of horses; what can he understand of their qualities?"

Bo Luo said:

"Everyone knows how to distinguish sex and color. This *Gao* always goes straight to the bottom of things, without worrying about incidental details. He only considers the inside, only what is important, neglecting everything else. If he has chosen a horse, it is undoubtedly an animal of great value."

When the horse was brought in, it turned out to be a horse worthy of a prince.

M. King *Zhuang* of *Chu* asked *Zhan He*:

"What must I do to rule well?"

"I only know how to rule myself, not the State," said *Zhan He*.

"Then," asked the king, "tell me what I should do to preserve the temple of my ancestors, the burial mounds of the Patron of the Earth and the Patron of the Harvest."

Zhan He replied:

"The domain of the well-ordered man, is always in good order; that of the disordered man, is always in disorder. The root is internal. Please draw your own conclusions."

The king of *Chu* said:

"You have spoken well."

N. *Hu Qiu Zhang Ren* said to *Sun Shu Ao*:

"Three things attract envy, hatred and misfortune; namely, high dignity, great power and considerable income."

"Not necessarily," said *Sun Shu Ao*. "The higher my dignity, the more humble I behaved. The greater my power, the more discreet I have been. The more my wealth increased, the more generous I was. Thus I incurred neither envy, nor hatred, nor disgrace."

When *Sun Shu Ao* was about to die, he said to his son:

"The king tried several times to get me to accept a fief. I have always refused. After my death, he will probably offer you an assignment. I forbid you to accept any good land. If you must accept anything, between *Chu* and *Yue* is the hill of *Qin Qiu* of ill fame, where those of *Chu* and *Yue* go to evoke the dead; ask for that land; no one will envy you."

In fact, when *Sun Shu Ao* died, the king offered a beautiful fief to his son, who begged him to give *Qin Qiu* Hill instead. His descendants still own it today.

O. *Niu Que* was a famous scholar of *Shang Di*. When he went down to *Han Dan*, in the middle of the countryside, he was attacked by robbers who stripped him of everything, including his clothes, without him defending himself. Then he left without showing any sadness. A thief, surprised, ran after him and asked him why he was not distressed.

"It is because the Sage prefers life to possessions," said *Niu Que*.

"Ah," said the thief, "you are a sage."

When he told the other thieves, they said:

"If he is a Wise Man, he may go to the prince of *Zhao*. He will accuse us and lose us. Let's kill him without wasting time..."

They ran after *Niu Que* and killed him. — A man from *Yen*, hearing this story, gathered his relatives and said to them.

"If you ever meet robbers, don't do what *Niu Que* of *Shang Di* did..."

Some time later, this man's younger brother, going to *Qin*, encountered bandits near the passes. Remembering his elder brother's instruction, he endeavored to resist. When the robbers left, he ran after them, demanding what they had taken from him, with many insults. This was too much.

"We had left you alive, contrary to custom," they told him. "But since, by pursuing us, you expose us to being caught, we must kill you. Four or five persons accompanying him were killed with him. Moral, do not boast; stand aside."

P. A certain *Yu*, a rich man from *Liang*, did not know what to do with his wealth. After building a terrace near the main road, he set up an orchestra there and spent his time drinking and playing chess with guests of all kinds, mostly adventurers or swordsmen. One day, when one of these guests made a good move in the game, *Yu* said, laughing and without thinking of the damage:

"Oh, a vulture has picked up a dead mouse (this is a stroke of luck)."

The players took it badly. This *Yu*, they said among themselves, has been rich for too long. That makes him arrogant. Let's set him straight! We've been insulted; let's wash our honor. — They seized the day, gathered in arms and destroyed the *Yu* family with iron and fire. Morality, luxury and arrogance lead to ruin.

Q. In the East, a certain *Yuan Xing Mu*, who was on a journey, fainted from hunger on the road. A thief of *Hu Fu*, named *Qiu*, who was passing by, put food in his mouth. After the third mouthful, *Yuan Xing Mu* came to himself.

"Who are you?" he asked.

"I am *Qiu* of *Hu Fu*," said the other.

"Oh," said *Yuan Xing Mu*, "aren't you a thief? And you made me eat your food? I am an honest man, I will not keep it!"

And, leaning on his two hands, our man began to make such violent efforts to vomit that he expired on the spot. — He acted like a fool. Although *Qiu* of *Hu Fu* was a bandit, his food was not contaminated by his evil doings. By applying to the food what belonged to the thief, this *Yuan Xing Mu* proved that he lacked logic.

R. *Zhu Li Shu* served Duke *Ao* of *Ju*. Seeing that the latter treated him too coldly, he abandoned him and went to live as a hermit by the sea, eating aquatic herbs in summer and acorns and chestnuts in winter. When Duke *Ao* died, *Zhu Li Shu* took leave of his friends and declared that he was going to commit suicide. — His friends said to him:

"You left the Duke because he treated you coldly, and now you want to commit suicide because he is dead; you lack logic."

"It is not like that," said *Zhu Li Shu*. "I left the Duke because he showed me too little favor. I am committing suicide because he can never show me favor again. I want to teach the masters of the future to treat their officers properly, and leave the officers an example of more than ordinary devotion."

Zhu Li Shu really sacrificed his life for a high ideal.

S. *Yang Zhu* said:

"When the good goes, the bad comes. Inner feelings have repercussions on the outside. Therefore, the Sages watch over all that emanates from them."

T. A neighbor of *Yang Zhu*, having lost a sheep, gathered all his people and even called *Yang Zhu*'s servants to help him look for it. *Yang Zhu* said to him:

"For one sheep, is it necessary to have so many people?"

"There are many roads in the mountains," said the other.

When the searchers returned, *Yang Zhu* asked:

"Did you find the sheep?"

"No," they said.

"Why not?"

"Because the paths are infinitely subdivided and it is impossible to travel them all."

Yang Zhu became sad. He stopped talking and laughing. After several days, astonished by this melancholy, his disciples said to him:

"Losing a sheep is not a great loss; and besides, it was not your sheep; why do you feel so bad?"

Yang Zhu did not answer. The disciples did not understand anything. *Men Sun Yang* went out and told the matter to *Xin Du Zi*. A few days later, *Xin Du Zi* went in with *Meng Sun Yang* to see *Yang Zhu*, and spoke to him in these terms:

"In the country of *Lu*, three brothers studied goodness and fairness under the same teacher. When they returned home, their father asked them:"

"What is goodness and equity?"

"It is," said the oldest son, "sacrificing one's reputation for the sake of oneself."

"It is," said the youngest, "to sacrifice oneself for the sake of a good reputation."

It is," said the youngest, "to take care of oneself and one's good reputation…"

Thus, these three students of the same scholar supported three different theses. Whose fault was it, the teacher's or theirs?

Yang Zhu replied:

"Many of those who live along the rivers are boatmen or ferrymen. These men have apprentices, whom they teach to operate boats and ferries. Almost half of these apprentices drown. Whose fault is it, the master's or theirs? Did the master teach them to drown?"

Xin Du Zi left without saying anything. Outside, *Men Sun Yang* was displeased and said to him:

"Why did you talk like that? We don't know any more than we knew before."

"You didn't understand anything," said *Xin Du Zi*, "Don't you see that I made the master tell his secret? The lost sheep on the many mountain paths had made him think of the disciples lost in the infinite diversity of schools. It is for the lost minds that he laments. In short, science is one and true, but among the many deductions to be drawn from it, some are erroneous. The teacher who errs leads his pupils astray; the disciples who err go astray in spite of their teacher.

U. *Yang Bu*, brother of *Yang Zhu*, having gone out in white cloth, got wet in the rain, changed and came back in black cloth. The dog of the house that had seen him go out in white, barked at him when he returned in black. Irritated, *Yang Bu* went to hit him.

"Don't hit him," said *Yang Zhu*, "You have changed from white to black. How could I recognize you?"

(Profound moral: The change of a moral being, for example from good to evil, breaks his usual relationship with other beings; he is no longer the same.)

V. *Yang Zhu* said:

"Even if he does not intend it, he who does good to others, attracts good reputation, this reputation attracts fortune, and fortune attracts enemies. Therefore, the Sages look several times before doing good to others."

W. Someone once claimed to have the recipe for not dying. The prince of *Yen* sent a delegate to ask for it. When the delegate arrived, the man with the recipe was dead. The prince was angry with the delegate for being too late, and was about to have him punished, when one of his favorites said to him.

"If this man had really had the recipe for not dying, surely he would not have deprived himself of using it for himself. But he died. So he didn't have the formula. So he would not have given you immortality…"

The prince gave up punishing the delegate.

A certain *Qi*, who also had a great desire not to die, was equally grieved by this man's death. One *Fu* mocked him, saying that, the man having died, to lament his ineffectual secrecy was to act without reason. A certain *Hu* said that *Fu* had spoken wrongly; for, he said, it sometimes happens that one who possesses a secret does not know how to use it; just as it happens that someone produces such and such a result (by chance or invention), without having had the formula.

A *Wei* man was a skillful charmer. When he was about to die, he taught his formulas to his son. The latter recited the formulas perfectly, but they had no effect. He taught them to another, who recited them with the same effect as his late father… Since a living person was able to act effectively with the formula of a dead person, I wonder (said *Lie Zi*) if the dead could not act effectively with the formulae of the living… (Death and life are two forms of the same being).

X. On New Year's Day, the inhabitants of *Han Dan* offered doves to *Jian Zi*, who received them gladly and paid them well. One of his guests asked him why. It is to show, by releasing them on New Year's Day, how good I am. The host said:

"People capture them to let them go. But in capturing them, they kill many. If you valued their lives, you would do better to forbid capturing them. In this way, you would show much better how good you are."

"You are right," said *Jian Zi*.

Y. *Tian* of *Qi*, after making offerings to his ancestors, gave a great banquet to a thousand guests, each of whom brought a gift according to custom. One of the guests offered fish and wild geese. Seeing them, *Tian* sighed piteously and said:

"See how well heaven treats men; it not only makes the various grains grow; it also brings forth fish and birds, for men to use…"

All the guests chorused slavishly. Only the son of the *Bao* family, a twelve-year-old boy, stepped forward and said:

"What you just said is not correct. Even heaven and earth are beings like all beings. There are no superior or inferior beings. It is a fact that the cleverer and stronger eat the dumber and weaker, but this does not mean that the latter were made or born for the use of the former. Man eats the beings he can eat, but heaven did not bring these beings into existence for man to eat them. Otherwise, it would also have to be said that heaven brought men into being so that mosquitoes would bite them and tigers and wolves would devour them."

Z. In the principality of *Qi* there was a poor man who was always begging in the city market. Bored with his pleas, the townspeople ended up giving him nothing more. So the poor man went to work for the veterinarian of the princely family, *Tian*, and so he earned enough to keep him from starving. Then they told him that serving a veterinarian was a disgrace. He replied:

"To be reduced to begging is considered the worst shame. But I was a beggar. How can it be shameful for me to serve a veterinarian? It is an advancement in the social ladder."

A man from *Song* found on the road half of a cut contract, which its owner had lost. He kept it carefully, watching closely how it had been clipped, and told his neighbor that he was going to get a fortune. He was mistaken in thinking that fate, which had given him half a contract, must also give him the other half.

A man had a dead tree in his garden. His neighbor said to him:

"A dead tree is a bad thing."

The man cut down the tree. Then the neighbor asked him to give him the wood. The man then suspected that the neighbor had made him cut the tree with that intention, and was offended. He was wrong. The request, which followed the initial comment, does not show that there was any prior intent.

A man lost his axe and suspected that his neighbor's son had stolen it. The more he thought about it, the more he believed it to have been so. The more he thought about it, the more it seemed to him that the boy's gait, his face, his words, and all his actions were those of a thief. But when he emptied his dung pit, he found his axe in it. The next day, when he saw his neighbor's son again, he found him to be the most honest boy he could find (autosuggestion).

When *Bai Gong* was plotting his revenge (in the previous paragraph, H), he suffered a fall in which the sting attached to the handle of his whip pierced his chin, without him feeling anything. When *Zheng*'s people heard about this, they said:

"If he did not feel this, what will he feel? He must be absorbed in his plans for revenge, not to have noticed his fall and his wound!" (transport).

A man from *Qi* was so eager to have gold that he got up early in the morning, got dressed, went to the market, went straight to a money exchange booth, picked up a gold piece and left. The guards grabbed him and asked:

"How do you try to steal in a place so crowded with people?"

"I only saw the gold," he said, "I didn't see the rest of the world" (transport).

Zhuangzi[1]
(The Treatise of the Transcendent Master from *Nan Hua*)

ZHUANG ZHOU

CHAPTER 1 - TOWARDS THE IDEAL

A, B. According to ancient legends, in the northern ocean lives a huge fish that can take the form of a bird. When this bird takes off, its wings spread in the sky like clouds, skimming the waves it flies southward, a distance of three thousand stades, and then soars with the wind to the height of ninety thousand stades in the space of six months[2].

Are we seeing up there in the sky troops of wild horses running? Is it powdery matter fluttering? Are they the breaths[3] that give birth to beings? And is the blue Heaven itself? Or is it only the color of distant infinity, in which Heaven hides, the personal being of the Annals and the Odes? And from above do we see this earth? And under what aspect? Mysteries!

Be that as it may, rising from the vast ocean, and dragged by the great mass of air, the only support capable of sustaining its immensity, the great bird glides at a prodigious height.

A cicada just hatched, and a very young pigeon, on seeing it, laughed at the great bird and said:

"What is the use of soaring so high, why expose oneself thus? We, who are content to fly from branch to branch, without leaving the suburbs; when we fall

---

1   *Zhuangzi* is attributed to *Zhuang Zhou*, also known as *Chuang Tzu* (according to the Wade-Giles romanization, now in disuse) (Translator Note).

2   Allegory analogous to that of the annual rise and fall of the dragon. Clouds from the North, condensed into rain in the South. Vapors returned by the South to the North. An annual cycle comprised of two periods of six months.

3   Blows of the great bellows of nature. *Lao Zi*, ch. 5 C.

to the ground, we do ourselves no harm; every day, without fatigue, we satisfy our needs. Why go so far? Why climb so high? Do not our worries increase in proportion to the distance and the height?"

Observations of two little beasts, on a subject beyond their competence. A small mind does not comprehend what a large mind embraces. A short experience does not extend to distant facts. The mushroom that lasts only one morning does not know what a lunation is. The insect that lives only one summer knows nothing of the succession of seasons. Do not ask the ephemeral beings for information about the great turtle whose period is five centuries, about the great tree whose cycle is eight thousand years. Even the old *Peng Zu*[4] will not tell you anything beyond the eight centuries that tradition attributes to him. Each being has his own formula of development[5].

C. There are men who are almost as narrow-minded as the two little beasts mentioned above. Understanding nothing but the routine of vulgar life, they are fit only to be mandarins of a district, or lords of a fief, at best.

Master *Rong* of *Song* was superior to this species, and more like the great bird. He lived, equally indifferent to praise and blame. He held to his own judgment and was not swayed by the opinions of others. He never distinguished between glory and disgrace. He was free from the bonds of human prejudice.

Master *Lie* of *Zheng* was superior to Master *Rong*, and even more like the great bird. His soul flew on the wings of contemplation, sometimes for a fortnight, leaving his body inert and insensible. He was almost free from earthly bonds. But not entirely, for he had to wait for ecstasy; a remnant of dependence.

Let us now suppose a man entirely absorbed by the immense cosmic gyration, and moving within it in infinity. He will no longer depend on anything. He will be perfectly free, in the sense that his person and his action will be united to the person and action of the great Whole. Thus, it is rightly said: the superior man no longer has his own self; the transcendent man no longer has his own action; the Sage no longer even has a name of his own. For he is one with the Whole.

D. Once the emperor *Yao* wanted to hand over the empire to his minister *Xu You*. He said to him:

"When the sun or the moon shines, we put out the torch. When the rain falls, we put aside the watering can. It is because of you that the empire prospers. Why should I remain on the throne? Please take it."

"Thank you," said *Xu You*, "please keep it! It is with you ruling, that the empire has prospered. What is the importance of my personal reputation? A branch in the forest is enough for the bird to lodge. A little water taken from the river quenches the thirst of the rat. I have no other needs than these little creatures. Let us stay in our respective places, you and me."

---

4   According to legends, *Peng Zu* was 767 years old in 1123 BC.

5   Here, everything preceding paragraph A is repeated a second time in B. Same background, same form. Fragment added to the first part, probably in the final version.

These two men reached the level of Master *Rong* of *Song*. The Daoist ideal is higher than that.

One day *Jian Wu* said to *Lian Shu*:

"I have heard *Jie Yu* say some exaggerated and extravagant things…"

"What did he say?" asked *Lian Shu*.

"He said that on the distant island of *Gu She* live transcendental men, white as snow, fresh as children, who eat no food at all, but breathe the wind and drink the dew. They ride through space, with clouds as chariots and dragons as mounts. By the influx of their transcendence, they preserve men from disease and make the harvest ripen. This is obviously madness. So I did not believe it."

Lian Shu replied:

"The blind man does not see, because he has no eyes. The deaf man does not hear, because he has no ears. You have not understood *Jie Yu*, because you have no spirit. The superior men of whom he spoke do exist. They even possess virtues far more wonderful than those you have just described. But they care so little about diseases and crops that if the empire fell into ruin and everyone asked them for help, they would not bother, because they are so indifferent to everything… The superior man is not affected by anything. A universal deluge would not overwhelm him. A universal conflagration would not consume him[6]. So high are they above all. We could make *Yaos* and *Shuns*[7] out of their refuse. And would these men be concerned with lesser matters, such as the harvest and the government of a State? Come on! — Each one imagines the ideal in his own way. For *Song* people, the ideal is to be well-dressed and well-groomed; for *Yue* people, the ideal is to be shaven and covered with tattoos. Emperor *Yao* took pains and imagined that he had ruled ideally well. After having visited the four Masters on the remote island of *Gu She*, he recognized that he had messed everything up. The ideal is the indifference of the superior man, who lets the cosmic wheel turn.

E. Vulgar princes do not know how to employ men of this stature, who do not excel in small offices, for their genius is cramped there.

Master *Hui*[8], having obtained in his garden enormous gourds, cut them into two halves which he used as basins. Finding these basins too large, he cut them into two quarters each. These quarters no longer stood upright and could not hold anything. He broke them.

"You are nothing but a fool," said *Zhuang Zhou*. "You have failed to make good use of these rare gourds. They should have made floats out of them, with which you could have crossed rivers and lakes. By wanting to make them smaller, you put them out of use."

It's the same with men as with things; it all depends on what use you make of them.

---

6   Allegorical phrases, later taken literally.

7   A swipe at Confucian paragons, who are regarded as inferior beings by the Daoists.

8   *Hui Zi*, minister of *Liang*, sophist, perpetual contradictor of *Zhuang Zhou*, and one of the usual recipients of his ridicule.

A *Song* family who raised silkworms had a recipe for an ointment that kept the hands of those who unrolled the cocoons in hot water from cracking. They sold their recipe to a foreigner for a hundred coins, and considered that they had made a good profit. Now the foreigner, who had become admiral to the king of *Wu*, ordered a naval expedition against *Yue*. It was winter. Having preserved, thanks to his ointment, the hands of his sailors from any frostbite, he won a great victory, which procured him a vast fief. Thus, two applications of the same ointment produced, one a small sum and the other an immense fortune.

He who knows how to use the superior man, gets much out of it. He who does not know, gets nothing.

F. Master *Hui* said to Master *Zhuang*:

"Your theories have breadth, but they have no practical value; that is why no one wants them. It is like the great ailanthus tree,[9] whose fibrous wood cannot be cut into planks, whose gnarled branches are useless."

"Good for me," said Master Zhuang. "For everything of practical use perishes for this reason. The marten may use a thousand stratagems, but in the end it perishes, its skin is sought after. The yak, despite being so powerful, ends up being killed and its tail is used to make banners. Whereas the ailanthus to which you do me the honor of comparing me, planted in barren soil, will grow as much as it wants, will shade the traveler and the sleeper, unafraid of the axe, precisely because, as you say, it is good for nothing. Is not being fit for nothing a state one should rejoice in?"

CHAPTER 2 - UNIVERSAL HARMONY

A. Master Qi[10] was sitting on a ladder, his eyes raised to heaven, breathing faintly. His soul must have been absent[11].

Amazed, the disciple *You*[12] who was serving him, said to himself:

"What is this, can it be that, without being dead, a living being should become like this, as insensible as a withered tree, as inert as extinguished ash? He is no longer my master."

"Yes," said *Qi*, returning from his ecstasy, "I am still him. I had only lost myself, for a time[13]. But what can you understand of this, you who know only human arrangements, not even earthly ones, much less celestial ones?

"Please try to make me understand by some comparison," said *You*.

---

9   Ailanthus (*Ailanthus altissima*), commonly known as tree of heaven, varnish tree, or in Chinese as *chouchun*, is an ornamental tree widely used in public gardens in southern Europe, originating in China (Translator Note).

10   *Qi*, the master of the southern suburbs, where he lived.

11   Comment: his body seemed to have lost its companion, the soul. Compare with chapter 24 H.

12   Master *Yen You*, *Yen Cheng*, or *Yen Nou*.

13   Commentary: The state of one who is absorbed in universal being, in unity. He loses the notion of distinct beings.

"So be it," said Master *Qi*. "The great indeterminate breath of nature is the wind. By itself, the wind has no sound. But when it moves them, all beings become to it like a set of reeds. Mountains, forests, rocks, trees, every roughness, every crevice, resound like so many mouths, softly when the wind is gentle, loudly when the wind is strong. They are roars, booms, whistles, commands, complaints, outbursts, shouts, tears. The call answers the call. It is an ensemble, a harmony. Then, when the wind stops, all these accents fall silent. Have you not observed this on a stormy day?"

"I understand," said *You*. "Human strings are those of man-made musical instruments. The earthly chords are those of nature's voices. But the celestial chords, Master, what are they?"

B. Master *Qi* said:

"It is the harmony of all beings, in their common nature, in their common becoming. There is no contrast there, because there is no distinction. Great science embraces, great words embrace. Science and words of a lower order distinguish. All is one. During sleep, the undistracted soul is absorbed in this unity; during wakefulness, distracted, it distinguishes diverse beings. — And what is the reason for these distinctions? What causes them is the activity, the relationships, the conflicts of life. Hence the theories, the errors. From crossbow shooting we derived the notion of good and evil. From contracts was derived the notion of right and wrong[14]. Credence was given to these imaginary notions; they were even attributed to Heaven. It is impossible to make humans abandon them. And yet, yes, complacency and resentment, sorrow and joy, plans and regrets; passion and reason, indolence and firmness, action and laziness, all these contrasts, are so many sounds coming from the same instrument, so many mushrooms born of the same moisture, fleeting modalities of the universal being. All this has come about during the course of time. Where does it come from? It developed! It was born, between a morning and an afternoon, of itself, not as a real being, but as an appearance. There are no distinct real beings. There is an *I*, only in contrast to a *he*. There being *he* and *me* only beings of reason, there is also not, in reality, that something nearer which is called *mine*, and that something farther away which is called *yours*. But who is the agent of this state of affairs, the mover of the great whole? Everything happens as if there were a real governor, but whose personality cannot be determined. The hypothesis which explains the phenomena is acceptable, provided we do not make this universal governor a distinct material being[15]. It is a tendency without palpable form, the inherent norm of the universe, its immanent evolutionary formula. Norms of all kinds, such as that which causes a body to have many organs[16], a family many persons, a state many subjects, are all participants in the universal ruler thus understood. These participants neither increase nor diminish it, for they

---

14   To hit or miss the target. Conformity or non-conformity with the source.

15   Denial of the High or Heavenly Sovereign from the Annals and Odes. Compare with *Lao Zi*, chapter 4 E.

16   The human soul falls into this category.

are communicated by it, they are not detached from it. As an extension of the universal ruler, the rule of such a being, which is its being, does not cease to be when it ends. It was before him, it will continue after it, unalterable, indestructible. The rest of it was only appearance. From ignorance of this principle derive all the pains of men, the struggle for existence, the fear of death, the apprehension of the mysterious beyond. Blindness is almost general, but not universal. There are still men, few, whom conventional traditionalism has not seduced, who recognize no master but their reason, and who, by the effort of the latter, have deduced the above doctrine from their meditations on the universe. These know that there is nothing real but the universal standard. The unthinking vulgar believe in the real existence of everything. Modern error has choked the ancient truth. It is so ingrained, so inveterate, that the greatest sages of the world, including *Yu* the Great[17], have been deceived by it. In support of the truth, I find myself almost alone.

C. But, if everything is one, if everything is reduced to a single standard, this standard will simultaneously include truth and error, all opposites; and if the facts of which men speak are unreal, human speech is therefore only a vain sound, no more than the clucking of a hen. I answer, no, there is no error in the standard, but for the narrow-minded; yes, the distinctions of the disciples of Confucius and *Mo Zi*, are no more than vain cackling. There is, in reality, neither truth nor error, neither yes nor no, nor any other distinction at all, all being one, even opposites. There are only various aspects, which depend on the point of view. From my point of view, I see it this way; from another point of view, I would see it differently. I and others have two different positions, which make each one to judge and talk differently. So we talk about life and death, the possible and the impossible, the lawful and the unlawful. There are discussions, some say yes and others no. Subjective errors of apprehension, due to the point of view. The wise man, on the contrary, begins by illuminating the object with the light of his reason. First he points out that this is that, and that it this, that all is one. Then he points out that, nevertheless, there is a yes and a no, an opposition, a contrast. He concludes that unity is real, that diversity is not real. His point of view is a point, from which this and that, yes and the no, continue to appear without distinguishing themselves. This point is the pivot of the norm. It is the immovable center of a circumference, on whose contour all contingencies, distinctions and individualities roll; from which alone an infinity is seen, which is neither this nor that, neither yes nor no. To see all things in the primordial unity, as yet undifferentiated, or at such a distance that all things merge into one, is true intelligence. — The sophists err in pretending to achieve this by positive and negative arguments, by analysis or synthesis. They only arrive at subjective ways of seeing, which, added together, form opinion and pass for principles. Just as a road is formed by the many steps of the passers-by, things end up being qualified by what many have said about them. It is so, they say, because it is so; it is a principle. — It is not so, they say, because it is not so; it is a

---

17   Attack on a Confucian paragon.

principle. Is it really so, in reality? Not at all. Considered in the standard, a straw and a beam, an ugly thing and a beautiful thing, all opposites are one. Prosperity and ruin, successive states, are but phases; all is one. But only great minds can understand this. Let us not trouble ourselves to distinguish, but see all in the unity of the norm. Let us not argue to prevail, but employ, with others, the procedure of the monkey breeder. This man said to the monkeys he was breeding, "I will give you three taros in the morning and four in the afternoon." All the monkeys were disgusted[18]. "Then," he said, "I will give you four taros in the morning and three in the evening." The monkeys were all pleased. With the advantage of having satisfied them, this man finally gave them only the seven taros a day that he had originally intended for them. This is how the Wise Man does it. He says yes or no, for the sake of peace, and remains calm at the center of the universal wheel, indifferent to the direction in which it turns.

D. Among the ancients, some thought that there was nothing pre-existent in the beginning. This is an extreme position. — Others thought there was something pre-existent. This is the opposite extreme position. Others thought that there was something indistinct, undifferentiated. This is the intermediate position, the true position. This undifferentiated primordial being is the norm. When distinctions were imagined, their notion was ruined. After distinctions came arts and tastes, subjective impressions and preferences that cannot be defined or taught. Thus the three musicians, *Zhao Wen, Kuang Zi* and *Hui Zi*, loved their music, for it was their own music, which they found different from that of others, and superior, of course. They could never define what this difference and superiority consisted of; they could never teach their own children to play like them. For the subjective cannot be defined or taught. The Sage scorns these vanities, remains in the penumbra of synthetic vision, is content with practical common sense.

E. It might be objected that there are no distinctions. Let us say that the distinction between these terms is only apparent. But how can absolutely opposite terms be reduced to simple unity? So how can we reconcile these terms: origin of being, being without origin, origin of being without origin; and these others: being and nothingness, being before nothingness, nothingness before being. These terms are mutually exclusive; it is either yes or no. — I answer: these terms are only mutually exclusive if we consider them as existent. Before becoming, in the unity of the primordial principle, there is no opposition. Considered in this position, a hair is not small, a mountain is not great; a stillborn child is not young, a centenarian is not old. Heaven, earth and I are of the same age. All beings, and I, are one in origin. Since everything is one objectively and in reality, why distinguish entities by words, which only express subjective and imaginary appreciations? If we start naming and counting, we will not stop, the series of subjective points of view is infinite.

---

18   Disgusted at having to wait until evening to receive the strong half of their pitanza. Compare *Lie Zi*, ch. 2 Q.

— Before time, everything was one, in principle closed like a sealed fold. Then, as language, there was only one general verb. All that has been added since then is subjective, imaginary. Like the difference between right and left, distinctions, oppositions, duties. So many beings of reason, which we designate with words, to which nothing responds in reality. Therefore, the wise man studies everything, in the material world and in the world of ideas, but without pronouncing himself on anything, so as not to add one more subjective opinion to those already formulated. He keeps silent, while the vulgar man prattles on, not for truth, but for show, says the adage. — What can be said of the universal being, except that it is? Is it to affirm anything, to say that Being is? Does it teach anything to say that humanity is humane, modesty is modest, courage is brave? Are these not empty phrases that mean nothing? If one could distinguish in principle, and apply attributes to it, it would not be the universal principle. To know how to stop where intelligence and words are lacking, that is wisdom. What is the use of looking for impossible terms to express an ineffable being? He who understands that he has it all in one, has conquered the heavenly treasure, inexhaustible, but also inscrutable. He has the integral illumination, which illuminates the whole without making the details appear. It is this light, superior to that of ten suns, that *Shun* once praised to old Yao[19].

F. "Everything in the world is personal and subjective", said *Wang Ni* to *Nie Que*. "A man lying in the mud will have lumbago, while an eel will feel no better anywhere than there. A man perched in a tree will feel uncomfortable there, while a monkey will find this position perfect. Some eat this, some eat that. Some seek this and some seek that. All the men ran after the two famous beauties *Mao Qiang* and *Li Ji*; while at the sight of them, the fish dived in horror, the birds took refuge in the air, and the antelopes fled at full gallop. You do not know what effect this thing has on me, and I do not know what impression it makes on you. This question of feelings and tastes, being entirely subjective, is mainly insoluble. It can only be set aside. Men will never agree on this point."

"The vulgar men, so be it", said *Nie Que*; "but the superior man?"

"The superior man," said Wang Ni, "is above such trifles. In his lofty transcendence he is above all impressions and emotions. In a boiling lake he does not feel the heat; in a frozen river he does not feel the cold[20]. If the lightning splits the mountains, if the hurricane shakes the ocean, he does not care. He rides on the clouds, he rides on the sun and moon, he rides through the universe; what interest can he have in lesser distinctions, for whom life and death are all one[21]?"

G. Master *Qu Qiao* said to Master *Qiu* of *Zhang Wu*: "It is said of the Sage that he is not bothered by the things of this world; that he does not seek his own advantage and does not shrink from danger; that he does not cling to anything; that he does not seek approval; that he keeps himself aloof from dust and mud…"

---

19   Imaginary anecdote. Attack on two Confucian paragons.
20   Metaphors that were taken literally later.
21   Two alternative phases of existence.

"I will define it better, in fewer words," said Master K'iou. "The Sage is abstracted from time and sees all in one. He keeps silent, keeping his personal impressions to himself, refraining from dissertation on obscure and insoluble questions. This recollection, this concentration, gives him, in the midst of the passionate business of vulgar men, an apathetic, almost silly air. In reality, inwardly, he applies himself to the highest occupation, the synthesis of all ages, the reduction of all beings to unity."

H. And as for the distinction which most torments men, that of life and death? Is not the love of life an illusion? is not the fear of death a mistake? is not this departure really a misfortune? does it not lead, like the bride who leaves her father's house, to another happiness? In the past, when the beautiful *Qi* of *Li* was kidnapped, she cried so much that she wet her dress. When she became the favorite of the king of *Jin*, she realized that she had been wrong to cry. Is this not the case with many dead people? Have they not gone away repentant and now think that they were wrong to love life? Is not life a dream? Some, awakening from a happy dream, mourn; others, freed by awakening from a sad dream, rejoice. Both, while dreaming, believed in the reality of their dream. After awakening, they told themselves that it was only a vain dream. So it is with the great awakening, death, after which we say of life that it has been but a long dream. But few of the living understand this. Almost all believe that they are wide awake. Truly, some think they are kings, others servants. We are all dreaming, you and me. I, who tell you that you are dreaming, am also dreaming my dream. The identity of life and death seems incredible to many people. It is unlikely that they can be convinced. For, in this matter, there is no obvious demonstration, no decisive authority, only an accumulation of subjective feelings. Only the heavenly rule will resolve this question. And what is this heavenly rule? It is to situate oneself, in order to judge, in the infinite… It is impossible to resolve the conflict of contradictions, to decide what is true and what is false. So let us place ourselves outside of time, beyond reasoning. Let us consider the question in infinity, the distance at which everything merges into an indeterminate whole.

I. The actions of all beings belonging to the Whole are not free, but required by its laws… One day the penumbra asked the shadow: why do you move in such a direction? I do not move, said the shadow. I am projected by some body, which produces and orients me, according to the laws of opacity and movement… So it is with all acts.

J. There are no real individuals, but only extensions of the norm… — Once, said *Zhuang Zhou*, one night I was a butterfly, fluttering contented with my fate. Then I woke up, being *Zhuang Zhou*. Who am I really, a butterfly who dreams it is *Zhuang Zhou*, or *Zhuang Zhou* who imagines he was a butterfly? In my case, are there two real individuals? Was there a real transformation of one individual into the other? — Neither one nor the other, says the commentary. There have been two unreal modifications of the one being, of the universal norm, in which all beings in all their states are one.

CHAPTER 3 - MAINTENANCE OF THE VITAL PRINCIPLE

A. Vital energy is limited. The mind is insatiable. To place a limited instrument at the discretion of an insatiable master is always dangerous, is often fatal. The master will wear out the instrument. Prolonged and exaggerated intellectual effort will exhaust the life. — To kill oneself for doing good for the love of glory, or to perish for a crime at the hands of the executioner, amounts to the same thing; it is death, by excess, in both cases. He who wants to last, must moderate himself, not to go to the end of anything, to remain always halfway. In this way, he will be able to preserve his body intact, maintain his life to the end, feed his parents until his death, and last himself to the end of his lot.

B. The butcher of Prince *Hui* of *Liang* was butchering an ox. Effortlessly, methodically, his knife was peeling away the skin, slicing the meat, separating the joints.

"You are really skillful," said the prince, who was watching him.

"My whole art," replied the butcher, "consists in considering only the principle of cutting. When I began, I was thinking of beef. After three years of practice, I began to forget the object. Now, when I cut, I have only the principle in mind. My senses no longer act; only my will is active. Following the natural lines of the ox, my knife penetrates and divides, cutting through the soft flesh, skirting the bones, doing its work as if it were natural and effortless. And it does so without wearing down, because it does not attack the hard parts. A beginner wears out one knife in a month. A mediocre butcher wears out one knife in a year. I have used the same knife for nineteen years. It has killed several thousand oxen without any wear and tear. Because I only let it go where it can go."

"Thank you," said Prince *Hui* to the butcher; "you have just taught me how to make life last, by making it serve only for what does not wear it out."

C. Affliction is another cause of wearing out the vital principle. Omitting the minor subjects of affliction, *Zhuang Zhou* indicates three serious causes, common in his time of feudal strife: mutilations, exile and death.

Resigning oneself to mutilation, like the secretary of the prince of *Liang*, who had a foot cut off, and who did not reproach his master for his mutilation, but consoled himself with the thought that it had been willed by heaven.

Resign yourself to banishment, like the swamp pheasant, which lives contentedly in its needy and restless existence, not desiring the ease of an aviary.

Resign yourself to death, for it is only a change, often for the better. When *Lao Dan* died, *Qin Shi*, after going to mourn him, made only the three laments that the ritual requires of everyone. When he had gone out, the disciples asked him: "Weren't you *Lao Dan*'s friend?" "I was," said *Qin*-cheu. "Then," said the disciples, "why didn't you cry any more?" "Because," said *Qin Shi*, "this corpse is no longer my friend. All these mourners who fill the house, shouting at the top of their voices, act out of pure sentimentality, in an irrational, almost condemnable manner. The law, forgotten by the common man, but remembered by the Sage, is that each one comes into this world in his own time, and leaves it in his own time. Therefore the Sage neither rejoices at births, nor grieves at deaths. The ancients have compared man to a bundle which the Lord ties up (birth) and unties (death)[22]. When the flame has consumed one bundle, it passes to another, and is not extinguished[23]."

Chapter 4 - The World of Men

A. *Yen Hui*, the favorite disciple, asked permission of his master Confucius.
"To go where?" asked the latter.
"To *Wei*," said the disciple. "The prince of that country is young and willful. He governs badly, accepts no critic, and causes his subjects to die for little. His principality is strewn with corpses. His people are plunged in despair… Now I have heard you say many times, that one must leave a well-ordered country, to go and help one that is ill-governed. It is the sick that the doctor goes to see. I would like to dedicate what I have learned from you to the salvation of the principality of *Wei*."
"Don't go," said Confucius. "You will be lost. The great principle is that one does not complicate oneself with multiple problems. The superior men of antiquity never worried about others to the point of disturbing themselves. They did not waste their time trying to make amends to a brutal tyrant… There is nothing more dangerous than to speak insistently of justice and charity to a violent man who delights in evil. His advisors will make common cause with him and unite to intimidate you. If you hesitate or weaken, they will triumph and the evil will be worse. If you attack them with force, the tyrant will have you killed. This is how the minister *Guang Long Feng* was killed by the tyrant *Jie*, and the prince *Bin Gan* was killed by the tyrant *Zhou*. Both, for taking the side of the oppressed people, against the oppressor princes. In the past, the great emperors *Yao* and *Yu* could not persuade the vassals greedy for glory and wealth; they had to reduce them by force of arms… Now the present prince of *Wei* is a man of the same class. In what tone are you going to speak to him, to impress him?"
"I will speak to him," said *Yen Hui*, "with modesty and frankness."
"You will waste your time," said Confucius. "This man is full of himself. Moreover he is a consummate cheat. Evil does not repulse him, virtue does not

---

22   Of which ancients does he speak? Chinese or Indians? — Which Lord: the Chinese High Sovereign of the Annals and Odes, or the Vedic *Prajapati*, master of life and death? The bundle recalls the *skandhas* (*Skandhas* [Sanskrit] means "heaps, aggregates, collections, groupings").

23   Daoist concept of survival, immortality of the soul. Commentary: state of life, state of death; bundle tied, bundle untied. Death and life, succession of comings and goings. The being remains the same; he who is one with the universal being, wherever he goes, maintains his being. Fire is to wood what the soul is to the body; it passes into a new body, as fire passes into another log, so fire spreads without going out, life continues unceasingly.

affect him. Either he will openly contradict you; or he will pretend to listen to you, but will not believe you."

"Then," said *Yen Hui*, "preserving my inner righteousness, I will accommodate myself to him outwardly. I will explain to him the heavenly reason, which will perhaps move him, since he is, like me, a child of heaven. Without trying to please him, I will speak to him with the simplicity of a child, as a disciple of heaven. With the respect that no one may accuse me of having failed him in the least, I will gently explain to him the doctrine of the Ancients. If this doctrine condemns his conduct, he cannot blame me, for it is not mine. Don't you think, Master, that I can correct the Prince of *Wei* in this way?"

"You will not be able to correct him," said Confucius. "This is the didactic procedure known to all masters, and it converts no one. By speaking in this way, you may not suffer reprisals, but that is all you will get."

"Then," asked *Yen Hui*, "how can you convert someone?"

"By preparing for it," said Confucius, "through abstinence."

"Oh," said *Yen Hui*, "I know that. My family is poor. We went for months without drinking wine or eating meat."

"This," said Confucius, "is the abstinence preparatory to the sacrifices. That is not what I mean, but abstinence of the heart."

"What is that?" asked Yen Hui.

"Concentrate all your intellectual energy as in a mass," said Confucius. "Listen not with the ears, not with the heart, but only with the mind. Intercept the path of the senses, keep the mirror of the heart pure; let the mind occupy itself, in the inner emptiness, only with abstract objects. The vision of the principle requires emptiness. To keep empty, that is the abstinence of the heart."

"Ah," said *Yen Hui*, "I did not know, that is why I am only *Yen Hui*. If I were to reach that point, I would no longer be *Yen Hui*; I would become a superior man. But, in practice, can one empty oneself to that point?"

"It is possible," said Confucius, "and I will show you how to do it. To do this it is necessary, to let enter from outside, into the domain of the heart, only beings which no longer have a name; abstract ideas, not concrete cases. The heart should only vibrate when it comes into contact with them (objective notions), never spontaneously (subjective emotions). One should keep oneself closed, simple, naturally pure, without any admixture of the artificial. In this way, one can remain unemotional, while it is difficult to calm down after having been moved; just as it is easier not to walk than to erase the traces of one's steps after having walked. Everything artificial is false and ineffective. Only the natural is true and effective. To expect an effect from human processes is to want to fly without wings or to understand without intelligence... Observe how the light that enters from the outside through this hole in the wall, spreads out in the emptiness of this floor, and fades quietly, without producing images. Thus, abstract knowledge must spread out in peace, without disturbing it. If the knowledge that remains concrete creates images or is reflected, man may remain still, but his heart will wander madly. The empty heart attracts spirits, who make their home there. It has an omnipotent effect on the living. It alone is the instrument of moral transformation, being a pure parcel of the Principle, the universal transformer. Thus one must explain the action exercised by *Yao* and *Shun* upon men, after *Fu Xi, Ji Jiu* and many others[24].

B. *Another discourse of Confucius on Daoist apathy…* Sent as ambassador by his lord the king of *Chu* to the prince of *Qi, Zi Gao* asked Confucius for advice.

"My king," he said, "has entrusted me with a very important mission. It will be exhausting; and I wonder if I will succeed. I fear for my health and for my head. The truth is that I am very worried… I have always lived soberly, with a healthy body and a calm heart. However, since the day I was appointed ambassador, my insides burn so hot that I have to drink ice water at night to calm my inner fire. If I am like this before I leave for my mission, what will it be like afterwards? To succeed, I will have to go through countless worries. And if I don't succeed, how will I save my head? Master, what advice can you give me?"

"Piety to parents and fidelity to the prince are the two fundamental natural duties," said Confucius, "which may never be dispensed with. To obey the parents and to serve the prince are the duties of the child and of the minister. And this, in all things, and come what may. In this matter, therefore, you must banish all consideration of pain or pleasure, and regard the duty itself, not as optional, but as fatal, for which you must devote yourself, if necessary to the point of sacrificing your life and accepting death. This being so, you are obliged to accept your mission, and to dedicate yourself to its fulfillment… It is true that the role of an ambassador, of a diplomatic matchmaker, is difficult and dangerous. To add pleasant and indiscreet words to a pleasant message; to add hurtful unpleasant words to an unpleasant message; to pose, to rush, to exaggerate, to overstep one's mandate; that is what usually causes the misfortune of ambassadors. Any excess is disastrous. That is why it is said in the Rules of Speech, 'convey the meaning of what you are asked to say, but not the terms, if they are harsh; *a fortiori*, do not add gratuitous hurtful words.' If you act that way, your life will probably be saved… It is usually passion that messes things up. Wrestlers start by fighting by the rules; then, when they get excited, they beat each other up. Drinkers start by drinking in moderation; then, when they get hot, they get drunk. The vulgar begin by being polite; then, with familiarity comes incivilities. Many matters, at first, are exaggerated, all because passion has interfered. The same can happen with message carriers. Woe to them if they get heated about their subject. If they add their own words, it will be their fault. As it is with water and wind, which lifts the waves easily, so when the speaker gets excited speeches swell easily. Nothing is so dangerous as words produced by passion. They can come to resemble the fury of the beast fallen into a trap. They provoke the breakdown of negotiations, hatred and revenge. So the Rules of Discourse say: 'Do not overdo your command. Don't try too hard out of a desire to succeed. Don't try to get more than you should ask for.' Otherwise, you will do no good and put yourself in danger. But, avoiding all passion, do your duty with

---

24   In this piece, *Yen Hui* professes Confucianism. Confucius teaches him Daoism.

a clear heart. Whatever happens. Question yourself constantly, asking: How will I respond to the kindness of my prince? Finally, be prepared to make the most difficult sacrifice, that of your life, if necessary. This is my advice."

C. *Another lesson in Daoist moderation.* — The philosopher *Yen He*, of *Lu*, having been appointed tutor to the eldest son of Duke *Ling* of *Wei*, asked *Ju Boyu* for advice.

"My pupil," he said, "is as bad as he can be. If I let him, he will ruin his country. If I try to restrain him, it may cost me my life. He sees the evils of others, but not his own. What can I do with such a disciple?"

Ju Boyu said:

"First be circumspect, be correct, don't lend yourself to criticism. Then you will seek to win him over. Adapt yourself to him, without condescending to act badly with him, but also without taking him too seriously. If he has a young character, be young with him. If he doesn't like restrictions, don't bother him. If he doesn't like domination, don't try to impose it on him. Above all, don't set yourself against him, don't make him angry with you... Don't try to fight him by force. That would be to imitate the stupid mantis, who tried to stop a chariot and was crushed... Only deal with him when he is well disposed. You know what tiger breeders do with their dangerous wards. They never give them a live prey, because the satisfaction of killing it would exalt their brutal cruelty. They do not even give them a large piece of meat, for the act of tearing it would overexcite their bloodthirsty instincts. They give them their food in small portions, and only approach them when, full and calm, they are in as good a mood as a tiger can be. Thus they are less likely to be eaten... However, don't make your disciple ornery by coddling him, either. Some manic horse breeders love their animals to the point of keeping their droppings. What happens then? It so happens that, having become capricious to the point of frenzy, these horses get carried away and break everything when approached even gently and with the best of intentions. The more you pamper them, the less appreciative they are."

The Daoist principles for managing people and businesses, outlined above, boil down to this: Treat everything from afar and from above, generally not in detail, without applying yourself too much, without worrying. Prudence, condescension, patience, a certain looseness; but not cowardice; and, if necessary, do not fear death, which is nothing to fear for the Daoist. — The rest (compare with chapter 1 F) is dedicated to abstention, to withdrawal, which the Daoists always put above action, because inaction preserves, while action wears away.

D. Master carpenter *Shi*, on his way to the country of *Qi*, passed the famous oak tree that shaded the mound of the earth genie in *Qu Yuan*. The trunk of this famous tree could hide an ox. It rose straight up, eighty feet high, and then stretched out a dozen master branches, from each of which a canoe could have been carved. People flocked to admire it. The carpenter passed him by, without a glance.

"But look," said his apprentice. "Since I began to handle the axe, I have not seen such a beautiful piece of wood. And you don't even look at it!"

"I have seen it," said the master. "It is not good for making a ship, a coffin, a piece of furniture, a door, or a column. It is wood of no practical use. It will live a long time."

When the master carpenter *Shi* returned from *Qi*, he spent the night at *Qu Yuan*. The tree appeared to him in a dream and said:

"Yes, trees whose wood is beautiful are cut young. The branches of fruit trees are broken in the eagerness to steal their fruit. For all their usefulness is fatal. So I am happy to be useless. Besides, it is the same for you men as it is for us trees. If you are a useful man, you will not live long."

The next morning, the apprentice asked the master:

"If this great tree is glad to be useless, why has it allowed itself to be made the genie of the place?" he asked.

"They put it there," said the master, "without asking its opinion, and it does not care. It is not popular veneration that protects its existence, it is its incapacity for common use. Its tutelary action is reduced to doing nothing. Like the Daoist sage, placed in his place in spite of himself, and refraining from action."

E. There follows another variation on the same theme, almost identical, a similar fragment added to the previous one, which ends thus: this tree, not being fit for common use, was able to grow to these dimensions. The same incapacity gives some men the possibility of reaching perfect transcendence.

F. In the country of the *Song*, in *Jing Shi*, trees grow thickly. The smaller ones are cut down to make cages for monkeys. The medium ones are cut to make houses for men. The large ones are cut down to make coffins for the dead. All perish, by the axe, before their time, because they can be used. If they were useless, they would grow old at ease. The treatise on victims declares that white-headed oxen, snub-nosed pigs, and men with fistulas, cannot be sacrificed to the Genie of the River; for, say the haruspices, these beings are harmful. Transcendental men think it is good for them, for it saves their lives.

G. The legless cripple *Shu*, a real monster, earned a living and supported a family of ten by mending, basket making, etc. When his country was mobilized, he remained in peace. In the days of hard work, nothing was asked of him. When there was a distribution of aid to the poor, he received grain and wood. His inability to perform ordinary services caused him to live to the end of his days. In the same way, his incapacity for vulgar duties will make the transcendent man live to the end of his allotted time.

H. While Confucius was visiting the country of *Chu*, the madman *Jie Yu*[25] cried out to him.

---

25   He was a Daoist sage, who was considered mad.

"Phoenix! Phoenix! No doubt, the world is decadent; but what can be done? The future has not yet come, the past is already far away. In times of good order, the Sage works for the State; in times of disorder, he is concerned with his own salvation. At present, times are such that escaping from death is difficult. There is no longer happiness for anyone; misfortune crushes everyone. This is not the time to show off. In vain shalt thou speak of virtue, and in vain shalt thou show your sober manners. I like to run like a madman; don't get in my way. I like to walk crooked; don't hinder my feet. It is time to let things happen."

I. By producing forests, the mountain attracts those who despoil it. By dripping its fat, the roast activates the fire that roasts it. The cinnamon tree is cut down because its bark is a coveted spice. The varnish tree is cut down to remove its precious sap. Almost all men imagine that being considered fit for something is a good thing. In reality, it is an advantage to be judged unfit for anything.

CHAPTER 5 - PERFECT ACTION

A. In the principality of *Lu*, a certain *Wang Tai*, who had suffered the amputation of both feet (a common punishment at the time), gathered around him more disciples than Confucius. *Chang Ji* was astonished at this and said to the Master:

"This *Wang Tai* neither speaks nor discusses; and yet those who went to him empty, return from him full. Could there be a way of teaching without words, an impalpable process of forming hearts? Where does this man's influence come from?"

"From his transcendence," replied Confucius. "I met him too late. I should go to his school. Everyone should take him as a teacher."

"How exactly is he superior to you?" Asked *Chang Ji*.

"In that," replied Confucius, "he has attained perfect impassibility. Since life and death are equally indifferent to him, the collapse of the universe would cause him no emotion. By dint of inquiry, he arrived at the immutable abstract truth, the knowledge of the one universal principle. It allows all beings to evolve according to their destinies, and he himself stands at the immovable center of all destinies[26]."

"I do not understand," said *Chang Ji*.

Confucius continued:

"There are two ways of looking at beings: as separate entities, or as being one in the great whole. For those who have risen to the latter kind of consideration, it matters little what their senses perceive. Their spirits fly, with all their action concentrated. In this global and abstract vision, the detail of deficits disappears. Therein lies the transcendence of this *Wang Tai*, which the mutilation of his body cannot diminish."

"Ah," said *Chang Ji*, "I understand. His reflections have made him master of his senses, and so he has attained impassibility. But is there anything in all that, any reason for running after him?"

---

26   Compare with chapter 2 C.

"Yes," replied Confucius, "mental fixity attracts those who seek wisdom, as still water attracts those who wish to be reflected. No one goes and reflects himself in running water. No one asks to learn from an unstable mind. It is the immutability that characterizes the Sage in the midst of the crowd. Thus, among the deciduous trees, are the evergreen pines and cypresses. As, among the vulgar men, the emperor *Shun*, always upright and correcting the others... The outward sign of this inner state is imperturbability. Not that of the brave who, for the sake of glory, throws himself alone into battle with an army. But that of the spirit which, superior to heaven, to earth, to all beings, dwells in a body to which it does not adhere, ignores the images provided by its senses, knows everything by global knowledge in its immobile unity. This spirit, absolutely independent, is master of men. If it pleases him to summon them en masse, on the appointed day they will all come running. But he does not want to be attended."

B. *Shentu Jia* had also suffered the amputation of his feet, for a real or supposed fault. In the principality of *Zheng* he followed, with *Zi Chan*, the lessons of *Bo Hun Wu Ren*. *Zi Chan*, despising this mutilated man, demanded that he give him the precedence...

"There are no ranks in our master's school," said *Shentu Jia*. "If you care about etiquette, go elsewhere. Dust does not stick to a perfectly clean mirror; if it does, the mirror is damp or greasy. Your demand for ritual shows that you are not yet free of flaws."

"You are a mutilated man," said *Zi Chan*, "but it seems to me that you want to pass yourself off as a *Yao*. If you were to examine yourself, you might find reason to be silent."

"You allude," said *Shentu Jia*, "to the punishment I have suffered, and think I have deserved it for some serious fault. Most of those in my case say very loudly that this should not have happened to them. Wiser than them, I say nothing, and resign myself in peace to my fate. Whoever passed within the field of vision of the famous archer, had to be pierced by an arrow; if it did not happen, it was because fate did not want it. Fate wanted me to lose my feet and others to keep theirs. Men who have their feet, laugh at me who have lost mine. This used to affect me. Now I have overcome this weakness. For nineteen years I have been studying with our master, who is very attentive to my inner self, and has never made any reference to my outer self. You, his disciple, do the opposite, aren't you mistaken?"

Zi Chan[27] felt the rebuke, changed his countenance and said:

"I will never mention it again."

C. In the principality of *Lu*, a certain *Shu Shan*, who had had his toes amputated, went to ask Confucius to instruct him.

---

27   The *Zi Chan* shown here in such a bad light is a Confucian paragon. Prince of *Zheng*, 6th century BC, celebrated in various offices; especially as an administrator. Confucius mourned his death bitterly.

"What good would it do you?" said the latter, "since you have not been able to preserve your bodily integrity."

"I wanted to learn from you how to preserve my mental integrity to compensate for this loss," said *Shu Shan*. "Heaven and earth are lavished on all beings, whoever they are, without distinction. I thought you were like them. I did not expect you to reject me."

"Excuse my incivility, please come in," said Confucius, "I will tell you what I know."

After the interview, when *Shu Shan* had gone away, Confucius said to his disciples:

"May this example encourage you to good, children! You see, this cripple is trying to make up for his past faults. Do not commit faults."

However, *Shu Shan*, ill-tempered with Confucius, went to speak with *Lao Dan*.

"This Confucius," he said to him, "is not a superior man. He attracts disciples, pretends to be a master, and openly worries about his reputation. But the superior man regards worries as handcuffs and fetters."

"Why," said *Lao Dan*, "have you not taken advantage of your meeting with him to tell him bluntly that life and death are one and the same thing; that there is no distinction between yes and no? You could have freed him from his handcuffs and fetters."

"Impossible," said *Shu Shan*. "This man is too full of himself. Heaven has punished him by blinding him. No one will make him see clearly again."

D. Duke *Ai*, of *Lu* said to Confucius:

"In the country of *Wei* there lived a man called *Tuo* the ugly. Indeed he was very ugly, a real scarecrow. And yet his wives, his fellow citizens, everyone who knew him, loved him. Why? Not because of his genius, because he always thought the same as everyone else. Not for his nobility, because he was a man of the people. Not for his wealth, because he was poor. Not for his knowledge, because he only knew his village... I wanted to see him. Of course he was frighteningly ugly. In spite of that, he charmed me, as he charmed everyone. After a few months, I was his friend. Within a year he had my full confidence. I offered him to be my minister. He reluctantly accepted and soon left me. I cannot console myself for losing him. To what do I attribute this man's fascination?"

"Once in the country of *Chu*," said Confucius, "I saw the following scene. A sow had just died. Her young were still sucking at its teats. Suddenly, they ran away in terror. They had realized that their mother was no longer looking at them, that she was no longer their mother. What they had loved in her with filial love was not her body, it was what animated her body and had just disappeared, the maternal virtue that resided in her... In the body of the ugly *Tuo*, there lived a perfect latent virtue. It was this virtue that attracted you, despite the repulsive form of his body."

"And what," asked Duke *Ai*, "is perfect virtue?"

"It is," replied Confucius, "an affable impassivity. Death and life, prosperity and decay, success and failure, poverty and wealth, superiority and inferiority, guilt and praise, hunger and thirst, cold and heat, are the alternate vicissitudes of which destiny is made. They follow one another, unpredictable, without known cause. These things must be ignored; they must not be allowed to penetrate the palace of the spirit, whose quiet peace they would disturb. To keep this peace steadily, without allowing it to be disturbed even by joy; to contemplate everything equanimously, to accept everything; this is perfect virtue."

"Why," asked Duke *Ai*, "do you call it latent?"

"Because," said Confucius, "it is impalpable, like the calm that draws in the water of a pond. Thus the calm peace of character, not otherwise definable, draws all to itself."

A few days later, Duke *Ai*, who had been converted to Daoism by Confucius, confided to Master *Min* the impression this conversation had made on him.

"Until now," he said, "I had believed that to rule, to control statistics and to protect the lives of my subjects, was my stately duty. But as I have heard a superior man (Confucius) speak, I think I have been mistaken. I have harmed myself by being too restless, and my principality by being too concerned about it. From now on, Confucius is no longer my subject, but my friend, for the service he has rendered me by opening my eyes."

E. One legless man won the confidence of Duke *Ling* of *Wei* to such an extent that the latter preferred him to better-trained men. Another, afflicted with a huge goiter, was the favorite adviser of Duke *Huan*, of *Qi*. The glory of a superior capacity eclipses the bodily forms to which it adheres. To pay attention to the body and not to virtue is the worst mistake. Placed in his field of all-embracing science, the Sage despises knowledge of details, all convention, all affection, all art. Free from these artificial and distracting things, he nourishes his being with heavenly food (pure reason, says the commentary), indifferent to human affairs. In the body of a man, he is no longer a man. He lives with men, but is absolutely indifferent to their approval and disapproval, because he no longer has their feelings. The infinitely small is what makes him still a man (his body); the infinitely great is what makes him one with heaven (his reason).

F. *Hui Zi* (musician and sophist) objected:

"A man cannot become, as you say, without affections."

"He can," answered *Zhuang Zhou*.

"Then," said *Hui Zi*, "he is no longer a man."

"He is still a man," said *Zhuang Zhou*; "for the Principle and Heaven have given him what makes a man."

"If he has lost feelings," replied *Hui Zi*, "he has ceased to be a man."

"If he had lost even the power of feeling, perhaps," said *Zhuang Zhou*, "(for this power is merged in nature); but it is not so. The power remains in him, but he does not use it to distinguish, to take sides, to love or hate. And consequently he does not use in vain the body, which the Principle and heaven have given him. This is not your case. You who kill yourself making music and inventing sophistry."

CHAPTER 6 - THE PRINCIPLE, FIRST MASTER

A. To know how to distinguish between the action of heaven and the action of man is the summit of teaching and science. — To know what one has received from heaven and what one must add, that is the culmination. — The gift of heaven is the nature received at birth. Man's role is to try, from what he knows, to learn what he does not know; it is to maintain his life to the end of the years allotted by heaven, without shortening it by his own fault. To know this, is the climax. — And what will be the criterion of these statements, the truth of which is not self-evident? On what is the certainty of this distinction between the heavenly and the human in man based? On the teaching of True Men. From them comes True Knowledge.

B. What are these True Men? The True Men of old even accepted the advice of minorities. They sought no glory, neither military nor political. Their failures did not afflict them, their successes did not make them proud. No height made them dizzy. Water did not wet them, fire did not burn them; for they had risen to the sublime regions of the Principle[28].

The ancient True Men were not disturbed by any dreams during their sleep, nor by any sadness (which marred their waking hours). Refined food was unknown to them. Their calm and deep breathing penetrated their organism to the heels; whereas the vulgar breathe only through the throat, as is proved by the spasms of the glottis of those who argue; the more passionate a man is, the more shallow is his breathing[29].

The ancient True Men ignored the love of life and the horror of death. Their entrance upon the scene of life, caused them no joy; their return, behind the scenes of the scene, at death, caused them no horror. Calmly they came, calmly they went, smoothly, without startle, as if they were gliding away. Remembering only their last beginning (birth), they did not worry about their next end (death). They loved this life while it lasted, and forgot it when they departed for another life at death. Thus their human feelings did not frustrate the Principle in them; the human in them did not drive the heavenly. Such were True Men.

Therefore their hearts were steadfast, their attitude was collected, their countenance was simple, their conduct was temperate, their feelings were regulated. They did, on all occasions, what had to be done, without confiding to anyone their inner motives. They waged war without hatred, and did good without loving. He is not a wise man who takes pleasure in communicating, who makes friends, who calculates times and circumstances, who is not indifferent to success or failure, who exposes his person for glory or favor. *Hu Bu Xie, Wu Guang, Bo Yi, Shu Qi,*

---

28   Because they were one, in this principle, with the natural forces, which only wet, burn, wound, and destroy their opposites. He who is one with the universal Principle, is one with fire and water, neither burns nor wets, etc.

29   Illusions, passions, preferences, all these are contrary to truth. For Daoists, pure air is the food par excellence of the vital forces.

Ji Zi, Zu Yu, Ji Tuo, and *Shen Tu Di*, served all and did good to all, without any emotion in their hearts vitiating their acts of charity.

The ancient True Men were always just, never kind; always modest, never flattering. They stood firm, but without harshness. Their contempt for everything was manifest, but unaffected. Their exterior was peacefully cheerful. All their actions seemed natural and spontaneous. They inspired affection for their manners and respect for their virtues. Under an air of apparent condescension, they kept distinctly aloof from the vulgar. They liked to withdraw and never prepared their speeches. For them, punishments were the essential part of government, but they applied them without anger. They considered rites as an accessory, which they performed as much as necessary so as not to offend the vulgar. They considered it a science to let time do its work, and a virtue to go with the flow. Those who thought they were actively moving were wrong. In reality, they let themselves be carried along by the current of time and events. For them, love and hate were one and the same thing; or rather, they neither loved nor hated. They regarded everything as essentially one, in the manner of heaven, and artificially distinguished particular cases, in the manner of men. Thus, in them there was no conflict between the heavenly and the human. And this is precisely what the true man does.

C. The alternation of life and death is predetermined, like that of day and night, by Heaven. Let man stoically submit to fate, and nothing will happen against his will. If anything happens that hurts him, it is because he conceived an affection for some being. Let him love nothing, and he will be invulnerable. There are higher feelings than the loves that are considered noble. Instead of loving Heaven as a father, let him revere it as the universal summit. Instead of loving his prince, even at the point of dying for him, let him sacrifice himself for the one abstract motive of absolute devotion. When the streams dry up, the fish gather in the holes and try to keep themselves wet by pressing each other. And we admire this mutual charity. Would it not have been better for them to seek salvation in the deep waters, each on his own side? Instead of always citing the goodness of *Yao* as an example, and the malice of *Jie*, would it not be better for men to forget these two characters, and direct their morals solely toward the abstract perfection of the Principle?

My body is part of the great mass (of the cosmos, of nature, of the whole). It has been the support of my childhood, the activity of my maturity, the peace in my old age, and the rest in my death. Good it was for me in the state of life, good it will be for me in the state of death. An object deposited may be stolen from any specific place; but an object entrusted to the same All, will not be stolen. Identify yourself with the great mass; in it is permanence. Permanence is not immobile. There is a chain of transformations, with the Self persisting through endless mutations. This time I am glad to be in human form[30]. I have experienced before and will experience afterwards the same contentment of being, in an unlimited succession

---

30   Commentary: To be man today is an episode in the chain of ten thousand successive transformations.

of different forms, an infinite succession of contentments. Why then should I hate death, the beginning of my next contentment? The Sage adheres to the whole of which he is a part, which contains him, in which he evolves. Surrendering himself to the thread of this evolution, he smiles at premature death, smiles at old age, smiles at the beginning, smiles at the end; he smiles and wants us to smile at all vicissitudes. Because it knows that all beings are part of the whole that evolves.

D. Now, this Whole is the Principle, the will, the reality, non-acting, non-apparent. It can be transmitted but not grasped, grasped but not seen. It has in itself its essence and its root. It always existed, unchanged, before heaven and earth existed. It is the source of the transcendence of the Manes and the High Sovereign of the Annals and the Odes. It begot the heaven and earth of the Annals and Odes. It was before formless matter, before space, before the world, before time; without being called for that reason high, profound, enduring, ancient[31]. *Xi Wei* knew this, and derived the astronomical laws from this knowledge. *Fu Xi* knew it, and derived physical laws from this knowledge. The Little Dipper (the pole-star, or Little Bear) owes to it its imperturbable fixity. To it the sun and moon owe their regular course. Through it *Kan Pi* settled in the *Kun Lun* mountains, *Ping Yi* followed the course of the Yellow River, *Jian Wu* settled on Mount *Tai Shan*, *Huang Di* ascended to heaven, *Zhuan Xu* inhabited the blue palace, *Yu Qiang* became the genie of the north pole, *Xi Wang Mu* settled in *Shao Guang*[32]. No one knows anything of its beginning or its end. Through it *Peng Zu* lived, from the time of the emperor *Shun*, to that of the five hegemons Through it ruled *Fu Yue* the empire of his master, the emperor *Wu Ding*, and became after his death a star (in the constellation Sagittarius).

E. Master *Kui*, also known as *Nan Bo*, asked *Nu Yu*:
"How is it that, in spite of your great age, you have the freshness of a child?"
"It is because," said *Nu Yu*, "having lived according to the doctrine of the Principle, I have not worn out."
"Could I learn this doctrine?" asked Master *Kui*.
"You do not have what it takes," replied *Nu Yu*. "*Bu Liang Yi*, on the other hand, had the necessary disposition. I taught him. After three days he had forgotten the outside world. Seven days later he lost his sense of the objects around him. Nine days more, and he lost track of his own existence. Then he acquired clear penetration, and through it the knowledge of momentary existence in the unbroken chain. Acquiring this knowledge, he ceased to distinguish past from present and future, life from death[33]. He understood that, in reality, killing does not cause death, begetting does not cause birth, the Principle sustains being through its ends and becomings. That is why he is rightly called the permanent fixer. From it, from the fixed, derive all mutations."

---

31   Since the absolute does not admit of relative epithets.
32   Memory or fiction? It cannot be determined from the comments. I pass the question to the scholars.
33   Phases, periods, of the one evolution.

"Have you invented this doctrine?" asked the master *Kui*.

"I learned it from the son of *Fu Mei*, disciple of the grandson of *Lao Song*, disciple of *Zhan Ming*, disciple of *Nie Xu*, disciple of *Su Yi*, disciple of *Yu Nou*, disciple of *Huan Ming*, disciple of *San Liao*, disciple of *Yi Shi*[34]."

F. *Zi Si*, *Zi Yu*, *Zi Li* and *Zi Lai*, were talking together. One of them said:

"Whoever thinks as I do, that every being is eternal, that life and death follow one another, that to be alive or dead are two phases of one and the same being, that one I would make my friend."

The other three thought the same, so the four men laughed together and became close friends.

Then it happened that *Zi Yu* fell seriously ill. He was horribly hunchbacked and deformed. *Zi Si* went to visit him. Breathing heavily, but with a calm heart, the dying man said to him:

"Good is the author of beings (the Principle, Nature), who made me as I am this time. I do not complain of it. If, when I have left this form, it makes my left arm into a cock, I will crow to herald the dawn. If it makes my right arm a crossbow, I'll shoot owls. If it makes my torso a carriage, and harnesses my spirit to a horse, I shall still be satisfied. Every being receives his form in due time, and leaves it in due time. This being so, why conceive joy or sorrow in these vicissitudes? It is not necessary. As the ancients used to say, the bundle is successively tied and untied. The being is not untied, nor is it tied. It depends on heaven for death and life. I, who am a being among beings, why should I complain about dying?"

Then *Zi Lai* also fell ill. He gasped and was about to expire. His wife and children surrounded him, weeping. *Zi Li* went to visit him and said to these intruders:

"Shut up, get out, don't hinder his passage[35]!" Then, leaning on the door-post, he said to the patient:

"Good is transformation. What will it do with you? Where will you go? Will you become the organ of a rat, or the leg of an insect?"

"I don't care," said the dying man. "In whatever direction his parents send him, the child must go. Now *yin* and *yang* are more to man than his parents[36]. When their revolution has brought my death, if I do not voluntarily submit, I would be a rebel... The great mass (the cosmos) has carried me through this existence, has served to make me live, has comforted me in my old age, gives me peace in my death. Good it has been to me in life, good it is to me in death... Let us suppose a smelter is busy stirring his molten metal. If a part of this metal, jumping out of the crucible, were to say to him: 'I want to become a sword, not something else!' The smelter would consider that metal unsuitable. It would be the same if a dying

---

34   Are they names of men? It is possible, but not probable. These words mean, and may be interpreted, as follows: I have not drawn this doctrine from my imagination, I discovered it by dint of meditating on the mystery of origin.

35   Which rather requires calm, as entering into sleep.

36   The two alternations of the cosmic revolution, higher agents of the Principle, give life or death while the parents, lower agents, determine only life.

man, at the moment of his transformation, would cry out: 'I want to become a man again, not something else!' Heaven and earth (the cosmos) are the great furnace, transformation is the great melter; whatever it does with us must be acceptable to us. Let us surrender to it with peace. Life ends in a dream, which is followed by a new awakening."

G. The masters *Sang Hu, Meng Zi Fan*, and *Qin Zhang*, were friends. One of them said:

"Who is perfectly indifferent to all influence, to all action? Who can soar to the heavens by abstraction, loiter in the clouds by speculation, play in the ether, forget his present life and the coming death?"

The three men looked at each other and laughed, for they were like that, and became best friends.

Having died one of the three, Master *Sang Hu*, Confucius sent his disciple *Zi Gong* to the funeral home to ask if he was needed for the funeral. When *Zi Gong* arrived, the two surviving friends were singing the following refrain before the corpse, to the accompaniment of the zither:

"Oh, *Sang Hu*! Oh, *Sang Hu*!… Here you join the transcendent, while we remain men, alas!"

Zi Gong approached them and asked:

"It is in conformity with the rites to chant like this in the presence of a corpse?"

The two men looked at each other, burst out laughing and said:

"What can this man understand about our rites?"

Zi Gong returned to Confucius, told him what he had seen and asked:

"Who are these people, without manners, without composure, who sing before a corpse, without a trace of grief? I do not understand."

"These people," said Confucius, "move outside the world, while I move in the world. There can be nothing in common between me and them. I was wrong to send you there. According to them, man must live in communion with the author of beings (the cosmic Principle), referring to the time when heaven and earth were not yet separated. For them, the form they have during this existence is an accessory, an appendage, from which death will deliver them, until they are reborn in another. Consequently, for them there is neither death nor life, neither past nor future, in the usual sense of these words. According to them, the matter of their body has served, and will serve successively, many different beings. Their viscera and organs are of little importance to people who believe in a continuous succession of beginnings and endings. They wander in spirit out of this dusty world, and abstain from any interference in its affairs. Why should they take the trouble to perform the vulgar rites, or maintain the appearance of performing them?"

"But you, master," asked *Zi Gong*, "why do you make these rites the basis of your morals?"

"Because Heaven has condemned me to this painful task," said Confucius. "I say it, but deep down, like you, I no longer believe it. Fish are born in water, men in the Principle. Fish live on water, men on non-action. Every man for himself in the waters, every man for himself in the Principle. The truly superior man is he who has broken with all else, to cleave to heaven alone. He alone should be called Wise by men. Too often he who is called Wise by men is only a vulgar being as far as Heaven is concerned."

H. *Yen Hui* asked Confucius:

"When *Mengsun Cai's* mother died, at her funeral, her son made the usual lamentations without shedding a tear, and read all the ceremonies without the least sorrow. However, in *Lu's* country, he is said to have satisfied filial piety. I do not understand this."

"Indeed, he has satisfied it," replied Confucius, "enlightened as he is, he could not refrain from external ceremonies, for that would be too shocking to the vulgar; but he refrained from the internal sentiments of the vulgar, which he does not share. For him, the state of life and the state of death are one and the same thing, and he does not distinguish between these states, neither anteriority nor posteriority, for he considers them links in an infinite chain. He believes that beings inevitably undergo successive transformations, which they have only to undergo in peace, without worrying about them. Immersed in the current of these transformations, the being has only a confused knowledge of what is happening to him. All life is like a dream. You and I who are speaking at this hour are two dreamers who are not awake... Therefore, as death is only a change of form for *Mengsun Cai*, it is not worth grieving over; any more than one would grieve at leaving a home in which he lived only one day. Thus, he confined himself to strict observance of the outward ritual. Thus, he shocked neither the public nor his convictions."

"No one knows exactly what the intimate nature of his being is like. The same man who has just dreamed that he is a bird soaring through the skies, then dreams that he is a fish plunging into the abyss. He cannot be sure whether he is awake or asleep. Nothing that happens is worth worrying about. Peace consists in submissively awaiting the dispositions of the Principle. At the moment of leaving the present life, the being enters the stream of transformations. This is the meaning of the formula 'enter into union with the celestial infinite'"[37].

I. When *Yi Er Zi* visited *Xu You*[38], the latter asked him what *Yao* had taught him.

"He told me," replied *Yi Er Zi*, "to cultivate goodness and fairness, to distinguish well between good and evil."

"Then," asked *Xu You*, "why do you come to me now? After *Yao* imbued you with his practical principles, you are no longer capable of rising to higher ideas."

"Yet that is my wish," said *Yi Er Zi*.

"An unattainable desire," said *Xu You*. "A man who has had his eyes gouged out can learn nothing about colors."

---

37   With Heaven, Nature, the Principle, adds the commentary.
38   Compare with chapter 1 D.

"You have reformed," said *Yi Er Zi*, "others who were deformed; why should you not succeed in reforming me, too?"

"There is little hope," said *Xu You*. "However, here is the summary of my doctrine: O Principle! You have given to all beings what is right for them, and never pretended to be called righteous. You, whose benefits extend to all times, and never pretended to be called charitable. You who were before the origin, and who do not pretend to be called venerable; you who enfold and sustain the universe, producing all forms, without pretending to be called skillful; it is in you that I move."

J. *Yen Hui*, the beloved disciple, said to his master Confucius:
"I am advancing..."
"How do you know?" asked Confucius...
"I am losing," said *Yen Hui*, "the notion of goodness and justice..."
"That is good," said Confucius, "but that is not all."
On another occasion, *Yen Hui* said to Confucius:
"I am getting better..."
"How do you know?" asked Confucius...
"I forgot the rites and the music," said *Yen Hui*...
"That's good," said Confucius, "but that's not all."
On another occasion, *Yen Hui* said to Confucius:
"I am making progress..."
"What tells you that?" asked Confucius...
"Now," said *Yen Hui*, "when I sit down to meditate, I forget everything[39]."
Confucius was moved and asked:
"What does that mean?"
Yen Hui replied:
"Stripping myself of my body, erasing my intelligence, giving up all form, expelling all knowledge, I unite myself with the one who pervades everything. This is what I mean when I say that I sit down and forget everything."
Confucius said:
"This is the union in which desire ceases; this is the transformation in which individuality is lost. You have attained true wisdom. Be my master from now on!"

K. *Zi Yu* and *Zi Sang* were friends. Once it rained heavily for ten days in a row. Fearing that *Zi Sang*, who was very poor, could not go out and was without provisions, *Zi Yu* packed a bundle of food and went to take it to him. As he approached her door, he heard his voice, half singing, half crying, saying, accompanying herself with the zither:
"O father, O mother, O heaven, O mankind!"
The voice was wavering and the singing was spasmodic. *Zi Yu* entered and found *Zi Sang* starving.

---

39   As soon as he has freed himself from what essentially constitutes Confucianism, goodness, equity, rites, and music, *Yen Hui* attains Daoist contemplation, and Confucius is compelled to approve of it!

"What were you singing?"

"I was thinking," said *Zi Sang*, "about the possible causes of my extreme distress. It certainly does not come from the will of my father and mother. Nor from the will of heaven and earth, which cover and sustain all beings. There is no logical cause of my misery. So it was my fate[40]!"

CHAPTER 7 - THE GOVERNMENT OF PRINCES

A. *Nie Que* asked *Wang Ni* four questions, to which the latter could not answer. Jumping with joy, *Nie Que* informed *Pu Yi Zi* of his triumph.

"Are you really superior to him?" *Pu Yi Zi* said. "Emperor *Shun* was not equal to the former ruler *Tai Shi*. *Shun* was infatuated by the virtues he thought he possessed, and always criticized others. The old *Tai Shi* was not so malicious. He slept peacefully and had no worries when he was awake. He valued himself no more than a horse or an ox. He was simple and peaceful and did not criticize anyone. You are more like *Shun*."

B. *Jian Wu* went to see the mad *Jie Yu*[41], who asked him:

"What have you learned from *Ren Zhong Shi*?"

"I learned from him," said *Jian Wu*, "that when princes make rules and force people to obey them, all is well."

"Everything seems to be fine," said *Jie Yu*. "Only the outside is regulated, not the inside. To rule by this method would be like trying to ford the sea, to contain the Yellow River in a bed, to make a mosquito carry away a mountain, all things absolutely impossible. The Sage does not regulate the outside. He sets the example of righteousness, which men will follow, if it pleases them. He is too careful to do more. Like the bird that flies high to avoid the arrow, the rat that digs a hole so deep that it cannot be smoked or dug out. Legislating is useless and dangerous."

C. *Tian Gen*, wandering south of Mount *Yin* toward the *Liao* River, met *Wu Ming Ren* and asked him point-blank:

"How can one rule the empire?"

Wu Ming Ren said to him:

"You are rude to ask like that. Besides, why should I care about the government of the empire, I who, disgusted with the world, live in contemplation of the Principle, wander in space like the birds, and soar into the void beyond space."

Tian Gen insisted. Then *Wu Ming Ren* said to him:

"Remain in simplicity, remain in vagueness, let all things be as they are, desire nothing for yourself, and the empire will be well governed, for everything will follow its natural course."

---

40   This is the final cry; blind acquiescence to the turning of the universal wheel, which always drags and sometimes crushes him; Daoist fatalism.

41   Compare chapter 4 H.

D. *Yang Zi Ju* having gone to see *Lao Dan*, asked him:

"Would not an intelligent man, with courage and zeal, be the equal of the wise kings of antiquity?"

"No," said *Lao Dan*. "His fate would be that of the non-commissioned officers, burdened with work and tormented by worries. His qualities would bring about his downfall. The tiger and the leopard are killed because their skin is beautiful. The monkey and the dog are enslaved because their skill."

Puzzled, *Yang Zi Ju* asked:

"But then, what did the wise kings do?"

"The wise kings," said *Lao Dan*, "covered the empire with their benefits, without making it clear that they were the authors of the benefits. They improved all beings, not by sensible actions, but by imperceptible influence. Without being known to anyone, they made everyone happy, remained in the abyss, and wandered through nothingness" (i.e., they did nothing definite, but let universal evolution take place).

E. In *Zheng* there was a transcendental sorcerer named *Ji Xian*[42]. This man knew everything concerning death and life, prosperity and misfortune of individuals, even predicting the exact day of someone's death as accurately as a genie could. So the inhabitants of *Zheng*, who did not want to know so much, fled as soon as they saw him approaching.

Lie Zi went to see him and was fascinated by this man. On his return, he said to his master *Hu Zi*:

"Until now I have considered your teaching to be the most perfect, but now I have found something better."

"Are you very sure about this?" said *Hu Zi*; "when you have only received my exoteric teaching, and not yet the esoteric, which is the fertile germ, the principle of life. Your knowledge is like the infertile eggs laid by hens deprived of roosters; it lacks the essentials... And as for the divinatory power of this sorcerer, could he not have read your interior? Bring him to me, and I'll show you that he only sees what we let him see."

The next day *Lie Zi* brought the sorcerer, who saw *Hu Zi* as a doctor sees a patient. After the visit, the sorcerer said to *Lie Zi*:

"Your master is a dead man; he will be finished before ten days; I had a vision of wet ashes when I saw him."

Lie Zi returned weeping and told *Hu Zi* what the sorcerer had said.

"I manifested before him in the form of winter earth," said *Hu Zi*, "with all my energies immobilized. As this phenomenon only occurs in the case of the common man when he is about to die, he concluded that my end was near. Bring him back again and see what happens then."

The next day, *Lie Zi* brought back the sorcerer. After the visit, the latter said:

---

42   This important piece does not belong here. It is likely to be displaced. Compare *Lie Zi*, chapter 2 L.

"It is fortunate that your master came to me. He is better now. Today I only saw signs of life in him; what I saw yesterday was therefore only an episode, not the end."

When *Lie Zi* informed him of these words, *Hu Zi*, said:

"It is that I have manifested myself to him, under the figure of a sunny land, acting all the springs of my energies. Bring him again."

The next day, *Lie Zi* brought back the sorcerer. After the visit, the latter said:

"It is too indeterminate a state. I cannot make any prognosis. After the determination, I will make a pronouncement."

Lie Zi reported these words to *Hu Zi*, and the latter said:

"It is that I manifested myself before him, in the figure of the great chaos, all my energies being in equilibrium. He could not distinguish anything. A whirlpool, a whirlwind, may be caused by a sea monster, or by a reef, or by a current, or by six other causes; it is an indeterminate thing, susceptible of nine different explanations. *A fortiori* the great chaos. Bring it back."

The next day, *Lie Zi* brought back the soothsayer. At first sight, the soothsayer fled in madness. *Lie Zi* ran after him, but could not catch up with him.

"He will not return," said *Hu Zi*. "I have manifested before him in the state of my emanation of the Principle. He saw, in an immense void, something like a snake unraveling; a projection, a torrent. This spectacle, unintelligible to him, terrified him and made him flee."

Convinced that he was still ignorant, *Lie Zi* secluded himself at home for three consecutive years. He did housework for his wife and served the pigs with respect, to destroy in himself the vanity that had almost made him abandon his master. He detached himself from all interest, freed himself from all artificial culture, and strove with all his might for original simplicity. Finally, he became as coarse as a clod of earth, closed and insensible to all that went on around him, and persevered in this state to his end.

F. Make non-action your glory, your ambition, your profession, your science. Non-action does not wear out. It is impersonal. It gives back what it has received from heaven, keeping nothing for itself. It is essentially an emptiness.

The superior man exercises his intelligence only in the manner of a mirror. He knows and understands without attraction or repulsion, without any lasting impression. Being so, he is superior to all things, and neutral with respect to them.

G. Carried Away, the king of the South Sea, and Thoughtless, the king of the North Sea, met Chaos, the king of the Center. They wondered what service they could render him.

"Men," they said to each other, "have seven orifices (the sense organs: two eyes, two ears, two nostrils, one mouth). Poor Chaos has none. We will make him some."

So they set to work and made him an orifice every day. On the seventh day, Chaos died (ceased to be Chaos, because it differentiated).

It is necessary to leave all beings in their natural, raw state, without trying to perfect them artificially, otherwise they cease to be what they are and must remain what they are.

CHAPTER 8 - WEBBED FEET

A. The body sometimes produces a membrane connecting the toes, or a supernumerary toe, it is true, but in excess of what it should normally be. The same is true of an excrescence, a tumor; although they originate in the body, these excesses are not natural. The same must be said of the various theories of goodness and equity (virtues) that are born of the mind, and of the tastes that emanate from the five viscera (temperament) of a person. These things are not natural, but artificial, morbid. They do not conform to the norm. Yes, just as the membrane connecting the toes of a man's feet, and the extra finger of his hand, interfere with his natural physical movements; so the tastes emanating from his viscera, and the virtues imagined by his mind, interfere with his natural moral functioning.

The perversion of the sense of sight led to excesses of color and ornamentation, of which the painter *Li Zu* was the promoter. The perversion of the sense of hearing produced abuses in the use of instruments and in tuning, of which the musician *Shi Kuang* was the instigator. Theories of goodness and fairness produced those fame-hunters, such as *Zeng Shen* and *Shi Qiu*[43] and others, who made flutes and drums throughout the empire celebrate their unattainable utopias. The abuse of argumentation produced men like *Yang Zhu* and *Mo Zi*, who fabricated reasons and reeled out deductions as one who molds tiles and plaits ropes; for whom arguing about substances and accidents, similarities and differences, was a game of wits; sophists and rhetoricians who exhausted themselves in useless efforts and words. All these are vain excesses, contrary to the truth, which consists in retaining what is natural, to the exclusion of what is artificial. Nature must not be violated, not even under the pretext of rectifying it. Let the compound remain compound, and the simple simple. Let the long remain long, and the short remain short. Beware of wanting to lengthen the legs of the duck, or shorten those of the crane. To attempt to do so would cause them pain, which is the characteristic note of all that is unnatural, while pleasure is the mark of the natural.

B. From these principles, it follows that the artificial goodness and equity of Confucius, are not natural feelings for man, for their acquisition and exercise are accompanied by shame and suffering. Those who have webbed feet or extra toes suffer, when they move, from their physical deficit or excess. Those who today defend goodness and justice suffer when they see the course of things, because they struggle with human passions. No, goodness and equity are not natural sentiments; otherwise there would be more of them in the world, which for the last eighteen centuries has been nothing but strife and noise. — The use of the quadrant and the line, of the compass and the set square, produces regular forms, only at the

---

43   *Si Yu*, aka *Shi Qiu*. *Entretiens de Confucius*, book VIII, chapter XV.

price of the resection of the natural elements. The ties that bind them together, the glue that fixes them, the varnish that covers them, do violence to the material of the products of art. The rhythm in rituals and music, the official declamations on goodness and equity intended to influence the hearts of men, all this is unnatural, artificial, pure convention. Nature governs the world. By the effect of this nature, curved beings have become so, without the intervention of the quadrant; straight beings, without the use of the line; round and square, without the compass and the set square. Everything holds together in nature, without ties, without glue, without varnish. Everything becomes, without violence, the result of a kind of irresistible call or attraction. Beings do not realize why they come to be; they develop without knowing how; the norm of their becoming and development is intrinsic. It has always been so; it continues to be so; it is an invariable law. Why then do we pretend to bind men and tie them together, with artificial ties of goodness and equity, with rites and music, with the glue and varnish of political philosophers? Why not let them follow their nature? Why should we try to make them forget this nature? Ever since the emperor *Shun* (about 2255 BC) disoriented the empire with his false formula of "goodness and equity", human nature has suffered, suffocated by the artificial, by the conventional.

C. Yes, from *Shun* to the present day, men follow various callings, not their own nature. The vulgar kill each other for money, the learned kill each other for reputation, the noble kill each other for the glory of their house, the Wise kill each other for the empire. Famous men, of various conditions, have this in common, that they have acted against nature and have ruined themselves in this way. What does it matter the diversity of the mode, if the fatal result is the same? — Two shepherds who lost their sheep, one by studying, the other by gambling, in the end suffered the same loss.

Bo Yi perished for love of glory, and *Zhi* for banditry; different motive, same result.

However, official history says of *Bo Yi* that he was a noble character, because he sacrificed himself for goodness and fairness; on the contrary, it says of *Zhi* that he was a vulgar man, because he perished for the love of gain. In short, since the end to which they arrived was the same, it is not necessary to use the distinction between noble and vulgar in their regard. Both did the same outrage to their nature, both perished in the same way. So why praise *Bo Yi* and blame *Zhi*?

D. No, it is the same with *Zeng Shen* and *Shi Qiu*; I will not speak well of him who has violated his nature by practicing goodness and equity. I will not speak well of him who has applied himself to the study of tastes, or sounds, or colors, even if he is famous as *Yu Er*, as *Shi Kuang*, or as *Li Zu*. No, man is not good because he practices artificial goodness and fairness; he is good by the exercise of his natural faculties. He makes good use of taste who follows his natural appetites. He makes good use of his hearing who listens to his inner sense. He who looks only at himself makes good use of his sight. Those who look and listen to others inevitably take something from the manner and judgments of others, to the detriment of the rightness of their natural sense. If they have deviated from their natural rectitude, it matters not to me whether they have the reputation of thieves like *Zhi* or of sages like *Bo Yi*; in my eyes, they are only astray. Because, for me, the rule is conformity or non-conformity with nature. Artificial goodness and fairness are as odious to me as vice and depravity.

CHAPTER 9 - TRAINED HORSES

A. Horses naturally have hooves capable of treading snow and a coat impenetrable to the wind. They graze in the grass, drink water, run and jump. That is their true nature. They have no use for palaces and dormitories... When *Bo Lao*, the first squire, declared that he alone understood how to treat horses; when he taught men to brand, shear, shoe, bridle, chain, and pen these poor beasts, then two or three horses out of every ten died prematurely, as a result of this violence done to their nature. When, as the art of training advanced, they were made to starve and thirst to harden them; when they were made to gallop in herds, in order and measure, to harden them; when the bit tormented their mouths, when the whip stung their loins; then, out of every ten horses, five died prematurely, as a result of these unnatural violences. — When the first potter announced that he was skilled in the working of clay, round pots were made from it on the wheel, and rectangular bricks in the mold. — When the first carpenter said he was skilled at woodworking, they made curved and straight shapes with the curvigraph and the chalk line. — Is this really treating horses, clay and wood according to their nature? Of course not! And yet, throughout the ages, men have praised the first groom, the first potter and the first carpenter for their genius and inventions.

B. Similarly, those who devised the modern form of government are praised for their genius and inventions. This is a mistake, in my opinion. The condition of men was very different under the good rulers of antiquity. People followed their nature, and nothing but their nature. All men, uniformly, obtained their clothing by weaving and their food by plowing. They were an indivisible whole, governed solely by natural law. In those days of perfect naturalism, men walked as they pleased and let their eyes roam freely, with no rituals to regulate their gait and their looks. In the mountains there were no roads or trenches; in the waters there were no ships or dams. All beings were born and lived together. Birds and quadrupeds lived on the grass that grew spontaneously. Man did not harm them, the animals let themselves be led by him without distrust, the birds did not worry about anyone looking into their nests. In those days of perfect naturalism, man lived as a brother of the animals, on an equal footing with all beings. Fortunately, Confucius' famous distinction between the wise man and the vulgar man was ignored. Equally devoid of science, all men acted according to their nature. Equally devoid of ambition, all acted with simplicity. Nature flourished freely everywhere.

C. This was discarded when the first Sage appeared. Seeing him twist and twist ritually, hearing him speak of goodness and fairness, men were amazed and wondered if they had not been mistaken so far. Then came the intoxication of music and the infatuation of ceremonies. Unfortunately, the artificial prevailed over the natural. As a result, peace and charity disappeared from the world. Man made war on animals, sacrificed them to his luxury. To make offering vessels, he tortured wood. To make ritual scepters, he inflicted cuts on jade. Under the pretext of goodness and fairness, he violated nature. Rituals and music ruined the naturalness of movement. The rules of painting made a mess of colors. The official scale muddled the tones. In short, artists are guilty of tormenting matter to execute their works of art, and the Wise are execrable for substituting nature with artificial goodness and fairness. — In the past, in the state of nature, horses grazed on grass and drank water. When they were happy, they rubbed their necks. When angry, they turned around and kicked each other. Knowing nothing else, they were perfectly simple and natural. But when *Bo Lao* harnessed them, they became deceitful and malicious, out of hatred of the bit and bridle. This man is guilty of the crime of horse perversion.

In the time of the ancient emperor *He Xu*, men stayed in their dwellings doing nothing, or wandered about without knowing where they were going. When their mouths were full, they patted their bellies in satisfaction. Knowing no more, they were perfectly simple and natural. But when the first sage taught them to make ritual bows to the sound of music, and sentimental contortions in the name of goodness and equity, then began the competition for knowledge and wealth, the inordinate pretensions and insatiable ambitions. It is a crime of the Sage to have thus confounded mankind.

CHAPTER 10 - THIEVES, SMALL AND GREAT

A. The common man locks his purses and chests with ropes and strong padlocks, lest petty thieves get their hands into them. When he does this, he thinks he is wise. A big thief comes along and takes his wallets and chests with their ropes and padlocks, very happy that they are well packed. And it turns out that the wisdom of these vulgar people consisted in preparing the thief's loot.

The same is true of government and administration. Those who are commonly called Wise Men are nothing more than the packers of the bandits to come. Example: In the principality of *Qi*, everything was regulated according to the laws of the Sages. The population was so dense that each village could hear the roosters and dogs of the neighboring villages. The waters were exploited with nets and traps, the land with plows and hoes. Everywhere were the temples of the ancestors, of the genie of the earth and the patron of the harvest, the inhabited centers; the countryside, even the farthest corners, was in the most perfect order. One fine day, *Tian Cheng Zi* murdered the prince of *Qi* (in 482 BC), and seized his principality, with all that the Sages had placed there. Then this bandit enjoyed the fruit of his crime, as quietly as *Yao* and *Shun*. No prince, great or small, dared to try to make him pay. At his death, he bequeathed the principality to his successors (who retained it until 221 BC). This is thanks to the Sages, who advise submission to the *fait accompli*.

The most renowned of the historical sages worked for great robbers, to the point of sacrificing their lives. *Long Feng* was beheaded, *Bin Gan* was disemboweled, *Chang Long* was tore apart, *Zi Xu* perished in the water.

The worst thing is that the bandits by profession also applied, in their own way, the principles of the Sages. This is what the famous *Zhi* taught his pupils: to guess where a great treasure is, that is wisdom; to enter first, that is courage; to leave last, that is propriety; to judge whether the coup is feasible or not, that is prudence; to divide the spoils equally, that is kindness and equity; only those who combine these qualities are worthy robbers.

Thus, if the principles of the Sages have occasionally benefited honest people, they have also, and more often, benefited rogues, to the disgrace of honest people. As proof of this, I will only cite the two historical facts that recall the phrases, "when the lips are cut, the teeth grow cold", and "the bad wine of *Lu* provoked the siege of *Han Dan*".

Yes, the appearance of the Sages causes the appearance of the bandits, and the disappearance of the Sages causes the disappearance of the bandits. Sages and bandits, these two terms are correlative, one calls the other, like torrent and flood, embankment and ditch.

I repeat, if the race of the Sages were to become extinct, the thieves would disappear; there would be perfect peace in this world, without quarrels. Because the race of the Sages is not extinguished there are always thieves. The more Sages are employed to govern the State, the more the thieves will multiply. For it is the inventions of the Sage that produce them. By the invention of measures of capacity, of scales and weights, of contracts divided in two and seals, they have taught many a fraud. By the invention of goodness and equity, they have taught many a malice and deceit.

If a poor devil steals the belt buckle, he shall be beheaded. If a great thief steals a principality, he will become a lord, and the preachers of goodness and equity (Sages, politicians for hire) will flock to him, and put all their wisdom at his service. The logical conclusion from this is that one should not waste time starting with petty thefts, but should begin at once by stealing a principality. Then one will no longer have to bother to steal again, and will no longer have to fear the executioner's axe. Then one will have all the Sages with all their inventions for oneself. Yes, to make bandits, and to prevent them from being defeated, is the work of the Sages (professional politicians).

B. It has been said[44]:

"Let the fish not come up out of the depths, where it lives unconscious but secure; let a state not show its resources, lest it be robbed."

---

44   *Lao Zi*, chapter 36.

But the Sages (politicians) are considered a resource of the state. Therefore, they must be hidden, kept in obscurity, not used. Thus the race of Sages would become extinct, and with it the race of bandits. Pulverize the jade and pearls, and there will be no more thieves. Burn the contracts, break the seals, and men will be honest again. Smite measures and weights, and there will be no more quarrels. Destroy radically all the artificial institutions of the Wise Men, and the people will regain their natural good sense. Shatter the scale of tones, smash the musical instruments, stop up the ears of the musicians, and men will regain their natural hearing. Abolish the scale of colors and the laws of painting, pluck out the eyes of painters, and men will regain their natural sight. Forbid the curvigraph and the chalk line, the compass and the set square; break the fingers of carpenters, and men shall regain natural processes, those known as[45]: "skill disguised as clumsiness."

Brand *Zeng Shen* and *Shi Qiu* (Legists), gag *Yang Zhu* and *Mo Zi* (Sophists), banish the goodness-equity formula (of the Confucians), and the natural propensities may again exercise their mysterious and unifying virtue. Yes, let us return to sight, to hearing, to common sense, to natural instincts, and there will be no more dazzling and false faces. Philosophers, musicians, painters, various artists, have done nothing but deceive and pervert men with deceptive appearances. They have been of no real use to mankind.

C. It was very different in the time of perfect nature, in the time of the ancient rulers, before *Fu Xi Shen Nong* and *Huang Di*. At that time, men only used knotted ropes for annals. They thought their coarse food and simple clothes were good. They were happy with their primitive customs and were quiet in their poor dwellings. The need to have relations with others did not torment them. They died of old age, before they had visited the neighboring principality, which they had seen from afar all their lives, and whose roosters and dogs they had heard every day[46]. At that time, thanks to these customs, peace and order were absolute.

Why is it so different today? Because the rulers are infatuated with the Sages and their inventions. People stretch their necks and stand on tiptoe to look in the direction from which some Sage is said to come. One abandons one's parents, or leaves one's master, to run toward this man. Pedestrians follow one after another in a queue, a line of carts digs deep ruts in the road leading to his door. All this is because, imitating the princes, the common man has also become infatuated with science. And nothing is more fatal to the States than this unfortunate infatuation.

D. It is artificial science, contrary to nature, that has caused all the evils of this world, and the misfortune of all who inhabit it. The invention of bows, crossbows, captive arrows, and spring traps, has caused the misfortune of the birds of the

---

45   *Lao Zi*, chapter 45. Each species of being, says the commentary, has its natural kind. Thus each species of spider has its form of web, each species of dung beetle has its special but invariable form of ball. Thus man must confine himself to a few simple and natural types, without multiplying or embellishing them. All art is perversion.

46   *Lao Zi*, chapter 80.

air. The invention of hooks, baits, nets and traps has caused the misfortune of the fish in the waters. The invention of nets and traps, has made the misfortune of quadrupeds in their thickets. The invention of sophistry, treacherous and poisonous, with its theories about substance and accidents, with its arguments about identity and difference, has disturbed the simplicity of the vulgar. Yes, the love of science, of inventions and innovations, is responsible for all the evils of this world. Preoccupied with learning what they do not know (the vain science of the sophists), men unlearn what they know (the natural truths of common sense). Preoccupied with criticizing the opinions of others, they close their eyes to their own errors. The result is a moral disorder, which is reflected in the sky in the sun and moon, on earth in the mountains and rivers, in the intermediate space in the four seasons, and even in the insects that tingle and swarm against the clock (locusts, etc.). All beings are losing ownership of their nature. It is the love of science that has brought about this disorder. It has lasted since the three dynasties. For eighteen centuries, people have been accustomed to despise natural simplicity, to make use of ritual trickery; or they have been accustomed to prefer verbose and fallacious politics to frank and loyal non-action. It is the talkers (wise men, politicians, rhetoricians) who have dirtied the world.

CHAPTER 11 - TRUE AND FALSE POLITICS

A. It is necessary to let the world go its way, and not to pretend to rule it. Otherwise, the vitiated natures will no longer act naturally (but artificially, legally, ritually, etc.). When all natures, being wholesome, stand and act in their own sphere, then the world is governed, naturally and by itself; there is no need to intervene.

In the past, by his rule, the good *Yao* delighted his subjects. But joy, which is a passion, breaks natural apathy. Therefore, *Yao's* rule was defective, for it excited his subjects.

The wicked *Jie* afflicted his subjects. Now affliction, which is a passion, breaks the natural placidity. Therefore, *Jie's* rule was defective, for it excited his subjects.

All emotion, being unnatural, is unstable and cannot last. Pleasure, complacency, are emotions of the *yang* principle. Displeasure, resentment, are emotions of the *yin* principle. In the macrocosm, the disturbance of *yin* and *yang* means that the four seasons do not come at the right time, that the succession of cold and heat does not come at the right time. In the human microcosm, the imbalance of *yin* and *yang* caused by the passions also causes great disturbances. Bodies suffer, minds suffer. People become unstable, lose control of their thoughts and desires, undertake and fail to complete (their moving passions constantly move to other objects). Then, in the empire, ambitious pretensions arise, struggles for dominance. Then, some become *Zhi* (bandits), others *Zeng Shen* and *Shi Qiu* (politicians). Then they legislate, with the aim of rewarding the good and punishing the bad. This is a superhuman task, an impossible attempt, given the number of people involved.

Unfortunately, the rulers of the three dynasties have wasted their time and effort on this, instead of quietly following the course of their nature and destiny.

Every theory, every convention, is wrong and false. Optical theories have distorted the natural notion of colors. Acoustic theories have distorted the true notion of sounds. Goodness theories have perverted the spontaneity of relationships. Theories of fairness have erased the innate sense of justice. Theories of ritual have produced subtlety, theories of music have developed lasciviousness. Theories of wisdom have multiplied politicians, theories of science have multiplied arguers. It would be all right if, sticking practically to natural laws, one speculated theoretically on the above subjects; it would be quite indifferent. But if, having forgotten the natural laws, these speculations are allowed to influence practice, there will be disorder and anarchy; and if we come to honor them, to give them the force of law, alas, poor world!

Let's see what government has come to today. It has become an uninterrupted succession of rituals. As soon as one ceremony is over, abstinence must be maintained in preparation for the next, and then go through the whole series of bowing, singing and dancing, etc., without rest and without end. A true Sage would do the opposite, if, in spite of everything, he had to take care of the empire. Holding himself to non-action, he would take advantage of the leisure of his non-intervention to give free rein to his natural propensities. The empire would be well served by being placed in the hands of this man[47]. Without using his organs, without using his bodily senses, he would sit still and see everything with his transcendent eye; absorbed in contemplation, he would shake everything as thunder does; the physical sky would obediently adapt itself to the movements of his mind; all beings would follow the (negative) impulse of his non-intervention, as dust follows the wind. Why should man apply himself to manipulating the empire, when complacency is enough?

B. *Cui Zhu* asked *Lao Dan*:
"How does one govern men, without positive action?"
Lao Dan said:
"By doing no violence to their hearts. The heart of man is made in such a way that every oppression depresses it, every excitement elevates it. Depressed, it becomes inert; excited, it becomes carried away. Sometimes it is flexible and yields to everything; at other times it is so hard that it breaks everything. Sometimes it burns like fire, sometimes it becomes as cold as ice. Its expansion is so rapid that, in the time it takes one to bow and turn one's head, it has gone to the end of the four seas and back. Its concentration is as deep as an abyss. His movements are free and uncontrollable, like those of celestial bodies. Proud of its freedom and unbound, such is the human heart, such is its nature."

Now, in ancient times (around 3000 BC), *Huang Di* was the first one to do violence to the human heart with his theories of goodness and fairness. Then *Yao*

---

47   *Lao Zi*, chapter 13.

and *Shun* used up the fat on their thighs and the hair on their legs, hastening for the material good of their subjects. They afflicted all their viscera in the exercise of goodness and equity, and exhausted their blood and breath in discussing the rules of these artificial virtues. All in vain. They had to banish *Huan Dou* at *Chong Shan*, the *San Miaos* at *San Wei*, and *Gong Gong* at *You Du*; a violent expedient, showing that, in spite of their goodness and equity, the empire was not devotedly subject to them. It was much worse under the three dynasties. Under them appeared the *Jie* (tyrants), the *Zhi* (bandits), the *Zeng Shen* and *Shi Qiu* (politicians), and finally the two races of the *Ru* (disciples of Confucius) and the *Mei* (disciples of *Mo Zi*). What a time! The theorists for and against looked at each other with animosity; the wise and the foolish contradicted each other; the good and the bad persecuted each other; the liars and the truthful mocked each other. The empire fell into decadence. They could no longer agree on first principles, and what was left of natural truths disappeared, as if consumed by fire, as if swept away by the great waters. Everyone wanted to become a sage in order to succeed, and people exhausted themselves in vain efforts.

It was then that the mathematical system of government was invented. The empire was squared with axe and saw. The penalty for anyone who deviated from the straight line was death. The hammer and chisel were applied to morality. The result was general upheaval and collapse. The lawgiver had erred in violating the human heart. The people attacked the Sages and the princes. The sages had to hide in mountain caves, and the princes were no longer safe in their family temples. Violent reactions followed, when the sages and princes returned to power. At present, the corpses of the tortured are piled in heaps, those who bear the yoke march in chains, and everywhere one sees only men punished by various torments. And in the midst of this atrocious scene, amidst the handcuffs, fetters, and instruments of torture, the disciples of Confucius and *Mo Zi* stand on tiptoe to make themselves taller, and roll up their sleeves complacently, admiring their work. Ah, how extreme is the hardening of these men! How extreme is their effrontery! Does the yoke sum up the wisdom of the Sages? Would handcuffs, shackles, and torture be the expression of their goodness and fairness? Would not *Zeng Shen* and *Shi Qiu*, these typical sages, have been more wicked than the tyrant *Jie* and the bandit *Zhi*? The adage is right: exterminate wisdom, destroy science, and the empire will spontaneously return to order.

C. *Huang Di* had been reigning for nineteen years, and his orders were obeyed throughout the empire, when he heard of the master *Guang Cheng*, who resided on Mount *Kong Tong*. Addressing him, he spoke to him as follows:

"I have heard, Master, that you have reached the Supreme Principle. I dare to ask you to communicate to me the quintessence of it. I will use it to return to the fields the cereals that feed the people, I will regulate the heat and the cold for the good of all living beings. Please give me the recipe."

Master *Guang Cheng* replied:

"You are so ambitious as to want to rule nature. To entrust its forces to you would be to lose all beings. Passionate man, if you ruled the world, you would want it to rain before the clouds form, you would make the leaves fall when they are still green, the sun and moon go out early. Selfish and self-interested heart, what do you have in common with the Supreme Principle?"

Huang Di withdrew in confusion, renounced the government and took up residence in an adobe hut, with a reed mat as furniture. After spending three months in this retreat of reflection and meditation, he returned to master *Guang Cheng*, whom he found lying with his head to the north (facing south, the master's position). Taking the student's place, very humbly, *Huang Di* approached on his knees, prostrated himself, applied his forehead to the ground, and then said:

"I know, Master that you have penetrated to the Supreme Principle. Please teach me how to conduct and preserve myself."

"This time, you have asked well," said Master *Guang Cheng*, "Come closer! I am going to reveal to you the basis of the Principle. Its essence is mystery, it is darkness, it is indistinction, it is silence. When one looks at nothing, listens to nothing, wraps one's mind in recollection, matter (the body) straightens itself spontaneously. Be recollected, be detached, do not tire your body, do not move your instincts, and you will be able to last forever. When your eyes no longer look at anything, when your ears no longer listen to anything, when your heart (intelligence and will) no longer knows or desires anything, when your spirit has enveloped and as it were absorbed your matter, then this matter (your body) will last forever. Watch your inner self, defend your outer self. Wanting to learn many things is what wears out… Follow me in spirit, beyond light, to the *yang* principle of all splendor; and beyond darkness, to the *yin* principle of darkness. Follow me now, beyond these two principles, to the unity (the supreme principle) which governs heaven and earth, which contains in germ and from which emanate, *yin* and *yang*, all beings. To know this Principle is the all-embracing science, which does not exhaust itself. Remaining at rest, in its contemplation, is what makes it last forever. Every being that preserves itself, maintains its vigor. I have embraced Unity, I have established myself in Harmony. I have lived for fifteen hundred years and my body has not weakened."

"You are a celestial being," said *Huang Di*, again resting his forehead on the ground.

"Listen," said Master *Guang Cheng*, "without interrupting me. The first Principle is essentially infinite and unfathomable; it is by mistake that men use the terms end and apogee when speaking of it. Those who have known it have become the emperors and kings of the heroic age, and have ended in apotheosis. Those who did not know it remained earthly men, ignorant and carnal. Now the first Principle is so forgotten, that all beings, having left the earth, return to the earth. Therefore, I will no longer remain in this world. I leave you to go beyond the gate of infinity, to wander through the immeasurable spaces. I will unite my light with that of the sun and the moon; I will merge my duration with that of heaven and earth. I don't even want to know if men think like me or differently. When they are all dead, I alone will survive, for I alone, in these times of decadence, have achieved union with Unity."

D. The politician *Yun Jiang*, wandering in the East, beyond the river *Fu Yao*, unexpectedly encountered the immortal *Hong Meng*, who was prancing about, beating rhythm on his flanks[48]. Surprised, *Yun Jiang* stopped, stood in ritual posture and asked:

"Venerable one, who are you, what are you doing here?"

Without ceasing to jump and beat his sides, *Hong Meng* replied:

"I am walking around."

Convinced that he was dealing with a transcendent being, *Yun Jiang* said:

"I want to ask you a question."

"Bah," said *Hong Meng*.

"Yes," said *Yun Jiang*. "The inflow of heaven is disturbed, that of the earth is obstructed; the six emanations are obstructed, the four seasons are disturbed. I would like to restore order in the universe, for the sake of the beings who inhabit it. Please tell me how I should do it."

"I don't know, I don't know," said *Hong Meng*, shaking his head, slapping his sides and jumping up and down.

Yun Jiang could get nothing more out of him.

Three years later, while still wandering in the East, beyond the plain of *You Song*, *Yun Jiang* unexpectedly met *Hong Meng* again. In the height of joy, he ran to him and said.

"Do you still remember me?"

Then, after prostrating herself twice, bowing her head, he added:

"I want to ask you a question."

"What can I teach you?" said *Hong Meng*. "I, who walk without knowing why, who wander about without knowing where I am going; me, I just wander about, not taking care of anything, lest I cause harm by some unwelcome intrusion."

"I, too," said *Yun Jiang*, "would like to wander free and carefree as you do; but people chase me wherever I go; it is a real servitude; they have hardly let me go; I take advantage of this respite to question you."

"Poor fellow!" said *Hong Meng*; "what shall I say to you, who meddle with the government of men? Who disturbs the empire, who violates nature, who hinders the action of heaven and earth? Who disturbs the animals, troubles the sleep of the birds, harms even the plants and insects? Who acts in this way, if not politicians, with their systems for governing men?"

"Is this how you judge me?" said *Yun Jiang*.

"Yes," said *Hong Meng*, "you are a poisoner; let me go my way."

"Heavenly Being," said *Yun Jiang*, "I have had great difficulty in finding you; please instruct me."

---

48   Daoist immortals are almost always depicted with eccentric poses and gestures, a sign of their contempt for the commonplace.

"Indeed," said *Hong Meng*, "you have a great need to learn, so listen! Start by not interfering with anything, and everything will take its natural course. Detach yourself from your personality (literally, drop your body like clothing), renounce the use of your senses, forget relations and contingencies, drown yourself in the great whole, cast off your will and your intelligence, animate yourself by abstraction until you have no soul. What is the use of speculating, unconsciousness being the universal law? The multitude of beings returns unconscious to its origin. He who has spent his life in unconsciousness will have followed his nature. If he acquires knowledge, he will have vitiated his nature. For he was born spontaneously, without being asked who and what he wanted to be. And nature wants him to return in the same way, without having known either who or what."

"Ah," cried *Yun Jiang*, "Heavenly Being, you have enlightened me, you have transformed me. All my life I had been searching in vain for the solution to the problem, and here I have it…"

Having said this, *Yun Jiang* prostrated himself with his forehead on the ground, then got up and went on his way.

E. The great concern of vulgar politicians is how to attach themselves to men; they are offended when someone does not want to make common cause with them. The fact that they love those who are of their opinion and hate those who are contrary to them, comes from the fact that, at the end, they only seek their own elevation. When they have attained the object of their ambition, are they really superior to the common people? Is it not worse to impose on the people what politicians call "their experience" than to abandon them to themselves? Fascinated by the idea of making the principality they administer benefit from the system of the three ancient dynasties, they pay no attention to the vices of this system. Their enterprise exposes the principality to the most serious risks. It is fortunate, if it escapes. It has one chance of salvation, against ten thousand. For a principality in which they will have succeeded imperfectly, they will absolutely ruin ten thousand others. It is sad enough that the masters of the earth do not see this danger The most important thing of all is in their hands. They must not entrust it to narrow-minded and self-interested men. Let them give their trust to transcendent men; to those who, free from all earthly interest, go to and fro in space, walk the nine regions, are citizens not of a country but of the universe. Such men are the noblest of all[49]. The esteem of vulgar men adheres to them, as unerringly as the shadow follows the opaque body, as the echo follows the sound. When he is consulted, the answer of the transcendent man exhausts the question and fulfills the wishes of the querent. He is the resource of the whole empire. His repose is calm and quiet, his comings and goings have no fixed purpose. He leads and brings back his interlocutors, without startling, by an impalpable influence. His movements have no fixed rules. Like the sun, he always shines. The substantial praise of this

---

49   Commentary: supreme nobility consists in absolute contempt for men and earthly things.

man is summed up by saying that he is one with the great whole. He is the great whole, and is no longer himself. No longer having any particular existence, he has no property. The ancient emperors still had some properties. It is necessary to have nothing, to be a friend of heaven and earth (to attain union).

F. Small but respectable are the beings that fill the world. Humble but necessary are the people. The affairs are uncertain but important. Laws are harsh but indispensable. Justice is unkind but obligatory. Sympathy is an affection that is not selfish. Rites are minor, but they must be done. These aphorisms summarize vulgar wisdom.

And I add: At the center of all things and superior to all, is the productive action of the Supreme Principle, unique and transforming itself into productive action. Transcendent and in constant action, is Heaven (the physical instrument of the productive action of the Principle). Therefore, the rule of the true Sages is to let Heaven do its work without helping it, to let the productive action act without interfering, to let the first Principle be free without pretending to guess for it. That is the important thing, in their eyes. Otherwise, in common practice, they are affectionate without affectation, just without pretense, ritualistic without scrupulousness, active without mannerism, legal without passion, devoted to the people and respectful of the rights of all. They regard no being as a particularly suitable means, and yet they use it for lack of anything better. The ignorance of those who understand nothing of the action of Heaven, arises from the fact that they do not clearly understand that of the Supreme Principle, of which Heaven is the instrument. Those who have no notion of this Principle itself are of no use; they are to be pitied.

There are two paths, the heavenly and the human. To concentrate nobly on non-action is the heavenly way. To be scattered and to toil in details, that is the human way. The heavenly way is superior, the human way is inferior. The two forms are very different. We will examine them closely in the following chapters.

CHAPTER 12 - HEAVEN AND EARTH

A. A uniform transforming force emanates from the immense complex of heaven and earth; a single ruler governs the multitude of beings; a single ruler governs the numerous mankind. The power of the ruler derives from the Principle; his person is chosen by Heaven; hence he is called Mysterious, like the Principle. The rulers of antiquity, abstaining from all personal intervention, let Heaven rule through them. The Principle acting through the ruler, his ministers and officials. To this just and enlightened right government all beings respond with absolute submission. In the apex of the universe, the first Principle influences heaven and earth, which transmit to all beings this influence, which in the world of men becomes good government, causing talents and capacities to flourish there. On the contrary, all prosperity comes from government, the efficacy of which is derived from the Principle, through heaven and earth. Therefore, since the ancient rulers desired nothing, the world was in abundance; they did not act, and everything evolved; they remained immersed in their meditation, and the people were kept in the most perfect order. This is what sums up the ancient adage: for the one who is united to Unity, everything prospers; even the spirits are subject to the one who has no personal interest.

B. How true are these words of the Master; how great, how immense is the Principle that covers and carries all beings; let the sovereign beware of following its particular meaning! Natural action is celestial action; spontaneous speech is celestial influence; loving all men and doing good to all beings is true goodness; merging all differences into one is true greatness; not wishing to dominate others in anything is true broadmindedness; possessing several things without dividing the heart is true wealth; following the celestial influx is the continuation of operations. To operate under this influence, this is effective operation; to serve as a docile intermediary to the Principle, this is perfection; not to let his determination be weakened by anything, this is constancy. Let the ruler concentrate these ten principles in himself, and then apply them to government, and all will follow its normal course. Let him leave the gold in the rocks and the pearls in the abyss, let him despise riches and honors, let him not care whether he lives to old age or dies young, let him not take pride in prosperity and not humble himself in the face of adversity, let him despise all worldly goods, let him not glory in his exaltation. Let his glory be in having understood that all beings are a universal complex, that death and life are two modes of the same being.

C. The Master said:

"The action of the Principle through Heaven is infinite in its expansion, elusive in its subtlety. It resides, imperceptible, in all beings, as the cause of their being and of all their qualities. It is in the resonance of metals and sounding flints. It is also in the shock that makes them resonate. Without it, nothing would be… The man who derives from it the qualities of a king walks in simplicity and refrains from occupying himself with many things. Being at the origin, at the source, united with unity, he knows like the geniuses, by intuition in the Principle. Consequently, his capacity extends to everything. When his mind has gone out through the door of a sense, for example through sight, as soon as he encounters a being, he grasps it, penetrates it, knows it thoroughly. For beings that have come into being by participation in the Principle, are known by participation in the virtue of the Principle. To preserve beings with full knowledge of their nature, to act upon them with full intelligence of the Principle, these are the powers of the being born to be king. He appears unexpectedly on the world stage, plays his role and all beings surrender to him. This is because he has received from the Principle the qualities that make the king. He sees in the darkness of the Principle, he hears the silent word of the Principle. For him, darkness is light, silence is harmony. He grasps being, in the depth of being; and his reason for being, in the highest abstraction, in the Principle. Standing on this height, utterly empty and devoid, he gives to all their due. Its action extends in space and time."

D. The emperor *Huang Di* had gone as far north as the red river and climbed the mountain *Kun Lun* to examine the southern regions, when he lost his black pearl (his treasure, the notion of the Principle, because he had given himself up to his ambitious dreams). He had Science search for it, but he did not find it. Research and Debate did not find it either. Finally Abstraction found it. *Huang Di* said to himself:

"Is it not strange that it is Abstraction that has found it? She whom the common people regard as the least practical of the faculties."

E. *Yao* was taught by *Xu You*, disciple of *Nie Que*, disciple of *Wang Ni*, disciple of *Pi Yi*. *Yao*, who was thinking of abdicating to give himself to contemplation, asked *Xu You*:

"Does *Nie Que* have what it takes to collaborate with Heaven (to be emperor in my place)? If so, I will have his master *Wang Ni*[50] impose the office on him."

"This," said *Xu You*, "would be doing something at the very least risky, perhaps disastrous. *Nie Que* is too clever and cunning. He will apply his human intelligence and skill to government, thus preventing Heaven, the Principle, from ruling. He will multiply charges, make concessions to scholars, make decisions, worry about traditions, get entangled in complications, take opinion into account, apply *a priori* theories about the evolution of things, etc. This man is too intelligent to be an emperor. Although he is qualified for the position by his nobility, because of his excessive ability he is only fit to be a minor officer. He has what it takes to stand up to bandits. If he were to become a minister, it would be a disgrace; if he were to come to the throne, it would be the ruin of the country."

F. While *Yao* was inspecting the territory of *Hua*, the officer in charge of that territory said to him:

"O sage, I wish you prosperity and longevity!"

"Be silent!" said *Yao*.

But the official continued:

"I wish you wealth!"

"Be silent!" said *Yao*.

"And many male children!" concluded the officer.

"Be silent!" said *Yao* for the third time.

The officer continued:

"Longevity, wealth, male posterity, all men want this; why only you don't want it?"

"Because," said Yao, "he who has many children, has many troubles; he who has much wealth, has many worries; he who lives long, suffers many contradictions. These three inconveniences make it difficult to cultivate moral virtue, so I did not want what you wished for me."

---

50   The authority of the teacher is, in China, equal or superior to that of the parents.

"Then," said the officer, "I no longer consider you a sage, but a common man. To all the individuals It procreates, Heaven gives the necessary sense to conduct themselves; that is why your children would manage on their own. To get rid of the cumbersome wealth, it would only be necessary to distribute it. You are more concerned than befits a Sage. The true sage lives in this world as a quail lives in a field, without attachment to a home, without worrying about his food. In times of peace, he takes his share of the common prosperity. In times of trouble, he takes care of himself and is not interested in business. After a thousand years, tired of this world, he leaves it and ascends to the Immortals. Riding on a white cloud, he arrives in the region of the Sovereign[51]. There none of the three misfortunes overtake him; his body lasts a long time without suffering; he no longer suffers contradictions."

Having said this, the officer went away. Recognizing in him a hidden Sage, *Yao* ran after him and said:

"I have some questions to ask you."

"Leave me alone," said the officer.

G. While *Yao* ruled the empire, the master *Gao*, known as *Bo Cheng*, received a fief from him. *Yao* passed the empire to *Shun*, who passed it to Yu[52]. Then master *Gao*, having renounced his fief, began to cultivate the land. *Yu* went to see him and found him busy plowing on the plain. After approaching him respectfully, he said:

"Master, the emperor *Yao* has invested you with a fief, which you have held until now. Why do you want to get rid of it now?"

"Because the world is no longer what it was with *Yao*," said Master *Gao*. "With *Yao* the people behaved well, without being rewarded for good behavior; they were obedient, without having to be coerced with punishments. Now they are systematically rewarded and punished, which has caused the people to lose their natural qualities. Nature has disappeared, laws have replaced it, hence all the disorders. Why do you waste my time? Why do you hinder my work?"

And bending over his plow, master *Gao* continued the furrow he had begun, and did not look back at *Yu*.

H. In the great beginning of all things all was formless, an imperceptible being; there was no sentient being, and therefore no name[53]. The first being that was, was the One, non-sensible, the Principle. The virtue emanating from the One, which gave rise to all beings, is called *de*. Multiplying ceaselessly in its products, this shared virtue, is called in each of them *ming*, its part, its lot, its destiny. It is by the alternation of concentration and expansion that the norm thus gives birth to beings. In the being that is born, certain determined lines specify its bodily form. In this bodily form is contained the vital principle. Each being has its own way of doing things, which constitutes its own nature. This is how beings descend

---

51   The High Sovereign of the Annals and Odes. Compare chapter 4 E of *Lao Zi*.
52   The nightmare of the Daoists, who blame him for the invention of systematic politics.
53   Compare chapter 1 of *Lao Zi*.

from the Principle. They return to it through Daoist mental and moral cultivation, which brings the individual nature back into conformity with the universal acting virtue, and the particular being into union with the primordial Principle, the great Void, the great All. This return, this union, is made, not by action, but by cessation. Like a bird that, closing its beak, ceases its song, becomes silent. Silent fusion with heaven and earth, in an apathy that seems stupid to those who do not understand it, but which in reality is a mystical virtue, communion with cosmic evolution.

I. Confucius asked *Lao Dan*:

"Some apply themselves to identify everything, and assert that, lawful and unlawful, yes and no, are the same thing. Others apply themselves to distinguish everything, and declare that the non-identity of substance and accidents is self-evident. Are these the Sages?"

"They are," replied *Lao Dan* "men who tire themselves without deriving profit for themselves, like the adjuncts of officials, the dogs of hunters, the monkeys of the street entertainers. *Qiu*[54], I am going to tell you a truth, which you will not be able to understand, nor even to repeat correctly. There are no more Wise Men! Now there are many men who, having head and feet, have neither mind nor ears. But you will look in vain for those who, in their material bodies, have preserved intact their part of the original principle. These (the Sages, when there are any) neither act nor rest, neither live nor die, neither rise nor fall, by any positive effort, but are carried along by the current of universal evolution. To do this (and thus to become a true Daoist sage) is within the reach of every man. To become a Sage, one need only forget (individual) beings, forget Heaven (causes) and forget oneself (interests). Through this universal forgetfulness, man becomes one with Heaven, merging into the Cosmos."

J. *Jianglü Mian* visited master *Ji Che* and said to him:

"The prince of *Lu* has asked me to advise him for the good government of his principality. I replied that he had not given me a commission for that. He insisted on knowing my personal opinion. This is what I told him; judge whether I spoke well or badly... I told the prince: Be dignified and sober; employ devoted officials and dismiss self-interested egoists; if you do this, everyone will be in your favor."

Ji Che laughed.

"Your policy," he said, "is as good as the gestures of that mantis who tried to stop a car. Absolutely ineffective; it might even become detrimental."

"But then," said *Jianglü Mian*, "what is the art of governing?"

"This is how the great sages did it," said *Ji Che*; "they stimulated the people to make amends, to advance, inspiring in them a taste for amendment, for advancement; then they let them evolve spontaneously; they let them believe that they wanted and acted for themselves. These are the great politicians. These are not based on the ancient *Yao* and *Shun* (as Confucius defends), for they are older than

---

54   Confucius' given name. A somewhat derogatory familiarity.

these Venerables, being of primordial origin, their policy consists in reviving in all hearts the spark of cosmic virtue that resides in each one."

K. *Zi Gong*, a disciple of Confucius, having gone to the principality of *Chu*, returned to that of *Jin*. Near the river *Han*, he saw a man busy watering his garden. He was filling a pitcher at the well, which he then emptied into the gutters of his flowerbeds; a laborious task and with little result.

"Don't you know," said *Zi Gong*, "that there is a machine with which you can water a hundred flowerbeds in a day easily and without fatigue?"

"How is it done?" asked the man.

"It is," said *Zi Gong*, "a counterbalanced ladle. It draws water from one side and pours it out the other."

"Too clever to be good," said the gardener, dissatisfied. "I learned from my master that every machine contains a formula, an artifice. Now formulas and contrivances destroy native ingenuity, disturb the vital spirits, prevent the Principle from dwelling in peace in the heart. I do not want your counterbalanced ladle."

Zi Gong bowed his head and did not answer. In turn, the gardener asked him:

"Who are you?"

"A disciple of Confucius," said *Zi Gong*.

"Ah," said the gardener, "one of those pedants who think they are superior to the people, and who pretend to be interesting by singing laments about the bad state of the empire. Come, forget your mind, forget your body, and you will have taken the first step on the road to wisdom. If you are incapable of mending yourself, what right have you to mend the empire? Now go! You have wasted enough of my time!"

Zi Gong left, pale with emotion. He did not recover until he had traveled thirty stades. Then the disciples accompanying him asked him:

"What is this man that has troubled you so much?"

"Ah," said *Zi Gong*, "until now I thought there was only one man in the empire worthy of his name, my master Confucius. But then I did not know this other man. I explained to him the Confucian theory of the tendency towards the goal by the most expedient means, with the least effort. I took this as the formula of wisdom. But he refuted me and gave me to understand, that wisdom consists in the integration of the vital spirits, the conservation of nature, the union with the Principle. These true Sages do not differ from the common man outwardly; inwardly their distinguishing feature is aimlessness, letting life flow without wanting to know where it flows. Every effort, every tendency, every art, is for them the effect of forgetting what man should be. According to them, the true man moves only under the impulse of his natural instinct. They also despise praise and blame, which neither benefit nor harm them. This is the stable wisdom, while I am tossed by winds and waves."

When he returned to the principality of *Lu*, *Zi Gong*, who had converted to Daoism, told Confucius of his adventure. The latter said:

"This man pretends to practice what was the wisdom of the primordial age. He sticks to the principle, to the formula, pretending to ignore applications and modifications. Certainly, if in today's world there still existed a way of living without thinking or acting, only attentive to one's own well-being, there would be reason to admire him. But you and I were born in a century of intrigues and struggles, in which it is no longer worthwhile to study the wisdom of the primordial age, because it no longer has any application."

L. *Zhun Mang*, who was on his way to the eastern ocean, met *Yuan Feng*, who asked him:

"Master, where are you going?"

"To the sea," said *Zhun Mang*.

"Why?" asked *Yuan Feng*.

"Because it is the image of the Principle," said *Zhun Mang*. "All waters flow into it, without filling it. All waters flow out of it, without emptying it. Just as beings come out of the Principle and return to it. That is why I go to the sea."

"And mankind," asked *Yuan Feng*, "what do you think, what is the policy of the lower sages, the Confucians?"

"It is," said *Zhun Mang*, "to do good to all, to favor all talents, to regulate the empire and be obeyed; that is the policy of the Sages of this kind."

"And the policy of the Taoist Sages, who collaborate with the cosmic influx?" asked *Yuan Feng*.

"It is," said *Zhun Mang*, "not to make plans; to act according to the inspiration of the moment; not to count at all on artificial distinctions of right and wrong, of good and evil; to give to all, as to orphans, as to the lost, to satisfy them, without claiming any return, without being thanked, without even making themselves known."

"And what about the policy of transcendental men who are totally superior?" asked *Yuan Feng*.

"These," said *Zhun Mang*, "merge their spirit with light, and their body with the universe. Luminous emptiness is the total abnegation of self. Subjected to their destiny, free from all attachment, these men enjoy the selfless joy of heaven and earth, who let things happen without love or hate, and let all things go spontaneously to their natural solution. Thus governed, all beings would return to their innate instinct, and the world would return to its primordial state."

M. When *Men Wu Gui* and *Chi Zhang Man Ji* saw the army of Emperor *Wu* passing by, the latter said to the former:

"If this emperor were as good as *Shun*, he would not have had to wage war."

"Did *Shun* reign in a peaceful or troubled age?" asked *Wu Gui*.

"You are right," said *Man Ji*; "they cannot be compared. *Shun* reigned in such a peaceful age that they could have done without an emperor. He wasted his time on trifles, such as dressing the wounds of ulcer patients, growing the hair of the bald, and curing the sick. He drugged the empire, with all the anxiety of a son drugging his father. Confucians praise him for having done so. A true Sage would have been ashamed to do so... In the days of perfect action, neither wisdom nor skill was valued. The rulers were like the branches of great trees, which shade and protect without knowing or wanting it; the people were like wild animals, which shelter under those branches and enjoy their shade without thanks. The rulers acted with equity without knowing the term equity, with charity without knowing the term kindness, with loyalty and fidelity, with simplicity and without asking for payments in return. Because of their extreme simplicity, no outstanding fact of these times has been preserved, and no history has been written about them."

N. A son, a minister, who does not approve of what his father or his prince does wrong, is proclaimed a good son, a good minister, by the public voice, by authority, without argument; and the mass obediently adopts this verdict, each believing that he has pronounced it himself[55]. If you tell these people that their judgment is not their own, that it has been suggested to them, they will be disturbed and offended. So it is, in most cases, with most men. Almost all of them receive their ideas ready-made, and follow all their lives the opinion of others. They speak in the style of the time, they dress according to the fashion of the time, not to follow any principle, but to do what others do. They are servile imitators, who say yes or no according to what has been suggested to them, and then believe that they have made up their minds. Is this not madness? An incurable madness, because men do not suspect that they are afflicted with this mania for imitation. General madness, because the whole empire is afflicted with this mania. And so it is in vain that I try to bring men back to the path of spontaneous personal action, which emanates from the self, from their own instinct. Alas!

Noble music leaves the villagers indifferent, while a trivial song makes them faint. Likewise, lofty thoughts do not enter minds filled with vulgar ideas. The sound of two clay drums covers the sound of a bronze bell. How can I make myself heard by the madmen who populate the empire? If I expected to be able to do so, I would be mad too. So I will leave them alone, doing nothing to enlighten them. None of them, moreover, will hold it against me, for they cling to their common madness. Like the leper to whom a son was born at midnight, who went to look for a light to see if the child was a leper like himself, and did not caress it until he saw that it was.

O. Consider a tree that is centuries old. A branch is cut from it. A piece of this branch is used to make a chiseled and painted ritual vase; the rest is thrown into the ditch and rots there. Then they will say, the vase is beautiful, the rest is ugly. And I say, both the vase and the rest are ugly, for they are no longer natural wood, but deformed artificial objects. I judge in the same way, the thief *Zhi*, as the Sages *Zeng Shen* and *Shi Qiu*. One is called vicious, the other virtuous. In my eyes, they are also wrong in that they are no longer men, for they have acted against nature, regardless of whether they acted right or wrong.

---

55   Although this is not obvious, since one could argue that the height of piety and devotion is to approve of everything, even evil, says the commentary.

And what are the causes of this ruin of human nature? They are the artificial theories of color (painting), which have perverted sight; the theories of sound (music), which have perverted hearing; the theories of smell (perfumery), which have perverted the sense of smell; the theories of taste (culinary art), which have perverted taste; and literary artifices (rhetoric and poetics), which have distressed the heart and distorted nature (through lyricism and enthusiasm). These are the enemies of human nature, dear to *Yang Zhu* and *Mo Zi*. I will not be the one to consider the arts as goods. Artificial rules embrace and imprison; how could they make one happy? Is the ideal of happiness the state of a bird locked in a cage? Is it not rather the state of a bird free in the air? Poor people! Their theories are a fire that torments their interior, their rites are a corset that tightens their exterior. Thus tortured and bound, to whom shall I compare them? To tenacious criminals? To caged beasts? Is this happiness?

CHAPTER 13 - THE INFLUENCE OF HEAVEN

A. The influence of heaven acts freely, producing all beings. The imperial influence, which spreads impartially, draws to itself all citizens. The influence of the Sage, which spreads evenly, causes all to submit to it. Those who have the understanding of the mode of this influence of heaven, of the Sage, of the ideal head of state, concentrate on meditative peace, which is the source of natural action. This peace is not a goal which the Sage attains by direct effort. It consists in the negative fact that no being moves his heart any longer, and is acquired by abstraction. It is the principle of the clear vision of the Sage. Like perfectly still water, it is so clear that it reflects even the hairs of the beard and eyebrows of the person who is reflected in it. Nothing tends more to equilibrium, to repose, than water; so much so, that from it the perfect level (water level) has been derived. Now, as repose clears the water, so it clears the vital spirits, among which is intelligence. The heart of the Sage, perfectly tranquil, is like a mirror reflecting heaven and earth, all beings. Emptiness, peace, contentment, apathy, silence, global vision, non-intervention; all this is the formula of the influence of heaven and earth, the Principle. The emperors and sages of antiquity knew this formula. Empty (of all passion), they grasped the truth of the general laws. Peaceful (without any emotion), they acted effectively. Not intervening themselves, leaving the details to their officers, they were free of pleasures and pains, and consequently lived long. Is it not obvious that emptiness, peace, contentment, apathy, silence, global vision, non-intervention, are the root of all good? Whoever understands this will be worth as much as *Yao* as emperor and *Shun* as minister. He will be able to reign, as a king, over the destiny of men; or, as a sage, over their minds. Whether he lives in seclusion, as an anchorite, by the waters, in the mountains, in the forests; or whether he serves as an educator of the world; in either case he will be recognized and attract all beings. Yes, from peace emanate the speculations of the great sages and the actions of the great kings; non-intervention makes one famous; abstraction elevates one above all. Understanding the nature of the influence of heaven and earth, which is benevolent and tolerant non-interference, is the great root, understanding with heaven. To practice a similar non-interference in the government of empire is the principle of agreement with men. Now agreement with men is human joy, happiness on earth; agreement with heaven is heavenly joy, supreme happiness.

In a paroxysm of admiration for his ideal, the Emptiness, the Rest, the Principle, *Zhuang Zhou* exclaimed:

"Oh, my Master! My Master! You who destroy without being evil! You who build without being good! You who were before time, and are not old! You who cover everything like the sky, who bear everything like the earth, who are the author of everything without being intelligent (unconscious action)! To understand you in this way is a heavenly joy. To know that I was born through your influence, that at my death I will return to your path; that by resting I commune with *yin*, your passive modality, that by acting I commune with *yang*, your active modality; this is supreme happiness. For the enlightened one who possesses this happiness, complaints against heaven (a fatal and unintelligent intermediary), resentment against men (who follow their own ways, like me), worries about business (which are not worthwhile), fear of ghosts (who can do nothing) are over. The action of the enlightened one merges with the action of heaven, his rest with the rest of the earth; his steady mind dominates the world; at death his lower soul will not be evil (it will dissipate peacefully), his higher soul will not wander hungry (it will pass into another form). Yes, to follow the evolution of the Principle, in heaven and on earth, in all beings, that is the heavenly joy. This joy is the depth of the heart of the Sage. From it he draws his principles of government."

B. As faithful imitators of heaven and earth, of the Principle and its influence, the ancient rulers did not intervene directly, did not concern themselves with details. Hence they could rule the whole empire. Inactive, they let their subjects act. Immobile, they let men move. Their thought extended to everything, without their thinking of anything; they saw everything in the principle, without distinguishing anything in detail; their power, capable of everything, applied to nothing. As heaven does not give birth, so beings are born; as the earth does not cause to grow, so beings grow. Thus, as the sovereign does not act, so the subjects prosper. How transcendent is the influence of heaven, earth, and the sovereign, thus understood! And how right it is to say, in this sense, that the influence of the sovereign is united with that of heaven and earth! Indefinite as that of heaven and earth, it attracts all beings and moves the multitude of men.

Unique, in its superior sphere, this influence extends, descending. The sovereign formulates the abstract law; his ministers apply it to concrete cases. Military art, laws and penalties, rites and customs, music and dances, weddings and funerals, and other things that torment Confucians, are minutiae that the Sage leaves to his officials.

It should not be thought, however, that in human things there are no degrees, no subordination, no succession. There is a natural order, based on the reciprocal relationship of heaven and earth, and on cosmic evolution. The ruler is superior to the minister, the father to his children, the old to the young, the man to the woman, the husband to the wife; for heaven is superior to earth. In the cycle of the seasons, the two productive seasons precede the two unproductive ones; every being passes through the two successive phases of vigor and decay; this is due to cosmic evolution; and as a result, the fathers have priority in the family, in the court it is the rank that gives priority, in the villages the elders are honored, in business the wisest is deferred to. To fail in these things would be to fail in the Principle, of which these rules have been derived.

C. The ancients considered the Principle in the heaven-earth binomial. From the mode of action of this binomial they derived the natural notions of goodness (blind) and fairness (unconscious), (opposed to the artificial notions of goodness and fairness of the Confucians); then the notions of functions and offices; then those of capacity, responsibility, sanction, and so on. As abstract notions increased, intellectuals were distinguished from fools; there were superior men and inferior men. All were treated according to their degree. The Wise served the sovereign, fed the fools, and amended them by their example, without compulsion, like the action of heaven and earth. It was the time of absolute peace, of perfect government. They did not argue or quarrel over entities and names, as sophists do today. They did not pretend to reward or punish adequately all good or all evil, as our Legists pretend. They looked to the root, to the origin, to the Principle which contains them all, for all solutions; and it was this view from above which obtained the superiority of their government. Whereas, for the sake of losing themselves in details, our sophists and our Legists are of no use.

D. In the past, *Shun*, still a minister, asked Emperor *Yao*:
"Emperor appointed by heaven, how do you perform your duties?"
Yao replied:
"I do not oppress the little ones, I do not harm the poor, I care for widows and orphans."
"All right," said Shun, "but that is not very elevated."
"Then," asked Yao, "what am I to do?"
"The influx of heaven," said *Shun*, "pacifies by its own emanation. To produce the succession of the seasons, the days and nights, the clouds and rain, the sun and moon simply shine."
"I understand," said Yao, "I have been too restless and too eager to please."

E. Confucius was on his way from the principality of *Lu*, in the east, to the capital of the *Zhou* (then *Lao Yang*), in the west. He wanted to offer his books to the imperial library. His disciple *Zi Lu* said to him:
"I have heard that a certain *Lao Dan* was for a long time the guardian of this library. Now he lives in retirement. Visit him. He will be able to help you receive your books."

"So be it," said Confucius; and went to *Lao Dan*. The latter flatly refused to patronize his books. To soften him, Confucius began to explain to him the contents of them.

"Do not talk so much," said *Lao Dan*; "tell me, in two words, what they contain."

"Goodness and fairness," said Confucius.

"Ah," said *Lao Dan*, "is it natural goodness and fairness?"

"But yes," said Confucius, "those that make man."

"Then define them," said *Lao Dan*.

"To love all beings and treat them well, without selfishness, that is kindness and fairness," said Confucius.

"And you preach this, being ambitious and selfish," said Lao Dan. "Master, if you really want to do good to the empire, begin by studying the unchanging influence of heaven and earth, the constant illumination of the sun and moon, the perfect order of the stars, the stability of the animal and vegetable species; observe that everything in nature is sequence and uniformity, the Principle pervades everything with its peaceful influence. You, too, must unite your influence with that of Principle, and you will be able to accomplish something. Stop trying to introduce by force your artificial and unnatural virtues… A man whose son had run away had the drum beaten to drive him away, instead of trying to bring him back gently. The result was that the fugitive wandered far away and could never be found. Your efforts to bring back the goodness and justice of the world to the sound of the drum will, I fear, have the same negative result. Master, you are causing what is left of nature to escape."

F. *Shi Cheng Qi* went to *Lao Zi* and said:

"Having heard that you are a Sage, I made a long journey to come to see you. I have walked for a hundred days, so long that the soles of my feet are calloused, and now I find that you are not a Sage. Because you keep the left-overs from your meals indefinitely; you have mistreated your sister because the rats have stolen the remains of the vegetables."

Lao Zi, looking distracted, let him say this, and answered nothing.

The next day *Shi Cheng Qi* returned to *Lao Zi* and said:

"Yesterday I blamed you. Your silence has made me think. I apologize."

"I pay as little attention to your apology as to your accusations," said Lao Zi. "I have renounced all desire to be called learned, transcendent, wise. You would call me an ox or a horse and I would not answer you. Whether what they say is true or false, to let men say it is to save oneself the trouble of answering them. My principle is to always let them say what they will. My silence yesterday was an application of this principle."

Then *Shi Cheng Qi* walked around *Lao Zi*, avoiding stepping on his shadow; then, presenting himself face to face, he asked him what he should do to make amends. *Lao Zi* turned him down with these words:

"False being, whose air and gesture denote untamed passions and unbridled intentions, do you intend to force me and make me believe that you want and can cultivate yourself? Go away! I have no more confidence in you than in any bandit of the frontiers."

G. *Lao Zi* said:

"Infinite in itself, the Principle penetrates by its virtue into the smallest of beings. All are filled with it. Immense is its expanse, deep as an abyss, all-encompassing and bottomless. All sentient beings and their qualities, all abstractions such as goodness and equity, are offshoots of the Principle, but derived, remote. This is what only the superior man understands; Confucius, the common sage, was wrong on this point. Therefore, when he governs, the superior man does not concern himself with these details and, consequently, the government of the world is only a light weight to him. He cares only for the tiller, and disregards any others affairs. From above, his glance dominates everything. No particular interest moves him. He inquires only into the essence of things. He lets heaven and earth pass by, he lets all beings pass by, without the least fatigue of mind, for he has no passion. Having penetrated into the Principle and identified its action with his own, he rejects artificial goodness and equity, conventional rites and music. For the mind of the superior man is dominated by one fixed idea, not to intervene, to let nature and time act."

H. In today's world, books (Confucian anthologies) are in fashion. Books are only sets of words. Words translate ideas. But true ideas are derived from a non-sensible principle, and can hardly be expressed in words. The formulas that fill books only express conventional ideas, which have little or no relation to the nature of things, to truth. Those who know nature do not attempt to express it in words; and those who attempt to do so show that they do not know it. The vulgar err in seeking truths in books, which contain only invented ideas.

I. One day, while Duke *Huan*, of *Qi*, was reading, sitting in the upper room, the wheelwright *Pian* was working on a wheel in the courtyard. Suddenly, leaving the hammer and chisel, he went up the steps, approached the duke and asked:

"What are you reading there?"

"The words of the Wise Men," replied the Duke.

"Of the living sages?" asked *Pian*.

"The dead sages," said the Duke.

"Ah," said *Pian*, "the detritus of the ancients."

The duke became irritated and said

"Wheelwright, what are you getting into? Explain what you mean, or I will have you executed."

"I will make myself clear as a man of my trade," said the wheelwright. "When I make a wheel, if I work weakly, the result will be weak; if I work harder, the result will be solid; if I work without thinking about what I am doing, the result will conform to my ideal, a good and beautiful wheel; I cannot define this method; it is a trick that cannot be expressed; so much so that I could not teach it to my son, since, at seventy years of age, to have a good wheel, I still have to make it myself. Could the ancient deceased sages whose books you read do better than I? They were able to deposit, in their writings, their trick, their genius, what made them superior to the vulgar. If not, the books you read are, as I have said, only the detritus of the ancients, the waste of their spirit, what has ceased to be."

Chapter 14 - Natural Evolution

A. The starry heaven revolves; the earth is fixed. The sun and moon follow each other alternately. Who governs all this? Who maintains this harmony? Where is the motionless engine that moves everything? Is the cosmic movement free, or is it forced? The clouds resolve themselves into rain, and the evaporated rain forms again into clouds. Who thus diffuses, without moving, abundance and well-being? From the North, the wind blows to the West, to the East, in all directions. Who moves this mighty breath? Who, motionless, gives it these varieties? "I will tell you," said *Wuxian Tiao*. "It is heaven, through the revolution of the five elements, in the six regions of space. It is this revolution that maintains order in nature; and in human affairs, there will be good order if the government conforms to it, and disorder if it does not. When the ancient rulers applied the nine laws[56], their government was prosperous and efficient. They enlightened the empire, which was perfectly subject to them. These were the so-called august rulers."

B. *Tang*, the prime minister of *Shang*, asked *Zhuang Zhou*: "What is goodness?"
"It is," said the latter, "the virtue of the tigers and wolves."
"How so?" said *Tang*.
"Don't tigers and wolves love their young?"
"And what about the supreme goodness?" said *Tang*.
"The supreme goodness," answered *Zhuang Zhou*, "consists in not loving."
"Then," said *Tang*, "the man who possesses supreme goodness is devoid of filial piety?"
"You are wrong," said *Zhuang Zhou*. "The supreme goodness is the abstract, undifferentiated, all-embracing benevolence, which is not contrary to concrete and determinate benevolences, but abstracts from them. It is to love, from so high, from so far away, that the object is lost sight of. Thus, from *Ying*, we cannot see the *Min Shan* mountains in the north. Yet they are there. It is an effect of distance. For filial piety to approach supreme goodness, it would be necessary for the son to love without regard for his parents, and for his parents to love him without regard for him. To love the whole empire without thought of it, and to be loved by it without being known by it, comes nearer to supreme goodness. To be more benevolent than *Yao* and *Shun* without realizing it, to do good to everyone without anyone suspecting it, this is supreme goodness, similar to the unconscious influence of heaven and earth, which makes everything evolve spontaneously. You see, it is not

---

56   On the Great Rule. See *Annals, Zhou* chapter 4; and *Textes Philosophiques*, page 25.

enough to appreciate filial piety to understand this... No doubt, filial and fraternal piety, ordinary kindness and fairness, faithfulness and loyalty, uprightness and constancy, all these virtues are somehow part of the supreme goodness, but they are very small in comparison with its greatness. It is said that to him who has all beauty, adornments add nothing; to him who has all wealth, gratification adds nothing; to him who has all honors, no distinction adds anything. It is the same with him who possesses absolute goodness, which is none other than Principle; he will occasionally practice all your lower order goodnesses, but they add nothing to him. And it is not from these details that we will define supreme goodness *a posteriori*; it is better to define it *a priori*, starting from the Principle."

C. *Biemen Cheng* said to the emperor *Huang Di*:

"When I heard your symphony *Xian Chi* performed near *Dong Ting* Lake, the first part frightened me, the second made me dizzy, and the third gave me a vague sensation from which I have not yet recovered."

"So it was meant to be," said the emperor. "This symphony contains everything. It is a human expression of celestial action, of universal evolution. — The first part expresses the contrast of terrestrial events occurring under celestial influence; the struggle of the five elements; the succession of the four seasons; the birth and decay of plants; the action and reaction of light and heaviness, of light and darkness, of sound and silence; the renewal of animal life, every spring, at the bursting of the thunder, after the lethargy of winter; the institution of human laws, of civil and military offices, and so on. All this is the sudden result of a series of events that take place during the year. All this, suddenly, without introductions, without transitions; in abrupt sounds, a succession of dissonances, as is the chain of deaths and births, appearances and disappearances, of all the ephemeral terrestrial realities. It must have frightened you. — The second part of the symphony reproduces, in soft or loud, prolonged and elongated sounds, the continuity of the action of *yin* and *yang*, the course of the two great luminaries, the arrival of the living and the departure of the dead. It is this continuous sequence as far as the eye can see, which stuns you with its infinity, to the point that, not knowing where you are standing, you lean against the trunk of a tree and sigh, overcome by the vertigo and anxiety caused by the emptiness. — The third part of the symphony expresses the productions of nature, the future of destinies. Hence the effervescence followed by calms; the murmur of the great forests, then a mysterious silence. For this is how beings go out from who knows where, and return to who knows where, in currents and waves. Only the Sage can understand this harmony, for only he understands nature and destiny. To grasp the threads of becoming, before being, when they are still taut in the cosmic loom, that is the celestial joy, which is felt but cannot be expressed. It consists, as Master *Yen* sang, in hearing that which has no sound yet, in seeing that which has no form yet, that which fills heaven and earth, that which encompasses space, the Principle, the engine of cosmic evolution. Without knowing it, you have remained in darkness. — My explanations have just led you from this vagueness to the knowledge of the Principle. Guard it well."

D. While Confucius was traveling to the west of the principality of *Wei*, his disciple *Yen Yuan* asked the master musician *Jin*:

"What do you think of my master's future?"

"I think," said master *Jin*, with a sigh, "that he will accomplish nothing."

"Why?" said *Yen Yuan*.

"Look," said *Jin*, "the straw dogs used in the offerings[57]. Before the offering, they are kept in chests, wrapped in beautiful cloths, while the representative of the deceased and the prior purify themselves by abstinence. After the offering, they are thrown away, trampled and burned. If they were put back into the chests, to be used on another occasion, all the inhabitants of the house would be tormented by nightmares, for these filters of evil would pour out the noxious influences with which they were filled. Now Confucius collects in his school the straw dogs of the rulers of antiquity (their books, filled with old memories that have become outdated and harmful). Hence the persecutions to which he was subjected in various places; the nightmares caused by his old straw dogs."

"To go by water, one takes a boat; to go by land, one takes a cart; impossible to travel by water in a cart, by land in a boat. Now the past times are like the present, like water and land; the empire of the *Zhou* and the duchy of *Lu* could be compared to a boat and a cart. To want to apply now the antiquated principles of the ancients, to pretend to use in the duchy of *Lu* the procedures of the empire of the *Zhou*, is like wanting to travel by boat on dry land, it is to attempt the impossible. Confucius labored in vain and brought misfortune upon himself, as did all those who tried to apply a certain system in different circumstances."

"Today, the bucket of the ancients has been abandoned for the counterbalanced ladle to raise the water, and no one feels the need to return to the bucket. Thus, the governmental procedures of the ancient emperors, which were appropriate in their time and are outdated now, should not be forcibly imposed in the present age. In every season certain fruits are eaten, the taste of which is agreeable at that time, while it would not be agreeable at another. The same is true of regulations and customs; they should vary with the times."

"Put the robe of the Duke of *Zhou* on a monkey. What will happen? He will tear it in rage, with his teeth and claws, and will not stand still until he has torn off the last shred. Now, antiquity and the present age are as different as the Duke of *Zhou* and a monkey. One should not dress the moderns in the costume of the ancients."

"In the past, when the beautiful *Xi Shi* had her tantrums, she was even more seductive. A very bad-looking woman, having seen her in this state, one day did the same thing she had seen her do. The result was that the rich villagers barricaded themselves in their homes, and the poor fled in terror with their wives and children. The ugly woman had only reproduced the fury, not the beauty of the beautiful woman. The same is true of Confucius' parody of antiquity. It makes people run away. This man will not succeed."

---

57   And funerals. See *Lao Zi*, chapter 5.

E. At the age of fifty-one, Confucius still had no notion of the Principle. Then he went to *Pei*, and visited *Lao Dan*.

"Ah, there you are!" said *Lao Dan*. "Are you the Sage of the North? What do you know about the Principle?"

"Nothing," said Confucius.

"Then," said *Lao Dan*, "why don't you look for it?"

"I have searched for it," said Confucius, "for five whole years, in the formulæ and numbers, without finding it."

"And so?" said *Lao Dan*.

"Then," said Confucius, "I searched for twelve whole years in the *yin* and the *yang*, also to no avail."

"I am not surprised," said *Lao Dan*, "if the Principle could be found in this way, it would long ago have become a gift among friends. Knowledge of the Principle is not so easily found or communicated. It assumes, in fact, that man is perfectly regulated."

"One should not try to monopolize the reputation to which so many men aspire. One must not take for oneself, exclusively, the notions of goodness and equity, which have already served so many ancients. One should only take one's share of these things, in due time. Otherwise, you will have the whole world against you, for others also want their share. The ancients did not accumulate anything. They wanted only one thing, the freedom to roam in the void, to speculate without restraint, to have no ties and no affairs. Thus they came to the knowledge of the Principle, which presupposes this detachment. Anyone who has been bound by the love of wealth, fame and power, is too distracted to be able to even strive for it. And as for government, which must consist in following exactly the movement of natural evolution, it is for the upright to rectify others. Of him who pretends to rectify others, not yet being himself upright, it must be said that reason does not yet shine in him[58]."

F. On another occasion, Confucius, having visited *Lao Dan*, explained to him his ideas on goodness and fairness.

"Listen," said the latter, "winnowers cannot see, because of the dust; when the mosquitoes are legion, it is impossible to rest. Your speeches about goodness and fairness have a similar effect on me; they blind me and make me panic. Come on! Leave the people alone! Believe what you will, in theory; but in practice, bend to the wind, accept the changes that have taken place in the world, do not beat the drum to remember the runaway son (what is left of antiquity; compare with chapter 13 E). Wild geese are naturally white, crows are naturally black; no dissertation will change this fact. The same is true of successive epochs, and of the men of those epochs. Your speeches will not turn the crows of today into the geese of yesteryear. You will not save what remains of the ancient world; its time has come. When the

---

58   How many blows to Confucius, who, ambitious and intriguing, pretended to have the secret of goodness and equity; pretended to monopolize, for himself and his disciples, the government of the fiefs and of the empire; etc.

waters dry up, the fish gather in the holes and try to save their lives by coating each other with the slime that covers them. Poor things! They should have scattered in time and gone into the deep water."

After this visit, Confucius remained for three days without speaking. At the end his disciples asked him:

"Master, how did you refute *Lao Dan*?"

"In the person of this man I saw the dragon," said Confucius. "The dragon folds visibly and then spreads invisibly, producing cloudy or serene weather, with no one understanding its powerful but mysterious action. I was surprised by this elusive man. He is too big for me, what could I say to refute him?"

G. "Then," said the disciple *Zi Gong*, "could not this man be the Sage, who is said to be withdrawn and silent, who spreads his influence everywhere, who is as mighty as thunder and as deep as the abyss, who acts like heaven and earth? Please allow me to go and see him."

With Confucius' permission, *Zi Gong* went to *Lao Dan*. The latter, after looking at him, said:

"I am very old and you are very young! What have you to teach me?"

Zi Gong said:

"The three great emperors and the five great kings did not rule in the same way, it is true, but they are all called Sages. Why do you alone deny them this title?"

"Come closer, boy, so that I may look at you more closely," said old *Lao Dan*. "So you say that these ancients did not rule in the same way."

"No doubt," said *Zi Gong*. "*Yao* abdicated. *Shun* appointed *Yu* as his successor. *Yu* and *Tang* waged war. King *Wen* surrendered to the tyrant *Zhou*. On the contrary, *Cheng Wang* overthrew him. Aren't these differences?"

"Come closer, boy, so that I can see you better," said old *Lao Dan* again. "Is this all you know of history? Then listen!"

"*Huang Di* organized his people into an empire, and therefore he wounded nature; but he did not care about the rest, not even about what Confucius considers most essential, such as mourning for dead parents; in his time, whether rites were performed or not, no one cared about that."

"*Yao* forced his people to perform mourning rites for their parents, but did not care about the rest."

"*Shun* pressured them to reproduce. By his command, women were to bear a child every ten months; children were to speak at five months and meet their fellow citizens before the age of three. Overwork introduced premature death into the world."

"*Yu* completely perverted the hearts of men. He legitimized murder, declaring that in war one killed bandits, not men, and therefore there was no evil. He then seized the empire for his family (he made it hereditary). From then on, the disorder got worse and worse. It was at its peak when the followers of Confucius and *Mo Zi* appeared, who invented what they call social relations, marriage laws, etc."

"And you say the ancients ruled the empire. No, they turned it upside down. They ruined, with their innovations, the basis of all stability, the strong influence of the sun and moon, of the mountains and rivers, of the four seasons. Their artificial knowledge was more fatal than the sting of a scorpion, than the tooth of a beast. And these men, who have failed to recognize the laws of nature and human destiny, arrogate to themselves the title of Sages! This is really too brazen!"

Zi Gong was stunned and uncomfortable by this outburst of *Lao Dan*.

H. Confucius said to *Lao Dan*:

"I have occupied myself with the Odes, the Annals, the Rites, the Music, the Mutations, and the Chronicles. I applied myself for a long time to the study of these six treatises, and became familiar with them. I spoke before seventy-two misguided princes, expounding to them the principles of the ancient rulers, the Dukes of *Zhou* and *Shao*, for their correction. None of them took advantage of my speeches. It is difficult to persuade these people."

"How fortunate!" said *Lao Zi*, "that none of them listened to you! If they had, they would have gotten worse. The six treatises are all garbage, accounts of events that happened in circumstances that no longer exist, of gestures that would be out of place in present circumstances. What can we deduce from a footprint, except that it was made by a foot? By whom? Why? How? and other circumstances, the print says nothing about all this. The same is true of the footprints left by events in history; they do not tell us about reality as it was, living and true."

"Each time has its own nature, as each being has its own nature; a nature that nothing can change. Herons fecundate by looking at each other, some insects buzz, others are hermaphrodites, others do the opposite. Just let them do it, each species according to its nature. Nature cannot be altered, destiny cannot be changed, time cannot be stopped, evolution cannot be obstructed. Let everything take its natural course, and you will only succeed: go against it, and you will only fail."

Confucius secluded himself in his house for three months to meditate on this lesson. At the end of this time, he went to *Lao Zi*.

"I understand now," he said to him. "Crows and magpies brood, fishes fertilize their young, digger wasps are born by transformation of a spider; men have successive sons, the birth of each makes the eldest weep. For a long time, I, *Qiu*, have kept out of the way of natural evolution, or even tried to push it back. That is why I failed to evolve mankind."

"Well," said Lao Zi. "Now, *Qiu*, you have found the key."

CHAPTER 15 - WISDOM AND STULTIFICATION

A. To have stultified ideas in the brain, and a high opinion of one's own singular morality; to break with the world and withdraw from it; to speak loudly and criticize others; in a word, to behave like pedants; this is what those do who live like anchorites in the mountains and in the valleys, despising the common paths, who end up dying of hunger, or drowned in some torrent.

To speak of goodness and equity, of loyalty and fidelity; to practice respect for others, simplicity, modesty; in a word, to constrain oneself in everything; this is what those who seek to pacify the world and mortify men do, whether they are itinerant or sedentary teachers. They frequent the courts exalt their merits, work to make a name for themselves, argue about rites and etiquette, wanting to regulate everything, they are politicians in search of a master to serve, a principality to organize, alliances to mediate.

To retire to the waters or to solitary places, to fish with a line or to do nothing, that is what lovers of nature and idleness do.

Breathing with moderation, evacuating the air contained in the lungs and replacing it with fresh air, helping one's own breathing with gestures similar to those of the climbing bear or the flying bird, this is what those who wish to live a long life do, the imitators of *Peng Zu*.

All these people are crazy. Let us now talk about serious men.

B. To have lofty aspirations, without preconceived prejudices; to aspire to perfection, but not according to the goodness-equity scheme; to rule without pretending to make a name for oneself; not to withdraw from the world; to live without breathing gymnastics; to have everything, and not to make a fuss about anything; to attract everyone, without doing anything for it, this is the way of heaven and earth, the way followed by the Daoist Sage.

Emptiness, peace, contentment, apathy, silence, global vision, non-intervention[59], this is the formula of heaven and earth, the secret of the Principle and its virtue. The Daoist sage acts in the same way. Calm, simple, selfless, no sadness creeps into his heart, no lust can move him; his conduct is perfect; his vital spirits remain intact. Throughout his life he acts like heaven; at death he enters into the great transformation. At rest, or in motion, he communes with the *yin* or the *yang* mode of the universe. It causes neither happiness nor misfortune to others. He only decides to act when he is forced to, when he cannot do otherwise. It rejects all science, all tradition, all precedent. It imitates in everything the indifferent opportunism of heaven. So he has nothing to suffer, neither from heaven, nor from beings, nor from men, nor from ghosts. During life he sails according to events; at death he stops. He does not think of the future, nor does he make plans. It shines without dazzling; it is faithful without compromise. In sleep he has no dreams, in wakefulness he is not melancholy. His vital spirits are always ready, his soul is always ready to act. Empty, peaceful, contented, simple, he communes with celestial virtue.

Pain and joy are similar vices, affection and resentment are similar excesses; he who loves or hates, has lost his balance. To know neither displeasure nor pleasure is the height of virtue; to be always the same, unchanged, is the height of peace; to cling to nothing is the height of emptiness; to have no relations with anyone is the height of apathy; to let go, to let be, is the height of disinterest.

---

59   Compare with chapter 13 A.

Incessant muscular fatigue wears out the body; incessant expenditure of energy exhausts it. Look at water. By its nature it is pure and calm. It is only impure or agitated when disturbed by violence. It is the perfect image of heavenly virtue, calm spontaneity. Purity without mixture, repose without alteration, apathy without action; movement conforming to that of heaven, unconscious, without expenditure of thought or effort; this is what preserves vital spirits. The possessor of an excellent *Gan Yue* sword keeps it carefully in a scabbard, and uses it only on great occasions, so as not to use it in vain. Curiously enough, most men take less trouble to preserve their vital spirit, which is more valuable than the best *Gan Yue* blade. For this life principle extends to everything, from the heaven above to the earth below, to the transformations of all beings, being so insignificant that it cannot be imagined, confusing its action with that of the Sovereign (the cosmic Sovereign, the soul of the world). Integrity and purity are what preserve the soul and prevent it from wasting away. In its state of integrity and purity, it communes with the celestial rule (synonymous with the High or Heavenly Sovereign). Hence the following aphorisms: the vulgar esteem fortune, the educated reputation, the learned the offices, the wise the integrity of his vital spirit; the principle of life is the purity and integrity which preserve it; purity means the absence of any mixture, integrity means the absence of any deficit; he whose vital spirit is perfectly pure and unadulterated, is a true Man.

CHAPTER 16 - NATURE AND CONVENTION

A. To pretend to amend nature by restoring it to its original state, by means of the studies made in the present schools; to wish to regulate the inclinations, by illuminating them with classical reasonings, is to show great blindness. The ancient sages knew no other science than that which emanated spontaneously from the calm of their nature, the simple apprehension of things, which did not disturb them. Their natural reason, derived from the Principle, functioned normally in their inner peace. Thus were born these simple notions: goodness, to bear all things; equity, to be reasonable. Equity was answered by loyalty; frank truth produced joy and its expression music; mutual trust produced courtesy and its expression rites. Later, having been distorted, rites and music became an element of perversion, as happens with everything that ceases to be in conformity with nature.

In the beginning, men were simple, like nature in its beginnings. Then there was no disturbance in the natural movements, no disorder of physical forces. The course of the seasons was regular, no being suffered, there were no untimely deaths, no theories or sciences. It was the age of perfect unity and union, of man with nature and of men with each other. No one intervened in the natural order. Everything followed its course spontaneously.

However, the decadence came. It began with the institutions of *Sui Ren* and *Fu Xi* (the artificial production of fire, marriage and family laws), which seemed to be a step forward, but inaugurated the ruin of the original simplicity and promiscuity. The decline was accentuated in the time of *Shen Nong* and *Huang Di* (abandonment of nomadic life, agriculture, formation of the state), increasing welfare, but at the cost of the former spontaneity. It was further accentuated when *Yao* and *Shun* reigned and introduced systematic modification (through laws and schools), compulsory practice of a so-called conventional good. This was the end of primitive morality. From then on, men substituted innate instinct for their theories, and peace disappeared from the empire. Finally, the progress of letters and sciences completed the extinction of what was left of natural simplicity, and filled minds with distractions. So now everything is nothing but disorder and perversion.

B. From this historical review it follows that the adoption of conventional morality was the ruin of primitive morality, and that this ruin of primitive nature was the ruin of the world. Nature and convention are two irreconcilable contradictions. The followers of these two paths cannot coexist. They cannot even understand each other, for they neither think nor speak alike. A sage of the party of nature (Daoist) will not need to go and hide in the mountains and forests; living in the midst of his fellow citizens, he will be unknown, because he is misunderstood. This situation is not recent; it goes back a long time. The ancient Sages, commonly called the Hidden Ones, did not become invisible, did not keep their mouths shut, did not deliberately hide their wisdom. They did not hide. It was their total opposition to their time that made them hidden, unnoticed, unknown and misunderstood. In good times they could have reshaped the world, giving it back its lost simplicity. But unfavorable times prevented them from doing so, so they spent their lives guarding the notion of primitive perfection and waiting in peace.

These men did not seek varied knowledge through subtle disquisitions, as do the sophists of today; they did not want to know everything or be able to do everything. Rather, they were reserved, almost timid, and remained in their place, meditating on their nature. The subject is vast enough to occupy a man, and difficult enough to demand reserve. To pretend to be teachers of the doctrine of the Principle, with imperfect science and conduct, would be to injure the doctrine, not to serve it. Therefore they labored in their own person, rejoicing in their approach to their goal. They did not dream, like the ambitious of our day (Confucians), of ranks and distinctions. What can these artificial things do for the perfection of nature? Nothing at all! They are even a poor satisfaction, because they are so precarious, for he who has obtained them cannot be sure that he will keep them. The Wise are equally indifferent in fortune and distress, neither rejoicing nor grieving over anything. When a gain makes someone happy, or a loss saddens him, it is a sign that the object was loved by him; affection and affliction are two disorders. Those who give their affections to any being, who do violence to their natural instincts by any convention, these are doing the opposite of what they ought to do. They should follow only their instinct, and live absolutely detached.

CHAPTER 17 - THE AUTUMN FLOOD

A. It was the time of the autumn flood. Hundreds of swollen rivers poured their waters into the Yellow River, whose bed had widened so much that, from one bank to the other, one could not distinguish an ox from a horse. This sight delighted the Genie of the River, who thought that there was nothing in the world better than his domain. Following the current, he went down to the North Sea. At the sight of its waters, which stretched eastward without limit, he observed that there was something better than his domains, and said with a sigh to the Genie of the Sea:

"The adage 'he who knows little, thinks himself great,' applies to me. I have heard it said that there was better than Confucius and his heroes, but I did not believe it. Now that I have seen the extent of your empire, I also begin to believe that your doctrine is superior to that of Confucius[60]. I was right to come to you to be taught by you, otherwise the true scholars would have ended up laughing at me."

"Welcome," said the Genie of the Sea. "Yes, the frog that lives at the bottom of a well has no idea what the sea can be; it only knows his hole. The ephemeral being, born and dead in summer, knows not what ice is; it has known but one season. A narrow-minded scholar like Confucius knows nothing of the higher science of the Principle, brutalized as he is by the prejudices of his caste. Having emerged from your narrow bed, you have seen the boundless ocean. Convinced now of your imperfection, you have become capable of the higher science. Listen then!... Of all waters, the greatest is the ocean. Innumerable rivers pour their waters into it without ceasing, without increasing it. It flows continuously down the eastern ravine without diminishing. It neither rises nor falls, like the great rivers; its level is always the same, immutable. Such is my empire. Well, its immensity has never inspired me with any pride. Why not? Because, in comparison with heaven and earth, the physical cosmos, I find it small. I feel that I am but a pebble, a bush on a mountain. Being so small, why should I value myself so much? Compared to the universe, the abysses of the four oceans are reduced to small holes in an immense surface. Compared to the earth, our China is reduced to the proportional dimensions of a grain in a huge barn. The totality of existing beings being expressed by the number ten thousand, humanity is worth only one unit. In fact, nowhere on the whole inhabited earth does the proportion of mankind to other beings exceed this number. Thus, mankind is to the mass of the universe what a hair is to the body of a horse. This is what has so troubled the ancient rulers, tormented the wise, and wearied the politicians; it is reduced to a fetus. *Bo Yi*, the Confucian hero, is reputed to be great for the part he played on this small stage; and Confucius is reputed to be a scholar, for having declaimed there. These men believed themselves to be something, because they knew no better; just as you believed yourself to be the first of the genies of water, before you had seen the sea."

Remembering the discussions of the sophists of the time, on the notion of the great and the small, the Genie of the River asked the Genie of the Sea:

---

60   School on the banks of the Yellow River. The Genie of the Sea is Daoist. The River Genie is Confucian and will convert to Daoism.

"So from now on I shall consider the universe as the expression of absolute greatness, and a hair as the symbol of absolute smallness, shall I not?"

"No," said the Genie of the Sea, "it is not so. The actual universe is not the expression of absolute greatness. For this quantity is not constant. It varies in the course of time, in the course of evolution, according to genesis and cessation. Considered thus, by high science, things change their aspect, the absolute becomes relative. Thus, the difference between the great and the small disappears in the vision of infinite distance. The difference between the past and the present is likewise erased, anteriority and posteriority disappearing, in the unlimited chain; and consequently the past no longer inspires melancholy, and the present is no longer of interest. The difference between prosperity and misery vanishes likewise, these ephemeral phases disappearing in the eternal evolution; and consequently, possession no longer causes pleasure, losing no longer causes sadness. For those who see from this distance and height, life is no longer a happiness, death is no longer a misfortune; for they know that periods succeed one another, that nothing can last. Man ignores much more than he knows. Compared to the universe, he is infinitely small. To conclude from the little we know, from the little we are, to what we do not know, to the universality of beings, is a process that leads to nothing. So do not use, in your speculations, the hair that you are, as a pattern of smallness; and the changing cosmos, as a pattern of greatness."

Satisfied that he had found such a good teacher, the Genie of the River continued his interrogations.

"The philosophers affirm," he said, "that an extremely attenuated being becomes zero; and that the same extremely amplified one becomes infinite."

"Yes and no," said the Genie of the Sea. "The notions of extreme attenuation and amplification are not clearly established by taking the same being as an example. The extremely faint conceivable is the abstract essence. The basis of measurable amplification is concrete matter. Essence and matter are two different things, which coexist in every sentient being, superior to zero. Zero is what calculus can no longer divide; infinity is what numbers can no longer encompass. Speech can describe concrete matter, thought reaches the abstract essence. Beyond this, metaphysical intuitions, inner dictates, which are neither matter nor essence, are only known by subjective appreciation. Following these inexpressible intuitions, the superior man does many things in a very different way from the vulgar, but without despising the latter, because he does not have the same lights. It is these that place him above honor and ignominy, above rewards and punishments. They make him forget the distinctions between the great and the small, between good and evil. Hence it is said that the man of the Principle remains silent; the perfect man seeks nothing; the great man has no more self, for he has united all parts into one; an ecstatic contemplation of universal unity."

The Genie of the River insisted again, wanting to know on what the distinctions between the noble and the vile, the great and the small, etc., are based. The Genie of the Sea replied:

"If we consider beings in the light of the Principle, these distinctions do not exist, being all one. In their own eyes, beings are all noble, and regard others as vile, in relation to themselves; a subjective point of view. In the eyes of the vulgar, they are noble or vile, according to a certain routine appreciation, independent of reality; following the conventional point of view. Considered objectively and relatively, all beings are great in relation to those smaller than themselves, all are small in relation to those larger than themselves; heaven and earth are but a grain, a hair is a mountain. Considered in terms of utility, all beings are useful for what they can do, all are useless for what they cannot; East and West coexist, by opposition, necessarily, each having its own attributes which the other does not have. Finally, in relation to the observer's taste, all beings have some facet in which they please some, and some in which they displease others; both *Yao* and *Jie* had admirers and detractors."

"The abdication ruined neither *Yao* nor *Shun*, but it ruined Baron *Kuai*. The revolt benefited emperors *Tang* and *Wu*, while it lost duke *Bo*. Depending on the time and circumstances, the result of the same actions is not the same; what is convenient for someone or in certain circumstances, is not convenient for another or in other circumstances. The same is true of the qualification of acts; what is noble in someone or in certain circumstances will be vile in another or in other circumstances. All this is relative and variable."

"A battering ram is the best thing for opening a wall, while for plugging a hole it would be an absolutely inept instrument; the means differ. The steeds of the emperor *Mu*, which traveled a thousand stades a day, would not have been worth as much as a cat if it had been a matter of catching a rat; the qualities are different. The owl counts its feathers and gathers its fleas at night, while in daylight it cannot see a mountain; the natures are different. *A fortiori*, nothing is fixed in moral things, esteem, opinion, and so on. Everything has a double aspect."

"Consequently, to want good without evil, right without wrong, order without disorder, is to show that one understands nothing of the laws of the universe; it is to dream of a heaven without earth, a *yin* without a *yang*; the double aspect coexists for everything. To wish to distinguish, as real entities, these two inseparable correlatives, is to show weak reason; heaven and earth are one, *yin* and *yang* are one; and likewise so are the opposite aspects of all opposites. Of the ancient rulers, some obtained the throne by succession, others by usurpation. All are called good rulers, because they acted according to the taste of the people of their time, and pleased their time. Those who act in the wrong time, against the taste of their contemporaries, are called usurpers. Meditate on these things, O Genie of the River, and you will understand that there is neither greatness nor littleness, neither nobility nor baseness, neither absolute good nor absolute evil; but that all these things are relative, depend upon times and circumstances, upon the appreciation of men, upon opportunity."

"But then," replied the Genie of the River, "practically, what shall I do? What shall I not do? What shall I admit? What shall I reject? Is there, yes or no, a morality, a rule of morality?"

"From the point of view of the Principle," replied the Genie of the Sea, "there is only an absolute unity, and changeable aspects. To put anything absolute outside of the Principle would be to err about the Principle. So there is no absolute morality, but opportunistic expediency only. In practice, follow the times and circumstances. Be uniformly just as a ruling prince, uniformly beneficent as an earth god, uniformly indifferent as an individual; embrace all beings, for all are one."

"The Principle is immutable, it has no beginning and no end. Beings are changeable, they are born and die, without stable permanence. From non-being they pass into being, without rest in any form, in the course of years and times. Beginnings and endings, growth and decay, follow one another. This is all we can see, as to the norm, the law, that governs beings. Their life passes on the world stage, as a snatched horse passes before our eyes. There is not a moment without change, without vicissitudes. And you ask yourself, what to do, what not to do? To follow the course of the transformations, to act according to the circumstances of the moment, that is all there is to do."

"Finally," said the Genie of the River, "please show me the advantages of the intelligence of the Principle."

"These advantages, said the Genie of the Sea, are as follows: He who knows the Principle, knows the law derived from it, applies it correctly, and is consequently respected by all beings. To the man whose conduct is completely wise, fire does not burn him, water does not drown him, cold and heat do not harm him, wild beasts do not hurt him. It is not that he has nothing to fear from these dangers. But his wisdom calculates so well that he avoids all misfortune; conducting himself with such circumspection that no harm overtakes him[61]."

"This wisdom, which results from the knowledge of the Principle, is what has been called the heavenly (natural) element in man, as opposed to the human (artificial) element. This heavenly element (nature) must predominate, if action is to be in conformity with the original perfection."

"Please make me more sensitive to the difference between the celestial and the human," insisted the Genie of the River.

"Behold," said the Genie of the Sea. "Oxen and horses are four-footed, that is the heavenly element (their nature). That they have a bit in their mouth or a ring in their nose, that is the human element (artificial, unnatural). The human must not suffocate the celestial, the artificial must not extinguish the natural, the artifact must not destroy the entity of truth. To restore one's own nature is to return to the first truth of being."

B. A *Kui* (a fabulous animal) with one leg, asked a millipede:
"How did you manage to have so many feet?"
The millipede said:

---

61   So not invulnerability, as later interpreted; but, such great prudence that he succeeds in evading all danger.

"Nature made me like this, with a central body, and thread-like legs all around. I move my heavenly springs (what nature gave me), without knowing why or how."

The millipede said to the snake:

"Without one foot, you move faster than I who have so many; how do you do it?"

"I don't know," said the snake. "I glide naturally."

The snake said to the wind:

"I move forward by means of my vertebrae and my sides; you have none, and yet you go from the North Sea to the South Sea faster than I do by slithering; how do you do it?"

"I blow naturally," said the wind, "even to the breaking of trees and the blowing down of houses. But you little beings, I have no control over you, you dominate me. Only one being is not dominated by anything; he is the Sage, possessor of the Principle."

C. Confucius passed by *Kuang*, and an armed troop of *Song* men surrounded him in such a way that escape was impossible. Confucius took his lute and began to sing. His disciple *Zi Lu* asked him:

"Master, how can you be so cheerful, under the present circumstances?"

"I did what I could to avoid this adventure," said Confucius; "therefore, it is not my fault, but that of fate. I also did what I could to break through; if I did not succeed, it was not because of my negligence, but because of the misfortune of the times. Under *Yao* and *Shun*, none of the Sages of that time were reduced to the extreme which now affects me, not because of their greater prudence, but because fate was then favorable to all. Under *Jie* and *Zhou*, none of the Sages of the time broke through, not because of their lesser ability, but because fate was then unfavorable to all… Not to fear sea monsters is the courage of fishermen. Not to fear ferocious beasts, is the courage of hunters. Not to fear drawn swords, to look with the same countenance on death and life, is the courage of warriors… To know that no happiness comes but in due time, that all misfortune is written in destiny, and consequently not to fear even in the face of imminent danger, but to trust stoically in destiny, that is the courage of the Wise. You, wait a moment, and you will see what is written in my destiny."

A few moments after the sage had thus spoken, the chief of the men-at-arms came up and said.

"We had mistaken you for one *Yang Hu*, whom we have to arrest; please excuse our mistake"… And they left[62].

D. *Gong Sun Long* the sophist, said to Prince *Mou* of *Wei*:

"As a young man, I first studied the doctrine of the ancient rulers of the classical traditions; then I delved into the question of goodness and equity (Confucianism);

---

62   This fragment is the Daoist counterpart of a Confucian text. In reality, Confucius believed that he would escape, because he saw himself as the ark destined to save the rites and other antiquities. Here he acts out of sheer fatalism.

then I examined resemblances and dissimilarities, substances and accidents, yes and no, lawful and unlawful (logic, morality); I got to the bottom of the theories and arguments of all the schools, and thought myself really very strong, when a certain *Zhuang Zhou* stunned and confused me. I do not know whether it was a defect in my dialectics or a deficit in my science; but the fact remains that I, the rhetorical sophist, remained mute before him, unable to reply and not daring to question him."

Prince *Mou* took a seat, heaved a sigh, raised his eyes to heaven, smiled and said:

"Do you know the story of the frog in the old well, and the turtle in the eastern sea?" 'How happy I am in my well,' said the frog to the turtle; 'I can jump over the curbstone, curl up in the holes between the bricks, swim on the surface, dive in the mud; of all the inhabitants of this well, larvae, tadpoles, none can do so much as I; so I prefer my well to your sea; try a little of its charms'... To please the frog, the turtle tried. But once it got its right leg into the well, it was impossible for it to get its left leg in, so narrow was the well. After pulling its leg out, it gave the frog the following information about the sea. 'It is more than a thousand stades long. It is deeper than the height of a thousand men standing on top of each other. In the time of Emperor *Yu*, in ten years there were nine floods; all this water flowed into the sea, without the sea rising. In the time of the emperor *Tang*, in eight years there were seven droughts; no water entered the sea, and yet the sea did not experience the slightest decrease. Duration, quantity, these terms do not apply to the sea. This constant immobility is the charm of my dwelling'... At these words, the frog in the well became dizzy and lost his head. — And you who, not knowing well the difference between yes and no, are examining the statements of *Zhuang Zhou*, are you not like the frog who tried to understand the sea? You are trying to do what you cannot do. It is like getting a mosquito to caress a mountain, or trying to get an earthworm to fight a torrent. What do you hear in the sublime language of this man? Frog of the old well! It descends to the subterranean springs and ascends to the firmament. It stretches beyond space, unfathomably deep, immeasurably mysterious. Its dialectical rules and logical distinctions are not instruments proportionate to such an object. It is as if you wanted to embrace the heavens with a pipe, or cut the earth with an awl. — Go now and ask no more questions, lest the same thing happen to you as to those sons of *Shou Ling*, who were sent to be educated at *Han Dan*. They unlearned the rude way of walking of *Shou Ling*, and did not learn the distinguished way of walking of *Han Dan*; so they returned to their native land walking on all fours. Do not ask for more, for you would forget your vulgar sophist knowledge, without understanding anything of the higher science of *Zhuang Zhou*."

Gong Sun Long, having listened to this peroration with his mouth open and his tongue lolling out, fled in dismay.

E. While *Zhuang Zhou* was fishing on the banks of the river *Pu*, the king of *Chu* sent two of his great officials to offer him the position of minister. Without lifting his line, without taking his eyes off his float, *Zhuang Zhou* said to them.

"I have heard that the king of *Chu* preciously preserves in the temple of his ancestors the shell of a transcendental tortoise, sacrificed, to serve for divination, three thousand years ago. Tell me, if given a choice, would this turtle have preferred to die so that its shell would be honored, or would it have preferred to live dragging its tail in the mud of the swamps?"

"It would have preferred to live dragging its tail in the mud of the swamps," said the two great officers, in unison.

"Then," said *Zhuang Zhou*, "go back to where you came from; I, too, would rather drag my tail in the swamp mud. I will go on living obscurely but freely; I do not want a burden, which often costs the bearer his life, and which always costs him peace."

F. Being *Hui Zi* minister of the principality of *Liang*, *Zhuang Zhou* went to visit him. Someone made *Hui Zi* believe that *Zhuang Zhou* came with the intention of supplanting him. Immediately, *Hui Zi* ordered a three-day and three-night search throughout the principality in order to apprehend him. *Zhuang Zhou*, who had not yet entered *Liang*, was not captured, but learned of it. Later, having found *Hui Zi*, he said to him:

"Do you know this southern bird, which is called *argus*? When it flies from the south to the north, it only perches on *eleococca* trees, only feeds on the seeds of the *melia* tree, only drinks from the purest springs. However, one day as it flew by, an owl devouring a dead field mouse in a field feared that it would fight for its carrion and let out a cry to intimidate it. The minister of *Liang* did the same to me."

G. *Zhuang Zhou* and *Hui Zi* were recreating on the bridge of a stream. *Zhuang Zhou* said:

"Look how the fish jump! That is the pleasure of fish."

"You are not a fish," said *Hui Zi*, "how do you know what the pleasure of fish is?"

"You are not me," said *Zhuang Zhou*; "how do you know that I do not know the pleasure of fish?"

"I am not you," said *Hui Zi*, "and, consequently, I do not know all that you know or do not know, I grant you; but, at any rate, I know that you are not a fish, and it is established, therefore, that you do not know what the pleasure of fish is."

"You are trapped," said *Zhuang Zhou*. "Let us return to your first question. You asked me, 'How do you know what the pleasure of fish is?' By this sentence you admitted that I knew; for you would not have asked me the how of what you knew that I did not know. And now, how did I know it? By direct observation, at the bridge of the stream. A way unknown to the sophists of the time, charlatans who observed nothing."

CHAPTER 18 - PERFECT JOY

A. Is there, or is there not, a state of perfect contentment under heaven? Is there, or is there not, a way to make the life of the body last? To achieve this, what should we do, what should we avoid, what should we use, and what should we abstain from?

The common people seek their satisfaction in riches, dignities, longevity, and the esteem of others; in rest, good food, good clothes, beauty, music, and the like. They fear poverty, obscurity, short life and disrespect from others; deprivation of rest; they seek good food, good clothing, good sights and sounds. If they don't get these things, they grieve and are saddened... Isn't it silly to relate everything to the body? Some of these things are even external and foreign to the body; such as riches accumulated beyond the use one can put them to, the dignities and esteem of others. And yet the common people exhaust their strength and torture themselves over these things day and night. In truth, worries are born with man and follow him throughout his life; even in the daze of old age, the fear of death does not leave him. Only military officers do not fear death, and are esteemed by the common people for it; rightly or wrongly, I do not know; for, if their bravery deprives them of life, it preserves that of their fellow-citizens; there are pros and cons. Civil officials who attract death by their impertinent censures, on the other hand, are blamed by the vulgar; rightly or wrongly, I do not know; for, if their frankness deprives them of life, it assures them of glory; there are pros and cons. As for the common people, I confess that I do not understand how one can derive satisfaction from what makes them happy; the fact is that the objects that make them happy do not make me happy. For me, happiness consists in inaction, while the vulgar people struggle. The adage is true: the supreme satisfaction is to have nothing to satisfy; the supreme glory is not to be glorified. Every act is disputed, and will be called good by some, bad by others. Only what has not been done cannot be criticized. Inaction is the supreme satisfaction, that is what keeps the body alive. Let me support my assertion with an illustrious example. Heaven owes its clarity to non-action, earth owes its stability to non-action; together, these two non-actions, the heavenly and the earthly, produce all beings. Heaven and earth, the saying goes, do everything without doing anything. Where is the man who manages to do nothing? This man will also be able to do everything.

B. When *Zhuang Zhou*'s wife died, *Hui Zi* went to mourn her, according to custom. He found *Zhuang Zhou* bent over, chanting, and beating the rhythm in a bowl, which he held between his legs. Surprised, *Hui Zi* said to him:

"That you do not mourn the death of the woman who was the companion of your life and who bore you children is strange enough; but that you sing and drum before her corpse is too much."

"At the time of her death I was affected for a moment," said *Zhuang Zhou*. "Then, reflecting on the event, I understood that it was not reason for it. There was a time when this being had not been born, had no organized body, had not even a place of tenuous matter, but was contained indistinctly in the great mass. A turn of this mass gave her her subtle matter, which became an organized body, which became animated and was born. Another turn of the mass, and she died. The phases of death and life follow each other, like the periods of the four seasons. She who was my wife sleeps now in the great bedroom (the intermediate of heaven and earth), awaiting her new transformation. If I were to mourn her, I would seem to know nothing of destiny (of the universal and inescapable law of transformations). But since I know something about it, I do not mourn her."

C. *Zhi Li* and *Hua Ji* (fictitious characters) were contemplating together the tombs of the ancients, scattered on the plain at the foot of the mountains of *Kun Lun*, where *Huang Di* settled and found his rest. Suddenly, they both realized that they had anthrax in their left arm (a disease that used to be fatal in China). After the first moment of surprise. *Zhi Li* asked:

"Does it scare you?"

"Why should it scare me? *Hua Ji* replied."Life is a borrowed thing, a passing state, a stage in the dust and dirt of this world. Death and life follow each other, like day and night. And then, have we not just contemplated, in the tombs of the ancients, the effect of the law of transformation? When this law comes to us in our turn, why should we complain?"

D. On his way to the kingdom of *Chu*, *Zhuang Zhou* saw, by the side of the road, a skull lying, emaciated but intact. Stroking it with his riding crop, he asked:

"Did you die out of banditry or out of devotion to your country? Out of misconduct or out of misery? Or did you die naturally, your time having come?"

Then, after picking up the skull, he used it as a pillow the next night.

At midnight the skull appeared to him in a dream and said:

"You have spoken to me in the style of sophists and rhetoricians, as one who holds human things to be true. Now, after death, these things are finished. Do you want me to speak to you about the hereafter?"

"With pleasure," answered *Zhuang Zhou*.

The skull said:

"After death, there are no more superiors or inferiors, no seasons or works. It is rest, the constant time of heaven and earth. This peace surpasses the happiness of kings."

"Bah!" said *Zhuang Zhou*, "if you obtained from the governor of destiny (the Principle) that your body, bones, flesh and skin; that your father, mother, wife, children, people and acquaintances were returned to you, I believe you would not be angry."

The skull looked at him with sunken eye sockets, sneered and said.

"No! I would not give up my royal peace, to return to human misery."

E. When *Yen Yuan*, his beloved disciple, departed for the principality of *Qi*, Confucius looked sad. The disciple *Zi Gong* rose from his mat and said:

"May I dare to ask you why you are saddened by this journey of *Hui*?"

"I will tell you," replied Confucius. "Once, *Guan Zi* said these words, which have always seemed to me very true: 'A small bag cannot contain a large object; a short rope cannot reach the bottom of the well.' Yes, the capacity of every being is included in its destiny, nothing can be taken away from it, nothing can be added to it. That is why I fear that if, following his convictions and his zeal, *Hui* exposes to the Marquis of *Qi* the theories of *Yao* and *Shun*, of *Huang Di*, of *Sui Ren*, of *Shen Nong*, the latter, a man of limited capacity, will see in his speeches a criticism of his government, will become angry and will put him to death."

"Opportunism is the only success factor. Not everything suits everyone. One should not judge others by oneself. Once a sea bird flew to the gates of the capital of *Lu*. As the phenomenon was extraordinary, the marquis thought that perhaps it was a transcendent being visiting his principality. Therefore, he went in person to look for the bird and took it to the temple of his ancestors, where he gave it a banquet. Before it was played the *Giu Shao* symphony of the emperor *Shun*. They offered it the great sacrifice, an ox, a goat and a pig. However, the bird, with haggard eyes and anguished look, did not touch the minced meat or taste the wine. After three days, it died of hunger and thirst. The marquis, judging the bird's tastes by his own, had treated it as he treated himself, and not as one treats a bird. A seabird needs space, forests and plains, rivers and lakes, fish for food, freedom to fly its own way and perch where it pleases. To hear men talk was a torment to this poor bird; how much more the music they played to it, and all the movement they made around it. If the symphony *Giu Shao* by *Shun*, or even the symphony *Xian Chi* by *Huang Di*, were played on the shores of *Dong Ting* Lake, the birds would take flight, the quadrupeds would flee, the fish would plunge into the depths of the waters, and men would listen in wonder. This is because fish live in water and men die in it. The nature of beings being diverse, their tastes are not the same. Even among men there are differences, and what pleases some does not please others. Therefore, the ancient sages did not suppose that all men had the same capacity, and they did not employ just anyone for anything. They classified men according to their works and treated them according to their results. This fair evaluation of individuals is the condition of all success. If *Yen Hui* correctly appreciates the Marquis of *Qi* and speaks to him accordingly, he will succeed; otherwise he will perish."

F. While *Lie Zi*, who was on a journey, was taking his meal by the roadside, he saw an old skull[63], picked it up and said to it.

"You and I know what death and life are; that this distinction is not real, but only modal; that it is not necessary to say of you that you rest, and of me that I move; the wheel turning and transformations succeed each other without ceasing. The germs of life are numerous and indeterminate. Thus a germ will become a duckweed leaf if it falls into a pond, a carpet of moss if it is thrown on a hill. As it rises, the moss becomes the *Wu Tu* plant, whose roots become worms, whose leaves become butterflies. These butterflies produce a larva, which lives under the hearths, and is called *Qu Tuo*. After a thousand days, this *Qu Tuo* becomes the bird *Qian Wu Gu*, whose saliva gives rise to the insect *Si Mi*. This becomes *Shi Xi*, then *Mou Rui*, then *Fu Kuan*… The plants *Yang Xi* and *Bu Sun* are two alternate

---

63   Compare *Lie Zi*, ch. 1 E, and above, paragraph D.

forms. From the old bamboos emerges the insect *Qing Ning*, which becomes a leopard, then a horse, then a man. Man enters the loom of the incessant universal revolution. In turn, all beings come out of the great cosmic loom, to return to it in due course; and so on[64]."

CHAPTER 19 - THE MEANING OF LIFE

A. He who has penetrated into the meaning of life, is no longer anxious about that which does not contribute to life. He who has penetrated into the nature of destiny, no longer seeks to scrutinize that inscrutable entity. To maintain the body, one must use the proper means, but not in excess, for any excess is useless. Moreover, one must strive to maintain the vital spirit, without which the body is doomed. The living being cannot oppose its vivification (when it is born); neither can it oppose that one day (when it dies) its life will be withdrawn. The common man imagines that to preserve life it is enough to maintain the body. He is mistaken. Besides, and above all, it is necessary to avoid the wearing out of the vital spirit, which is practically impossible amidst the worries of the world. Therefore, in order to preserve and maintain life, it is necessary to abandon the world and its worries. It is in the tranquility of a regulated existence, in peaceful communion with nature, that one finds a renewal of vitality, a renewal of life. This is the fruit of understanding the meaning of life.

Let us repeat: it is the abandonment of cares and concerns that preserves life; for this abandonment preserves the body from fatigue and the vital spirit from wear and tear. He whose body and vital spirit are intact and ready, is united with nature. Now nature is the mother-father of all beings. The being is formed by condensation; it dissolves by dissipation, to become another being. And if, at the moment of this dissipation, its body and vital spirit are intact, it is able to transmigrate. Quintessentialized, he becomes a collaborator of heaven[65].

B. *Lie Zi* asked *Yin* (*Yin Xi*), the guardian of the passage, confidant of *Lao Zi*:

"The superior man penetrates all bodies (stone, metal, says the commentary) without experiencing any resistance from them; he is not burned by fire; no altitude gives him vertigo; for what reason is this so, tell me?"

"Only because," said *Yin*, "it has kept pure and intact the original vital spirit received at its birth; not by any process, no formula. Sit down, I will explain. All material beings have their own form, shape, sound and color. From these various qualities come their mutual enmities (fire destroys wood, etc.). In the primordial state of universal unity and immobility, these oppositions did not exist. They

---

64   Daoist transformism; compare *Lie Zi*, ch. 1 E. Neither death nor life, but indestructible germs, constituting individuals; but continuous transformation of the forms of the sensible sheath of these individuals.

65   That is to say, says the commentary, that it passes from the category of beings influenced by heaven and earth, to the mass influencing heaven and earth, to the great whole as an integral part. Daoist notion of cooperation with heaven, can be compared with the Indian notion of withdrawal in *Brahman*.

all derive from the diversification of beings, and from their contacts caused by the universal turning. They would cease if diversity and motion ceased, which immediately cease to affect the being that has reduced its individual being and its particular motion to almost nothing. This being (the perfect daoist sage) no longer conflicts with any other being, because it is established in the infinite, erased in the indefinite. It has reached and is at the starting point of transformations, a neutral point where no conflicts occur (which only occur on certain paths). By the concentration of his nature, by the nourishment of his vital spirit, by the gathering of all his powers, he has united himself to the beginning of all genesis. His nature being complete, his vital spirit intact, no being can touch him."

"For example, if a man who is absolutely drunk falls from a car, he may be bruised, but not killed. Why, are his bones and joints different from those of other men? No, but at the moment of the fall, this man's vital spirit, concentrated by unconsciousness, was absolutely intact. At the moment of the fall, in view of his unconsciousness, the idea of life and death, fear and hope, did not move this man's heart. He himself did not stiffen, and the ground was not hard for him, so he did not break any limbs. This drunkard owed the integrity of his body to his drunken state. Thus the perfect Sage will be preserved intact by his state of union with nature. The Sage is hidden in nature, so nothing can harm him."

"However, he who is wounded must not blame that which has wounded him; he must blame himself, for his vulnerability is a proof of imperfection. A reasonable man does not blame the sword that wounded him, or the tile that fell on him. If all men would contemplate their imperfection as the cause of their misfortunes, there would be perfect peace, the end of wars and torments. It would be the end of the reign of this false human nature (artificial nature invented by politicians), which has filled the world with bandits; it would be the beginning of the reign of the true heavenly nature (natural nature), the source of all good deeds. Not to repress one's own nature, not to believe men, is the way to return to the truth (to the original integrity)."

C. When Confucius was on his way to the kingdom of *Chu*, he came out of a forest and saw a hunchback catching cicadas on the fly, with a rod[66], as surely as one catches an object with one's hand.

"You are very clever," said Confucius, "tell me your secret."

"My secret," said the hunchback, "is this: For about six months I practiced keeping several balls balanced on the end of my rod. When I succeeded in balancing two of them, few cicadas escaped me. When I managed to balance three, only one out of ten escaped. When I managed to balance five, I didn't miss any more. My secret is to concentrate all my energies on the target. I have mastered my arm, my whole body, so that they feel no more excitement or distraction than a piece of

---

66   Commentators explain it in two ways. He poked them in the air, some say, which is hardly credible. The end of the rod was coated with glue, say others, which is more likely. Compare with *Lie Zi*, ch. 2 J.

wood. In the vast universe full of things, I only see the cicada I want to catch. Since there is nothing to distract me, I naturally catch it."

Addressing his disciples, Confucius said:

"Unify intentions; have a single intention, which merges with the vital energy; this is the summary of this hunchback's speech."

D. *Yen Yuan*, the favorite disciple, said to Confucius:

"While crossing the *Shang* rapids[67], the boatman maneuvered his boat with marvelous skill. I asked him:"

"How do you manage to maneuver so well!"

"A swimmer," he said, "learns it easily; a diver knows it without having learned it…"

"What is the meaning of this answer, which I did not understand?"

"Here is the meaning," said Confucius (speaking as a Daoist master). "A swimmer thinks little of the water, since he is familiar with its dangers, which he no longer fears; a diver does not think of it at all, since he is in the water as in his element. The sense of danger affects little the swimmer, who has almost full use of his natural faculties. As the diver is not affected by the sensation of danger at all, he is completely at ease in the water and consequently rules it perfectly."

"In archery, if the prize offered is a baked clay object of little value, the archer will not be influenced and will have free use of all his skill. If the prize is a bronze or jade brooch for the belt, the archer being disturbed, his aim will be more uncertain. If the prize offered is a gold object, his aim, strongly influenced, will be quite uncertain. In each case it is the same man, with the same skill, but more or less affected by an external object. Any distraction stuns and irritates."

E. Duke *Wei* of *Zhou*, receiving *Tian Kai Zhi* in audience, said to him:

"I have heard that your master *Zhu Xian* studied the problem of the preservation of life. Please repeat to me what you heard him say on this subject."

"What can I tell you?" said *Tian Kai Zhi*. "I was a sweeper in *Zhu Xian*'s[68] house!"

"Don't evade me, master *Tian*," said the duke; "I want to be satisfied."

Then *Tian Kai Zhi* said:

"*Zhu Xian* said that, in order to preserve one's own life, one should do like shepherds, who, when a sheep goes astray, whip it to rejoin the flock, where it is safe."

"What does that mean?" said the duke.

"That is all," said *Tian Kai Zhi*. "In the principality of *Lu*, one *Shan Bao* spent his life in the mountains, drinking only water, having no contact with men. Thanks to this diet, at seventy years of age, he was still as fresh as a child. A hungry tiger came out to meet him and devoured him… Doctor *Zhang Yi* was one of the most skilled doctors. Rich and poor competed for his consultations. At the age of forty, he died

---

67   Compare *Lie Zi*, ch. 2 H.

68   Ritual humility of the disciple, who should fear to do wrong to his teacher by misrepresenting his teaching.

of a contagious fever, which he caught at the bedside of a patient… *Shan Bao* cured his vital spirit, but let his body be devoured by a tiger. *Zhang Yi* cured his body, but let the fever destroy his vital spirit. Both were wrong not to flog their sheep (not to watch over their safety). Confucius said, 'Neither too much isolation, nor too much relationship; the right balance is wisdom.' When, on a dangerous pass, accidents happen often enough, men warn each other, pass only in a group and with due care. While not warning each other of the dangers inherent in eccentric behavior or diet. This is unreasonable!"

F. The official in charge of the sacrifices, having gone to visit the pen of the pigs destined for slaughter, in full official dress, made the following speech to these animals:

"Why do you die with such bad grace, when your death brings you so many advantages and honors? I fatten you for three months. Before the sacrifice, I keep ten days of continence and three days of abstinence for you. After the sacrifice, I arrange your limbs in a beautiful order, on white carpets, on the carved sideboards. Are you not wrong to show such a bad face?"

If this man had really thought of the good of the pigs, he would have let them live in his pen until the end of his days, even with straw and bran as food. But he thought of his own good, of his office, of his emoluments, of his funeral as a civil servant after his death. Since he was happy because he had what was good for him, he thought that pigs should be happy even if they were treated unnaturally. Optical illusion caused by selfishness.

G. Duke *Huan* of *Qi* was hunting near a swamp, with the minister *Guan Zhong* driving his chariot. Suddenly, the duke saw a specter. Placing his hand on *Guan Zhong*'s hand he said:

"Do you see it?" he asked in a low voice.

"I see nothing," said the minister.

When he returned to his palace, the duke became delirious, said he was ill and did not leave his room for several days. Then the officer *Gao Ao* (of imperial blood) addressed the following speech to him:

"You are only sick with terror; a specter cannot harm a character like you. When too much vital spirit has been spent in an attack of passion (anger or terror), a deficit occurs. When the vital spirit accumulated in the upper body (excess *yang*) cannot descend, man becomes irascible. When the vital spirit accumulated in the lower part of the body (excess of *yin*) cannot rise, man becomes forgetful. When the vital spirit accumulated in the center cannot go up or down, then the man feels sick (his heart is obstructed, says the commentary). This is your case: too much concentration. You must distract yourself!"

"Perhaps," said the duke, "but, tell me, are there no specters?"

"Yes, there are," said the officer. "There is the *Li* of the sewers, the *Jie* of the boiler rooms, the *Lei Ting* of the dunghills. To the northeast are the *Bei A* and the *Wa Long*; to the northwest, the *Yi Yang*. On the waters, there is the *Wang Xiang*; on the hills, the *Zhen*; on the mountains, the *Kui*; on the steppes, the *Fang Huang*; on the marshes, the *Wei Tuo*[69]."

"Ah," said the duke, who had seen his specter near a swamp, "what does the *Wei Tuo* look like?"

"He is thick," said *Gao Ao*, "like a shaft, long as a cart pole, dressed in purple and wearing a red headdress. He doesn't like the rolling of carts. When he hears it, he stands up and covers his ears. His appearance is splendid. Whoever has seen him becomes a hegemon (the great ambition of the duke of *Qi*)."

"Ah," said the duke, laughing loudly, "it was really a *Wei Tuo* the specter I saw."

He immediately began to dress, without ceasing to talk to the officer. Before night, he found himself completely cured, by suggestion, without having taken any medicine[70].

H. *Ji Xing Zi* trained a fighting cock for Emperor *Xuan*, of the *Zhou* dynasty[71]. After ten days, when asked about it, he replied:

"The training is not yet completed; the animal is still vain and willful."

Ten days later, when questioned again, he said:

"Not yet; the animal still responds to the crowing of the other roosters, and gets excited at the sight of them".

Ten days later, when questioned again, he said:

"Not yet; it is too passionate, too nervous."

Ten days later, on being questioned again, he said:

"It is ready! The crowing and the sight of its companions do not move it any more than if it were made of wood. No rooster will be able to cope with it[72]."

I. Confucius was admiring the waterfall of *Lu Liang*[73], which falls from a height equal to thirty times the height of a man; it produced a foaming torrent in a channel forty stades long, so turbulent that neither turtles, alligators, nor even fish could frolic in it. Suddenly, Confucius saw a man swimming among the eddies. Mistaking him for a desperate man who had tried to drown himself, he told his disciples to follow the shore, to pull him out of the water, if possible. A few hundred paces further down, the man pulled himself out of the water, untied his hair to dry it and began to walk, singing. Confucius joined him and said:

"I almost took you for a transcendent being, but now I see that you are a man. How can one move in water with such ease? Please tell me your secret."

"I have no secret," said the man. "I began by swimming methodically; then it became natural to me; now I float like an aquatic being; I am one with the water,

---

69   Folklore of the time. The *Wei Tuo*, alias *Wei Yi*.

70   Health and sanity are the result of the perfect balance of nature. Specters are subjective, not objective, the externalization of internal disturbances, such as dreams, hallucinations, etc.

71   Compare *Lie Zi*, chapter 2 Q.

72   Meaning: He is concentrated on one, on one thing. Its reentrant activity is fused with its vital principle.

73   Compare *Lie Zi*, chapter 2 I.

going down with the whirlpool, rising in the whirlpool. I follow the movement of the water, not my own will. That is my secret… I wanted to learn to swim, since I was born at the water's edge. By dint of swimming, it became natural to me. Since I have lost all notion of what I do to swim, I am in the water as in my element, and the water sustains me because I am one with it."

J. The sculptor *Qing* made a support for a set of bells and gongs, a belfry whose harmonious beauty surprised everyone. The Marquis of *Lu* went to admire it and asked *Qing* how he had made it.

"I did it this way," said *Qing*, "when I was commissioned to make the belfry, I applied myself to concentrate all my vital forces, to gather myself entirely in my heart. After three days of this exercise, I had forgotten all the praise and emoluments that my work would bring me. After five days, I no longer expected success, nor feared failure. After seven days, having lost the notion of my body and limbs, having completely forgotten his Highness and his courtiers, all my faculties being concentrated on their object, I felt that the time had come to act. I went into the forest and began to contemplate the natural forms of the trees, the bearing of the most perfect. When I fully understood this ideal, only then did I set to work. That is what directed my work. It is through the fusion in one, of my nature with that of the trees, that this belfry has acquired the qualities that make it admired."

K. *Dong Ye Ji* appeared before Duke *Zhuang*, to show him his carriage and his talent as a driver. His horses advanced and retreated without deviating in the slightest from the straight line. They described, on the right or on the left, circles as perfect as if they had been drawn with a compass. The duke admired this precision, and then, wanting to make sure of their constancy, asked *Ji* to do a hundred laps in a row, on a given track. *Ji* was foolish enough to agree. *Yen He*, who saw, in passing, this forced ride, said to the duke:

"*Ji*'s horses will be exhausted."

The duke did not reply. Soon after, in fact, *Ji*'s horses had to be removed from the track. Then the duke asked *Yen He*:

"How could you foresee what would happen?"

"Because," said *Yen He*, "I saw *Ji* spurring already tired horses[74]."

L. The craftsman *Chui* drew, freehand, circles as perfect as if they had been traced with a compass. This was because he drew them without thinking about them; consequently, his circles were perfect as the products of nature. His mind was concentrated on one, with no worries or distractions.

A shoe is perfect when the foot does not feel it. A belt is perfect when the waist does not feel it. A heart is perfect when, having lost the artificial notion of good and evil, it naturally does good and naturally abstains from evil. A mind is perfect when

---

74   All effort is against nature. Nothing that goes against nature can last, because it goes against nature, and only nature lasts.

it has no internal perception, with no tendency to anything external. Perfection is to be perfect without knowing that one is perfect (Nature, plus unconsciousness).

M. *Sun Xiu* went to see Master *Bian Qing Zi* and made this strange speech to him:

"I have been unjustly given the reputation of useless, of a bad citizen. Now, if my lands do not yield, it is because the years have been bad; if I have done nothing for my prince, it is because I have missed the opportunity. And now I am no longer wanted, neither in the village nor in the city. Oh, heaven! What have I done to bring about such a fate?"

"The superior man," said *Bian Zi*, "forgets himself, so much so that he does not know whether he has viscera and senses or not. He is out of the dust and dirt of this world, far from the affairs of men. He acts without claiming success, and rules without wishing to dominate. Is this how you have behaved? Have you not rather flaunted your knowledge to the point of offending the ignorant? Have you not flaunted your superiority, and sought to shine, even to the eclipsing of the sun and moon, thus driving everyone away? And after that, you blame heaven! Hasn't heaven given you everything that is good for you, a well-formed body, a normal life and the rest? Isn't it to heaven that you owe it not to be deaf, blind or lame, like so many others? What right have you to blame heaven? Go on your way!"

When *Sun Xiu* left, *Bian Zi* sat up, pulled himself together, looked at the sky and sighed.

"What is wrong with you, Master?" his disciples asked.

Bian Zi said:

"I told *Sun Xiu* about the qualities of the superior man. It is too much for him. He may lose his head."

"Don't worry, master," said the disciples. "*Sun Xiu* is right or wrong. If he is right, he will realize it, and what you have said will not make any unpleasant impression on him. If he is wrong, what you have said will torment him, and he will come back to learn more, which will be beneficial to him."

"I was wrong, nevertheless," said *Bian Zi*. "You must not tell a man what you yourself understand, if he is not able to understand it... Once the Prince of *Lu* made offerings and gave a concert to a sea-bird that had fallen at the gates of his city[75]. The bird died of hunger, thirst and terror. The prince should have treated it, not in his way, but in the way of the birds; then the result would have been different, favorable and not fatal. I acted like the Prince of *Lu*, when I talked to that fool of *Sun Xiu* about the superior man. Driving a mouse in a horse-drawn carriage, to give a quail a concert of bells and drums, is to frighten these little creatures. I must have frightened *Sun Xiu*.

---

75   Compare chapter 18 E.

CHAPTER 20 - VOLUNTARY OBSCURITY

A. As *Zhuang Zhou* was crossing the mountains, he saw a large tree with long, leafy branches. A woodcutter who was cutting wood nearby would not touch that tree.

"Why not? asked *Zhuang Zhou*.

"Because its wood is good for nothing," said the woodcutter.

"Therefore, the fact that it is good for nothing will allow this tree to live to its natural death," concluded *Zhuang Zhou*.

After crossing the mountains, *Zhuang Zhou* was greeted by a friendly family. Glad to see him again, the master of the house asked his servant to kill a duck and cook it.

"Which of our two ducks should I kill?" Asked the servant, "The one that can quack or the one that is mute?"

"The mute one," said the master.

The next day, the disciple who accompanied *Zhuang Zhou* said to him.

"Yesterday they spared this tree, because it was good for nothing; today they cut the throat of this duck, because it could not quack; so, to be able or unable, what saves?"

"It depends on the case," said *Zhuang Zhou*, laughing. "Only one thing saves in all cases; it is to have risen to the knowledge of the Principle and its action, and thus to remain in indifference and abstraction. The man who has reached this point pays as little attention to praise as to blame. He knows how to rise like the dragon and fall like the serpent, bending to circumstances, without being stubborn about anything. Whether his position is high or low, he adapts to his environment. It frolics in the bosom of the ancestor of all things (the Principle). It disposes of all beings as it sees fit, without being affectionate to any being. Whatever happens, it fears nothing. So said *Shen Nong* and *Huang Di*. Today's politicians (Confucius and his disciples) do the opposite, and that is why they experience setbacks. After condensation, dissipation; after success, ruin. Strength calls for attack, elevation attracts criticism, action is not without deficits, the counsel of wisdom is despised, nothing is stable or lasting. Remember, O disciple, that the only solid foundation is the knowledge of the Principle and its action (indifference and abstraction)."

B. The incorruptible *Xion Yiliao*, having visited the Marquis of *Lu*, noticed that he was sad and asked him the reason.

"It is because," said the marquis, "while I have studied the rules of the ancients and sought to do honor to my predecessors; while I have venerated the Manes and honored the Sages, personally and constantly, I am afflicted, blow after blow, by all sorts of misfortunes."

"This does not surprise me," said *Xion Yiliao*. "The means you have employed will not preserve you. Think of the fox and the leopard. These animals may retire into the depths of the forests and the caves of the mountains, coming out only at night and with great care, enduring hunger and thirst rather than venture into inhabited places; but they always end by perishing in a net or trap. Why do they hunt them? For their beautiful fur, which men covet. But you, Highness, the Marquisate of *Lu*, are the very fur that your neighbors covet. If you want to find peace, let go of it willingly, extinguish all the desires of your heart, retreat into solitude. In the country of *Nan Yue*, there is a city called the Seat of Solid Virtue. Its inhabitants are ignorant and frustrated, without self-interest or desire. They produce, but do not hoard; they give, but do not demand to be repaid. There is no etiquette or ceremony among them. Yet, despite their savage appearance, they practice the great natural laws, celebrate births and mourn deaths. Marquis, leave your marquisate, renounce the vulgar life; let us go and live there together!"

"It is far away," said the marquis, "the road is difficult, we have to cross mountains and rivers, I have neither boat nor cart."

Xion Yiliao said:

"If you were to cast off your dignities, if you did not care for your country, if you wished to go there, your desire would take you."

"It is far away," said the marquis, "How am I to get provisions? How can I detach myself from my companions?"

Xion Yiliao said:

"If you did not care for your luxuries, if you were not attached to your well-being, you would not worry about provisions; you would entrust yourself to the rivers, to the sea, without even fearing to lose sight of the land; and having to abandon your companions would not make you turn back. But I see, master of your subjects, that your subjects are your masters, for you care for them. You are not a *Yao*, who never considered anyone as his subject, and never was anyone's subject. I have tried to cure you of your melancholy; but you are not a man to employ the only effective remedy, which consists, after abandoning everything, in uniting yourself to the Principle, in abstraction. As long as one retains the notion of his personality, his conflicts with those of others will prevent peace. It is like a ferry crossing a river. If an empty boat drifting on the river hits it, even if they are irascible, the boatmen will not be angry, because no one has come into conflict with them, the boat being empty. If, on the contrary, there is a person in the boat, shouts and insults will immediately come out of the ferry. Why? Because there has been a conflict between people? A man who has been able to shed his personality can travel around the world without experiencing any confusion."

C. A certain *She* was commissioned by Duke *Ling* of *Wei* to raise the money necessary to found a bell tower. It was set up on a mound at the entrance to the city. After three months, the bells were cast and hung. *Qing Ji*, of the imperial blood of the *Zhou*, asked *She*:

"How did you manage to be so successful and so quickly?"

She said:

"I have been careful to do nothing. Does not the saying go that it is no good to chisel and polish, but to let nature do its work? Looking most indifferent, paying no attention to them, I let the people do it spontaneously, as nature does. They came, bringing their offerings, without my calling them, and left without my stopping them. I said nothing, neither to those who displeased me nor to those who pleased me. They all gave what they could or would, and I took it without comment. So everything went smoothly. The same way of doing things would make the most considerable undertaking (the government of a principality or an empire, says the commentary) equally successful."

D. After Confucius had been blockaded for seven days with his disciples on the border of the principalities of *Chen* and *Cai*, and had been on the point of perishing from starvation, the grand duke *Ren* offered his condolences in these terms:

"Master, this time you have seen death at close quarters."

"Yes," said Confucius.

"Did it frighten you?"

"Yes," said Confucius.

"Then," said the Grand Duke *Ren*, "I will give you the recipe that preserves you from the dangers of death… On the shore of the eastern sea is the bird *Yi Dai*, which lives in flocks. None of them relies on itself, they always fly leaning on each other. In perfect order, none of them leaves the flock, neither to advance, nor to retreat. When they eat, it is also like a troop, None of them turns aside to snatch a better morsel, Each pecks in his own place. This beautiful order protects them against animals and against men, against all accidents. So is man, who lives like and with others, who does not turn away, like you, Confucius. To avoid misfortune, one must also be careful not to affect extraordinary qualities or talents, as you do. The most upright tree will be the first to be cut down. The well with the sweetest water will be the first to dry up. Your science frightens the ignorant, your lights offend the foolish. Do not hoard the sun and the moon. It is your pretensions that bring you disgrace. I once heard this from a man of great merit: 'To boast is to close the way to fortune; if you already have merit and renown, you will be robbed. To disappear, to hide in the mass, that gives security…' To go with the flow without distinguishing oneself, to go along the road without being noticed, modestly, with simplicity, to the point of appearing vulgar; to erase the memory of one's own merits and to make one's own reputation be forgotten; this is the secret of living in peace with men. The superior man seeks obscurity. Why do you seek notoriety?"

"Thank you," said Confucius.

Then, interrupting his ordinary relations, after dismissing his disciples, Confucius hid himself among the reeds of a swamp, dressed himself in furs and fed on acorns and chestnuts. In time he returned so perfectly to the state of nature that his presence no longer frightened quadrupeds and birds. Even men found it bearable.

E. One day Confucius said to the master *Sang Hu*:

"I have been expelled twice from the principality of *Lu*. In *Song* they cut down the tree that sheltered me. Going to *Wei*, I was stopped between *Chen* and *Cai*. I had to flee from danger at *Shang* and *Zhou*. As a result of these successive misfortunes, my friends have turned away from me, my disciples have deserted me. What have I done to bring all this upon me?"

Sang Hu said:

"You know the story of *Lin Hui*, who, at the defeat of *Jia*, fled, throwing away his jade scepter worth a thousand bars of gold, but carrying on his back his little son. Certainly, the scepter was worth more than the child; the child was more difficult to save than the scepter; nevertheless, *Lin Hui* took the child and abandoned the scepter. Why did he do so? Because interest alone bound him to the scepter, while nature bound him to the child. Now, interest is a weak tie, which misfortune unties. Whereas nature is a strong bond, which withstands all trials. The same is true of interested friendship and transcendent friendship. The superior man, rather cold, attracts; the vulgar, though warm, repels. Relationships that have no deep profound reason, break down as they are formed. You are now only a vulgar man, and interest is the only tie that binds you to your disciples. Therefore your attachment ceases with adversity."

"I thank you," said Confucius.

He retired thoughtfully, closed his school and left the books. His disciples, on being dismissed, no longer bowed reverentially to him, but began to esteem him.

On another occasion *Sang Hu* said:

"When he was about to die, *Shun* said to *Yu* the following: 'Be careful! Affection that is based only on bodily forms is not solid. To be solid, affection must have serious reasons as its foundation. To be loved, through imposition is worthless. The ascendancy conquered by true qualities is the only lasting one. One is faithful to such a man, not for his beauty, nor for his favors, but for his intrinsic value.'"

F. Dressed in a robe of patched cloth, his shoes tied to his feet with strings, *Zhuang Zhou* met the king of *Wei*.

"In what tribulation I see you, master," said the king.

"Excuse me, king," said *Zhuang Zhou*, "it is poverty, not tribulation. He who possesses the knowledge of the Principle and its action is never in tribulation. He can experience poverty if he is born in unhappy times… Like a monkey, in a forest of beautiful trees with long, smooth branches, he frolics with such agility, that neither I nor *Peng Meng* (a famous archer) could hit him. But when it has to climb up stunted and thorny trees, how much less nimble is its stride! Yet it is the same animal; the same bones, the same sinews. Yes, but circumstances have become unfavorable, preventing it from making free use of its means… Thus will have to suffer the Sage born under a stupid prince surrounded by incapable ministers. This was the case of *Bin Gan*, whose heart was torn out by the tyrant *Zhou Xin*."

G. When Confucius was blocked between *Chen* and *Cai*, for seven days, unable to cook any food, he took in his left hand a piece of dry wood, and struck it with his right hand with a dead branch, singing the ode of Master *Piao*. Music without pitch or measure, the natural murmur of a wounded heart, reminiscent of that of the earth torn by the plowshare.

Yen Hui, his favorite disciple, stood in a desperate posture, arms folded, staring at his master. Fearing that he might become too exalted, Confucius said to him:

"*Hui*, resigning yourself to natural trials is easy. To remain indifferent to the favors of men is difficult. There is no beginning that is not followed by an end. Man is one with heaven. I who sing now, who am I?[76]"

Yen Hui, not understanding, asked for an explanation:

"What is the meaning of 'Resigning to natural trials is easy', master?"

Confucius said:

"Hunger, thirst, cold, heat, poverty, obstacles and contradictions, all these are included in cosmic evolution, in the law of transformations; every man, therefore, encounters these things on his path, and must resign himself to them. An inferior must not rebel against the dispositions of his superior. How much more does the duty of submission in relation to heaven correspond to every man!"

Yen Hui asked:

"What is the meaning of 'Remaining indifferent to the favors of men is difficult'?"

Confucius said:

"A man with an office attracts honors and money, everything is confused. External goods, which add nothing to his moral value, which change nothing in his destiny. He who allows himself to be seduced by them, from the rank of sage, falls to the level of thieves (whom money tempts). Now, to live in the midst of riches and honors, without being seduced by riches and honors, is very difficult. In this situation, the wise man needs the circumspection of the swallow. This bird never perches in a place that his keen eye has judged unsafe. When it has lost its prey, it neither stops nor turns back, but continues its flight at a run. It lives among the dwellings of men, but always distrustful of their inhabitants."

Yen Hui went on to ask:

"What is the meaning of 'There is no beginning that is not followed by an end'?"

Confucius said:

"Since all beings are constantly changing their form, the giver of these forms being unknown and the rules he follows being mysterious, what can be known of their end, what can be known of the new beginning that will follow this end? So we have only to wait for what will happen, keeping a right attitude."

Yen Hui asked again:

"What is the meaning of 'Man is one with heaven'?"

Confucius said:

"To be man is to be heaven (part of the universal norm). What prevents man from being heaven (melted into the mass with loss of his personality) is his own activity. So the Sage refrains from action and abandons himself to evolution, which in the end will absorb him into the great all."

---

76   Actually, I don't have a stable personality. I do not know who or what I was, nor do I know what or who I will become. Succession of exits and re-entries from and into the great whole.

H. While *Zhuang Zhou* was poaching in the reserved park of *Diao Ling* a large bird flew in from the south. Its wings were six feet long. Its eyes were more than an inch in circumference. It flew so close to *Zhuang Zhou* that its wing brushed his head, and finally descended into a grove of chestnut trees. *Zhuang Zhou* ran after it, cocking his crossbow. On a shady tree trunk, a cicada was taking a rest, absorbed in its music. A carnivorous mantis attacked it. The large bird swooped down on both of them, giving *Zhuang Zhou* the opportunity to shoot it. As he picked it up, he thought to himself how selfishness and antagonism lead beings, who are all of the same nature, to destroy each other. As he left the forest, the guard was about to catch him for poaching.

When he returned home, *Zhuang Zhou* locked himself up for three months. His disciple *Lin Zi* asked him the reason for this long confinement, and he said.

"I used this time to convince myself that, to live long, you don't have to fight with others, but do and think like everyone else. Always battling, you eventually end up being defeated in your turn. I learned this from the big bird and the ranger of *Diao Ling*[77]."

I. Master *Yang* (*Yang Zhu*) went to the principality of *Song* and spent the night at an inn. The innkeeper had two women, one beautiful and the other ugly. The ugly one was loved, the beautiful one was not.

"Why?" Master Yang asked.

"Because," said a servant girl, "the beautiful one, knowing that she is beautiful, poses, so that we deliberately ignore her beauty; while the ugly one, knowing that she is ugly, effaces herself, so that we deliberately ignore her ugliness."

"Remember this, disciples!" said Master *Yang*. "To stand out, without showing off one's excellence, is the conduct that makes one loved everywhere."

CHAPTER 21 - TRANSCENDENT ACTION

A. *Tian Zifang*, who assisted Marquis *Wen* of *Wei*, often quoted *Xi Gong*.

"Was he your master?" asked the marquis.

"No," said *Tian Zifang*. "We come from the same village. I have often been amazed at the precision of his speeches. That is why I quote him."

"Then," said the marquis, "you have had no master?"

"Of course I have had one," said *Tian Zifang*.

"Who?" asked the marquis.

"The master *Shun* of the eastern suburb."

"If he was your master," said the marquis, "why don't you ever quote him?"

"Because," said *Tian Zifang*, "this man does not speak. He is a transcendent man. He is heaven in human form. Empty of all contingency, he meditates within

---

77   The cicada, the mantis, the bird, the archer and the guard, represent the philosophical and political schools of the time, always at war and fighting. The cicada is Confucius, mesmerized by his monotonous rambling. The contemplative and scathing mantis is *Lao Zi*. The three months of *Zhuang Zhou's* retreat did not change him. He remained rebellious and combative.

himself his transcendence. He is kind to everyone, and when someone does not act as he should, he points it out to him with his correct attitude, and thus corrects him without words. You can see that I cannot quote this man."

When *Tian Zifang* came out, Marquis *Wen* was stunned and did not say a word for the rest of the day. Then he sent for his ordinary confidants and told them:

"How different from us is the man of perfect virtue. Until now I had believed that the study of the words of the sages and scholars, and the practice of goodness and fairness, were all an ideal (Confucianism). (But since I heard about the master of *Tian Zifang*, I am completely defeated and as if paralyzed, I can no longer open my mouth. Everything I have learned so far is not solid. The marquisate, whose worries prevent me from devoting myself to Daoism, has become hateful to me."

B. Master *Xue*, Count of *Wen* (Daoist), on his way from the south to *Qi*, passed through the capital of *Lu*, the land of Confucius, where several people asked to see him…

"What's the use?" he said. "The scholars of this country only study conventional rites, not human nature. I don't want to see them."

When he returned from *Qi*, Master *Xue* stopped again at *Lu*, and the same people asked to see him again. So he received them in the guest room, and then returned to his apartment with a sigh. The next day, another visit, another sigh after the visit. The disciple serving master *Xue* was intrigued and asked him:

"Why do you sigh like that every time you have visitors?"

"Because," said Master *Xue*, "I am more and more convinced that the scholars of this country, well versed in conventional rites, do not understand human nature. My visitors made their entrances and exits in the most studied and measured manner, with the airs of dragons and tigers. Then, instead of asking me anything, they reproached me like teachers and lectured me like (superior) parents. That is why I sighed."

Confucius (in the process of converting to Daoism, and represented here as more insightful than the other scholars of *Lu*,) also went to see master *Xue*, and withdrew without having said a word to him…

"Why did you keep silent?" asked his disciple *Zi Lu*…

"Because," said Confucius, "it was enough for me to look at this man. The higher science (transcendence) springs from his eyes and penetrates with his gaze; words cannot express it."

C. *Yen Yuan* (his most valued disciple) said to Confucius (completely converted to Daoism):

"Master, when you walk, I follow your walking; when you trot, I follow you at trot; when you gallop, I follow you at a gallop; but when you take off and move away from the ground, then I can only follow you with my eyes."

"Explain yourself, *Hui*," said Confucius.

"Behold," said *Yen Hui*. "The walk is your speech; I can follow it. The trot is your reasoning; I can follow it. The gallop is your speculation; I can follow it. But what

I cannot grasp is the transcendent (Daoist) influence by which you persuade and triumph. What is that?"

"That is," said Confucius, "the fascination exerted by my higher self, my part of the universal norm, upon the self, the part of the norm of my listener, if he has not extinguished it. Meditate well upon this! The most lamentable death is the death of the heart (the extinction of the norm); it is far worse than the death of the body. The man whose heart lives, acts upon the hearts that live, like the sun that vivifies the world. The sun rises in the east and sets in the west. It enlightens all beings, who are oriented towards it. With its appearance, its action begins; with its disappearance, they become inert. Thus is the diurnal rhythm, day and night. The rhythm of life and death resembles it. In turn, the being dies, and then lives (revives). When it has received a definite form, it retains it until the end of this existence, a period of daylight during which it acts. Then comes death for him, a period of night during which he rests. And so on, without interruption, like the chain of time. He becomes again a being according to his merit, but he only knows (in his new existence) that he is such because of his destiny, without being able to measure his previous mass (the mass of moral antecedents, the karma that weighs on him). At the end of this existence, the beings who were in intimate contact (shoulder to shoulder), leave each other in pain. If the survivor seeks to know the state of the deceased, it is in vain, for he has ceased to be him. To ask for him is, then, to look for a (stolen) horse at the fair, which has already found another master. To weep for the other is to show a grave (doctrinal) forgetfulness; it is to forget that the other no longer exists in his former personality. This cessation of personality is not to be lamented as a misfortune. For the annihilation is not total. The physical self has ceased to be, it is true, and it would be a mistake to think that it exists. But the transcendent self (the part of the norm that was this person) remains, and may be thought to exist... It is through this transcendent, almost impersonal self that I act upon my listeners. It is not unpleasant, like the personal self of Confucius."

D. Confucius went to visit *Lao Dan* and found him sitting motionless and ecstatic. Ecstasy seized him as he dried his hair after his ablutions[78]. Confucius waited discreetly until he came to himself, and then said:

"You had left things and men; you had withdrawn to the seclusion of the self!"

"Yes," said *Lao Dan*. "I was frolicking in the origin of things."

"What does that mean?" asked Confucius.

"I am not yet well," said *Lao Dan*; "my tired mind is not yet free to think, my tight mouth can hardly articulate; nevertheless, I shall try to satisfy you... The two modes of being having differentiated in the primordial being, its turning began and cosmic evolution ensued. The apogee of *yin* (condensed in the earth) is tranquil passivity. The culmination of *yang* (condensed in heaven) is fruitful activity. The passivity of the earth offering itself to heaven, the activity of heaven exerting itself on the earth, from both of which all beings were born. The invisible force, the

---

78   Compare chapter 3 A.

action and reaction of the binomial heaven-earth, produces all evolution. The beginning and the end, the fullness and the void, the astronomical revolutions, the phases of the sun and the moon, everything is produced by this one cause, which no one sees, but which always acts. Life unfolds towards a goal, death is a return to an end. Genesis goes on incessantly, without the origin being known, without the end being seen. The action and reaction of heaven and earth are the only motor of this movement. This is the beauty, the supreme joy. To frolic in this rapture is the lot of the superior man."

"But how to arrive at that?" asked Confucius.

"By utter indifference," continued *Lao Dan*. "The animals that inhabit the steppe feel no attraction for any particular grass; the fish that live in the waters are not attached to any particular habitat; consequently, no movement disturbs their peace. All beings are an immense whole. He who is attached to this unity to the point of having lost the sense of his own personality, sees his body in the same way as he sees dust, life and death in the same way as he sees day and night. What can move this man, for whom gain and loss, happiness and misfortune are nothing? He scorns dignities like clay, because he knows that he is nobler than these things. And this nobility of his being, no vicissitude can touch. Of all possible changes, none will alter his peace. He who has attained the Principle, understands it."

"Ah," said Confucius in bewilderment, "here is a teaching as wide as heaven and earth; can it be summed up in some formula, after the manner of the ancients?"

Lao Dan replied:

"Springs arise naturally. The superior man is equally spontaneous. Heaven is high, the earth is deep, the sun and the moon are bright, all without formulas."

When he went out, Confucius related all the above to his disciple *Yen Hui*.

"Up to now," he said, "I have known as much about the Principle as about the eels that live in vinegar. If the Master had not lifted the veil that covered my eyes, I would never have glimpsed the perfect heaven-earth complex (the great cosmic unity)."

E. When *Zhuang Zhou* visited Duke *Ai* of *Lu*, the latter said to him:

"There are many scholars in the duchy of *Lu*; but none, is comparable to you, Master."

"There are only a few scholars in the duchy of *Lu*," replied *Zhuang Zhou*.

"How can you talk like that," said the duke, "when all we see everywhere are men dressed in the garb of scholars?"

"The costume, yes," said *Zhuang Zhou*. "They announce, with their round caps, that they know the things of heaven; with their square shoes, that they know the things of earth; with their sonorous pendants, that they know how to carry harmony everywhere. Some know all this without the need to wear the suit. Others wear the suit, without knowing the thing. If you do not believe me, make this experiment: prohibit by edict, on pain of death, the wearing of the scholar's suit by anyone who is not competent."

Duke *Ai* did so. Five days later, all but one of *Lu*'s scholars had changed their clothes. The Duke himself asked that unique person about the government of the state. He answered everything pertinently, without it being possible to disturb him.

"You said," said *Zhuang Zhou* to the duke, "that there were many scholars in the duchy of *Lu*. One is not many."

F. *Bo Li Xi*, who was not interested in dignities and riches, became a breeder of cattle, and produced magnificent oxen, his natural instinct revealing to him how to treat them according to their nature. When Duke *Mu* of *Qin* saw this, he appointed him his minister, so that he could develop his people.

Shun did not like life and did not fear death. This is what made him worthy and capable of ruling men.

G. Prince *Yuan* of *Song* wished to have a map drawn for him; the scribes who had been summoned came, received their instructions and bowed; then some of them, discouraged, departed; others licked their brushes and pounded their ink, with a thousand and one gestures. A scribe, who arrived after the hour with carefree airs, also received his instructions, saluted, and immediately retired to his room. The duke sent to see what he was doing. It was ascertained that he had made himself comfortable, naked to the waist, with his legs crossed, and was beginning to rest. When the Duke learned this:

"This one, he said, will succeed; he is a man who knows how to do it[79]."

H. King *Wen*, ancestor of the *Zhou*, being in *Zang*, saw a man fishing with a rod and line, carelessly, mechanically, only his nature acting in him, without any admixture of passion. King *Wen* resolved at once to appoint him his minister. But, thinking then of the probable displeasure of his parents and officials, he wanted to put the idea out of his mind. But he could not! The fear that his people would be left without heaven (without a minister to rule it naturally like heaven), made it impossible for him to forget his intention. So he thought how to do it. In the morning, having summoned his officers, he said to them:

"Last night I saw in a dream a handsome man, of swarthy complexion, with a beard, riding on a speckled horse with red-tinted hooves, who cried to me: give your power to the man of *Zang*, and your people will be well."

The officials were greatly moved and shouted:

"It was the late king your father who appeared to you."

"Then," said King *Wen*, "do you want us to consult the tortoise-shell about this event?"

"No, no!" said the officials, unanimously. "A verbal order from the late king is not to be disputed."

Therefore, King *Wen* sent for the fisherman and handed over the government to him. The latter changed nothing, made no regulations, gave no orders. After

---

79   One can only succeed by letting one's own nature act. Restraint prevents success.

three years, when King *Wen* inspected his kingdom, he found that the bandits had disappeared, that the officials were honest, that taxes were respected. The common people lived together, the officials did their duty, the feudatories did not invade. Then King *Wen*, treating the man from *Zang* as his master, sat him down facing south, stood in front of him facing north and asked:

"Could you not do to an empire the good you have done to a kingdom?"

The *Zang* man only replied with a frightened look. That same day, before nightfall, he disappeared. No one ever knew what had become of him. However, one detail of this story surprised the honest *Yen Yuan*.

"How could it be," he asked Confucius, "that King *Wen* claimed a dream he had not had?"

"Shut up!" said Confucius. "Everything King *Wen* did was well done. We must not judge this man. Naturally straight, in this case he had to bow to circumstances[80]."

I. *Lie Yukou* (*Lie Zi*) drew his bow in the presence of *Bo Hun Wu Ren*. He held his bow with such a firm arm that, having a cup full of water fixed at his left elbow, at the moment he shot his arrow, the water did not spill out. His right hand was so active that, as soon as he released one arrow, he would set the next. And, all the time, his body remained as straight as a statue (the ideal of an archer of the old school)... This, said *Bo Hun Wu Ren* (the Daoist), is the shooting of an archer, of a man who wants to shoot, of a man who knows he is shooting (art, not nature). Come with me to some peak, to the edge of an abyss, and we'll see what's left of your poses.

They went together to a high mountain, to the edge of a precipice a hundred times the height of a man. There *Bo Hun Wu Ren* camped, on the edge of the abyss, with his heels sticking out into the void. Leaning only on the tips of his toes, he bowed to *Lie Yukou* and invited him to come over and take his place beside him. But the dizziness had already made him fall to all fours, sweat pouring down to his heels. *Bo Hun Wu Ren* said to him:

"The superior man carries his gaze to the depths of the celestial blue, to the depths of the earthly abysses, to the farthest reaches of the horizon, without his vital spirits being moved in the least. He who is not like this is not a superior man[81]. Seeing your haggard eyes, you make me dizzy."

J. *Jian Wu* said to *Sunshu Ao*:

"You have been put in front three times without being exalted, and you have been dismissed three times without being affected. At first I suspected that you were pretending to be indifferent. But, after convincing myself that, on these occasions, your breathing remained perfectly calm, I now believe that you are really indifferent. How did you become so?"

---

80   Confucian opportunism takes precedence over morality. We see that Confucius is not completely converted. Here he showed his true condition.

81   Every physical disturbance is a symptom of imperfection of nature. Compare *Lie Zi*, ch. 2 E.

"I have done nothing at all," said *Sunshu Ao*. "I had nothing to do with either my appointments or my demotions. In these adventures there was neither gain nor loss to me, so I was neither exalted nor affected by them. What is so extraordinary about this? Nothing more natural, on the contrary. My position was not myself, I was not my position. Favor and disfavor were due to my office, not to myself. Then why should I have taken the trouble and fatigue to worry about it? Would I not have wasted my time thinking of men's esteem or contempt?"

Having heard this answer, Confucius said:

"This is an ancient true man. Ancient men of this kind were neither impressed by the speeches of the learned, nor seduced by the charms of beauty, nor violated by the powerful and brutal. *Fu Xi* and *Huang Di* sought their friendship in vain. Neither love of life nor fear of death, those motives so powerful in the vulgar, made a dent in them. So what effect could dignities and riches have on them? Their minds were higher than the mountains, deeper than the abyss. It mattered not to them that their social position was infinitesimal. The whole universe being theirs by their union with the universal cosmos, the granting of dignities and riches to the vulgar did not impoverish them, the great whole remaining for them."

K. When the king of *Chu* was speaking to the dispossessed former prince of *Fan*, the courtiers said:

"*Fan* has already been ruined three times."

The prince of *Fan* interrupted them:

"The ruin of *Fan* has not taken my life. It is not certain that *Chu*'s prosperity will maintain yours. Do not trust present prosperity to the point of believing that you are safe from future ruin. Prosperity and ruin alternate. If we place ourselves high above the spinning wheel, *Fan* is not destroyed, *Chu* does not prosper. Everything passes alternately through the two phases of ruin and prosperity."

CHAPTER 22 - KNOWLEDGE OF THE PRINCIPLE

A. Knowledge went north to the black waters; he climbed the mountain of darkness, where he encountered Inaction. Knowledge said to Inaction:

"I have something to ask you. By what kind of thoughts and reflections does one come to know the Principle? What position should one adopt and what should one do to understand it? Where to begin and what path to take to reach it?"

To these three questions, Inaction did not answer. Not because he did not want to answer, but because he did not really know what to answer.

Getting no answer, Knowledge went to the white water, climbed the mountain of inquiry, where he saw Abstraction, and asked him the same three questions again.

"Ah," said Abstraction, "I will tell you this…"

As he was about to speak, it happened that he did not know what he was talking about.

Disappointed, Knowledge went to the imperial palace and asked *Huang Di* the three questions. The latter told him:

"To come to know the Principle, first there is no thinking, no pondering. To come to understand it, do not take any position, do nothing. To arrive at it, one must not start from any precise point, nor follow any determined path."

"Then," asked Knowledge, "between them and us, who acted better?"

"It was Inaction," said *Huang Di*, "for he said nothing at all. Then Abstraction, who almost spoke. The two of us were wrong to speak. The saying goes, 'He who knows, does not speak (because he knows that he will not be able to express what he knows); he who speaks, shows that he does not know.' The Sage does not speak, not even to teach. The Principle cannot be reached, its action cannot be grasped. All that can be taught and learned, such as goodness, equity and rites, is all that is posterior and inferior to the Principle, all that was invented only when the true notions about the Principle and its action were lost, at the beginning of the decadence. The saying goes: 'He who imitates the Principle diminishes his action day by day, until he no longer acts.' When he has reached this point (pure non-action), then he is equal to any task. But to return to the origin in this way is a very difficult thing, which only the superior man can do."

"Life follows death, death is the origin of life. The reason for this alternation is inscrutable… The life of a man is a condensation of matter, the dissipation of which will be his death, and so on and so forth. This being so, is there any reason to regret anything? All beings are a constantly changing whole. Some are called beautiful, others ugly. I abuse words, for nothing lasts. In its next metamorphosis, what was beautiful may become ugly, what was ugly may become beautiful… This is summed up in the saying: 'The whole universe is one and the same substance.' The Sage, without esteeming or despising any being in particular, gives all his esteem to the cosmic unity, to the great whole."

(*What follows appears to be an interjected fragment.*) Summarizing his conversation with *Huang Di*, Knowledge said:

"Inaction didn't know what to answer; Abstraction forgot to answer; you answered and then retracted your answer…"

"Yes," said *Huang Di*. "Nothing can be said about the Principle. Whoever speaks of it is mistaken…"

Inaction and Abstraction learned of this answer from *Huang Di*, and judged it good.

B. Heaven and earth, so majestic, are mute. The course of the stars and the seasons, so regular, is not deliberate. The evolution of beings follows an immanent law, not formulated. Imitating these models, the superior man, the Sage par excellence, does not intervene, does not act, lets everything follow its course. The transcendent binomial heaven-earth presides over all the transformations, the succession of deaths and lives, the mutations of all beings, without any of these beings having an explicit knowledge of the primary cause of all these movements, of the Principle that makes everything endure from the beginning. The immense space is the intermediate point between heaven and earth. The smallest fetus owes its existence to heaven and earth. Heaven and earth preside over the continuous evolution of beings, which in their turn rise or sink; the regular rotation of *yin* and *yang*, the four seasons, etc. Some beings seem to disappear and yet continue to exist; others, having lost their bodies, become even more transcendent. Heaven and earth nourish all beings, without their knowing it. From this notion of the universe, we can return to the confused knowledge of its cause, the Principle. This is the only way. We can only say of the Principle that it is the origin of everything, that it influences everything while remaining indifferent.

C. *Nie Que* asked *Pi Yi* to explain the Principle. *Pi Yi* told him:

"Regulate your morals, focus your perceptions, and universal harmony will spread to you. Attract your faculties, unify your thoughts, and the vital spirit of the universe will dwell in you as an extension. The action of the Principle communicating itself to you, will become in you the principle of your qualities. You will dwell in the Principle. You will acquire the simplicity of the calf that has just been born, and you will cease to worry about what you are and where you come from..."

Before *Pi Yi* finished his peroration, *Nie Que* fell fast asleep (ecstatic). Amazed, *Pi Yi* chanted:

"Here is his body turned into dead wood, and his heart into extinguished ash. Now he is transcendent, his true science no longer wavers. Having become blind, his reason no longer argues. He has reached the intuition of the Principle. What a man!"

D. *Shun* asked his minister *Cheng*:

"Can one come to possess the Principle?"

Cheng replied:

"If you do not possess your own body, how can you say that you possess the Principle?"

"If my body is not mine, whose is it?"

"Your body," said *Cheng*, "is a loan of gross matter, which heaven and earth have made for you for a time. Your life is a transitory combination of subtle matter, which you also receive from heaven and earth. Your destiny, your activity, is an integral part of the flow of beings, under the action of heaven and earth. Your children and grandchildren are a renewal (literally a change of skin) that heaven and earth have given you. You advance in life without knowing what pushes you, you flutter without knowing what stops you, you eat without knowing how you assimilate, the powerful but unknown action of heaven and earth moves you in everything; and would you pretend to appropriate anything?"

E. Confucius said to *Lao Dan*:

"As I have a little free time today, I would like to hear you speak of the essence of the Principle."

Lao Dan said:

"You should first have enlightened your heart by abstinence, purified your vital mind and discarded your preconceived ideas. Because the subject is abstruse, difficult to expound and difficult to listen to. But I will try to tell you something about it... The luminous was born from the dark, the forms were born from the amorphous. The vital spirit (universal, of which the particular vital spirits are participations) was born from the Principle; the prime matter was born from the sperm (universal, of which the particular sperm is a participation). Then the beings were mutually engendered, by communication of their matter, either by uterine gestation, or by the production of ova. Their entrance on the scene of life is not noticed, their exit makes no noise. There is no visible door, no definite home. They come from everywhere and fill the immensity of the world, contingent and ephemeral beings... Those who, knowing this, care for nothing, are well, have a free mind and keep their sensory organs in perfect condition[82]. Without tiring their mind, they are able to perform any task. For they act (or rather do not act, they let happen) spontaneously, naturally, as the sky is high by nature, as the earth is wide by nature, as the sun and the moon are bright by nature, as beings swarm naturally... Study and discussion don't teach us anything about the Principle, so the Sages refrain from study and discussion. Knowing that the Principle is an infinity that nothing can increase or diminish, the Sages are content to embrace it as a whole... Yes, it is immense as the ocean. What majesty in this incessant revolution, in which the restart immediately follows the cessation... To follow the flow of beings by doing good to all is the way of the ordinary Sages (Confucians). But to have taken a position outside this flow, and to do good to those who follow in its wake, is the way of the superior Sage (Daoist, who acts as the Principle). — Let us consider a human being, in the state of a barely conceived embryo, whose sex is not even determined yet. It has developed, between heaven and earth. As soon as it has developed, it can return to its origin (stillborn). Considered on this principle, what is it but a mixture of breath and sperm? And if it survives, it will be only for a few years. The difference between what is called a long life and a short life is so small! In short, it is a moment in the infinite course of time. Many do not even have the time to demonstrate whether they possess the spirit of a *Yao* (virtuous emperor) or a *Jie* (vicious tyrant). — The evolution of each individual in the plant kingdom follows a certain law. Likewise, the law governing human evolution is like a gear. The wise man follows the movement, without reluctance, without clinging. To foresee and calculate is to be artificial; to let oneself go is to follow the Principle. The emperors and kings of high antiquity rose and became famous by letting go. — The passage of man between heaven and earth, from life to death, is like the leap of a white steed, crossing a ravine from one side to the other; a matter of an instant. As by the effect of a bubbling, beings enter into life; as by the effect of a flow, they enter into death. A transformation has made them live, a transformation

---

82   Blindness and deafness are, for Daoists, premature wear and tear, due to immoderate use of the vital force.

makes them die. All the living find death unpleasant, men mourn it. And yet what is it but the loosening of the bow and its return to the sheath; the emptying of the body bag and the release of the two souls it imprisoned? After the embarrassments and vicissitudes of life, the two souls leave, the body follows them to rest. This is the great return (the souls and bodies return to the whole). — The notion that the incorporeal has produced the corporeal, that the body returns to the incorporeal, the notion of perpetual turning, is known to many men, but only the elite draw the practical consequences. The vulgar man willingly discusses this subject, while the superior man is profoundly silent. If he were to attempt to talk about it, he would have to renounce his science, by which he knows that it is impossible to talk about it, and that one can only meditate on it. To have realized that nothing is gained by asking about the Principle, but that one must contemplate it in silence, is what is called having attained the great result (having attained the goal)[83].

F. *Dong Guo Zi* asked *Zhuang Zhou*:
"Where is that which is called the Principle?"
"Everywhere," said *Zhuang Zhou*.
"Give me an example," asked *Dong Guo Zi*.
"For example, in this ant," said *Zhuang Zhou*.
"Could you give a more humble example?" asked *Dong Guo Zi*.
"For example, it is in this blade of grass."
"Still lower."
"It is on this fragment of tile."
"And lower?"
"It is in this excrement," said *Zhuang Zhou*.
Dong Guo Zi did not ask any more questions. Then *Zhuang Zhou* took the floor and said to him.

"Master, asking questions as you just did will get you nowhere. This procedure is too imperfect. It resembles that of those market experts who summarily judge the fatness of a pig by pressing their foot on it (the foot makes a more or less deep impression, depending on whether the pig is more or less fat). Do not ask whether the Principle is in this or in that. It is in all beings. That is why it receives the epithets great, supreme, whole, universal, total. All these different terms apply to one and the same reality, to cosmic unity. — Let us transport ourselves in spirit out of this universe of dimensions and locations, and there will be no need to attempt to locate the Principle. Let us transport ourselves out of the world of activity, into the realm of inaction, of indifference, of rest, of restlessness, of vagueness, of simplicity, of leisure, of harmony, and there will be no need to attempt to qualify the Principle. It is the indeterminate infinite. It is a lost cause to try to reach it, to try to locate it, to try to study its movements. Science does not get there. It (the Principle) who made beings to be beings is not subject to the same laws as beings. It (the Principle)

---

83   Confucius is thus dismissed from his questioning and returned to contemplation, which his busy life as a politician renders him incapable of doing.

who made all beings limited, is itself unlimited, infinite. Therefore, it is idle to ask where it is. — As to evolution and its phases, fullness and emptiness, prosperity and decay, the Principle produces this succession, but it is not this succession. It is the author of causes and effects (the first cause), but it is not the causes and effects. It is the author of condensations and dissipations (births and deaths), but it is not itself condensation or dissipation. Everything proceeds from it and evolves through and under its influence. It is in all beings, by a termination of norm; but it is not identical with beings, being neither differentiated nor limited."

G. *A He Gan* and the future emperor *Shen Nong* were studying under *Lao Long Ji*. Sitting on a stool, *Shen Nong* was napping with the door closed. *A He Gan* pushed open the door and told him point-blank that his master had died. *Shen Nong* jumped up, dropped his staff, burst out laughing and said:

"Will he have died of despair at his inability to lift me up with his great phrases?"

The Daoist *Yen Gang*, who had come to offer condolences, hearing these words, said to *Shen Nong*:

"The study of the Principle attracts the best subjects in the empire. You have what it takes to apply yourself to it. For, without having learned anything about it, you have proved for yourself, as your jest about the death of your teacher shows, that it is not great sentences that give intelligence, which is a fundamental Daoist axiom. The Principle is reached neither by sight nor by hearing. It can only be said to be a mystery. Whoever speaks of it shows that he does not understand it."

H. Purity asked Infinite[84]:

"Do you know the Principle?"

"I do not know it," said Infinite.

Then Purity asked Inaction:

"Do you know the Principle?"

"I know it," said Inaction.

"By reflection or by intuition?" asked Purity.

"By reflection," said Inaction.

"Explain yourself," said Purity.

"I think of the Principle as the confluence of contrasts, nobility and vulgarity, collection and dispersion; therefore I know it by reflection."

Purity went to consult Primordial State.

"Who," he asked, "has answered correctly? Who is right and who is wrong?"

Primordial State said:

"Infinite said, 'I do not know the Principle'; this answer is deep. Inaction said, 'I know the Principle'; this answer is superficial. Infinity was right in saying that it knew nothing of the essence of Principle. Inaction could only say that it knew it, as far as its external manifestations were concerned."

Surprised by this answer, Purity said:

---

84   Compare with paragraph A. Analogous piece.

"Ah, then, not to know it is to know it (its essence), to know it (its manifestations) is not to know it (as it really is). But how can we understand this contradiction, that it is by not knowing It that we know It?"

"It is thus," said Primordial State, "the Principle cannot be heard; what is heard is not it. The Principle cannot be seen; what is seen is not it. The Principle cannot be enunciated; what is enunciated is not it. Can we conceive, if not by reason (not by imagination), the non-sensible being that produced all sensible beings? No, certainly not! Therefore, the Principle, which is this non-sensible being, cannot be imagined, nor can it be described. Remember this: both he who asks questions about the Principle and he who answers them prove that they do not know what the Principle is. One can neither ask nor answer what the Principle is. These are vain questions and inane answers, implying ignorance of what the universe is and what the great origin was. These people will not rise above the heights of the earth (of Mount *Kun Lun*). They will not reach the absolute emptiness of perfect abstraction.

I. Diffused Light asked Formless Nothingness (the indeterminate infinite being, about the Principle):

"Does it exist or does it not exist?"

He heard no answer. After staring for a long time, he saw only a dark void, in which, despite all his efforts, he could distinguish nothing, perceive nothing, grasp nothing.

"This is the climax," he said, "and it is impossible to enter it. The notions of being and non-being are common. The nothingness of being cannot be conceived of as existing. But here, existing, is the nothingness of form (the indeterminate infinite being). This is the climax, this is the Beginning!"

J. At the age of eighty, the man who forged swords for the minister of war had not yet lost any of his skill[85]. The minister said to him:

"You are clever, tell me your secret."

"It only consists in the fact that I have always done the same work," replied the blacksmith. "When I was twenty years old, I became fond of forging swords. I had eyes only for that object. I applied myself to nothing else. By dint of forging swords, I ended up forging them without thinking about it. Everything that one does, when one does it incessantly, ends up becoming thoughtless, natural, spontaneous, (and consequently in conformity with the thoughtless and spontaneous influence of the Principle); then one always succeeds."

K. *Ran Qiu* asked Confucius:

"Is it possible to know what existed, before heaven and earth were formed?"

"Yes," said Confucius; "that which exists now (the eternal unchangeable Principle)."

---

85   Compare ch. 3 B.

Ran Qiu withdrew without asking for more. The next day, he saw Confucius again, and said to him:

"Yesterday I asked you what existed before heaven and earth, and you answered me what exists now. At first I thought I understood; but since then, the more I think about it, the less I understand. Please explain to me the meaning of your answer."

"Yesterday you used your natural faculty of apprehension," replied Confucius, "(the intuition arising from the emptiness of the heart, says the commentary), and consequently grasped the truth of my proposition. But since then you have reasoned with your artificial logic, which has obscured the evidence of your original intuition. I told you, what was is what is. For there is neither past nor present, neither beginning nor end, in relation to the Principle, which is always, in the present... But, in my turn, I will ask you a question. Tell me, can there be children and grandchildren who have no parents, no ancestors?"

As *Ran Qiu* was speechless, Confucius said to him:

"Among men, no. The human mode of begetting consists in certain beings communicating their vital principle to an offspring of the same nature. The genesis of heaven and earth (pseudo-children), of all beings (pseudo-grandchildren of the Principle) was very different. Was that which was before heaven and earth (the Principle) a determinate being, having form and shape? No! It who determined all beings (the Principle) was not itself a determinate being. It was the indeterminate primordial being, of which I said that what it was is what it is. It is illogical to think that sentient beings have been produced by other sentient beings in an infinite chain. (This chain had a beginning, the Principle, the non-sentient being, whose influence has extended since then until its unfolding)."

L. *Yen Yuan* said to Confucius:

"Master I have heard you say many times that one should not worry so much about relationships. What does that mean?"

Confucius replied:

"The ancients remained impassive before the vicissitudes of events, because they kept out of the current. The moderns, on the contrary, follow the current and, consequently, are tormented by diverse interests. There is, above the transformations, a unity (the Principle), which remains motionless, indifferent, undifferentiated, unmultiplied. It is from this Unity that the ancients, the true Sages, drew their model. It was the subject of conversation in the park of *Xi Wei*, in the garden of *Huang Di*, in the palace of *Shun*, in the residences of the emperors *Tang* and *Wu*. — *Interpolation:* Later, the so-called scholars, the masters among the disciples of Confucius and *Mo Zi*, began to argue about yes and no. Now the discussions are general. The ancients did not act like that. – Like Unity, the elders were calm and neutral. Since they did not harm anyone, no one wanted to harm them. This one rule of not making enemies is sufficient in matters of relations.

M. (*Additional fragment, probably out of place*)... When I rejoice at the sight of the wooded mountains, the high plateaus, suddenly sadness comes to disturb my joy. Sadness and joy come and go in my heart, without my being able to control them. I can neither withhold the one nor preserve myself from the other. Unfortunately, the human heart is like an inn open to all visitors. Some encounters can be foreseen, but others are unpredictable. Some things can be prevented, but others cannot. The unforeseen, the inevitable, has no remedy for these two evils. Whoever would struggle against them would make himself even more miserable, for failure is certain in the struggle to achieve the impossible. Therefore, there is nothing to be done but to submit to fate, which derives from the Principle. To be silent is the best use that can be made of the faculty of speech. To do nothing is the best use of the faculty to act. To learn nothing is the best use that can be made of intelligence. Wanting to learn too much, wanting to know everything (Confucius), is the worst mistake.

CHAPTER 23 - RETURN TO NATURE[86]

A. Among the disciples of *Lao Dan*, one *Geng Sang Chu Sang*, having finished receiving his teachings, went north, settled at the foot of Mount *Wei Lei*, and in turn taught his disciples. For the sake of Daoist simplicity, he dismissed those of his servants who gave themselves airs of intelligence, and eliminated those of his concubines who were kind, keeping around him only rustic and ordinary people. At the end of three years, as a result of his presence and his examples, the village of *Wei Lei* prospered greatly. The villagers said to each other:

"When Master *Geng Sang* came to live among us, we found him strange. It was because we did not know him well enough. Now that we have had time to get to know him, who among us does not consider him a Sage? Why not make him our local Sage, honoring him as we honor the representative of the dead, the genie of the earth and the genie of the harvest, with obeisances and offerings at certain times?"

Geng Sang Chu heard these words. Sitting in his school in his place as a teacher, he looked worried. His disciples asked him why.

"According to my master *Lao Dan*," he replied, "if spring revives the plants, if autumn ripens the fruits, these are natural effects produced by the great Principle operating in everything, and not the merits of the seasons. Like nature, the superior man must operate concealed (shut up in his house), and not allow himself to be acclaimed by the tumultuous populace. Now the people of this little town of *Wei Lei* are planning to bestow upon me, a vulgar man, the rank and offerings of the Sages. This shames me, for I do not wish to contravene the teachings of my master *Lao Dan*."

"Fear not," said his disciples; "you have all you need and the task is easy. In a channel a whale could not turn, but a smaller fish moves at ease. On a mound a buffalo would not be safe, but a fox lives very well. And then, should not the wise be honored, the skillful be elevated, the beneficent and the useful be distinguished?

---

86   The text of this chapter, very obscure, seems to have undergone many mutilations and transpositions.

Since *Yao* and *Shun*, this has been the rule. Master, let the little people of *Wei Lei* do so. Yield to their wish!"

Geng Sang Chu said:

"Come closer, my children, so that I can tell you… Showing oneself is always fatal. Even an animal big enough to swallow a carriage, if it leaves its lair in the mountains, will not avoid the nets and traps. Even if it were large enough to swallow a ship, the stranded fish will be devoured by ants. It is for the sake of their conservation that birds and wild animals seek the heights, fish and turtles the depths. In the same way, the man who wants to preserve his body and his life, must hide himself in seclusion and mystery… And as for the authority of *Yao* and *Shun* that you have quoted to me, it is null. What have those phrase-coiners, those innovators, those minds occupied with vulgarities and trifles, done for the good of mankind? They honored the Wise; this is the best way to make the people competitive. They elevated the intelligent; this is the best way to turn all citizens into bandits[87]. Of all their inventions, none improved the people. On the contrary, they overexcited the selfishness of the people, a passion that makes parricides, regicides, thieves and plunderers. I tell you that it is from the reign of these two men that all disorders date. If their policy continues, a time will come when men will devour one another."

B. *Nan Rong Zhu* (a man already advanced in age, who had entered the school of *Geng Sang Chu*), having assumed the most respectful position, asked his master:

"At my age, what should I do to become a superior man?"

Geng Sang Chu said to him:

"See to it that your healthy body hermetically imprisons your vital spirit; do not allow thoughts and images to buzz inside you; if you do this for three whole years, you will get what you desire."

Nan Rong Zhu replied:

"Eyes all seem identical, but those of the blind do not see. Ears all seem identical, but those of the deaf do not hear. Hearts seem all alike, but the foolish do not understand. Corporeally I am formed like you, but my mind must be made differently from yours. I do not understand the meaning of the words you have just uttered."

"This must be due to my inability to express myself," said *Geng Sang Chu*. "A mosquito can do nothing for a big butterfly. A small *Yue* hen cannot hatch a goose egg. Obviously I don't have what it takes to carry you to term. Why don't you go south and consult *Lao Zi*?"

C. Following *Geng Sang Chu*'s advice, *Nan Rong Zhu* provided himself with the necessary provisions, walked for seven days and seven nights, and arrived at the place where *Lao Zi* lived…

"Did *Geng Sang Chu* send you?" asked the latter.

---

87   Compare with *Lao Zi*, chapter 3.

"Yes," said *Nan Rong Zhu*.

"Why?" asked *Lao Zi*, "did you bring such a large group?"[88]

Nan Rong Zhu looked behind him, astonished.

"You have not understood my question," said Lao Zi.

Embarrassed, *Nan Rong Zhu* lowered his head and, after raising it, sighed and said:

"Because I didn't understand your question, are you going to forbid me to tell you what brought me here?"

"No," said *Lao Zi*, "tell me!"

Then *Nan Rong Zhu* said:

"If I remain ignorant, men will despise me; if I become learned, it will be by wearing out my body. If I remain bad, I will harm others; if I become good, I will have to wear myself out. If I do not practice fairness, I will harm others; if I do, I will harm myself. These three doubts torment me. What should I do and what should I avoid? *Geng Sang Chu* has sent me to ask your advice."

Lao Zi said:

"I read well in your eyes, at first glance, that you have lost your head. You look like a man trying to pull his sinking relatives from the bottom of the sea. I feel sorry for you."

After gaining admission to *Lao Zi*'s house as a boarder, *Nan Rong Zhu* began moral treatment. He first applied himself to fixing his qualities and eliminating his vices. After ten days of this exercise, which he found hard, he saw *Lao Zi* again.

"Is the work of your purification progressing? It seems to me that it is not yet perfect. Disturbances of external origin (introduced through the senses) can only be repelled by the opposition of an internal barrier (the memory). Disturbances of internal origin (originating in reason) can only be repelled by an external barrier (self-compulsion). Even those who are advanced in the science of the Principle, occasionally experience the attacks of these two kinds of emotions, and still have to guard against them; how much more those who, like you, have lived a long time without knowing the Principle, and are not very advanced."

"Alas," said *Nan Rong Zhu* discouraged, "when a peasant falls ill, he tells his illness to another and finds himself, if not cured, at least relieved. But every time I consult the great Principle, the evil that torments my heart increases, as if I had taken a medicine contrary to my illness. It is too strong for me. Please give me the prescription to make my life last; with that I shall be satisfied."

"And do you think," said *Lao Zi*, "that this can be passed from hand to hand? Making life last involves many things. Are you able to preserve your physical integrity, not to compromise it? Will you always be able to distinguish good from bad? Will you be able to stop, and refrain, at the limit? Will you be able to lose interest in others and concentrate on yourself? Will you be able to keep your mind free and calm? Can you return to the state of your early childhood? The newborn cries day and night without becoming hoarse, so solid is its new nature. It does not

---

88   Of prejudices, attachments, passions, illusions, and errors.

let go of what it has grasped, so concentrated is its will. He stares for a long time without blinking, unmoved by anything. It walks aimlessly and stops for no reason, it moves forward spontaneously, without reflection. To be indifferent and follow nature, that is the formula to make life last."

"The whole formula?" asked *Nan Rong Zhu.*

Lao Zi continued:

"This is the beginning of the superior man's career, what I call the thaw, the break, after which the river begins to run its course. The superior man lives, like other men, on the fruits of the earth, on the blessings of heaven. But he is attached neither to man nor to the thing. Profits and losses leave him equally indifferent. He takes no notice of anything, rejoices in nothing. He hovers in the air, concentrating on himself. This is the formula for making his life last."

"The whole formula?" asked *Nan Rong Zhu.*

Lao Zi continued:

"I said that one must become a small child again. In moving, in acting, the child has no aim, no intention. His body is indifferent like dry wood; his heart is inert like extinguished ash. For him, there is neither happiness nor misfortune. What harm can men do to him who is above these two great vicissitudes of destiny? The superior man is he who is lodged in the highest indifference."

D. (*In the following text, it is probably* Zhuang Zhou *who speaks*). He whose heart has reached this peak of immutability emits a natural light (pure reason, without anything conventional) which reveals to him what may still remain in him of artificiality. The more he detaches himself from this artificiality, the more stable he will be. In time, the artificial will disappear completely, leaving only the natural in him. Men who have reached this state are called celestial children, celestial persons; that is, men who have returned to their natural state, who have become again as heaven made them.

This cannot be learned by theory or practice, but by intuition or exclusion. To stop where no more can be learned (and to remain, says the commentary, in indifference and inaction) is to be perfectly wise. He who pretends to ignore (to decide, to act, at random), will be broken by the fatal course of things (for he will inevitably come into conflict with destiny).

When all provisions have been made and all precautions taken for the maintenance of the body, when one has not provoked others by any offense, then, if any misfortune occurs, it must be attributed to fate, not to men, and, consequently, care must be taken not to avoid it by doing any baseness, and even care must be taken not to grieve over it in the heart. It is in man's power to close the tower of his mind (his heart) well; it is in his power to keep it closed, provided he does not examine or discuss what is presented to him, but simply refuses access.

Every act of one who is not perfectly indifferent is a disorder. The object of the act, having entered his heart, lodges there and never leaves. With every new act, there is a new disorder.

He who does in the light of day what is not good, will be punished by men from time to time. If he has done it in the dark, the spirits will punish him from time to time. Remembering that when one is not observed by men, one is observed by the spirits, makes one behave well even in the secrecy of one's retreat.

Those who take care of their life do not move to become famous. Those who burn to acquire, extend their external activities. The former are men of reason, the latter are men of commerce. The latter strive to rise, to progress, to achieve their ambition. They are storehouses of worries and concerns. They are so full of themselves that there is no room in their hearts even for love of their fellow men. So they are hated as if they were no longer men.

Of all the instruments of death, desire is the most murderous; the famous sword *Mo Ye* has not killed so many men. The worst killers, it is said, are *yin* and *yang*, from which no one escapes, of all men who populate the in-between of heaven and earth. And yet it is true that while *yin* and *yang* kill men, it is because men's appetites give them over to these killers.

E. The one and universal Principle subsists in the multiplicity of beings, in their genesis and destruction. All the different beings are such by accidental and temporary differentiation (individuation) from the Whole, and their destiny is to return to this Whole, of which their essence is a participation. Of this return, the vulgar say that the living who are dead and have not found the way, wander like ghosts; and that those who are dead and have found the way, are defunct (extinct). Survival and extinction are two ways of speaking of an identical return, arising from the fact that we have applied to the state of the non-sentient being, the notions proper to the sentient being. The truth is that, having come out of the nothingness of form (indeterminate being) by their generation, and having returned to the nothingness of form by their death, beings retain a reality (that of the universal Whole) but no longer have a place; they retain a duration (that of the eternal Whole) but no longer have time. The reality without place, the duration without time, is the universe, the cosmic unity, the Whole, the Principle. It is within this unity that births and deaths, appearances and disappearances, silent and imperceptible, take place. It has been called the heavenly or natural gate, the doorway into and out of existence. This door is the non-being of form, the undefined being. Everything has come out of it. A sentient being cannot ultimately be derived from a sensible being. It necessarily derives from the non-being of form. This non-being of form is unity, the Principle. This is the secret of the Sages, the seed of esoteric science.

In their dissertations on the origin, the ancients who attained a higher degree of science, gave three opinions. Some thought that for all eternity there existed a definite, infinite being, author of all limited beings. Others, suppressing the infinite being, thought that, for all eternity, there existed limited beings who passed through alternate phases of life and death. Finally, others thought that first there was the formless nothingness (the indefinite infinite being), from which all definite beings emanated, with their genesis and cessations. Indefinite being, genesis, cessation, these three terms are together, like the head, the rump and tail of an animal. I (*Zhuang Zhou*) support this thesis. For me, the indefinite being, all becomings, all endings, form a complex, a whole. I shake hands with those who think so. However, at a given moment, the three opinions mentioned above could be reconciled. They are related, like branches of the same tree.

Particular being is to indefinite being what soot (palpable deposit) is to smoke (impalpable). When the soot is deposited, there has been no new production, but only a passage from the impalpable to the palpable, the soot being a concrete smoke. And likewise, if this soot dissipates again into smoke, there will still be only a conversion, with no essential modification. I know that the term conversion, which I use to express the succession of lives and deaths in the bosom of the Principle, is not a common term; but I must say so, or I shall not be able to express myself... The disarticulated limbs of a slaughtered ox are a victim. Several rooms are a house. Life and death are the same state. From life to death, there is no transformation, there is conversion. Philosophers get heated when it comes to defining the difference between these two states. For me, there is no difference; the two states are one.

F. In case of injury, the closer the injured person is to one, the less one apologizes. Forgiveness is asked of the peasant stranger whose foot has been stepped on; but the father does not ask forgiveness of his son in the same situation. The height of rituals is to do none. The height of decorum is to make fun of everything. The height of intelligence is to think of nothing. The height of goodness is to love nothing. The height of sincerity is to pay no deposits. Deviations of the appetites must be repressed. The aberrations of the mind must be corrected. Everything that impedes the free flow of the Principle must be discarded. Wanting to be noble, rich, distinguished, respected, recognized and advantaged are the six appetites. Air, posture, beauty, argument, breath and thought are the things that provoke the aberrations of the mind. Antipathy, sympathy, indulgence, anger, pain and joy, are the things that impede the free flow of the Principle. Repulsion and attraction, taking and giving, knowledge and power, are all obstacles. The interior from which these twenty-four causes of disorder have been removed, becomes settled, tranquil, luminous, empty, non-acting and capable of everything.

The Principle is the source of all active faculties, life is its manifestation, the particular nature is a modality of this life, its movements are the acts, the failed acts are the faults.

The learned guess and speculate; and when they cannot see more clearly, they do as little children do and stare at an object.

To act only when one cannot do otherwise is an ordered action. To act without being compelled to do so is dangerous interference. Knowledge and action must go hand in hand.

G. *Yi* was a very skilled archer (artificial art), and extremely stupid by nature. There are people very wise by nature, who do not understand any art. Nature is the basis of everything.

Freedom is part of natural perfection. It is not lost just by confinement in a cage. *Tang* encaged *Yi Yin*, making him his cook. Duke *Mu* of *Qin* caged *Bo Li Xi*, giving him five goatskins[89]. They encage men by offering them what they like. All favors enslave.

Freedom of spirit requires the absence of interest. He who has passed through the ordeal of having his feet amputated, no longer dresses; because he can no longer beautify himself, he no longer has that interest. He who is to be executed, no longer feels vertigo at any height; because he is no longer afraid of falling, he no longer has any interest in preserving his life.

To be a man who has returned to the state of nature, one must have renounced the friendship of men, and all the little means which serve to gain and maintain it. One must have become insensible to veneration and outrage; one must always maintain the natural equilibrium.

One must be indifferent, before making an effort, before acting; so that the effort, the action, which comes from non-effort, from non-action, is natural.

To enjoy peace, one must keep the body in a good state. For the vital spirits to function well, one must put the heart in order. To act always well, one must only give up rest when one can do nothing else. This is the way of the Wise.

CHAPTER 24 - SIMPLICITY

A. When the scholar *Nü Shang* introduced the anchorite *Xu Wugui* to the Marquis *Wu* of *Wei*, the latter addressed him with the words of interest required by the rites, saying:

"Your privations in the mountains and forests will no doubt have weakened you; you are no longer able to continue this kind of life and seek some social position; that is why you have come to me, is it not?"

"No," said *Xu Wugui*, "I have come to give you my condolences. If you continue to let your passions plague your inner self, your vital spirit will wear out. If you choose to repress them, given the hold you have allowed them to take, you will have to discipline yourself greatly. I offer you my condolences, in any case."

This speech displeased the marquis, who looked at *Xu Wugui* with a haughty air and did not respond.

Seeing that the marquis was unable to receive the abstract Daoist teaching, *Xu Wugui* tried to give it to him concretely.

"Let me add something else," he said. "I am a good judge of dogs. I consider those who are only concerned with satisfying their voracity (the sensual type) to be of the lowest class. I consider those who bask in the sun (the intellectuals) to be of the middle class. Lastly, I consider those who seem indifferent to everything to be of the higher class; for, once set in motion, no distractions will cause them to stray..."

---

89   Compare with *Mencius*, V. I. 7 — V. I. 9.

"I also know how to judge horses. Those that describe ingenious geometrical figures, I consider worthy of belonging to a prince. Those that charge with strength without worrying about danger, I consider them to be made for an emperor..."

"Marquis, free yourself from worries and distractions of a lower order; apply yourself to the essential."

Marquis *Wu* laughed out loud, happy to have understood this simple speech.

When *Xu Wugui* came out, *Nü Shang* said to him:

"You are the first who has succeeded in pleasing our prince. No matter how many times I have spoken to him about the Odes, the Annals, the Rituals, the Music, the Statistics, and the Military Art[90], I have never seen him smile until his teeth were bared. What must you have said to put him in such a good humor?"

"I spoke to him," said *Xu Wugui*, "of his own subjects, of dogs and horses."

"Bah!" said *Nü Shang*.

"You know the story of the man from the country of *Yue*, who was exiled to a distant region," said *Xu Wugui*. "After a few days, seeing a man from *Yue*, he was glad. After a few months, seeing a *Yue* object, he was pleased. After a few years, the sight of a man or an object that only resembled those of his country, pleased him. An effect of his growing nostalgia... For the man lost in the steppes of the north, living among the grasses and wild beasts, to hear the footsteps of a man is a joy; and how much more, when that man is a friend, a brother, with whom he can converse heart to heart... It was as a brother, by nature, that I spoke to your prince. It had been so long since this poor man, saturated with pedantic speeches, had listened to the simple and natural words of another man. That is why he was glad when he heard me, because it relieved his homesickness."

B. (*Another variation on the same theme*). Receiving *Xu Wugui* in audience, Marquis *Wu* said to him:

"Master, you have lived long in the mountains and forests, feeding on roots and chestnuts, onions and wild garlic. Now you are old, and you cannot continue with this kind of life. Doubtless the taste for wine and meat has returned to you. Is it not to have your share that you have come to offer me your advice for the good government of my marquisate[91]?"

"It is not for that," said *Xu Wugui*. "I have been accustomed to privation from my childhood, and have no desire for your wine or your meat. I have come to give you my condolences."

"For what misfortune?" asked the marquis in astonishment.

"For the ruin of your body and mind," said *Xu Wugui*. "Heaven and earth extend to all beings, whoever they may be, a uniform influence, which aims at making all attain their natural perfection, the highest as well as the lowest. Why then, lord of a marquisate, do you make your people suffer by your exactions, for the pleasure of your senses which ruins your body? Your spirit, naturally in consonance with

---

90   Confucian themes, deadly dull.
91   A blow at the paid politicians of the time.

the tendency of heaven and earth, cannot approve of this, and therefore suffers a violence that ruins it. It is for the double ruin, of your body and of your mind, that I give you my condolences."

Surprised by this speech, the marquis *Wu* said:

"I have long desired your visit. I would like to practice kindness to my people. I would like to be fair to my neighbors. What must I do for this?"

Xu Wugui said:

"Cease your fortress building, your maneuvers and exercises, which impoverish your people and worry their neighbors. Stop buying plans of conquest, estimates of stratagems. All war exhausts the people, the enemy and the warrior, by the anxieties it provokes. Like heaven and earth, be kind to all and harm none. All will be well, your people, your neighbors and yourself."

C. *Huang Di* was going to visit *Da Wei* on *Ju Ci* mountain, *Fang Ming* was driving his chariot, *Chang Yu* was acting as counterweight, *Zhang Ruo* and *Xi Peng* were in front, *Kun Hun* and *Hua Ji* were behind. On the plain of *Xian Cheng*, the seven Sages got lost. After meeting a boy herding horses, they asked him if he knew where *Ju Ci* mountain was and where *Da Wei* lived.

"I know," said the boy.

"Can it be," said *Huang Di*, "that, without having studied, this boy knows where Mount *Ju Ci* is, and knows *Da Wei*? Could he be a transcendent being?"

And *Huang Di* asked him how to rule the empire well.

"In the same way that I rule my horses," replied the boy; "I think it is no more difficult... I used to walk only within the confines of space, and the multitude of the particular beings I had to look at almost tired my eyes. Then, an old man advised me to ride the chariot of the sun and walk on the plain of *Xian Cheng* (to rise above the world of individuals, to see everything from as high as the sun). I followed his advice and my eyes were cured. Now I only walk outside the limits of real space, in the universal, in abstraction. It is from this point of view, it seems to me, that the empire can be ruled as I rule my horses."

As *Huang Di* insisted that he explain further, the mysterious boy told him.

"I keep away from my horses whatever may harm them; as for everything else, I leave them to their own devices. I think that, in the government of men, an emperor should confine himself to this."

Astonished, *Huang Di* prostrated himself, touched the earth with his forehead, called the child Heavenly Master, and went on his way.

D. It is in abstraction that the Principle must be sought. It is from the infinite that particular beings must be looked at. But most men do just the opposite.

Philosophers are lost in their speculations, sophists in their distinctions, investigators in their researches. All these men are captive in the limits of space, blinded by particular beings.

So it is with those who court princes in order to get a post, those who seek the favor of the people, those who strive for prizes. The same with the ascetics who macerate themselves to become famous; the legists, the ceremonialists, the musicians, who compete with each other; finally those who make a profession of exercising Confucian goodness and equity). The peasant is absorbed by his work, the merchant by his trade, the artisan by his profession, the commoner by his small daily business.

The more favorable the circumstances, the more they become immersed in their specialty. At every failure, at every disappointment, they grieve. They follow a fixed idea, never coming to an agreement about things. They exhaust their bodies and overwhelm their minds. And this, all their lives. Alas!

E. *Zhuang Zhou* said to *Hui Zi*:
"From the fact that an archer has reached by chance a goal he did not aim at, can we conclude that he is a good archer? And, since this chance can happen to anyone, can we say that all men are good archers?"

"Yes," said the sophist *Hui Zi*.

Zhuang Zhou continued:

"From the fact that in this world there is no universally accepted notion of what is good, and that every man calls what he likes good; from this fact, can we conclude that all men are good?"

"Yes," said *Hui Zi*.

"Then," said *Zhuang Zhou* "it must also be said that the five present Confucian schools, *Mo Zi*, *Yang Zhu*, *Gong Sun Long* and yours are right at the same time. But it is not possible for the truth to resonate in five different chords at the same time."

As someone boasted to *Lu Ju* that he could produce heat in winter and cold in summer, *Lu Ju* said to him, "What a great success, to cause a break in the cosmic balance! I do just the opposite, I put myself in unison with universal harmony. See for yourself."

Having tuned two zithers to the same note, *Lu Ju* placed one in the outer room and the other on an inner floor. When he played the chord *gong* on one, the same chord *gong* sounded on the other. The same was true for the chord *jue* and the others. Each zither made the other vibrate in unison from a distance...

"If *Lu Ju* had played a discordant note," said *Zhuang Zhou*, "not in accordance with the scale, the twenty-five strings of the other zither would not have resounded, but would have trembled, as this dissonance offended the established tuning of the strings. The same is true of the five schools (five zithers, each with a different tuning). Each one makes the others tremble. How is it possible that they are all right?"

"Even if one makes people tremble," said *Hui Zi*, "this does not prove one wrong. Whoever has the last word is right. For a long time now, the disciples of Confucius, of *Mo Zi*, of *Yang Zhu*, and of *Gong Sun Long*, have been picking apart my arguments, trying to stun me with their shouting. They have never been able to silence me; therefore, I am right."

"Listen to this story," said *Zhuang Zhou*. "In a moment of distress, a man of *Qi* sold his only son to the *Song*, to make him a eunuch. The same man kept with veneration the vessels for offerings to the ancestors. He kept the offering vessels and, by castration of his son, suppressed the descendants who would have made the offerings. You do the same as this father, sophist, you for whom an expedient is everything, the truth counts for nothing. — Listen again to the story of this servant of *Chu*, who was given an important mission by his master. Having to cross a river in a ferry at midnight in a lonely place, he could not suppress his quarrelsome temper and quarreled with the ferryman who threw him into the water. You will end up badly like this man, you who quarrel with everyone for the sake of quarrelling."

Even after *Hui Zi*'s death, *Zhuang Zhou* did not cease to persecute him with his taunts. A statue of *Hui Zi* was erected on *Hui Zi*'s grave. One day, following a funeral procession, *Zhuang Zhou*, who was passing by, suddenly said, pointing to the statue:

"See the lime speck on this man's nose!"

And he ordered *Shi*, the carpenter (who accompanied the procession, to make any repairs to the bier or coffin) to remove it. The carpenter struck a blow with his axe in front of the statue's nose, and the lime grain was carried away by the air current. Prince *Yuan* of *Song*, hearing of the fact, admired the carpenter's skill and said to him.

"Do your trick again on my person."

The carpenter drew back, saying:

"I only dare to do it on dead matter."

"For me," said *Zhuang Zhou*, "it is quite the opposite. Since *Hui Zi* died, I no longer have anyone to operate on."

(*The axe represents the powerful doctrine of* Zhuang Zhou, *the grain of lime represents the small spirit of* Hui Zi. *When* Zhuang Zhou *argued, without even touching* Hui Zi, *the little spirit of* Hui Zi *vanished. Commentary*).

F. When *Guan Zhong* (*Guan Zi*, 7th century BC) fell seriously ill, Duke *Huan* of *Qi*, whose minister he was, came to him and said.

"Father *Zhong*, your illness is serious. If it should worsen (euphemism, if you should die), tell me, to whom shall I entrust my dukedom?"

"You are the master," said *Guan Zhong*.

"Would *Bao Shu Ya* do well?" asked the duke.

"No," said *Guan Zhong*. "This man is too much of a purist, he is too exacting. He does not mix with anyone inferior to him. He forgives no one his faults. If you make him a minister, he will inevitably offend both his master and his subjects. You would have to get rid of him in a short time."

"Then whom shall I appoint?" asked the duke.

"Since you insist," said *Guan Zhong*, "take *Xi Peng*. This one (a good Daoist, he is so abstract, that) his prince will not notice his presence, and no one will be able to gainsay him. He always reproaches himself for not being as perfect as *Huang Di*, and dares not reproach anyone. The sages of the first order are those who differ from the common people by their transcendence; the sages of the second order are those who differ from them by their talent. If the latter want to impose themselves by their talent, they drive men away. If, in spite of their talent, they put themselves below men, they win them all over. *Xi Peng* is such a man. Besides, since his family and his person are not well known, no one envies him. Since I must advise you, I repeat, take *Xi Peng*[92]."

G. The king of *Wu*, sailing down the Blue River, landed on the island of the monkeys. When these animals saw him coming, they fled and hid in the bushes. Only one remained, frolicking as if mocking him. The king shot an arrow at it. The monkey caught it on the fly. Irritated, the king ordered his entire entourage to hunt down the impertinent monkey, who succumbed to their numbers. Before its corpse, the king gave the following lesson to his favorite *Yen Bu Yi*:

"This monkey has perished, for having provoked me with the ostentation of his skill. Take care of yourself! Do not imitate him! Do not bother me with your bravado!"

Frightened, *Yen Bu Yi* asked *Dong Wu* to train him in simplicity. After three years, everyone spoke highly of him.

H. *Nan Bo Zi Qi* was sitting, looking at the sky and sighing. Finding him in that state, *Yen Cheng Zi* said to him:

"You were in ecstasy[93]."

Zi Qi said:

"I once lived as a hermit in the mountain caves. The prince of *Qi* took me out to become a minister, and the people of *Qi* congratulated him. I must have betrayed myself so that he found me like this. I must have sold myself, for him to have acquired me in this way. Alas, my freedom is at an end. I pity those who lose themselves by accepting charges. I pity those who complain of not having a charge. I cannot run away. There is nothing left for me but to retreat into ecstasy."

I. When Confucius went to the kingdom of *Chu*, the king offered him the wine of welcome. *Sun Shu Ao* presented the cup, *Shi Nan Yi Liao* made the preliminary libation, and then said:

"It was at this time, the elders made a speech."

Confucius said:

"I shall apply today the method of speech without words, of which you, my masters, have made such good use. You *Yi Liao* avoided a battle and brought peace between *Chu* and *Song* by juggling bells. You, *Sun Shu Ao*, softened *Qin Qiu*'s bandits and led them to lay down their arms by dancing the pantomime before them. If I dared, in front of you, to speak otherwise than with my silence, may I be struck dumb for life!"

---

92   Compare with *Lie Zi*, ch. 6 C.
93   Compare with ch. 2 A.

Instead of seeking so much, stay with the unity of the Principle; stay in silence, before the ineffable; that is perfection. Those who do otherwise are evil men.

The greatness of the sea is that it gathers in its bosom all the currents of the eastern slope. So does the Sage, who embraces heaven and earth, and does good to all, without wishing to be known. He who has passed thus, without charges during his life, without titles after his death, without making a fortune, without becoming famous, is a great man.

A dog is not a good dog because he barks a lot, a man is not a wise man because he talks a lot. To be a great man, it is not enough to believe that one is great, it is not enough to pretend to make others believe that one is great. To be great means to be complete, like heaven and earth. We only become great by imitating the way of being and acting of heaven and earth. To strive for it without haste, but also without hesitation; not to be swayed by anything; to return to oneself without tiring, to study antiquity without saddening oneself; this is what makes a great man.

J. *Zi Qi* had eight sons. He lined them all up before the physiognomist *Jiu Fang Yin*, and said to him:

"Please examine these boys, and tell me which of them show signs of good omen."

The soothsayer said:

"This one, *Kun*."

Amazed and joyful, the father asked:

"What do you predict for him?"

"He will eat the food of a prince for the rest of his life," said the soothsayer.

At these words, *Zi Qi*'s joy was replaced by sadness. He said, weeping:

"What wrong has my son done, to have such a fate?"

"When someone eats from a prince's table, this honor goes back to the third generation of his ancestors. So you shall have your share of your son's good fortune. And do you weep, as if you were afraid of this happiness? Can it be that what is good for your son is bad for you?"

"Alas," said *Zi Qi*, "are you sure you interpret my son's destiny correctly? That he shall have all his life wine and meat at his discretion is well-being, no doubt, but at what price my son will get it is what you have perhaps not seen clearly. I distrust this omen, for only extraordinary things happen to me. Although I have no flocks, a sheep came to lamb at my house. Although I don't hunt, a quail has built its nest in my house. Aren't these things strange? I'm afraid my son has a strange future, too. I would have wished him to live as I do, free between heaven and earth, enjoying as I do the blessings of heaven and feeding on the fruits of the earth. I do not wish him, any more than myself, to have concerns, worries, or adventures. I wish, as I do, that he would soar so high in natural simplicity that no earthly thing could make any impression upon him. I wish him, like myself, had been absorbed in indifference, not in interest. And now you predict a most vulgar reward for him. This supposes that he will have rendered very vulgar services. Therefore, the omen is bad. An inevitable fate, probably, for neither my son nor I have sinned, so it must be a decree of destiny. That's why I'm crying."

Later, both the fortune-teller's prediction and the father's fears came true, as follows: *Zi Qi* had sent his son *Kun* to the country of *Yen*, and bandits captured him on the way. As it would have been difficult for them to sell him into slavery while he was whole, they cut off one of his feet and sold him into the principality of *Qi*, where he became road inspector of the capital. For the rest of his life he ate his share of Prince *Qi*'s leftovers, as the soothsayer had predicted; plagued by the vilest worries, as his father had foreseen.

K. *Nie Que* having found *Xu You*, asked him:
"Where are you going?"
"I am leaving the service of Emperor *Yao*," said *Xu You*.
"Why?" asked *Nie Que*.
"Because this man makes a fool of himself with his affected kindness. He thinks he is doing something wonderful by attracting men. What could be more banal than that? Show affection to men, and they will love you; do them good, and they will come running; flatter them, and they will exalt you; then, at the slightest displeasure, they will abandon you. Certainly, kindness attracts; but those who are attracted, come for the benefit it brings them, not for the love of the one who treats them well. Kindness is a man-trapping machine, similar to bird-traps. It is not possible to do good to all men, whose natures are so diverse, by the same procedure. *Yao* believes, with his goodness, that he is doing good to the empire, while he is ruining it. This is because he sees from within, subject to illusion. The Sages, who see from the outside, were right in this case."

Let us observe, among the diverse natures of men, the following three classes: the lazy, the adherent, and the affable... The lazy learn the phrases of a master, assimilate them, and repeat them, believing they are saying something, while, like mere parrots, they merely recite... Adherents become attached to the one who gives them life, like lice living on pigs. The day comes when the butcher, having killed the pig, sets it on fire. The same thing sometimes happens with the parasites of a patron... The affable type was *Shun*. He attracted people with some attraction, like fat attracts ants by its rancid smell. People loved the smell of *Shun*. Every time he changed his residence, people followed him. As a result, *Shun* never knew peace.

Well, the transcendent man is neither lazy, nor adherent, nor affable. He hates popularity above all else. He is not familiar. He does not give up. He is devoted to his abstract higher principles, he gets along with everyone, but he is a friend to no one. For him, ants are not simple enough. He is simple, like sheep, like fish. He takes as true what he sees, what he hears, what he thinks. When he acts spontaneously, his action is straight as a line drawn with a string. When he lets himself be carried along by events, he adapts himself to their course.

L. The true men of antiquity adjusted themselves to evolution, and never intervened, by an artificial effort, in the natural course of things. Living, they preferred life to death; dead, they preferred death to life. Each thing in its own time, as when you take a medicine.

To fight against the course of things is to seek ruin. Thus the minister *Wen Zhong*, in saving the kingdom of *Yue*, which was to perish, brought about his own destruction.

One should not wish that the owl had better eyesight and the crane shorter legs. Their natural lot is what suits them best.

He who knows how to make the most of his natural resources always comes out on top. Thus, although the wind and the sun make the water of the rivers evaporate, they continue to flow, because the springs, their natural reserves, feed their course.

Nothing is more constant, more faithful, than natural laws, such as that which says that water flows down slopes, such as that which causes opaque bodies to cast a shadow.

Let man beware of exhausting what nature has given him by excessive and immoderate use. Sight wears out the eyes, hearing wears out the ears, thought wears out the mind, all activity wears out the agent. And to think that some are proud of the abuses they have committed in this matter. Is this not a fatal delusion?

M. Man, whose body occupies so small a place on earth, reaches through space to heaven by his spirit. He knows the great unity, its first state of concentration, the multiplication of beings, the universal evolution, the immensity of the world, the reality of all that it contains, the firmness of the laws that govern it. At the bottom of everything is nature. In the depths of nature is the pivot of everything (the Principle), which seems dual (*yin* and *yang*) without really being so, which is knowable but not adequately so. Man came to know it by dint of seeking it. Extending beyond the limits of the world, his mind reached (the Principle) the elusive reality, always the same, always flawless. This is his greatest achievement. He achieved it by reasoning, from certainties already acquired, about things still uncertain, which gradually became certain in turn, the knowledge of the Principle being the ultimate final certainty.

Chapter 25 - Truth

A. Having gone *Ze Yang* (*Peng Zeyang*) to *Chu*, the minister *Yi Jie* announced his arrival to the king of that country, and then returned to his business. Failing to obtain an audience, *Ze Yang* turned to *Wang Guo*, a sage of the country, and asked him to speak on his behalf.

"Ask *Gong Yue Xiu* for this service," said *Wang Guo*.

"Who is it?" asked *Ze Yang*.

"He is," said *Wang Guo*, "a man who harpoons turtles in the river during the winter and rests in the forest during the summer (a Daoist sage). *Yi Jie* won't do anything for you. Ambitious, scheming, selfish, works only for himself. *Gong Yue Xiu*, absolutely selfless, imposes himself, by the elevation of his principles, on the brutal king of *Chu*."

"Through the charm of his conversation, the Sage makes the people forget the torments of misery and makes them resign themselves. By his moral ascendancy, he makes the great forget the elevation of their rank and renders them humble. He fraternizes with the small and converses with the great, giving to each what he can understand and keeping the rest for himself. Without speaking, he fills those around him with peace. Without preaching, he mends them. He does not disdain to remain, from time to time, with his family, to fulfill his role as a father and to do good to the people. Simple, firm, calm, he is oblivious to all worries and imposes himself on everyone. *Gong Yue Xiu is such a man. He alone will be able to make the king of* Chu, *who is ill-disposed toward you, receive you.*"

B. The Sage understands that, linked together, all beings form one body (one whole), but he does not pretend to penetrate into the intimate nature of this link, which is the mystery of the cosmic norm. Following in all his movements the universal law, he is the agent of heaven. Men call him Wise, because he cooperates with heaven. He does not concern himself with knowing what cannot be known, but acts with the knowledge he has, persistently, constantly. He does not reflect on what qualities he may have, but leaves them to the view of others, without ascribing to himself what is a gift of nature. He is benevolent to men, not from affection, but from instinct, and does not claim their gratitude.

C. When, after a long absence, a man has returned to his homeland, he feels a satisfaction that neither the sight of the graves that have multiplied, nor the ruins that vegetation invades, nor the disappearance of nine-tenths of his acquaintances, can alter. It is that he sees again in his mind what once was, abstracting himself from what is. It is that he rises above the present circumstances.

So does the Sage, unmoved by the vicissitudes of the world, contemplating in them the unchanging nature.

So did the legendary ruler *Ren Xiang*. He remained indifferent, in the center of the revolving circle of worldly things, letting himself be carried along by the eternal and undivided evolution, remaining non-transformed (because of his indifference) in the universal transformation. This position is unique.

One should not try to imitate heaven (in the manner of Confucius), with positive acts. One must imitate heaven by detaching oneself from everything. This is the way the Sage serves humanity. He abstracts himself from everything, and follows his time, without defect and without excess. This is the passive union with the Principle, the only possible one. To seek active union is to attempt the impossible[94]. The emperor's minister *Tang* regarded his office rather as honorary. He let everything pass, and was careful not to enforce the laws. This made his government successful. Now, on the contrary, Confucius would like everything to be thoroughly examined and many regulations to be enacted. He forgets the very true words of *Yong Cheng* (an ancient Daoist): "To add days to years, to suppose a

---

94   Here the text is probably mutilated.

substance behind accidents, are errors coming from a fictitious conception of the nature of time and beings. Reality is an eternal present, an essential unity." (The commentary adds that there is not even an *I* and a *you*).

D. The king of *Wei* had concluded a treaty with the king of *Qi*, who violated it. The king of *Wei*, furious, resolved to have him assassinated by a hired assassin (standard procedure at the time). *Gongsun Yen*, his minister of war, said to him:

"You who have ten thousand chariots, you are going to entrust your revenge to a vile assassin. Give me two hundred thousand men instead. I will lay waste the country of *Qi*, I will besiege its king in his capital, I will kill him in his defeat. This will be noble and complete."

The minister *Ji Zi* thought the advice bad and said to the king:

"Do not provoke *Qi*. We have just built a beautiful wall. If it were damaged, it would cause pain to the citizens working on it. Peace is the solid foundation of power. The Minister of War is a fool, who should not be listened to."

Minister *Hua Zi* (Daoist) found both opinions equally bad, and said to the king:

"He who, in order to have an opportunity to show his military skill, advised you to go to war, is a foolish one. He who, in order to show his eloquence, advised you to make peace, is also foolish. His two opinions are the same."

"But then, what shall I do?" asked the king.

"Meditate on the Principle," said *Hua Zi*, "and draw the conclusion."

As the king was unsuccessful, *Hui Zi* brought to him *Dai Jinren*, a sophist friend. The latter went into the matter with the following allegory:

"Imagine a slug. This slug has two horns. Its left horn is the principality of the Brutal king; its right horn is that of the Savage king. These two kingdoms are constantly at war. The dead, without number, are scattered on the ground. A fortnight after his defeat, the vanquished already seeks revenge."

"Nonsense!" said the king of *Wei*.

"I am sorry," said *Dai Jinren*. "O, king, do you consider that space is limited in any of its six dimensions?"

"No," said the king; "space is unlimited in all six dimensions."

"Thus," said *Dai Jinren*, "immense space has no boundaries; do the two small principalities of *Wei* and *Qi* have boundaries?"

"No," said the king, little given to dialectics, and judging that he could not grant to the lesser what he had denied to the greater."

"There are no boundaries, therefore there is no dispute," said *Dai Jinren*. "Now, O king, tell me how you differ from the wild king of the right horn."

"I see no difference," said the king.

Dai Jinren went away, leaving the king utterly bewildered. When *Hui Zi* returned, the king said to him:

"This is a superior man; only a wise man would know how to answer him."

"That's right," said *Hui Zi*. "When you blow on a clarinet, a bright sound comes out; when you blow on the hilt (hollow, shell-shaped) of a sword, only a whisper comes out. If *Dai Jinren* were to be appraised in his just measure, the praises of *Yao* and *Shun* would be reduced to a murmur, those of *Dai Jinren* would sound like a clarinet."

The affairs of *Wei* and *Qi* were left at that.

E. Confucius went to *Chu* and stayed at *Yi Qiu*, in the house of a condiment maker. Immediately, in the neighboring house, they climbed onto the roof (flat, to look into the courtyard of the house where Confucius was staying).

"Why do these people look so frightened?" asked the disciple *Zi Lu*, who accompanied Confucius.

"They are the family of a Sage, who willingly hides among the people and lives in obscurity," said Confucius. "The moral elevation of this man is sublime. He hides it carefully, speaking only of trivial matters, without betraying the secret of his heart. His views differed from those of the common people of the time, and he has little to do with men. He has been buried here, in life, in the manner of *Yi Liao*."

"May I go and invite him to come and see us?" asked *Zi Lu*.

"It would be a waste of time," said Confucius. "He just went up to the roof to see if it is really me who is passing by. Since I am engaged in politics, he must have little desire to converse with me. Knowing that I am going to visit the King of *Chu*, he must be afraid that I will reveal his retirement, and that the King will force him to take a job. I am sure he has just retired to a safe place."

Zi Lu went to see, and found the house deserted.

F. The farm manager of *Zhang Wu*, said to *Zi Lao*, a disciple of Confucius:

"If ever you are entrusted with a charge, be neither superficial nor meticulous. In the past, when I cultivated, I was guilty of both: insufficient plowing, excessive weeding, resulting in unsatisfactory harvests. Now I plow deeply, then weed moderately; hence the abundant harvest."

Hearing this, *Zhuang Zhou* said:

"At present, in cultivating their body and mind, many people fall into the faults indicated by this steward. Either they plow the soil of their nature insufficiently, and allow it to be overrun by passions. Or they weed it indiscriminately, uprooting what should be preserved, destroying its natural qualities."

"If care is not taken, vices invade a healthy nature, as ulcers invade a healthy body, by the effect of excessive internal heat revealing itself on the outside."

G. *Bo Ju*, who was studying with *Lao Dan*, said to him one day:

"Let me take a tour of the empire."

"What's the point?," said *Lao Dan*. "The empire is the same as here everywhere."

Bo Ju insisted and *Lao Dan* asked him:

"In which principality will you begin your tour?"

"The principality of *Qi*," said *Bo Ju*. "When I get there, I will go straight to the corpse of one of those tortured ones, whom the king of *Qi* leaves lying unburied; I will straighten him up, cover him with my mantle, cry to heaven on his behalf, say to him, shouting: Brother! brother! did you have to be a victim of the inconsistency of those who have the empire in their hands? The rulers forbid, on pain of death, to steal, to kill. And these same men encourage theft and murder by honoring nobility and wealth, which are the bait for crime. As long as distinctions and property are maintained, will there ever be an end to conflict among men?"

"In the past, princes were grateful for the order of their subjects and blamed each other for any disorder. When a man perished, they blamed each other for his loss. Now it is very different. Laws and ordinances are traps from which no one can escape. There is the death penalty for those who have not completed tasks that are impossible. Thus, reduced to the limit, the people lose their natural honesty and commit excesses. To whom are these excesses to be imputed? To the wretches who atone for them? or to the princes who have provoked them?"

H. In sixty years of life, *Qu Bo Yu* changed his mind sixty times. Fifty-nine times he had firmly believed that he was in possession of the truth, fifty-nine times he had suddenly recognized that he was in error. And who knows whether his sixtieth opinion, with which he died, was better founded than the previous fifty-nine? So it is with every man who is attached to beings in detail, who seeks something other than the confused knowledge of the Principle. Beings become, it is a fact; but the root of this becoming is invisible. From his false science of detail, the vulgar draw erroneous consequences; whereas, if he would start from his ignorance, he could arrive at the true science, that of the Principle, that of the Absolute, the origin of all. This is the great error. Unfortunately, there are few who get rid of it… So, when men say yes, is it really yes? When they say no, is it really no? What is the value, the truth, of human affirmations? Only the absolute is true, because it alone is.

I. Confucius asked the same question, first to the great historian *Da Tao*, then to *Bo Changqian* and finally to *Xi Wei*:

"Duke *Ling* of *Wei* was a drunkard and a libertine; he ruled badly and his word could not be trusted. He would have deserved a worse posthumous epithet than *Ling*. Why was his name *Ling*?"

"Because the people, who were quite fond of him, wanted it thus," answered *Da Tao*.

"Because the censors granted him extenuating circumstances," said *Bo Changqian*, "for the following fact: One day he was bathing with three of his wives in the same pool, when the minister *Shi Qiu* had to go in on urgent business, and the duke covered himself and his wives. It was concluded that this lecherous man still had a remnant of modesty, and they contented themselves with calling him *Ling*, thus improving his fame."

"You are mistaken," said *Xi Wei*. "This is the fact: After the Duke's death, the tortoise was consulted as to where he should be buried. The answer was: 'not in his family cemetery, but in *Sha Qiu*.' When his grave was dug at the indicated place, at the bottom they found an ancient tomb. When the slab enclosing it was brought to light and washed, the inscription was read: 'Neither you nor your descendants will rest here, for Duke *Ling* will take your place.' The epithet *Ling* was bestowed upon him by fate… In conclusion, historical truth is only sound when it is derived from the Principle."

J. *Shao Zhi* asked *Tai Gong Diao*:
"What are the maxims of the hamlets?"

"Hamlets," said *Tai Gong Diao*, "are the smallest human agglomerations, of about ten families, of a hundred individuals only, forming a body which has its traditions. These traditions were not invented suddenly, *a priori*. They have been formed by the distinguished members of the community, by the addition of particular experiences; as a mountain is made of handfuls of earth, a river of many streams of water. The verbal expression of these traditions is what are called the 'maxims of the hamlets.' They are the law. All is well in the empire, so long as it is allowed to flow freely. Such is the Principle, indifferent, impartial, letting all things take their course, without influencing them. It claims no title (lord, governor). It does not act. Doing nothing, there is nothing it cannot do (not actively intervening, but as an evolutionary norm contained in everything). On the surface, from our human way of seeing, times succeed each other, the universe transforms, adversity and prosperity alternate. In reality, these variations, effects of the same norm, do not modify the immutable whole. All contrasts find their place in this whole, without clashing; as, in a swamp, all kinds of grasses are next to each other; as, in a mountain, trees and rocks are mixed. — But let us return to the maxims of the hamlets. They are the expression of experience, resulting from the observation of natural phenomena.

"Then," said *Shao Zhi*, "why not say that these maxims are the expression of the Principle?"

"Because," said *Tai Gong Diao*, "as they extend only to the field of human affairs, these maxims have only a limited scope, whereas the Principle is infinite. They do not even extend to the affairs of other earthly beings, the sum of which is to mankind as ten thousand to one. Above terrestrial beings are heaven and earth, the visible immensity. Above heaven and earth are *yin* and *yang*, the invisible immensity. Above all, there is the Principle, common to all, which contains and pervades all, whose infinity is its own attribute, the only one by which it can be designated, for it has no name of its own."

"Then," said *Shao Zhi*, "explain to me how all that exists came out of this infinity."
Tai Gong Diao replied:

"Emanating from the Principle, *yin* and *yang* influenced each other, destroyed each other, reproduced each other. Hence the physical world, with the succession of seasons, mutually producing and destroying each other. Hence the moral world, with its attractions and repulsions, its loves and hates. Hence the distinction of the sexes and their union for procreation. Hence certain correlative and successive states, such as adversity and prosperity, security and danger. Hence abstract notions of mutual influence, of reciprocal causation, of a certain circular evolution in which beginnings succeed terminations. This is more or less the sum total of human knowledge, drawn from observation and expressed in words. Those who know the Principle do not scrutinize any further. They speculate neither on the nature of the primordial emanation nor on the possible end of the existing order of things."

Shao Zhi continued:

"Daoist authors, however, have discussed these questions. Thus, *Ji Zhen* maintains that it is a passive and unconscious emanation, while for *Jie Zi* it is an active and conscious production. Who is right?"

"Tell me," said *Tai Gong Diao*, "why do cocks go *cock-a-doodle-doo* and why do dogs go *bow-wow*? The fact of this difference is known to all men, but the most learned of men will never say why. It is so, by nature; that is all we know. Diminish an object to the point of invisibility, magnify it to the point of incomprehensibility, and you will not derive from it the reason of its being. And how much less will you get to the bottom of the question of the genesis of the universe, the most abstruse of all. It is the work of an author, said *Jie Zi*. It came from nothing, said *Ji Zhen*. Neither of them will ever prove their claim. They are both mistaken. It is impossible for the universe to have had a pre-existing author. It is impossible for being to have arisen from nothing. Man can do nothing about his own life, because the law governing life and death, his own transformations, escapes him; what then can he know of the law governing the great cosmic transformations, the universal evolution? To say of the universe that"someone made it" or that it "came out of nothing" are not demonstrable propositions, but gratuitous assumptions. For me, when I look to the origin, I see it lost in a distant infinity; when I look to the future, I see no end. But human words cannot express what is infinite, what has no end. Limited as are the beings who use them, they can only express the affairs of the limited world of those beings, limited and changing things. Now, after emanation, the Principle from which beings emanated, being inherent in those beings, cannot properly be called the author of beings; this refutes *Jie Zi*. The Principle inherent in all beings, having existed before beings, cannot properly be said to have come from nothing; this refutes *Ji Zhen*. When we now refer to the Principle, this term no longer designates the solitary being, as it was in primordial time; it designates the being that exists in all beings, the universal norm presiding over cosmic evolution. The nature of the Principle, the nature of Being, is incomprehensible and ineffable. Only the limited can be understood and expressed. The Principle acts as the pole, as the axis of the universality of beings; let us say of it only that it is the pole, that it is the axis of universal evolution, without attempting to understand or explain it."

CHAPTER 26 - FATE

A. Accidents coming from outside, can neither be foreseen nor avoided, neither by the good nor by the bad. Thus *Guan Longfeng* and *Bin Gan* were executed, *Ji Zi* saved his life only by feigning insanity, *E Lai* lost his, as did the tyrants *Jie* and *Zhou*. The most perfect loyalty did not prevent the ruin of ministers like *Wu Yuan* and *Chang Hong*. The most exemplary filial piety did not prevent *Xiao Yi* and *Zeng Shen* from being mistreated.

Ruin arises from the most seemingly harmless circumstances, from the most seemingly safe situations, just as fire arises from two rubbing woods, just as metal liquefies on contact with fire, just as thunder arises from the disruption of the balance of *yin* and *yang*, just as lightning fire arises from the water of a storm.

The worst thing is that there are cases in which man is caught between two fatalities, with no possible way out; between which he writhes, not knowing what to resolve; between which his mind, as if suspended between heaven and earth, does not know what to decide; consolation and affliction alternate, pros and cons clash, an inner fire devours him. This fire consumes his peace with a fervor that no water can quench. So much so, that his life perishes and his career comes to a premature end.

B. *Zhuang Zhou* knew these great extremes. One day misery reduced him to asking the intendant of the Yellow River for the alms of a little grain.

"As soon as the tax is collected, I will lend you three hundred taels."

Zhuang Zhou, irritated, said:

"Yesterday, on my way here, I heard a cry for help. It was a gudgeon, lying in a patch of rainwater at the bottom of a furrow, which was about to dry up. 'What do you want?' I asked it. 'I need water,' it said, 'so I can go on living.' 'Very well,' I said, 'I am going to the court of the kingdoms of *Wu* and *Yue*. When I return, I will bring you the waters of the western river.' 'Alas,' groaned the gudgeon, 'I only need a little water to live, but I need it now. If you can only do for me what you have just said, lift me up instead and deliver me to a dried fish merchant; then I shall suffer less time.'"

C. *When fate weighs upon him, the Sage must not give up. He must stand firm until fortune turns in his favor. Ren Gongzi* provided himself with a good hook, a strong line and fifty mussels for bait, stationed himself on the coast of *Hui Ji* and began fishing in the eastern sea. He persevered in this way every day for a whole year without catching anything. Finally, all of a sudden, a huge fish swallowed his hook. Duly hooked, it tried in vain to sink into the depths, but was brought to the surface, struck the water with its fins to make it foamy, made a diabolical noise which was heard in the distance; finally it was quartered, and the whole country ate it, and this story was told, sung, and admired in the following ages. Now suppose *Ren Gongzi*, tired of his long wait by the sea, had gone fishing for gudgeons in the ponds, he would never have caught this beautiful piece, nor acquired its fame. Such are those who, abandoning the ideal, stoop to flatter small lords."

D. *Some are victims of fate, even after their death.* Some young scholars were violating an ancient tomb, to see if the ancients really did for the dead all that is said in the Odes and Rituals. Their master, who was standing guard outside, shouted to them:

"Hurry! The east is whitening! What are you doing?"

From inside, the young men replied:

"We still have to inspect his vestments. But we have already seen that the corpse has, in his mouth, the pearl of which the Odes speak in the text: 'green, like the corn on the hills'; this man who did no good during his life, why does he have, after his death, a pearl in his mouth?"

Then, after separating the lips of the corpse by pulling his beard and whiskers, they loosened his jaws with the pick of an iron hammer; carefully, not for his sake, but so as not to damage the pearl, which they took.

E. *Criticizing, judging, attracts misfortune.* A disciple of *Lao Lai Zi*, having gone out to gather some firewood, met Confucius. When he returned, he said to his master:

"I saw a scholar, long-chested, short-legged, stooped, with his ears set quite far back, looking sorrowful for the whole universe. I do not know to what school he belongs."

"It is *Qiu*," said *Lao Lai Zi*; "call him."

When Confucius arrived, *Lao Lai Zi* said to him:

"*Qiu*, give up your stubbornness and your particular ideas; think and act like other scholars."

Confucius bowed, in gratitude for the advice received, as the rites demand; then, when the ritual smile faded, his face appeared sad and he asked:

"Do you think my plans for reform will not succeed?"

"Of course you will not succeed," said *Lao Lai Zi*. "Since you are unable to bear the criticisms of your contemporaries, why do you provoke those of all posterity? Are you deliberately trying to make yourself miserable, or do you not realize what you are doing? To solicit the favor of the great, to seek the affection of the young, as you do, is to act in a very vulgar manner. Your judgments and criticisms make you many enemies. The true Sages are much more reserved than you, and they achieve something through this reserve. Woe to you, who have given yourself the mission to provoke everyone, and who obstinately persevere in this dangerous path!"

F. *There are those who know how to foresee the doom that threatens others, and do not notice the doom that threatens themselves.* One night, Prince *Yuan* of *Song* saw in a dream an afflicted human figure approaching the door of his room and saying to him.

"I come from the abyss of *Zai Lu*. The genie of *Ceng Jiang* entrusted me to the genie of the Yellow River. On the way, I was taken by the fisherman *Yu Ju*."

When he awoke, Prince *Yuan* ordered the diviners to examine his dream. They replied:

"The being who appeared to you, is a transcendent turtle".

The prince asked:

"Is there among the fishermen here a man named *Yu Ju*?"

"Yes," said those present.

"Let him appear before me," said the prince.

The next day, at the official audience, the fisherman introduced himself.

"What did you catch?" asked the prince.

"I found in my net," said the fisherman, "a white turtle, the shell of which is five feet in circumference."

"Show me your turtle," commanded the prince.

When it was brought in, the prince asked himself whether he should kill it or keep it alive. He cast lots for the solution to his doubt. The answer was, "Killing the turtle will be advantageous for divination." So the tortoise was killed. Its shell was pierced in seventy-two places. No yarrow rod ever fell out.[95].

Having heard about this fact, Confucius said:

"Thus, this transcendental turtle was able to appear after his capture to Prince Yuan, but it could not foresee and prevent its capture! After its death, its shell continued to make infallible predictions to others, but it had failed to predict to itself that it would be killed! It is clear that science has its limits, that even transcendence does not reach everything."

Even the wisest man, if he has made many enemies, ends up becoming their victim. The fish that has escaped from the cormorants is caught in a net. What is the point of fretting with so many sterile worries, instead of just looking at things from above? What is the use of meddling and talking instead of sticking to natural prudence? The newborn child does not learn to speak artificially by the lessons of a teacher; it learns it naturally by its contact with its speaking parents. Thus, natural prudence is acquired by common experience, without effort. As for extraordinary accidents, there is no point in trying to calculate them, since nothing can prevent them. This is fate!

The following fragments, up to the end of the chapter, are dislocated, says the commentary, with reason.

G. The sophist *Hui Zi*, said to *Zhuang Zhou*:

"You only talk about useless things."

Giving him a taste of his own medicine, *Zhuang Zhou* said:

"If you know what is useless, you must also know, I think, what is useful. The earth is useful to man, for it supports his steps, is it not?"

"Yes," said *Hui Zi*.

"Suppose a chasm opens up before your feet, will it still be useful to you?" asked *Zhuang Zhou*.

"No," said *Hui Zi*.

"Then," said *Zhuang Zhou* "it is proved that useless and useful are synonymous, for you have just called the same land useful and useless. So I am only talking about useful things."

H. *Zhuang Zhou* said:

"The natural dispositions of men are diverse. He who is made for conversation with men will not be made to live in solitude; he who is made for solitude will

---

95   It means that none of its oracles granted a false answer (Translator Note).

not be made for conversation with men. But absolute solitude and immoderate conversation are an excess, not something natural. The misanthrope buries himself alive, the schemer throws himself into the fire. Extremes are to be avoided."

Nor should extraordinary acts be performed, for once the circumstances in which they were carried out are forgotten, history may judge them as eccentric rather than heroic.

One should not always exalt antiquity and depreciate the present time, as the bookish men do (Confucius). Since *Xi Wei*, we know that no one can go back in time. So let us follow the thread of time.

The superior man accommodates himself to the times and circumstances. He is neither eccentric, nor misanthropic, nor scheming. He lends himself to men, without giving himself away. He lets people think and express themselves, does not contradict them, but keeps his own opinion.

I. As long as there are no obstacles, the eye sees, the ear hears, the nose smells, the mouth tastes, the heart perceives, the mind produces the right acts. In any path, the essential thing is that there should be no obstruction. Any obstruction produces strangulation, cessation of functions, injury to life. For their vital acts, beings depend on breath. If this breath is not abundant in a man, the fault is not in heaven, which day and night penetrates him; it is in him, who obstructs his ways with physical or moral obstacles.

For conception, the hollow of the womb must be well permeable to the influence of heaven, which presupposes the permeability of its two avenues, the two (Fallopian) tubes. For the maintenance of life, the hollow of the heart must be well permeable to the influence of heaven, which presupposes the permeability of its six valves. When a house is untidy, the mother-in-law and daughter-in-law, for lack of space, quarrel. When the orifices of the heart are obstructed, their functioning becomes irregular.

The vision of beauty seduces the mind. Courage degenerates into ambition, ambition into brutality, prudence into obstinacy, science into strife, plenitude into excess. The public good has produced administration and bureaucracy.

In spring, under the combined action of rain and sun, grass and trees grow luxuriantly. The scythe and the pruning shears cut down half of them; the other half remain. Neither those that have been cut down nor those that have remained know the reason for their fate. Fate!

J. Rest restores health, continence repairs wear and tear, peace remedies nervousness. These are curative remedies. Preventive ones would be better.

The procedures are different. The transcendent man has his own. The ordinary wise man has his own procedures. The skilled people have theirs. The rulers and the ruled have their principles.

K. The same process does not always produce the same result. In the capital of *Song*, the father of *Yen Men*, the gatekeeper, passed away; his son grew so thin with grief that it was deemed necessary to give the office of Master of Officers to this paragon of filial piety. When the others saw this, they imitated him, but obtained no office and died of consumption.

To avoid the throne, *Xu You* was content to flee, while *Wu Gang* thought he should commit suicide. Disappointed in his ambition, *Ji Tuo* went into exile, and *Shen Tu Di* drowned himself.

L. When the fish is caught, the net is forgotten. When the hare is caught, the trap ceases to be of interest. When the idea is conveyed, it does not matter what words were used to convey it. How I would like (*Zhuang Zhou*) to deal only with men for whom ideas were everything, words being nothing[96].

CHAPTER 27 - SPEECH AND WORDS

A. "Of my words," said *Zhuang Zhou*[97], "many are allegories, many are relations of the speech of others. I have said, from day to day, what I have thought fit to say, according to my natural sense."

"I have used allegories taken from external objects, to make abstract things understood. I will not say that they are all perfect, for a father should not praise his son. Praise is only worthwhile when it comes from a third party. However, I think they are convincing. So much the worse for those who are not convinced."

"I have related the speeches of others, in order to bring out certain controversies; those who argue are inclined to value too much the thesis of their party, and to ignore too much that of the opposite party. The men I have quoted in this way are my elders, my predecessors. Not that I regard any elder as an authority. Far from it. He who has not got to the bottom of things, however old he may be, is not an authority in my eyes, nor should he have any influence on my opinion. He may be a narrator of ancient things (Confucius), but he is not a teacher of ancient things."

"I have spoken without artifice, naturally, following the impulse of my inner sense; for only such words please and endure. For before all speech, there is an innate harmony in all beings, their nature. Because of this pre-existing harmony, my word, if it is natural, will make others vibrate, with few or no words. Hence the well-known sayings: There is speech without words... Sometimes words are not necessary... Some people have spoken all their lives without saying a word... Some who have been silent all their lives have spoken a great deal."

"To the same natural sense is joined the fact of experience, since all men spontaneously perceive whether a thing is right or wrong, whether it is so or not so. This perception cannot be explained in any other way. It is so, because it is so; it is not so, because it is not so. It fits, because it fits; it does not fit, because it does not fit. Every man is endowed with this sense of approval and disapproval. It vibrates in

---

96   This paragraph is the dislocated beginning of the next chapter.
97   Some critics see in this paragraph the preface or appendix to *Zhuang Zhou's* work, which has been transposed here.

unison in all men. Words that conform to it are accepted because they sound good, and they endure because they are natural."

"And whence comes this unity of the natural sense? It comes from the unity of all natures. Beneath the many specific and individual distinctions, beneath the innumerable and ceaseless transformations, in the background of circular evolution without beginning or end, there is hidden a law, which has been called the natural wheel (of the potter), or simply nature (one, participated in by all beings, in which this common participation produces a common background of harmony)."

B. *Zhuang Zhou* said to *Hui Zi*:

"In his sixtieth year, Confucius was converted. He denied what he had affirmed up to then (artificial goodness and fairness). But did he believe what he then affirmed more firmly than what he had affirmed before?"

"I believe," said *Hui Zi*, "that Confucius always acted according to his convictions."

"I doubt it," said *Zhuang Zhou*. "But, at any rate, after his conversion he taught that everything comes to man from the great womb; that his song must agree with the scale and his conduct with the law; that, in speculative or practical moral doubt, one must make up one's mind what one is going to say; that one must submit wholeheartedly to the customs laid down by the state, whatever they may be; etc. I cannot follow it that far."

"To fare well, man must follow his natural instinct."

C. *Zeng Zi* was twice a civil servant, under different states of mind which he explains as follows:

"During my first post, I had a salary of only a little more than thirty bushels of grain; but, as my parents who were still living, they could profit by it, I occupied this post gladly. In my second post I had a salary of one hundred and ninety-two thousand bushels; but as my deceased relatives could no longer benefit from it, I occupied this post with displeasure."

His disciples asked Confucius:

"Is there not, in this conduct of *Zeng Shen*, some vicious attachment of the heart?"

"Undoubtedly; a sincere attachment to his pay," said Confucius, "which he should have not regarded more than a mosquito or a crane passing before his eyes."

In reality, it was heartfelt attachment to his parents. But filial piety being the basis of his system, Confucius would not say so. *Zhuang Zhou* brings this out, and hints that even attachment to parents is against pure nature, as it causes either pleasure or sorrow.

D. *Yen Cheng Zi You* said to *Dong Guo Zi Qi*:

"Since I have been your disciple, I have gone through the following states. After one year, I regained my native simplicity. After three years, I lost the sense of 'you' and 'I'. After four years, I was indifferent and insensitive. After five years, I began to live a superior life. After six years, my mind, totally focused on my body, did not wander. After seven years, I entered into communication with universal nature. After eight years, I stopped worrying about life and death. Finally, after nine years, the mystery was accomplished; I found myself united with the Principle. It is activity during life that causes death. It is the *yang* (nature) principle, which causes life. So life and death are vulgar things. Is there any reason to worry so much about them?"

"We calculate celestial phenomena, measure terrestrial surfaces; superficial sciences, which do not reach the deeper reason of the universe. Without knowing the beginning and the end, can we know whether or not the world is governed by a law, which presupposes an author? What is sometimes taken for sanctioned may be only a game of chance, so how can we know whether or not subtle spirits exist? The meaning is that we can know nothing of a cause outside ourselves; life is a matter of evolution; death is the fact of attrition."

E. Twilight (symbolizing the semi-wise) said to Shadow (Daoist ignorance):

"Sometimes you are stooped and then erect, gathered and then dispersed, sitting and then standing, moving and resting; what is the reason for all these changes?"

"I don't know," said Shadow. "I am like that, without knowing why. I am, like the sheath from which a cicada has emerged, like the skin from which the snake has shed its skin, an accessory, a thing that has no existence of its own. I am even less real than these objects. I appear in the light of day or fire, as soon as the light fades, I disappear. I depend, as to my being, on an object, which depends, as to its being, on universal being. When it appears, I also appear; when it disappears, I also disappear; when it dies, I die with it. I cannot account for my movements."

Thus everything is passive, exists through the Principle and depends upon the Principle. Knowing this, the disciple of wisdom must first of all be profoundly humble[98].

F. *Yang Ziju*, who was on his way to *Pei*, met *Lao Zi*, who was going to *Qin*, in *Liang*. Surprised by *Yang Ziju*'s smug air, *Lao Zi* looked up at the sky and said with a sigh:

"I don't think I should waste my time teaching you."

Yang Ziju did not reply. When they arrived at the inn, *Yang Ziju* first carried all the necessary toiletries himself. Then, after leaving his shoes in front of the door, he went on his knees to *Lao Zi* and said.

"I have long been looking forward to your instructions. I did not dare to stop you on the way to ask for them; but now that you have some free time, please explain to me the meaning of what you told me when I saw you."

Lao Zi said:

---

98   Compare *Zhuang Zhou*, chapter 2 I.

"You have a haughty look that makes people run away; while the disciple of wisdom looks confused, no matter how blameless he is, and feels his inadequacy, no matter how advanced he is."

Yang Ziju was greatly impressed and said:

"I will take advantage of your lesson."

He made such good use of it, and so humbled himself in the space of the one night he spent at the inn, that all the people of the house who had served him with awe and reverence on his arrival, no longer had any regard for him before his departure, (in China regard is proportionate to the insolence of the traveler)[99].

Chapter 28 - Independence[100]

A. When *Yao* wanted to give up his throne to *Xu You*, the latter refused. Then *Yao* offered it to *Zhou Zi Fu*, who also refused, not because he considered himself incapable, but because he was suffering from an illness, which government care would have aggravated. He preferred the care of his life to the care of the empire. How much more would he have preferred the care of his life to lesser care?

In turn, *Shun* offered his throne to *Zi Zhou Zhi Bo*. The latter refused on the pretext of his melancholy, which worries would aggravate. Of course he would not have harmed his life for a lesser thing. This is how the disciples of the Principle differ from the common man (by maintaining their life, which the vulgar wear out through ambition). Then *Shun* offered the empire to *Shen Quan*, who refused, saying:

"As an inhabitant of the universe and subject to its revolutions, in winter I dress in furs and in summer in muslin; in spring I cultivate without tiring myself too much, and in autumn I reap what is necessary for myself; I act by day and rest by night. I live thus, without attachment, between heaven and earth, happy and content. Why should I trouble myself with the empire? You have offered it to me because you know me so badly."

Having said this, to avoid any further entreaty, he departed and withdrew into the depths of the mountains. No one knew where he had settled.

Then *Shun* offered the empire to his old friend, the tenant farmer *Zhou Hu*, who refused, in these terms:

"If you, who are strong and skillful, are not able to handle it, how much less I, who am not worth as much as you..."

Having said this, so as not to be obliged, he set sail with his wife and children, and never returned.

Tai Wang Dan Fu, the ancestor of the *Zhou*, when he was settled in *Bin*, was constantly attacked by the *Di* nomads. Whatever tribute he paid them, furs and silks, dogs and horses, pearls and jade, they were never satisfied, for they coveted his lands. *Dan Fu* said to himself:

---

99   Compare *Lie Zi*, chapter 2 N.
100   There are doubts about the authenticity of this chapter.

"My subjects are my brothers, my sons; I do not want to be the cause of their loss."

So he summoned his people and said to them:

"Submit yourselves to the *Di*, and they will treat you well. Why should you worry about me? Nor do I want to live at your expense, at the risk of your lives…"

Having said this, he took his staff and left. All his people followed him and settled with him at the foot of Mount *Qi*[101]. This is a beautiful example of the respect the Sage has for the lives of others.

He who understands the respect to be had for life does not expose his own for the sake of wealth or for the horror of poverty. He does not expose it in order to progress. He remains in his condition, in his plot of land; while the vulgar exposes himself lightly, for a small and insignificant benefit.

Three times in a row, the people of *Yue* murdered their king. To avoid the same fate, Prince *Sou* fled and hid in the *Dan Xue* cave. Finding themselves without a king, the people of *Yue* went in search of him, discovered his retreat, smoked him to force him out, and hoisted him onto the royal chariot, while the prince cried out to heaven…

"If these people needed a prince, why did it have to be me?"

It was not the dignity of king that Prince *Sou* feared, but the misfortunes to which it exposed him. The throne of a principality was not worth the risk of his life in his eyes. Thus, the people of *Yue* were right to insist on having him as king.

B. The two principalities of *Han* and *Wei* disputed a plot of land commonly-owned. *Zi Hua Zi* went to visit Marquis *Zhao Xi* of *Han*, and finding him very concerned about this matter, said to him:

"Supposing there were an inexorable decree thus conceived… whoever puts his hand into the empire, will obtain the empire, but will lose the hand, left or right, whichever he has put into it… in that case, would you put your hand into the empire?"

"No," said the marquis.

"Perfect!" said *Zi Hua Zi*. "So you prefer your two hands to the empire. Now your life is worth even more than your two hands, *Han* is worth less than the empire, and the adjoining piece of land that is the cause of the dispute is worth even less than *Han*. So why do you sicken with sadness, to the point of compromising your life, for such a trivial object?"

"No one has so far spoken to me with so much wisdom as you," said the marquis.

In fact, *Zi Hua Zi* had clearly distinguished the futile (increase of territory) from the important (preservation of life).

C. The prince of *Lu*, having heard that *Yen He* possessed the science of the Principle, sent a messenger to bring him a sheet of silk as a gift. Dressed in coarse

---

101   1325 BC.

cloth, *Yen He* was feeding his ox at the door of his house. It was to himself that the prince's messenger, who did not know him, asked:

"Is this where *Yen He* lives?"

"Yes," said the latter, "it is I."

As the messenger showed him the silks, *Yen He* said to him:

"My friend, you must have misunderstood your instructions; confirm them, lest you get into a bad situation."

So the messenger returned to the city and made inquiries. When he returned, *Yen He* was nowhere to be found.

This is an example of true disregard for wealth. For the disciple of the Principle, the main thing is the preservation of his life. He devotes himself to the government of a principality or empire, when he is obliged to do so, and uses only the surplus of his vital energy, regarding his office as incidental, his main interest being the care of his life. The vulgar men of this time, on the contrary, compromise their life for their interest; it is pitiful!

Before doing anything, a true Sage examines the objective and chooses the means. Our moderns, on the contrary, are so thoughtless that, taking the Marquis of *Sui*'s pearl as a projectile, they shoot a sparrow a thousand meters away, becoming the laughing stock of all, because they expose such a precious object for such a mediocre and uncertain result. Actually, they do even worse, because the life they expose is more precious than the pearl of the Marquis of *Sui*[102].

D. *Lie Zi* was reduced to black misery, and the sufferings of hunger were visible on his face. A visitor spoke of him to *Zi Yang*, minister of the *Zheng* principality, in these terms:

"*Lie Yukou* is a scholar versed in the science of the Principle. His misery will cause it to be said that the prince of *Zheng* does not concern himself with the learned."

Indignant at this remark, *Zi Yang* immediately ordered his district official to send grain to *Lie Yukou*. When the official's envoy arrived at his house, *Lie Zi* greeted him very civilly, but refused the gift. When he left, *Lie Zi*'s wife, beating her chest in pain, said to him.

"The wife and children of a Sage, must live at ease and happy. Until now we have suffered from hunger, because the prince has forgotten us. But now, remembering us, he has sent us food, and you refused it! Have you not acted against fate?"

"No," said *Lie Zi*, laughing, "I have not acted against fate, for it was not the prince who sent us this grain. Someone spoke favorably of me to the minister, who sent this grain; if that someone had spoken unfavorably of me, he would have sent his henchmen, with the same stupidity. It was chance not fate, that's why I refused. I don't want to owe *Zi Yang* anything."

Soon after, *Zi Yang* was killed by the people in a riot[103].

---

102   Legend has it that after the Marquis of *Sui*, healed a wounded snake, the snake brought him a priceless pearl.

103   Compare *Lie Zi*, ch. 8 D.

E. King *Zhao* of *Chu* had been driven from his kingdom, and *Yue* the court butcher accompanied him in his flight. When the king had regained his kingdom, he had rewards distributed to those who had followed him. When it was *Yue* the butcher's turn, he refused any reward.

"I had lost my office by the king's departure," said he; "I have regained it by his return; I am, therefore, compensated; why give me any more reward?"

The king ordered the officers to insist, the butcher said:

"Not having deserved death for any fault, I did not wish to be killed by the rebels, so I followed the king; I saved my own life, and did nothing that was useful to the king; why should I accept a reward?"

Then the king ordered the butcher to be brought into his presence, in the hope of persuading him to accept. When the butcher heard this, he said:

"According to the law of *Chu*, only great rewards for extraordinary merit are conferred by the king himself. Now I, in terms of wisdom, did not prevent the loss of the kingdom, in terms of bravery I fled for my life. Strictly speaking, I do not even deserve the credit of having followed the king in his misfortune. And now the king wants, against the law and custom, to receive me in audience and reward me himself. No, I do not want this to be said of him and of me."

Informed of these words, the king said to the generalissimo *Zi Qi*:

"In his humble condition, this butcher has sublime feelings. Offer him a place in the hierarchy of the great vassals in my name."

Upon *Zi Qi* making him this offer, *Yue* replied:

"I know that a vassal is nobler than a butcher, and that the income of a fief is more than what I earn. But I do not want a favor, which would be reproached to my prince as illegal. Leave me to my butcher's shop!"

Whatever they did, *Yue* stood his ground and remained a butcher. *Example of Daoist moral independence.*

F. *Xun Xian* lived in the country of *Lu* in a round adobe hut, surrounded by a thorn hedge, and grass grew on its roof. A mat tied to a mulberry branch poorly closed the hole used as a door. Two broken jars, embedded in the wall, closed with a light stretched cloth, formed the windows of his two cells. The roof leaked, the floor was damp. In this miserable den, *Xun Xian* sat playing the zither, content.

Zi Gong came to visit him, riding in a chariot so wide it could not enter his alley, dressed in a white robe lined with purple. *Xun Xian* received him, with a broken cap on his head, worn-out shoes on his feet and leaning on a tree branch as a cane. Seeing him, *Zi Gong* exclaimed:

"How unfortunate you are!"

"I am sorry," said *Xun Xian*. "To lack goods is to be poor. To know and not to do is to be unhappy. I am very poor; but I am not unhappy."

Zi Gong remained silent. *Xun Xian* added:

"To act to please the world, to make particular friends under the guise of the general good, to study to be admired, to teach to become rich, to dress in a disguise of goodness and righteousness, to go about in sumptuous attire-all these things you do are things I will never resolve to do."

Zeng Zi lived in the country of *Wei*. He wore a robe of coarse unlined cloth. His face betrayed suffering and hunger. The calluses on his hands and feet showed how hard he worked for a living. He could not have a hot meal once every three days. He had worn the same garment for ten years. If he had tried to tie his hair up, the worn straps would have broken. If he had tried to put his whole foot into his shoes, the heel would have separated from the rest. If she had tugged at the sleeves of her dress, they would have stuck to her hands. And yet, dressed in rags and wearing slippers, he intoned the hymns of the *Shang* dynasty in a voice that echoed through space like the sound of a bronze or flint instrument. The emperor could not persuade him to serve him as a minister, the great feudatories could not persuade him to befriend them. He was of the type of independent and free spirits. He who values his freedom must renounce the comforts of the body. He who values his life must renounce dignities. He who values union with the Principle must renounce all attachments.

Confucius said to *Yen Hui*:

"*Yen Hui*, listen to me! Your family is poor; why don't you go and look for some position?"

"No," said *Yen Hui*, "I don't want any office. I have fifty acres in the countryside, which provide me with food, and ten acres in the suburbs, which provide me with clothes[104]. Meditating on your teachings while I play my zither is enough for my happiness. No, I will not seek office."

These words greatly impressed Confucius, who said:

"What a good mind *Hui* has! I knew well, that, in theory, he who has modest tastes, does not get into straits; that he who is concerned only with his inner progress, is not affected by any privation; that he who tends only to perfection, despises charges. Although I have taught these principles for a long time, I have only now seen them applied by *Hui*. Today I, the theoretician, have received a practical lesson."

G. *Mou*, the son of the Marquis of *Wei*, having been appointed to a post at *Zhong Shan* (near the sea), said to *Zhan Zi*:

"I have come here to the sea, but my heart has remained in the court of *Wei*."

Zhan Zi said:

"Stifle your pain, so that it will not wear out your life."

Prince *Mou* replied:

"I have tried, but to no avail. My pain is invincible."

"Then," said *Zhan Zi*, "give it free rein (by crying, shouting, etc.). For to react violently against an invincible feeling is to inflict a double wear and tear on oneself (the pain plus the reaction). None of those who do so live long."

---

104   Textile plants were grown near houses, so that they would not be cut down and stolen at night. Grain theft is less easy.

For this prince, accustomed to court, to have to live in a country of rocks and caves, was doubtless harder than it would have been for a man of low caste. Yet it is unfortunate for him that, having had what was necessary to tend towards the Principle, he did not attain it. There he would have found peace in indifference.

H. When Confucius was besieged and blockaded between *Chen* and *Cai*, he was without meat or grain for seven days, reduced to living on wild herbs. Despite his exhaustion, he never stopped playing the zither in the house where he had taken refuge.

Yen Hui, who was gathering herbs outside, heard the disciples *Zi Lu* and *Zi Gong* say among themselves:

"The Master has been expelled from *Lu* twice, intercepted at *Wei* once. The tree that sheltered him in *Song* was cut down. He has been in great danger in *Shang* and *Zhou*. Now he is besieged here. They want him to perish, not daring to kill him, but the one who does so will certainly not be punished. The Master knows this and plays the zither. Is he a wise man who is unaware of his situation?"

Yen Hui told these words to Confucius, who stopped playing, sighed and said:

"Their minds have little scope. Call them so that I can talk to them!"

When they had entered, *Zi Lu* said to Confucius:

"This time you are finished!"

"No," said Confucius. "As long as a Sage's doctrine has not been disproved, he is not finished with it. When I enter the struggle for good and righteousness in a time of passions and troubles, it is natural that I should experience violent opposition, but that does not mean that I am finished. My doctrine is irrefutable, and I will not be deflected from it by any persecution. The winter frosts only show the strength of resistance of the cypress, which does not lose its leaves. So will it be, with my doctrine, despite this incident between *Chen* and *Cai*..."

Having said this, Confucius again played his zither and sang with a dignified air. *Zi Lu*, convinced, took a shield and danced the pantomime. *Zi Gong* said:

"I did not know how high heaven is above the earth (the Sage above the vulgar)."

The ancients who possessed the science of the Principle were equally happy in success and failure. For success and failure were equally indifferent to them. Their satisfaction came from a higher cause, from the knowledge that success and failure proceed equally from the Principle, fatally, inevitably, like cold and heat, like wind and rain, in a succession and alternation to which one must submit. It was by virtue of this science that *Xu You* was content north of the river *Ying*, and *Gong Bo* at the foot of Mount *Qiu Shou* (suspicious paragraph, probably interpolated. Compare *Zhuang Zhou*, ch. 17 C; ch. 20 G and ch. 20 D).

I. When Shun[105] offered his empire to his former friend *Wu Ze*, the latter said:

"Oh no! You have left the fields for the court, and now you want me to degrade myself too. I don't know you any more!..."

---

105   Systematic demolition of Confucian paragons.

Having said this, *Wu Ze* went to throw himself into the abyss of *Qing Ling*.

Before attacking (the tyrant) *Jie*, *Tang* (the future emperor) consulted *Bian Sui*, who replied:

"That is none of my business…"

"Then whom should I consult?" asked *Tang*…"

"I don't know," said *Bian Sui*.

Tang turned to *Wu Wuang*, who also replied: "It's none of my business, I don't know…" Then *Tang* said:

"What if I ask *Yi Yin* for advice?…"

"Perfect!," said *Wu Wang*. "Coarse and dull, that man has what it takes to serve your purposes; besides, that's all he has."

Advised by *Yi Yin*, *Tang* attacked *Jie*, defeated him, and then offered the throne to *Bian Sui*. The latter said to him:

"My refusal to give you advice, should have made you understand that I want nothing to do with a thief; and now you offer me your booty! How wicked this century must be, for a man without conscience to come twice to try to sully me with his touch! I will not be insulted a third time…"

Having said this, *Bian Sui* drowned himself in the river *Chou*.

Then *Tang* offered the throne to *Wu Guang*, with this argument:

"A wise man (*Yi Yin*) made the plan (for the dethronement of *Jie*); a brave man (*Tang*) carried it out; now it is the turn of a good man (*Wu Guang*) to ascend the throne, in accordance with the traditions of the ancients…"

Wu Guang refused, saying:

"To dethrone an emperor is a lack of equity; to kill his subjects is a lack of kindness; to profit by the crimes of others is a lack of modesty. I cling to traditional maxims, which forbid accepting any office from an unjust master, and treading the soil of an unprincipled empire. I refuse to be honored by you, and I do not wish to see you again…"

Having said this, *Wu Guang* tied a large stone on his back and threw himself into the *Lu* river.

J. In the past, at the origin of the *Zhou* dynasty, the two scholar princes, *Bo Yi* and *Shu Qi*, lived in *Gu Zhu*. Upon hearing the news of the change of dynasty, they said to each other:

"It seems that in the West there is a man who is a Sage; let us go and see him!"

When they arrived south of Mount *Qi* (in the capital of the *Zhou*), Emperor *Wu* had them met by his brother *Dan*, who promised them riches and honors on oath if they would serve his house. The two brothers looked at each other, smiled scornfully and said:

"We were wrong! This is not what we were looking for…"

In the meantime, they had learned how the change of dynasty had come about, so they added:

"In former times the emperor *Shen Nong*, so devout and reverent, offered his sacrifices for his people, without making any special request for himself. From the government of his subjects, to which he applied himself so conscientiously, he derived neither glory nor benefit for himself. The *Zhou* who took advantage of the decline of the *Yin* to invade the empire, are very different men. They plotted against the emperor, won over his subjects, and used force. They swear to be believed (which goes against Daoist simplicity), they brag to please, they wage war for their own benefit. It is clear that the change in the empire has gone from bad to worse. In the past the elders served in times of order, and retired in times of disorder. Currently the empire is in darkness, the *Zhou* have no virtue. It is better that we retire to remain pure, rather than defile ourselves with the contact of these usurpers."

Having made this decision, the two sages went north to Mount *Shou Yang*, where they died of starvation. The example of these two men is admirable. When unexpectedly offered riches and honors, they did not allow themselves to be seduced, they did not deviate from their noble sentiments, which can be summed up in this maxim: do not enslave yourself to the world.

Chapter 29 - Politicians

A. Confucius was a friend of *Qi* of *Lua Xia*[106]. This one had a younger brother, who was known as the Brigand *Zhi*. This individual had organized an association of nine thousand followers, who did as they pleased in the empire, kidnapping princes, plundering individuals, seizing cattle, abducting women and girls, not sparing even their close relatives, pushing impiety to the point of not making offerings to their ancestors. As soon as they appeared, the cities were put in a state of defense and the inhabitants barricaded themselves. Everyone had to suffer these evildoers. Confucius said to *Liuxia Ji*:

"Parents should lecture their children, older brothers should lecture their younger brothers. If they do not do so, it is because they do not take their duty seriously. You are one of the best officers of this time, and your younger brother is the Brigand *Zhi*. This man is the scourge of the empire, and you don't give him lessons. I am ashamed of you. I warn you that I will go and lecture him in your place."

Liuxia Ji said:

"It is true that fathers and elders should lecture sons and younger brothers; but, when sons and younger brothers refuse to listen, even if the father or elder brother is as eloquent as you are, the result will be nil. Now, my younger brother, *Zhi*, is naturally fierce and rapturous. Moreover, he is so strong that he fears no one, and so eloquent that he knows how to show his misdeeds as if they were good deeds. He loves only those who flatter him, gets angry as soon as someone contradicts him and does not hesitate to insult. Believe me, don't mess with him."

---

106   The worthy *Zhan He*, alias *Zhan Ji*, posthumous name *Zhan Hui*. Better known as *Liuxia Hui* or *Liuxia Ji*, after his country.

Confucius did not follow this advice. He set off, with *Yen Hui* driving his chariot and *Zi Gong* acting as counterweight. He found *Zhi* sitting south of Mount *Tai Shu*, with his band chopping up human livers for his dinner. Climbing down from his chariot, Confucius went alone to the man on guard and said.

"I, *Kong Qiu* of *Lu*, have heard of the high sentiments of your general; I wish to speak with him…"

And having said this, he saluted the guard with reverence. The latter went to warn the Brigand *Zhi*, who was so enraged at this news that his eyes shone like stars and his bristling hair lifted his cap.

"This *Kong Qiu*," he said, "isn't he the sweet talker of *Lu*? Tell this to him: 'Charlatan, who attributes his buffoonery to King *Wen* and Emperor *Wu*. You who wear a headdress of woven cloth, and a leather belt. You who speak as much nonsense as words. You who eat without plowing, and dress without spinning. You who say that just by opening your lips and saying a few words, you can distinguish between good and evil. You who have led all the princes into error, and led astray all the wise men of the empire. You who, under the guise of preaching piety, flatter the mighty, the noble and the rich, you, the worst of evildoers, go quickly! Otherwise, I will have your liver added to the minced meat that is being prepared for our supper.'"

When the guard informed him of these words, Confucius insisted and said to *Zhi*:

"As your brother's friend, I wish to be received in your tent."

The watchman notified *Zhi*:

"Let him come," said the latter.

Confucius did not need to be told twice. He walked quickly, went straight to *Zhi* and greeted him.

At the height of his fury, *Zhi* stretched out both legs, placed his sword crosswise, turned his eyes toward Confucius and, with the tone of a perturbed tigress while nursing her cubs, said.

"Be careful *Qiu*! If you say things that please me, you shall live; if you say anything that displeases me, you shall die!"

Confucius said:

"Three qualities are especially prized in men: good looks, great intelligence, and military valor. Whoever possesses any one of these three qualities to a high degree is worthy to command men. Now, general, I see that you possess these three qualities in an eminent degree. You are eight feet two inches tall, your eyes are bright, your lips are ruddy, your teeth are white as cowries, your voice is as sonorous as a bell; and a man who combines all these qualities is called the Brigand *Zhi*! General, I am outraged! If you would take me as an adviser, I would use my credit to win the favor of all the neighboring princes; I would build a great city, to be your capital; I would gather hundreds of thousands of men, to be your subjects; I would make you a powerful and respected feudal prince. General, believe me, bring life back to the empire, stop making war, dismiss your soldiers, so that families can go in peace to their subsistence and ancestors' offerings. Follow my advice and you will acquire the reputation of a wise and brave man; the whole empire will applaud you."

Still furious, *Zhi* replied:

"Come here, *Qiu*, and know that you can only bamboozle small spirits. Do I need you to show me that the body my parents gave me is well made? Do you think your compliments move me, when I know that you will denigrate me elsewhere more than you have flattered me here? And besides, the chimerical bait with which you want to trap me, is really too crude. But suppose I get what you promised me, how long shall I keep it? Has not the empire of the descendants of *Yao* and *Shun* escaped, and has not the posterity of the emperors *Tang* and *Wu* been extinguished, precisely because their ancestors had left them a very rich and consequently much coveted inheritance? Power does not last, and happiness does not consist, as you and your fellow politicians would have us believe, in this thing. In the beginning there were many animals and few men. During the day, they gathered acorns and chestnuts; at night, they took refuge in the trees, for fear of wild beasts. This was the period known as the nesting period… Then came the time of the caves, during which men, still naked, gathered fuel in summer for warmth in winter, the first manifestation of care for the maintenance of life… Then came the time of *Shen Nong*, the first farmer, a time of absolute carelessness. Men knew only their mother, not their father (there was no marriage). They lived in peace, with elk and deer. They grew enough food to eat and spun enough clothes to wear. No one harmed anyone else. It was the time when everything followed its natural course, in perfection… *Huang Di* put an end to this happy time. He was the first to assume imperial power, to wage war, to give battle to *Chi You* on the plain of *Zhuo Lu*, and to shed blood over a space of a hundred stades (in pursuing the vanquished). Then *Yao* and *Shun* invented state ministers and administrative machinery. Then *Tang* overthrew and exiled his sovereign *Jie*, *Wu* dethroned and put to death the emperor *Zhou*. Since then, until now, the strong have oppressed the weak, the majority has tyrannized the minority. All emperors and princes have troubled the world, as the first of their kind. And you, *Qiu*, have set out to propagate the principles of King *Wen* and Emperor *Wu*, and intend to impose these principles on posterity. It is for this reason that you dress and gird yourself differently from the common mortals, that you lecture and pose, deceiving the princes, advancing your personal interests. You are indisputably the first of evildoers, and, instead of calling me, the Brigand *Zhi*, the people should call you, the Brigand *Qiu*… I appeal to the results of your teaching. Having cajoled *Zi Lu*, you made him lay down his arms, you made him study. The astonished world said: *Qiu* knows how to soften the violent. The illusion did not last. Having attempted to assassinate the prince of *Wei*, *Zi Lu* perished, and his salted corpse (to make it last longer) was exposed at the eastern gate of the capital of *Wei*. Shall I go on listing the successes of the talented man, the great Sage, whom you imagine yourself to be? In *Lu* you were defeated twice. You were expelled from *Wei*. In *Qi* you were almost mistreated. Between *Chen* and *Cai*, you were besieged. The whole empire refused to give asylum to the master who salted his disciple *Zi Lu*. In short, you have not been able to be useful, neither to yourself nor to others, and you pretend that your doctrine is esteemed! This doctrine, you say, is not my doctrine. It goes back, through the ancient sovereigns, to *Huang Di*. Famous paragons, by which alone you can deceive the vulgar. Unleashing his wild passions, *Huang Di* waged the first war and bloodied the plain of *Zhuo Lu*. *Yao* was a bad father. *Shun* was a bad son. *Yu* stole the empire to give it to his family. *Tang* banished his ruler. *Wu* killed his own. King *Wen* imprisoned *You-li*. These are the six paragons, whose admiration you impose on the vulgar. Closely considered, they were men whose love of their interests made them act against their conscience and against nature; men whose actions are worthy of the deepest contempt… And your other great men, did they not all perish as victims of their stupidity? Their utopias caused *Bo Yi* and *Shu Qi* to starve and remain unburied. Their idealism caused *Bao Jiao* to retreat into the woods, where he was found dead, on his knees, kissing a tree trunk. His frustration at not being listened to caused *Shen Tu Di* to tie a stone to his back and throw himself into the river, where fish and turtles devoured him. The faithful *Jie Zi Tui*, who had come to feed his duke *Wen* with a piece of his thigh, was so sensitive to the latter's ingratitude that he retreated into the forest, where he perished in the fire. *Wei Shang*, having made an appointment with a beautiful woman under a bridge, let himself be drowned by the rising water rather than break his word. In what way, I ask you, does the fate of these six men differ from that of a crushed dog, a slaughtered pig, or a beggar who died of misery? Their passions caused their deaths. Wouldn't they have done better to live their lives in peace? You keep holding up faithful ministers like *Bin Gan* and *Wu Zixu* as examples. Now *Bin Gan* was sentenced to death and had his heart ripped out; *Wu Zixu* had to commit suicide and his body was thrown into the river. This is what earned these followers their allegiance, becoming the laughing stock of public opinion… So, of all the real life examples you invoke as proof of your system, none of them convince me, quite the contrary. And if you invoke arguments from beyond the grave, these things prove nothing…"

"In my turn, I will give you a practical lesson, about what is, in fact, humanity. Man loves the satisfaction of his eyes, his ears, his mouth, his instincts. He has, to satisfy his inclinations, only the duration of his life, sixty years on the average, sometimes eighty, rarely a hundred. And from these years must be subtracted the times of sickness, sadness and misfortune. So much so that, in a month of life, a man has scarcely four or five days of real contentment and frank laughter. The course of time is infinite, but the lot of life allotted to each person is finite, and death puts an end to his time. An existence is, in the course of centuries, only the leap of a horse over a ditch. Now, my opinion is that he who does not know how to make this short life last as long as possible, and does not satisfy during this time all the inclinations of his nature, understands nothing of what humanity really is… Conclusion: I deny, *Qiu*, all that you assert, and support all that you deny. Don't answer a single word! Go quickly! You are a fool, a braggart, a utopian, a liar, and you offer nothing that can set men right. I will speak to you no more."

Confucius bowed humbly and hastened to retire. When he wanted to climb into his carriage, he had to try three times until he could grasp the railing, so bewildered was he. His eyes were wild-eyed, his face livid, and he leaned against the rail, his head bobbing and panting. On his way back to town, he met *Liuxia Ji* at the eastern gate.

"Ah, there you are," said the latter. "I haven't seen you for a long time. You look tired. Have you by any chance been to see *Zhi*?"

"I have gone to see him," said Confucius, looking up at the sky and sighing deeply.

"Ah," said *Liuxia Ji*, "and did he admit any of the things you told him?"

"He admitted none of them," said Confucius. "You were quite right. This time I, *Qiu*, acted like the man who cauterizes himself when he is not ill (I took pains and put myself in danger, in vain). I pulled the tiger's whisker, and I am lucky to have escaped his teeth."

B. *Zi Zhang*, who was studying with a view to entering politics, asked *Man Gou De*:

"Why don't you enter the path of opportunism (that of Confucius and the politicians of the time)? If you don't, no one will give you office, you will never achieve anything. This is the surest path to fame and fortune. And you will find yourself in distinguished company."

"Really?" said *Man Gou De*. "Politicians disturb me by the shamelessness with which they lie, by their intrigues to attract their supporters. I prefer natural freedom to their false opportunism."

"Freedom," said *Zi Zhang*, "was abused by *Jie* and *Zhou* in all things. Both were emperors, and yet if now it were said to a thief: you are a *Jie*, or you are a *Zhou*, that thief would be greatly offended, so much was their abuse of freedom that *Jie* and *Zhou* were despised by the lesser people… Whereas the Confucians and *Mo Zi*, commoners and paupers, have acquired such a reputation for their use of opportunism, that if you say to any minister of state, you are a Confucian, or you are a *Mo Zi*, this great personage will be proud of himself, holding himself in great honor. This shows that it is not the nobility of rank that imposes itself on men, but the wisdom of conduct."

"Is that really true?" said *Man Gou De*. "Those who have stolen little are locked up in jails. Those who have stolen much sit on thrones. Is it opportunism and wisdom to steal much? And so, are politicians really as pure as you say they are? It is at the gate of the great thieves (feudal princes), where we find them posted, begging. *Xiao Bo*, Duke *Huan* of *Qi*, killed his elder brother to marry his widow; in spite of this, *Guan Zhong* consented to become his minister and procured for him, by all means, precedence, as hegemon, over the other feudatories. Confucius accepted a gift of silks from *Tian Cheng Zi*, the murderer of his prince and usurper of his principality. Natural morality demanded that these two politicians censure their patrons. Instead, they acted like lapdogs before them. It was their opportunism (selfishness, seeking personal gain), which brought them down to suffocate their conscience. Of them this text was written: Oh! the good; oh! the bad… Those who have triumphed are the first; those who have not triumphed are the last."

Zi Zhang continued:

"If you abandon all things to natural freedom, if you admit no artificial institution, the whole order of the world will disappear; there will be no more ranks, no more grades, not even kinship."

Man Gou De said:

"Have your politicians, who attach so much importance to these things, observed them well? Let us see your paragons! *Yao* killed his eldest son. *Shun* exiled his maternal uncle. What respect for kinship! *Tang* exiled his ruler *Jie*, *Wu* killed *Zhou*. What respect for hierarchy! King *Qi* supplanted his elder brother, the duke of *Zhou* killed his own. What respect for precedence... Ah, yes, Confucius' disciples speak softly, *Mo Zi's* disciples preach universal charity, and this is how they act in practice."

When the discussion failed, *Zi Zhang* and *Man Gou De* appealed to an arbitrator, who said:

"Both of you are right and wrong, as happens when one takes an extreme position. The vulgar see only wealth; the politician esteems only reputation. To reach their goal, they fight and wear themselves out. Wise is he who considers the yes and the no, from the center of the circumference (compare ch. 2 C), and lets the wheel turn. Wise is the one who acts when circumstances are favorable, the one who stops acting when the time is right. Wise is he who is not impassioned by any ideal. Any pursuit of an ideal is fatal. His stubborn loyalty caused *Bin Gan* to tear out his heart and *Wu Zixu* to gouge out his eyes. His determination to tell the truth, to keep his word, caused *Zhi Gong* to testify in court against his father, and *Wei Sheng* to drown under a bridge. His uncompromising disinterest caused *Bao Zi* to die on his knees at the foot of a tree, and *Shen Zi* to be ruined by the artifices of *Ji* of *Li*. Confucius did not honor his mother's memory, *Kuang Zhang* was persecuted by his father because of his exaggerated ritual scruples. These are well-known historical facts. They show that any extreme position becomes false, that any exaggerated obstinacy ruins. Wisdom consists in remaining in the center, neutral and indifferent."

C. Inquietude said to Tranquility:

"Everyone values reputation and fortune. The crowd courts the victors, grovels before them and exalts them. The satisfaction they feel from it makes them live long. Why do you not strive? Is your apathy a lack of intelligence, a lack of ability, or a stubbornness in certain principles that are your own?"

Tranquility replied:

"I desire neither reputation nor fortune, for these things do not give happiness. It is all too obvious that men who always push forward, disregarding all inconvenient principles, forming their conscience on any historical precedent; clearly do not come to enjoy a long and happy life. Their life is, like that of the most vulgar, only a tissue of toil and rest, of sorrows and joys, of groping and uncertainties. However much they may progress, they are still exposed to mishaps and misfortunes."

"So be it," said Inquietude; "but still, while they possess, they enjoy. They can attain what the superior man and the wise man have not. He who has attained a high position depends upon whoever lends him his weapons, his intelligence, his talents. Even in a lesser position, the upstart remains privileged. He enjoys all the pleasures of the senses, all the satisfactions of nature."

"Selfishness," said Tranquility, "is that happiness? In my opinion, the Sage takes for himself only what is strictly necessary, and leaves the rest to others. He does not agitate, he does not struggle. All agitation, all competition, is a sign of morbid passion. After achieving something, the sage withdraws, renounces, without taking credit for it, without waiting to be forced to do so. When destiny has raised him to the top, he imposes himself on no one, weighs on no one; he thinks of the coming change, of the eventual turning of the wheel, and so he is modest. *Yao* and *Shun* acted that way. They did not treat people kindly, but neither did they harm them, out of abstraction and caution. *Shan Quan* and *Xu You* rejected the throne for the sake of security and peace. The world praises these four men, who never acted against their principles. They gained fame, without having sought it."

"In any case," says Inquietude, "it did not come for free. Instead of the sufferings of administration, they inflicted on themselves those of abstinence and deprivation, a way of life equivalent to a prolonged death."

"Not at all," said Tranquility. "They led a life together. And a life together is the only possible happiness. Anything else makes you unhappy. With his ears full of music and his mouth full of food, the upstart is not happy. The preoccupation with maintaining his position makes him like a beast of burden that climbs the same slope over and over again, sweating and blowing. All the riches, all the dignities, will not quench the hunger and thirst that torments him, the inner fever that devours him. His storehouses being full to overflowing, he will not cease to desire more, he will not consent to give up anything. His life will pass in guard around these useless accumulations, in worry, in fear. He will barricade himself in his house, and will not dare to go out without an escort (for fear of being kidnapped). Is this not a real misery? Well, those who suffer it, do not notice it. Unconscious of the present, they cannot foresee the future either. When the hour of misfortune comes, they will be caught unawares, and all their possessions will not be worth a day's respite. It is a fool who tires his mind and wears out his body to reach such an end."

Chapter 30 - Swordsmen

A. King *Wen* of *Zhao* was passionate about swordsmanship. Professional swordsmen flocked to his court. He gave hospitality to more than three thousand such men, who fought before him whenever he requested, day or night. Every year, more than a hundred people were killed or seriously injured in these jousts. But these accidents did not dampen the king's passion. As the kingdom was largely abandoned, his neighbors judged the time propitious to seize it. When the crown prince *Li* heard this, he was greatly distressed. He gathered his friends together and said to them:

"I will give a thousand taels as a reward to anyone who can persuade the king to put an end to these swordsmen's quarrels..."

"Only *Zhuang Zhou* is capable of doing so," said the prince's friends.

Immediately, the prince sent messengers to invite *Zhuang Zhou* and offer him a thousand taels. *Zhuang Zhou* refused the money, but followed the envoys.

"What do you want from me, and why do you offer me one thousand taels?," he asked the prince.

"I have heard that you are a wise man," said the latter, "so I began by respectfully sending you a thousand taels, in anticipation of what was to follow. You refused my gift; how dare I then tell you what I desire of you?"

"I have heard," said *Zhuang Zhou*, "that you wish me to cure the king your father of a certain passion. If I offend him, he will kill me; if I fail, perhaps you yourself will do it; in either case, your thousand taels will be left over (would of no use to me). If I please the king and you are pleased, then your thousand taels will be too little. That is why I have refused your money."

"Well," said the prince. "Our king only likes swordsmen."

"I know," said *Zhuang Zhou*. "I am a very good swordsman."

"Perfect," said the prince. "Only the king's swordsmen all wear a tasseled turban and a narrow doublet; they have fierce faces and are very noisy. The king accepts only this type. If you appear before him dressed as a scholar, he won't even look at you."

"Then," said Zhuang Zhou, "have a suit made for me."

Three days later, the prince presented *Zhuang Zhou* to the king, dressed as a swordsman. The king received him with a naked sword in his hand. *Zhuang Zhou* advanced toward him slowly (to avoid being taken for a disguised assassin), and did not greet him (for the same reason).

"Why," asked the king, "has my son introduced you?"

"I have heard," said *Zhuang Zhou*, "that you like sword duels. I would like to show you what I can do in this kind of combat."

"How strong are you?" asked the king.

"Place one swordsman after another, ten paces apart," said *Zhuang Zhou*, "a thousand stades in length; I will pass over the bodies of all of them in a row."

The king was delighted.

"You have no equal," he said.

"And this is my theory," said *Zhuang Zhou*. "I attack gently, let my adversary get close, let him get excited, pretend to retreat, he lets go, I skewer him. Would you allow me to show you how I do it?"

"Not so fast, master," said the king worriedly. "Go and rest first. When the preparations have been made, I will send for you."

B. Then the king had his soldiers drill for seven days straight. More than sixty were killed or wounded. The king chose the five or six most skilled and placed them at the back of the great hall, sword in hand, ready to fight, and after calling *Zhuang Zhou*, he said to him.

"I'm going to put you in the presence of these masters…"

"I have had to wait long enough," said *Zhuang Zhou*.

"What are the dimensions of your sword?" asked the king.

"Any sword is good enough for me," said *Zhuang Zhou*. "However, there are three that I prefer. You choose."

"Explain yourself," said the king.

"These are," said *Zhuang Zhou*, "the emperor's sword, the vassal's sword, and the commoner's sword."

"What is the sword of the emperor?" asked the king.

"It is that which covers everything within the four frontiers," said *Zhuang Zhou*, "that which extends to the border barbarians, that which reigns from the western mountains to the eastern sea. Following the course of the two principles and the five elements, of the laws of justice and clemency, it rests in spring and summer (seasons of labor), it rages in autumn and winter (seasons of executions and wars). Nothing resists this sword when it is drawn from its sheath and wielded. It forces all beings into submission. This is the sword of the emperor."

Surprised, the king asked:

"What is the vassal's sword?"

"It is," said *Zhuang Zhou*, "a weapon made of bravery, fidelity, courage, loyalty and wisdom. Wielded over a principality, in accordance with the laws of heaven, earth and time, this sword maintains peace and order. Feared as lightning, it prevents all rebellion. This is the sword of the vassal."

"And the sword of the commoner, what is it?" asked the king.

"It is iron in the hands of certain men who wear a tasseled turban and a narrow doublet," said *Zhuang Zhou*; "who roll their eyes and talk very loudly; who cut their throats, pierce their livers or their lungs, in senseless duels; who kill each other, like fighting cocks, without any use to their country. O king, you, who are perhaps predestined to become the master of the empire, is it not unworthy of you to value this weapon so highly?"

The king understood. He took *Zhuang Zhou* by the arm and led him to the upper part of the hall, where a banquet was being served. The king was beside himself as he paced the table… *Zhuang Zhou* said to him:

"Go back and take a seat; I will say no more about the swords (and will not embarrass you any more)."

Then King *Wen* shut himself up in his apartments for three months, reflecting on his conduct. During this time his swordsmen finished killing themselves. (Some commentators explain that they all committed suicide out of spite. In any case, the species died out and the abuse ceased).

Chapter 31 - The Old Fisherman

A. While walking through the forest of *Zi Wei*, Confucius sat down to rest near the *Xiang Tan* hill. The disciples took up their books. The master played his zither and began to sing.

The singing attracted an old fisherman. With his gray hair loose and his sleeves rolled up, the old man got out of his boat, went up to the shore, came over, put his left hand on his knee, rested his chin on his right hand and listened attentively. When the song ended, he waved his hand toward *Zi Gong* and *Zi Lu*. Both of them approached him:

"Who is he?" asked the old man, pointing to Confucius.

"He is the Sage of *Lu*," said *Zi Lu*.

"What is his name?" asked the old man.

"His name is *Kong*," said *Zi Lu*.

"And what does this *Kong* do?" asked the old man.

"He strives," said *Zi Gong*, "to revive sincerity, loyalty, goodness and fairness, rites and music, for the greater good of the principality of *Lu* and of the empire."

"Is he a prince?" asked the old man.

"No," said *Zi Gong*.

"Is he a minister?" asked the old man.

"No," said *Zi Gong*.

The old man smiled and withdrew. *Zi Gong* heard him mutter:

"Goodness, fairness! It is very nice, no doubt, but he will be lucky if he does not lose at this game. In any case, the worries and troubles he takes, by wearing out his mind and body, will impair his true perfection. How far he is from the science of the Principle!"

Zi Gong reported these words to Confucius, who quickly put away the zither from his lap, stood up and said:

"He is is a Sage," and went down to the bench to ask the old man for an interview. The latter was pushing the gaff of his boat to undock it. When he saw Confucius, he stopped and turned to him. Confucius approached and greeted.

"What do you want from me?" asked the old man.

"You have just spoken words whose meaning I do not understand," said Confucius. I respectfully beg you to instruct me for my own sake.

"That wish is most praiseworthy," said the old man.

B. Confucius prostrated himself, then, having risen, said:

"From my youth until this age of sixty-nine years (the penultimate year of his life), I *Qiu* have studied unceasingly, without being instructed in the supreme science (Daoism). Now that I have the opportunity, judge with what enthusiasm I will listen to you."

The old man said:

"I do not know whether we shall get along well; for the common law is that only get along those whose feelings are similar. In any case I will tell you my principles, and apply them to your conduct… You concern yourself exclusively with the affairs of men. The emperor, the lords, the officers, and the plebeians, these are your interests; let us talk of them. You intend to admonish these four types of men, to force them to behave well, the final result being a perfect order, in which all will live happily and contentedly. Will you really succeed in creating a world without evils and complaints? It is enough, to distress the plebeian, if his field does not yield, if his roof leaks, if he lacks food or clothing, if a new tax is imposed on him, if the women of the house quarrel, if the young men disrespect the old. Do you really expect to get rid of all these things? Officers complain about the difficulties of their duties, about their failures, about the negligence of their subordinates, about their merits not being recognized, about their failure to advance. Can you really change all this? The lords complain about the disloyalty of their officers, about the rebellions of their subjects, about the clumsiness of their craftsmen, about the poor quality of the royalties paid to them in kind, about the fact that they often have to present themselves at court with their hands full and that the emperor is not happy with their gifts. Are you really going to put an end to all this? The emperor laments the disorders of *yin* and *yang*, cold and heat, which harm agriculture and make the people suffer. He laments the quarrels and wars of his feudatories, which have cost the lives of many men. He laments that regulations on rites and music are badly observed, that his finances are depleted, that relations are little respected, that the people behave badly. How are you going to eliminate all these disorders? Do you have the capacity, the power, to do it? You who are neither emperor, nor lord, nor even minister; a mere private individual, you intend to reform humanity. Before seeing your dream realized, you would have to free men from the eight manias that I am going to enumerate: the mania of meddling in what does not concern one; the mania of speaking without prior consideration; the mania of lying; the mania of flattery; the mania of denigrating; the mania of sowing discord; the mania of giving friends a false reputation; the mania of intriguing and insinuating. Are you a man who can put an end to all these vices? And the four following abuses: the prurience to innovate in order to become famous; the usurpation of the merit of others in order to advance oneself; the stubbornness in faults in spite of admonitions; the obstinacy in ideas in spite of warnings; will you change all these? When you have done so, then you can begin to expound your theories of goodness and fairness to men, with some chance that they will understand something of them."

C. With an altered face and sighing with emotion, Confucius bowed in thanks for the lesson, rose and said:

"I may be a utopian, but I am not an evil one. Then why am I so universally reviled, persecuted and expelled? What is it that brings me all these evils? I do not understand."

"You understand nothing," said the old man in amazement; "you really are very limited. It is your mania for taking care of everyone and everything, for posing as a censor and universal teacher, that is causing you these tribulations. Listen to this story: A man was afraid of the shadow of his body and the trail of his footsteps. To get rid of them, he began to run away. But the more steps he took, the more footprints he left; no matter how fast he ran, his shadow would not leave him. Still, he thought he would eventually overtake them, and so he ran so fast that he died. The fool! If he had sat in a covered place, his body would not have cast a shadow; if he had remained still, his feet would have made no more footprints; he had only to remain at peace, and all his ills would disappear... And you who, instead of keeping the peace, devote yourself to arguing about goodness and equity, about similarities and dissimilarities, about I don't know what idle subtleties, are you surprised by the consequences of this mania, do you not understand that it is by annoying everybody that you have attracted universal hatred? Believe me, from the day when you take care only of yourself and apply yourself to cultivate your natural background; from the day when, giving others what they deserve, you leave them in peace; from that day, you will no longer have any trouble. By refusing to see yourself, and by observing others too much, you attract all your misfortunes.

D. Discomposed, Confucius asked:

"What is my natural basis?"

"The natural basis," said the old man, "is the simplicity, sincerity and uprightness that each one brings with him when he is born. This alone influences men. No one is moved by the spurious verbiage, the tears, the outbursts, the pathos of an actor. True feelings are communicated to others without the artifice of words or gestures. It is because they emanate from natural depths, from native truth. From this basis are born all true virtues, the affection of parents and the piety of children, loyalty to the prince, communicative joy at feasts, sincere compassion at funerals. These feelings are spontaneous and have nothing artificial about them, whereas the rituals in which you pretend to enclose all the acts of life are a sham. The natural basis is the part which every man has received from universal nature. Its dictum is invariable. It is the only rule of conduct for the Sage, who despises all human influence. Fools do just the opposite. They draw nothing from their own basis, and are at the mercy of the influence of others. They do not value the truth that is in them, but share the frivolous and fickle affections of the vulgar. It is a pity, Master, that you have spent your whole life in lies, and have only heard the truth exposed so late."

E. Confucius prostrated himself, rose, saluted, and said:

"How happy I am to have met you, what a favor from heaven! Ah, master, do not consider me unworthy to become your servant, so that by serving you I may have the opportunity to learn more. Tell me, please, where you live. I will come and stay with you, so that I may complete my education."

"No," said the old man. "The saying goes: reveal the mysteries only to those who can follow you; do not reveal them to those who cannot understand them. Your prejudices are too inveterate to be curable. Look elsewhere. I leave you."

And as he said this, the old man turned his boat and disappeared with it among the green reeds.

F. Although *Yen Yuan* had prepared the chariot for the return journey, and *Zi Lu* held the reins, Confucius could not tear himself away from the shore. At last, when the wake left by the boat had been obliterated, when no noise from the gaff reached his ears, he decided, as if regretting it, to take his place in the chariot. *Zi Lu*, who was walking beside him, said to him:

"Master, I have served you for a long time. I have never seen you show so much respect and deference to anyone. You have always been haughty and disdainful when princes and lords received you and treated you as an equal. And now, before this old man leaning on his gaff, you have bent your back at right angles to listen to him, you have bowed before answering him. Was there not something excessive in this show of reverence? How was this old fisherman worthy of such demonstrations?"

Leaning on the railing, Confucius sighed and said:

"You are decidedly incorrigible; my teachings slip, without effect, over your too coarse mind. Listen to me, not to venerate an elder is to fail in the rites. Not to honor a Sage is to lack judgment. Not to bow to the virtue that shines in another is to do harm to oneself. Remember that, fool! And if this is true of all virtue, how much more is it true of the knowledge of the Principle, by which all that is subsists, whose knowledge is life and ignorance death. To conform to the Principle gives success, to oppose it is certain ruin. The duty of the Sage is to honor the science of the Principle wherever he finds it. Now this old fisherman has it. Could I not honor it as I did?"

Chapter 32 - Wisdom

A. *Lie Yukou* (*Lie Zi*) was on his way to *Qi* when he returned halfway. He met *Bo Hun Wu Ren* who asked him:

"Why are you coming back this way?"

"Because I was afraid," said *Lie Yukou*.

"Afraid of what?" said *Bo Hun Wu Ren*.

"I went into ten soup kitchens," said *Lie Yukou*, "and five times I was served the first."

"And you were afraid," said *Bo Hun Wu Ren*, "of what?"

"I thought," said *Lie Yukou*, "that in spite of my strict incognito, my qualities were undoubtedly shown through my body. For how else could I explain this deference on the part of such vulgar people? If I had made it as far as *Qi*, perhaps the prince, also knowing of my ability, would have entrusted me with the care of his principality, which is wearing him out. It was this possibility that frightened me and made me retrace my steps."

"That is well thought out," said *Bo Hun Wu Ren*, "but I fear that will be repeated when you return to your home."

In fact, soon after, *Bo Hun Wu Ren*, who had gone to visit *Lie Yukou*, saw a quantity of shoes before his door. He stopped, rested his chin on the end of his cane, thought for a long time and withdrew. However, the doorman had warned *Lie Yukou* of his presence, who, without taking the time to put them on, grabbed his sandals and ran after his friend. After catching up with him at the outer door, he said:

"Is this how you leave without giving me any advice?"

"What's the use now?" said *Bo Hun Wu Ren*. "Didn't I warn you that it would be repeated at your home? I know you have done nothing to attract all those people, but you have done nothing to drive them away either. Now that you have given yourself over to dissipation, what good would my advice do you? No doubt your visitors will benefit from your qualities, but you will suffer from their conversation. Such people will teach you nothing. The talk of the vulgar is poison, not nourishment, to a man like you. Of what use is intimacy with people who feel and think differently? It is usual for the skilled to wear out, for the learned to tire, like you. And for whom? For frivolous beings who only know how to take a walk among their meals, wandering adventurously like a ship that has set sail and is going down the drain, occasionally buying themselves a conversation with a Sage to distract their boredom."

B. A certain *Huan* of the *Zheng* principality, after reading the official books for three years, was promoted to scholar. This promotion made his whole family famous. To prevent his younger brother from overshadowing him, the new scholar made him embrace the doctrines of *Mo Zi*. As a result, the two brothers argued constantly, and the father argued for the younger brother against the elder, so that there was a perpetual quarrel at home. After ten years of this life, *Huan* could stand it no longer and committed suicide. The animosity of father and brother survived his death. They did not visit his grave, nor did they make offerings to him. One day *Huan* appeared in a dream to his father and said:

"Why do you resent me so much? Was it not I who made your second son a follower of *Mo Zi*, whose doctrine you love so much? You ought to be grateful to me!"

Since then, *Huan* received his offerings.

This shows that the author of men (the Principle), does not so much reward their intentions, as the fulfillment by them of destiny. *Huan*, in making his brother a follower of *Mo Zi*, was carried away by a feeling of base selfishness, like those who forbid others to drink water from their well. However, in doing so, he did the right thing, for fate willed that his brother should become a follower of *Mo Zi*, and all that followed from that. Thus *Huan* escaped punishment from heaven, as the ancients said. His action was imputed to him, but his intention was not.

C. The wise man differs from the common man in that he keeps quiet and avoids what may disturb him. The vulgar man does the opposite, seeks trouble and avoids peace.

"For one who has known the Principle, it is still necessary to avoid talking about it, which is difficult, says *Zhuang Zhou*. To know and not to speak is perfection. To know and speak is imperfection. The ancients tended to perfection. *Zhu Pingman* learned from *Zhi Liyi* the art of dragon slaying. He paid a thousand taels for the recipe, his entire fortune. He practiced for three years. When he was sure of his business, he didn't do or say anything."

"Then what's the point? When one is capable, it is necessary to prove it, says the vulgar…"

The Wise Man never says "it is necessary".... From this are born troubles, wars and ruins.

Entangled in multiple details, embarrassed by material concerns, the mediocre man cannot tend towards the Principle of all things, towards the great incorporeal Unity. To the superior man it is reserved to concentrate his energy in the study of that which was before the beginning, to enjoy in the contemplation of the dark and indeterminate primordial being, such as it was when only the formless waters existed, gushing forth in unmixed purity. O men, you study the wisps of straw, and are ignorant of the great repose (in the general science of the Principle).

D. A certain *Cao Shang*, a politician of *Song*, was sent by his prince to the king of *Qin*. He set out with a rather modest crew and returned with a hundred wagons, laden with gifts received from the king of *Qin*, whom he had greatly pleased. He said to *Zhuang Zhou*:

"I would never dare to live like you in a village alley, ill-clad and ill-shod, thin and emaciated from hunger and misery. I prefer to court princes. This has brought me another hundred carloads of gifts."

Zhuang Zhou replied:

"I know the price of the king of *Qin*. To the surgeon who opens an abscess, he gives one cartload of gifts; to the one who licks his hemorrhoids, he gives five cartloads. The more vile the service rendered to him, the better the pay; what could you have done to him, to receive even more than the one who licks his hemorrhoids? Out of my presence!"

E. Duke *Ai*, of *Lu*, asked *Yen He*:

"If I were to make *Zhong Ni* (Confucius) my prime minister, would my duchy be all right?"

"I would be in great danger," said *Yen He*. "*Zhong Ni* is a man of small details (a painter of fans), a fine talker, who dresses to please, who flutters to make an effect. He only admits his own ideas, and only follows what is in his imagination. What good, then, could he do your people? If you made him a minister, you would soon regret it. It is not good to lead people away from the truth and teach them falsehood. And so, in what he does, this man seeks his own advantage. To act like this is not to act like heaven, so it benefits no one. If you were to introduce a merchant into the hierarchy of your officers, public opinion would be offended. It would be even more offended if you made this dealer a minister of politics. This man will not succeed in anything, and will not end well. There are external crimes, which the executioner punishes. There are inner crimes (Confucius' ambition), which *yin* and *yang* punish (the wasting away of the body, premature death). Only the Sage escapes penal sanction."

F. Confucius said:

"The human heart is more difficult to approach than mountains and rivers; its feelings are more uncertain than those of heaven. For heaven has outward motions, by which its intentions may be conjectured; while the exterior of man does not betray, when it does not wish to do so, his inward feelings. Some seem upright, while they are passionate; some seem frustrated, while they are skillful; some seem simple, while they are full of ambition; some seem firm, while they are too flexible; some seem slow, while they are hasty. Some who seem thirsty for righteousness, fear it as fire. Therefore, the Sage never trusts appearances. He puts men to the test; near him, to assure their reverence; on a distant mission, to assure their fidelity. By entrusting them with matters to discuss, he realizes their talent. By asking unexpected questions, he realizes their knowledge. By assigning them a date, he is aware of their accuracy. By enriching them, he knows their charitable spirit. By exposing them to danger, he tests their composure. By getting them drunk, he discovers their inner feelings. By bringing them in contact with women, he tests the degree of their continence. The above nine tests distinguish the superior man from the vulgar man[107]."

G. When *Kao Fu* the Righteous received his first post, he bowed his head; before the second, he bent his back; when a third was imposed on him, he fled; this is a good model. Vulgar men do things differently. At their first post, they raise their heads; at the second, they put on great airs in their chariot; at the third, they begin to speak contemptuously of those who are superior to them in kinship or age; the ancients never did that.

There is nothing more fatal than self-serving conduct, with intrigues and ulterior motives.

Nothing ruins so much as the admiration of one's own works, combined with the depreciation of those of others.

Eight things, which seem advantageous, are ruinous; namely, to excel in beauty, beard, height, corpulence, strength, eloquence, courage and audacity. Three things, which appear to be defects, on the contrary usually bring fortune; namely, lack of character, indecision and timidity. Six things fill the mind with thoughts, memories and worries; namely, affable trade which creates friends, violent conduct which makes enemies, concern for goodness and fairness which fills with distractions, care for health which breeds hypochondria, intercourse with scholars which gives a taste for study, intercourse with the great which awakens ambition, and the company of vulgar men which makes one want to take every opportunity to do one's own business.

H. A politician in search of a master to serve, having courted the king of *Song*, had received ten chariots of gifts, which he showed to *Zhuang Zhou* with childish ostentation. *Zhuang Zhou* said to him:

"On the banks of the river, a poor family lived pitifully weaving mats, (a very unprofitable trade). After diving into the water, the son of the family pulled out a

---

107   Cautious, cunning, and meticulous Confucianism. For the Daoist, it is union with the Principle that makes man superior, with consequent broadmindedness.

pearl worth a thousand taels. When his father saw it, he said to him: Quick, take a stone and break it! Pearls of this size can only be found at the bottom of the abyss, under the chin of the black dragon. When you took it, the dragon was probably sleeping. When it wakes up, it will look for it, and if it finds it here, it will be our undoing… But the kingdom of *Song* is also an abyss, and its king is worse than the black dragon. No doubt he was distracted when you got hold of those ten carts of pretty things. If he changes his mind, you will be crushed."

I. A prince invited *Zhuang Zhou* to be his minister, and the latter replied to the envoy:

"The ox[108] destined for sacrifice is clothed in embroidered cloth and receives choice fodder. But one day it is taken to the great temple (to be sacrificed there). At that time, he would rather be the commonest ox in the last of the pastures. So it is with the ministers of princes. Honors first, disgrace and death in due course."

J. When *Zhuang Zhou* was about to die, his disciples expressed the intention of contributing to his having a more decent funeral.

"None of that!" said the dying man. "I shall have enough with heaven and earth as a bier, the sun, moon and stars as jewels (they used to put them on the coffins), and all nature as a procession. Can you give me something better than this great luxury?"

"We will not leave your corpse unburied, to be preyed upon by crows and vultures," said the disciples.

"And to avoid this fate," said *Zhuang Zhou*, "you will bury it for the ants to devour. Is it right to deprive the birds of it and give it to the insects?"

With these supreme words, *Zhuang Zhou* showed his faith in the identity of life and death, his contempt for all vain and useless conventions. What is the sense of trying to level what is not flat? What is the sense of keeping up appearances? What proportion have rites and offerings to the mystery of the beyond? The senses are only sufficient for superficial observation; the mind alone penetrates and convinces. The vulgar, however, believe only what they see with their eyes and do not use their minds. Hence the vain rituals and false pretensions, for which the Sage feels only contempt.

CHAPTER 33 - VARIOUS SCHOOLS

A. Different authors have invented many recipes for governing the world, each giving his own as the most perfect. But it turned out that all of them were insufficient. There is only one effective procedure: let the Principle act, without frustrating it. It is everywhere, it permeates everything. If transcendent influences descend from heaven and rise from earth, if Sages are produced, it is thanks to it, immanent in the universal whole. The closer his union with Principle, the more perfect is man. The higher degrees of this union make celestial men, transcendent

---

108   Compare with the turtle, chapter 17 E.

men, superior men. Then come the Sages, who speculatively know that heaven, the sensible manifestation of the Principle, is the origin of everything; that its action is the root of everything; that everything comes out of the Principle, by way of evolution, and returns to it. Finally, the princes apply these ideas in practice, by their beneficent kindness, their rational equity, the rites that regulate conduct, the music that produces understanding, a perfume of benevolence that pervades everything. Thus did the princes of antiquity, advised by their wise men. They distinguished cases and applied laws to them. They qualified and designated. They went deep into all things by consideration and examination. Finally, all clarified, they took regulated measures as one can count one two three four. Because the hierarchy of officials worked, business went on and they were concerned with the care of the people, the raising of livestock was encouraged; the old and the children, the orphans and the widows, became the object of great solicitude; everything that needed to be done reasonably for the common good was done. In taking this trouble, the ancients collaborated with the transcendent celestial and terrestrial influences, with the action of heaven and earth. They nourished the living, maintained peace, extended their benefits to all. From the perfectly sounded principles, they extracted varied applications, acting in all directions, on the most diverse beings. The ancient laws handed down from generation to generation, which are preserved in great number in the histories, testify to the theoretical and practical science of the ancients.

Then came the Odes, the Annals, the Rites, and the treatises on music, by the scholars of *Zou* and *Lu*, the official masters of the principalities. In their idea, the Odes are a code of morals, the Annals a repertory of facts, the Rites a rule of conduct, Music a means of producing concord, the Mutations a procedure for knowing the movements of *yin* and *yang*, the Chronicles a means of distinguishing true reputations from false ones. These writings, which spread from the central provinces to the whole empire, became the subject on which scholars exercised themselves.

Then came a time when the empire had fallen into great disorder and was devoid of great scholars, other principles were invented, discussions were started and everyone pretended to be right. It was like the discussion of the ears and eyes with the nose and mouth, which could never agree, for each sense was right, but only as to its own object. Thus the various schools have each its specialty, good in its time and place; but none of them embraces everything, nor has any right to exclude the others. How can a single scholar, lurking in a corner, presume to judge the universe and its laws, all that the ancients did and said? Who is qualified to set himself up as judge of things and of intelligences? Since the science of the Principle has fallen into oblivion, men no longer act except under the influence of their passions, the leaders of the various schools arrogate to themselves the right to judge and condemn everything and everyone. They lose sight of the primordial unity which had been the great rule of the ancients. With their different explanations, they divide what once was the single doctrine of the empire.

B. Let us first speak of the followers of *Mo Zi*. To pass on to future generations a morality of integrity, not to overindulge in luxury and ceremonies, to avoid by great moderation the conflicts of life, all these are rules of the ancients. *Mo Zi* and his disciple *Qin Huali* were passionately in love with them and consequently exaggerated them. They absolutely outlawed music. Under the pretext of economy, they reduced the rules of mourning to nothing. In the name of universal charity, *Mo Zi* ordered to do good to all, and forbade all disputes and all anger. He did not condemn science, but ordered that scholars should remain without distinction, in the same rank as the vulgar. In so doing, he offended the ancients and himself… His symphonies, whose titles have been preserved in history, are sufficient proof that the ancients esteemed music. That they wanted, at funerals, a luxury proportioned to the condition, is shown by their rules about coffins. Thus, when *Mo Zi* forbade all music and wanted all coffins to be identical, he offended the ancients. He also violated his own law of universal charity, for he violated human nature by forbidding singing and weeping, which are for man an indispensable natural relief. Is it charity to intend that man should suffer incessantly and stoically, and finally be summarily buried? No, surely not… So the theories of *Mo Zi* were not as successful as those of other Sages, because they wounded men's hearts, who rejected them… In vain *Mo Zi* appealed to the example of *Yu* the Great, who devoted himself stoically to the good of the empire during the long years he spent in channeling the land and delimiting the fiefdoms. His doctrine made no impression on men, who had no inclination to imitate the disciples of *Mo Zi* and ignored those disciples who dressed in coarse furs and cloth, wore clogs or coarse shoes, and devoted themselves without rest or relaxation, to perfecting themselves in suffering for the sake of the great *Yu*.

Moreover, if at first they did not get along with other people, soon the followers of *Mo Zi* did not get along with each other either. *Qin* of *Xiang Li, Ku Huo, Ji Chin, Deng Lingzi* and others each claimed to be the repository of *Mo Zi*'s true ideas, and they attacked each other. Like the sophists, they disserted on substance and accidents, on similarities and dissimilarities, on the compatible and the incompatible. Their more able disciples founded as many small sects, which they hoped to make enduring. Their discussions continue to this day.

In short, the intentions of *Mo Zi* and *Qin Huali* were good, but they were wrong in practice. The obligation they imposed on everyone to surrender and sacrifice in the extreme would have produced, if it had found an echo, something superior to vile selfishness, but inferior to the natural system (do nothing and do not intervene). However, honor to *Mo Zi*! He was the best man in the empire. Although his efforts were unsuccessful, his name should not be forgotten. He was a talented scholar.

C. Let us now speak of the school of *Song Xing* and *Yin Wen*… Despise vulgar prejudices, avoid all luxury, offend no one, keep peace for the happiness of the people, possess no more than you need, keep your mind and heart free, all this the ancients did and said. *Song Xing* and *Yin Wen* made these maxims the basis of a new school, whose disciples wear a specially shaped cap to be recognized. They treated all men with kindness, whoever they were, believing that mutual support was the noblest of moral acts. This conduct, they thought, would win over all men and make them brothers, which was their chief aim. They accepted all outrages. They tried to pacify all disputes. They condemned all violence, especially the use of arms. Apostles of pacifism, they preached it everywhere, reprimanding the great and indoctrinating the small. Rejected, they were not discouraged. When they were rebuffed, they returned to the charge and ended up, by dint of insistence, getting people to listen to them.

In all this, there was undoubtedly some good, but also some error. These generous men forgot too much of themselves for the good of others. For the price of their services, they only accepted their food from those who deserved it. The result was that the teachers of the sect had to fast frequently. This did not frighten their young disciples, who were enthusiastic about devoting themselves to the common good, saying to themselves:

"Why should I not sacrifice my life, as my teacher did, for the salvation of the world?"

They were good people, they criticized no one, they harmed no one, they only despised the selfish who did nothing for the public good. They not only forbade war, but, rising above it, they discovered the cause in appetites and lust, and the remedy in temperance and self-denial. But they stopped there, and in their speculations did not know how to rise to the Principle (departing from their just deductions). They were aborted Daoists.

D. Let us speak now about the school of *Peng Meng, Tian Pian, Shen Dao* and others… Impartiality, altruism, patience, condescension, tranquility, indifference towards science, charity towards all, all this was practiced by the ancients. *Peng Meng* and his disciples made these maxims the basis of their doctrine. They postulated, as a first principle, universal union. Each one, they said, needs the others. The sky covers, but does not support; the earth must therefore help it. The earth bears, but does not cover; therefore, heaven must help it. No being is sufficient for itself, nor is it sufficient for everything. Like heaven and earth, the great doctrine must embrace everything and exclude nothing. in harmony, by mutual accommodation and tolerance.

Therefore, *Shen Dao* declared war on all selfishness, on all individualism, on all coercion of others. He demanded perfect selflessness in relationships. He declared all science useless and dangerous. He mocked the world's esteem for the intelligent, and its infatuation with the wise. Without definite theoretical principles, he accommodated everyone and everything. Distinctions of right and wrong, of lawful and unlawful, did not exist for him. He accepted no advice from anyone, took no precedent into account and ignored all counsel. To act, he waited for an external influence to set him in motion; just as a feather waits for the wind to lift it to fly, and a millstone waits to be turned to grind… *Shen Dao* was right and wrong. He was right when he condemned science, because it breeds doctrinal stubbornness, superfluous opinions, cliques and parties. He was wrong, and rightly laughed at, when he demanded that men should make no more use of their intelligence than a clod of earth. Taken to this degree of exaggeration, his system was more suitable for the dead than for the living.

Tian Pian held the same error, having been, like *Shen Dao*, a disciple of *Peng Meng*, whom he regarded as his master. This teacher was the cause of their believing that the ancients had not risen above the practical denial of the distinction between good and evil, between reason and evil; for he omitted to teach them that they denied this distinction because they had discovered the primordial unity. Now, since if one does not rise to unity, it is not possible to realize non-distinction, the fact that *Peng Meng* and his followers denied the distinction without giving proof, brought them into conflict with all others. Their doctrine was incomplete, flawed. However, they had some idea of the Principle and approached Daoism.

E. Let us now speak of the school of *Guan Yin Zi* and *Lao Zi*... To seek pure causality in the invisible root of sentient beings, and to regard these sentient beings as gross products. To regard their multitude as less than their Principle. To remain recollected in mind in emptiness and solitude. These are the maxims of the ancient masters of the science of the Principle. These maxims were propagated by *Guan Yin* and *Lao Dan*. They gave them a firm foundation in the pre-existence of the indeterminate infinite being, the union of all in the great unity. From the principle of being, of universal union, they deduced that the rules of human conduct should be submission, acquiescence, not wanting and not acting, letting go so as not to harm.

Guan Yin said:

"To him who is not blinded by his interests, all things appear in their truth. The movements of this man are natural like those of water. The repose of his heart makes him a mirror in which everything is concentrated. He responds to every event as an echo responds to sound. He withdraws, he fades away, he accommodates himself to everything, he wants nothing for himself. It takes precedence over no one, but insists on always being last."

Lao Dan said:

"Preserving your masculine energy, submit yourself as the female. Become the confluence of waters. Being perfectly pure, accept to appear not to be. Put yourself on a level with the world. While everyone desires to be first, wish to be the last, like the refuse of the empire. While everyone desires abundance, prefer destitution, seek deprivation and isolation. Do not spend yourself, do not interfere. Laugh at those whom the vulgar call intelligent. Regard nothing in yourself as meritorious, but be content to be blameless. Always rejoice in the Principle and respect its laws. Avoid even the appearance of strength and dexterity, for the strong are broken and the sharp are dulled by their enemies and the envious. Be broad and friendly to all. This is the apex." — O *Guan Yin*; O *Lao Dan*, you are the greatest men of all ages!

F. Let us now speak of *Zhuang Zhou*... All the ancient Daoists were concerned with the dark and indistinct primeval being, with its alternate mutations, with the two states of life and death, with the union with heaven and earth, with the outgoing of the spirit, with its comings and goings. *Zhuang Zhou* took up these themes and made them his delight. He spoke of them, in his own way, in original and daring terms, freely but without causing a schism. Considering that men hardly understand abstract explanations, he resorted to allegories, to comparisons, to the staging of characters and to the repetition of the same theme in various forms. Neglecting minor details, he focused on the crucial point of the union of the spirit with the universe. To avoid unnecessary discussion, he neither approved nor disapproved of anyone. His writings, full of verve, do not offend. His words, full of originality, are serious and worthy of attention. Everything he says makes sense. Two theses in particular had his preference, namely, the nature of the author of beings (the Principle), and the identity (successive phases) of life and death. He spoke about the origin, with breadth and freedom; and about the ancestor (the Principle), with breadth and elevation. His arguments on the genesis of beings and cosmic evolution are rich and solid. He plays in the unfathomable obscurities.

G. Let us now speak of the sophist *Hui Shi* (*Hui Zi*)... He was a man of fertile imagination. He wrote enough to load five wagons (in those days they wrote on wooden slats). But his principles were false, and his words were meaningless. He argued like a rhetorician, supporting or refuting paradoxical propositions such as these: The great unity is that which is so large that there is nothing outside; the small unity is that which is so small that there is nothing inside. The smallest is a thousand stades in extent. Heaven is lower than the earth; the mountains are flatter than the marshes. The sun in its fullness is the setting sun. A being can be born and die at the same time. The difference between a great and a small resemblance is the small resemblance-difference; when beings are totally alike and totally different, it is the great resemblance-difference. The limitless South is bounded. I went to *Yue* today and came back yesterday. The united rings are separable. The center of the world is north of *Yen* (north country) and south of *Yue* (south country). Love all beings, unite with heaven and earth.

Hui Shi loved these discussions, which earned him a reputation as a skilled sophist throughout the empire. In his imitation, others practiced the same jousting. Here are some examples of his favorite topics: An egg has hair. A rooster has three legs. *Ying* holds the empire. A dog can be called a sheep. Horses lay eggs. Fingernails have tails. Fire is not hot. Mountains have mouths. The wheels of a cart do not touch the ground. The eye does not see. The finger does not reach its object. The end is not the end. The turtle is longer than the snake. The set square not being square, the compass not being round, cannot draw squares and circles. The mortise does not hold the tenon. The shadow of a flying bird does not move. An arrow that hits the target does not advance and does not stop. A dog is not a dog. A brown horse plus a black ox is three. A white dog is black. An orphan foal has not had a mother. A length of a foot, which is reduced daily by half, will never be reduced to zero.

On these and similar topics these sophists argued throughout their lives, never running out of words. *Huan Duan* and *Gongsun Long* were noted for giving false impressions, sowing doubts, putting people on the spot, but without ever convincing anyone of anything, only wrapping their patients in the web of their fallacies, triumphant when they saw that they could not unravel them. *Hui Shi* spent all his time and intelligence in inventing paradoxes more subtle than those of his emulators. This was his glory. He knew he was very strong, and willingly claimed to have no equal in the world. Unfortunately, while he had the upper hand, *Hui Shi* was not right… One day, an intelligent southerner named *Huang Liao* asked him to explain why the sky did not fall, why the earth did not sink, why it was windy, raining, thundering, and so on. Gravely and bravely, *Hui Shi* undertook to satisfy this joker. Without a moment's thought, he began to talk and talk and talk, never taking a breath, never getting anywhere. To contradict was his happiness, to silence was his triumph. All the sophists and rhetoricians feared him… Poor man! His strength was only weakness, his path was narrow. His prodigious activity was only, for the universe, the buzzing of a mosquito, a useless noise. If he had used his energy to advance toward the Principle, how much better it would have been! But *Hui Shi* was not a man to find peace in serious considerations. He scattered himself in vain efforts and was only a verbose rhetorician. He did the opposite of what he should have done. He shouted to silence the echo and ran to catch up with his shadow. Poor man!

Subject Index

THE PRINCIPLE

Acts without acting: Zhu 25 j.
Author, motor, pivot, fixer of all: Lao 1 b, 4. — Zhu 2 b, 6 e, 14 a, 22 b, 23 e f.
Ineffable, unnameable, immutable: Lao 1 a, 5 d, 14, 21 b, 25, 32 a, 62, 70. - Lie 1 f. - Zhu 6 d i, 11 f, 12 a b c, 13 a g, 25 j.
Known by abstraction, not by effort: Lie 2 a. — Zhu 17 a, 22 a f g h i, 24 d m.
Non-produced: Lie 1 a b d.
The sea, image of the Principle: Zhu 12 l.
Universal mother: Lao 6. — Lie 1 b.
Universal norm: Zhu 2 b, 25 b.

THE VIRTUE OF THE PRINCIPLE

Beings: Lie 1 b, 1 c. **Real unit**: Zhu 23 e.
Apparent distinction: Lie 1 b, 3 a, 3 b, 3 c. **Snag and smoke**: Zhu 23 e.
Cosmic periods: Lie 1 n.

Evolution; the chain of transformations; revolutions: Lie 1 f, 1 m, 1 c, 1 g. — Zhu 6 c, 6 e f h, 18 b d, 21 k, 22 e k, 23 e, 25 j.
Its expansion: Lie 1 b. — Zhu 12 a b c, 13 a g, 25 j.
Its unfoldment: Lao 14 b e, 21 a c d, 32 b, 34 a.
Matter: Lie 1 c.
Metempsychosis: Lie 1 i, 1 m.
Mystery of the origin: Lao 1 c. - Zhu 2 d, 12 h, 22 e k, 25 j.
Becoming: Zhu 14 c.
The cosmic craft: Lie 1 e. — Zhu 18 f.
The Heaven-Earth binomy: Lao 5, 79 d. - Zhu 6 f k, 13 c, 21 d. **Between the two, the bellows**: Lao 5 c.
Man: Lie 1 o, 1 g.
Transformism: Lie 1 e, 5 e. — Zhu 18 f.
Yin and yang, two modes, alternation, the wheel: Lao 42 a. - Lie 1 a, 1 d, 1 p, 2 b, 2 c. - Zhu 6 f, 11 a, 11 a, 14 c, 17 a, 19 g, 21 d, 22 b, 23 d, 25 j, 26 a, 32 e, 33 a.

THE GREAT WHOLE

All is one; the cosmos: Lie 1 b, 3 a b c. - Zhu 2 b, 6 e, 6 f, 17 a, 23 e, 25 b j.

All unreal distinctions: Lie 1 b, 3 a b c.

Continuity, cohesion, consonance: Lie h to 5 q. — Zhu 24 e.

Of music: Lie 5 j. Zhu 14 c.

Identity of opposites: Lao 2 a. — Zhu 2 b c e h, 17 a, 25 j.

Reciprocity between macrocosm and microcosm: Lie 2 c.

The Universe: Lie 1 n, 5 a b. — Zhu 25 j.

Union with the whole: Lie 2 k, 3 b, 4 b. - Zhu 1 e, 2a à e, 6 c f g j, 11 c d, 22 e, 27 d.

NATURE

Becoming a little child again: Lao 55. — Zhu 23 c.

Conservation of his nature and knowledge of the principle, make the superior man: Zhu 19 b, 20 f, 21 a, 21 d.

Natural basis, natural sense: Zhu 27 a b, 31 d.

Natural state: Lao 3, 65, 80. — Lie 2 j q. — Zhu 16 a, 29 a.

Pure, whole, calm: Lie 2 d e f....

Return to nature: Zhu 10 b c, 23 d, 27 d.

She alone is good and true: Zhu 8 a b e d, 9 tot, 19 j l, 21 g,

United with the cosmos: Lie 2 k, 3 b, 4 b. Zhu 19 j, 20 g, 21 j.... **...with the elements:** Lie 2 d... **...with water:** Lie 2 h i, 8 g. Zhu 19 i... **...with fire:** Lie 2 k... **...with animals :** Lie 2 j q, 2 g, 22 j.

ARTIFICIAL, CONVENTIONAL

Confucian goodness and equity: Lao 18, 19, 38. Zhu 8 b, d, 9 c, 10 b.

Its fatal consequences: Zhu 8 a, b, c, d, 9 a, 9 b, 9 c, 10 d, 11 a, 12 o, 13 b, e, 17 a, 25 g.

Its genesis: Lao 18, 19, 38. — Zhu 9c, 11b, 16a, 16b, 21b, 21e, 33a.

Natural Taoism, artificial Confucianism: Zhu 31 b c d, 32 f g.

AGAINST NATURE

And pure convention: tastes: Zhu 8 a. — **...virtues:** Zhu 8 a. — **...art:** Zhu 9 a. — **...sciences:** Lao 20 a, 20 e. — Zhu 25 h. — **...government:** Zhu 9b. — **...politics:** Lao 27. Zhu 9 c, 10 a, 29 b. ... **all rules or customs:** Zhu 17 a, 24 e. — **...all effort:** Lao 23.

THE SAGE

Abstinence of the heart: Zhu 4 a, 4 h, 6 h g, 7 c.

All efficacy comes from emptiness: Lao 11. — **...in him true happiness is found:** Lie 1 h, 1 l. Zhu 18 a.

Does not do violence to its own nature: Lie 7 b, 7 f g.

Does not wear himself out: Lao 10, 12, 13, 44, 52. — Zhu 3a b c, 15 b, 19 a, 19 k, 24 l.

Folds himself, adapts himself: Lie 8 a. — Zhu 6 h, 14 f, 20 a, 26 h.

Hates vulgarity and avoids the vulgar: Lie 2 m. — Zhu 6 b, 24 j, 32 a.

He does not impose on himself, but leaves all things free: Lao 2 c, 2 d, 10 g, 27 c, 34 a, 51 c. - Lie 4 c.

He smiles above all: 6 c.

His affable impassivity: Lao 33. — Zhu 5 a d, 6b, 21 i j, 26 c.

His cold altruism, his total charity: Lao 5 b, 49, 67, 81. Lie 2 q. Zhu 14 b, 31 c.

His disdainful disinterestedness, his systematic effacement, voluntary ob-

scurity: Lao 7 a b, 9 c, 13, 8 c, 24, 28, 40, 61, 66, 68 . 41 b c, 42 b, 54, 71, 72, 76, 77, 78. - Lie 2 n o p, 4 k, 8 i o p. - Zhu 20 b d, 27 f, 32 c.

His model is water: Lao 8 a b, 78.

His perfect abstraction, concentration and indifference: Lao 52, 56.... 20 d, 34 b, 50. — Lie 4 e g h h n, 81. Zhu 1 a c, 2 g, 3 b, 11 d, 19 a, 19 c , 19 d, 19 h, 20 b, 23 c g.

His non-acting government: Lao 17, 29, 37, 57, 63, 64. — Zhu 24 c.

His union with the Principle: Zhu 12i, 12k, 16b, 17a.

His way: Lao 15. Zhu 15 a b, 16 b, 19 e, 22 e, 23 b c, 26 h.

Its central view, its total science: Lie 4 h. — Zhu 2 c h, 5 e, 11 c, 25 b c, 32 c.

Its independence: Lao 56. — Zhu 14 e, 17 b, 17 e, 28 a to j, 29 c.

Its indulgent greatness: Lie 8 f.

Its non-action, letting go: Lao 10 d. 43, 48, 73. Zhu 7 f, 11 f, 12 l, 13 b, 25 c.

Its simplicity: Lao 39, 40. — Zhu 24 a.

Its transcendent inclusiveness: Lao 45, 47.

Never disputes: Lao 79. — Zhu 7 a, 20 h, 221, 26 e.

Recovers by breathing exercises: Lao 52 b. — Zhu 15 a.

Straw dogs: Lao 5. Zhu 14 d.

The attraction it exerts: Lao 22, 35.

The incapacity preserves: Zhu 1 f, 4 d à i, 20 a.

The sage abhors war: Lao 30, 31, 69.

PSYCHICAL STATES

Death of the heart: Zhu 21 c.

Dreams, wanderings of the soul: Lie 2 c ; ...real: Lie 3 d.

Ecstatic rapture and etherealization, its preparation: Lie 2 c, 3 a, 4 f. - Zhu 1 c, 2 a, 6 j, 7 c, 17 a, 21 d, 24 h.

Inner sight, made visible to others: Lie 2l. Zhu 7 e.

Peace of mind and speech is indispensable to attain the Principle; all passion and emotion makes one incapable: Lao 1 c, 20 c, 55. Lie 2 m. Zhu 12 n, 19 d. - ...repose of water and mind, Zhu 13 a.

Speaking without words: Zhu 27 a.

Suggestion: Lie 8 z. Zhu 19 g.

Unconsciousness, protective sheath: Lie 2 d, 3 f. - Zhu 19 h.

—

Destiny, fate: Lie 4 a, 6 a-i, 8 e j k. — Zhu 6 f g k, 24 j, 25 i, 26 a-f, 32 b.

Fortune and misfortune, phases: Lao 9, 36 a. — Lie 4 i. — Zhu 21 k.

Life and death, phases: Lao 16. - Lie 1 e f i k, 3 b,7 b c. - Zhu 2h, 6 b c, 12 b, 21 c d, 22 a, 27 d.

Repose in death: Lie 1 j, 7 e.

Self, personality, bundle of firewood: Zhu 2 j, 3 c, 6 c h, 21 c.

Survival? Soul? Shades? The faggot: Lao 10 a b, 33 b. — Lie 3 b. — Zhu 3 c, 6 d, 13 a-i, 18 d f, 20 b, 23 d, 27 d.

—

The Sovereign: Lao 4e. — Lie 5 b. — Zhu 1 a, 3 c, 6 c d, g.

The superior man: Lie 2 d. - Zhu 1 d e, 2 f, 6 g, 7 f, 13 g, 23 b, 23 c.

Transcendent men: Lie 2 b. - Zhu 11 e, 12 c. - His heavenly palace: Lie 3 a. — His islands: Lie 5 b. Zhu 1 d. The higher man: Lie 2 b. — Zhu 2 e, 12 c.

True Men: Zhu 6 b, 15 b.

—

Sophists and sophisms: Lie 2 r, 4 l. — — Zhu 17 g, 25 d, 33 g.

Systems: Zhu 33. — from Mo Zi: 33 b. — of Song Xing and

— of Guan Yin Zi and Lao Dan: Zhu 33 e. — of Zhuang Zi: 33 f. - of Hui Zi, sophists: 33 g.
Yin Wen: 33 c. - of Peng Meng, Tian Pian, Shen Dao: Zhu 33 d.

SINGLE ANECDOTES

Archery: Lie 5 n, Lie 8 b, Lie 2 e. Zhu 21 i.
Asbestos fabric: Lie 5 q.
Auto-suggestion: Lie 8 z.
Books, detritus of the elders: Zhu 13 i.
Dead deer in a dream: Lie 3 e.
Emperor Mu's puppets: Lie 5 m.
Exchange of hearts: Lie 5 i.
Giant tortoises: Lie 5 b.
Guao and Xiang, the rich and the poor: Lie 1 p.
Imagination and suggestion: Lie 3 h.
Oracle turtle captured : Zhu 26 f.
Sacrificial oxen: Zhu 32 i.
Sacrificial pigs: Zhu 19 f.
Sacrificed turtle: Zhu 17 e.
Sea turtle: Zhu 17 d.
Seabird: Zhu 18 e.
Smoke and soot : Zhu 23 e.
Specters ; Zhu 19 g.
Stealing from nature, stealing from others: Lie 1 p.
Confucius surrounded : Zhu 17 c, Zhu 20 d, Zhu 20 g, Zhu 28 h.
The autumn flood: Zhu 17 a.
The black pearl: Zhu 12 d.
The butterfly: Zhu 2 j.
The children of Han Dan: Zhu 17 d.
The crushed pearl: Zhu 32 h.
The fighting rooster: Lie 2 q.
The frog in the well: Zhu 17 d.
The island of the monkeys : Zhu 24 g.
The language of animals: Lie 2 q.
The magic sword: Lie 5 p.

The cream: Zhu 1 e.
Chaos operated: Zhu 7 g.
The pleasure of the fishes: Zhu 17 g.
The prescription against death: Lie 8 w.
The pumpkins: Zhu 1 e.
Violated corpse : Zhu 26 d.
The rich man and his servant: Lie 3 d.
The scrupulous: Lie 8 q.
The shadow and gloom: Zhu 2 i, Zhu 27 e.
The symphony of Huang Di: Zhu 14 c.
The three doctors: Lie 6 e.
The useless tree: Zhu 1 f, Zhu 4 d e f.
Counterbalanced ladle: Zhu 12 k, Zhu 14 d.
Universal folly: Lie 3 g.
Wise men of the West: Lie 4 c.

REPEATED ANECDOTES

Archery: Lie 2 e. Zhu 21 i.
Gift of grain for Lie Zi: Lie 8 d. Zhu 28 d.
Hunting cicadas : Lie 2 j. Zhu 19 c.
Lie Zi becomes popular: Lie 2 m. Zhu 32 a.
Lu Liang's waterfall: Lie 2 i, 8 g. Zhu 19 d.
Meeting of Lao Dan and Yang Zhu: Lie 2 n. Zhu 27 f.
The beautiful and the ugly : Lie 2 o. Zhu 20 i.
The death of Guang Zhong : Lie 6 c. Zhu 24 f.
The deceived seer : Lie 2 l Zhu 7 e.
The Fighting Cock : Lie 2 q. Zhu 19 h.
The monkey breeder : Lie 2 q. Zhu 2 e.
The Shang Rapids: Lie 2 h. Zhu 19 d.
The skull: Lie 4 e. Zhu 18 d. f.
Transformism : Lie 1 e. Zhu 18 f.

Index of Names

A

A He Gan: Zhu 22 g.

B

Bai Feng Zi: Lie 4 j.
Bai Gong: Lie B h,B z.
Ban Shu: Lie 5 m.
Bao Shu Ya: Lie 6 c. Zhu 24 f.
Bi Gan, prince, put to death by the tyrant Zhou in 1122 B.C. Lie 6 a. Zhu 4 a, 10a, 20 f, 26 a, 29 ab.
Bian Qing Zi: Zhu 19 m.
Bian Sui: Zhu 28 i.
Bo Changqian: Zhu 25 i.
Bo Gao Zi: Lie 2 c.
Bo Hun Wu Ren: Lie 1 a, 2 e m, 4 e. Zhu 5 b, 21 i, 32 a.
Bo Lao: Zhu 9 a.
Bo Li Xi: Zhu 21 f, 23 g.
Bo Ya, musician: Lie 5 l.
Bo Yi and Shu Qi, purists, died in 1122 B.C. Lie 6 a, 7 d. Zhu 6 b, B c, 17 a, 28 j, 29 a.

Bu Liang Yi: Zhu 6 e.

C

Cao Shang: Zhu 32 d.
Chang Ji: Zhu S a .
Chang Lu Zi: Lie 1 n.
Cheng, emperor, 1115-1079 B.C., son of Wu, nephew of Zhou Gong: Lie 7 j. Zhu 14 g.
Chi Zhang Man Ji: Zhu 12 m.
Confucius, 551-479 B.C.: Lie 1 h i j, 2 f r, 3 e f, 4 a b d, 5 g, 7 j, 8 h. Zhu 2 c, 4 a, 5 c d, 6 g, 9 b, 11 b, 12 i k, 13 e, 14 d e f g h, 17 a, 20 d e g, 21 b c d, 22 e k, 25 e, 26 e f, 27 b c, 28 f h, 29 a b, 31 a-f , 32 e f.

D

Dai Jinren, sophist: Zhu 25 d.
Dan Fu: Zhu 28 a.
Deng Ling Zi: Zhu 33 b.
Deng Xi, philosopher: Lie 4 j, 6 d, 7 f.
Dong Guo Zi Qi,: Zhu 27 d.
Dong Ye Ji, coachman: Zhu 19 k.

Duan Gan Sheng: Lie 7 g.
Duan Mushu: Lie 7 g.

E

E Lai: Zhu 26 a.
Er Han, singer: Lie 5 k.

F

Fei Wei, archer: Lie 5 n.
Fu Xi, legendary emperor of the fifth millennium B.C.: Lie 2 q, Zhu 4 a, 6 d, 10 c, 16 a, 21 j.
Fu Yue, minister: Zhu 6 d.

G

Gan Ying, archer: Lie 5 n.
Gao Bo Cheng: Zhu 12 g.
Geng Sang Chu: Zhu 23 a b.
Geng Sang Zi: Lie 4 b.
Gong Gong: Lie 5 a. Zhu 11 b.
Gong Hu: Lie 5 i.
Gong Sun Long, sophist: Lie 4 1. Zhu 17 d, 33 g.
Gong Sun Yen: Zhu 25 d.
Gong Yi: Lie 4 k.
Gong Yue Xiu: Zhu 25 a.
Guan Long Feng: Zhu 4 a, 26 a.
Guan Yin Zi: see Yin Xi.
Guan Zhong, Guan Yi Wu, Guan Zi, minister, seventh century B.C. Lie 5 f, 6 c, 7 a e. Zhu 18 e, 19 g, 24 f, 29 b.
Guang Cheng: Zhu 11 c.

H

He Xu: Zhu 9 c.
Hei Luan, assassin: Lie 5 p.
Hong Meng: Zhu 11 d.
Hu Bu Xie: Zhu 6 b.
Hu Zi, Master Lin or Hu Qiu: Lie 1 a, 21, 4 e g, 8 a. Zhu 7 e.
Hua Jie: Zhu 18 c.
Hua Zi, man with amnesia: Lie 3 f.

Huan Dou: Zhu 11 b.
Huan, Duke of Lu: Lie 2 q.
Huang Di, Yellow Emperor, founder of the Chinese Empire, probably towards 3000 B.C.: Lie 1 b f, 2 a q, 3 e, 5 c, 6 f. Zhu 6 d, 10 c, 11 b c, 12 d, 14 g, 16 a, 18 c e, 21 j, 22 a l, 24 c f, 29 a.
Hui Ang, father of Hui Zi: Lie 2 r.
Hui Zi, sophist: Zhu 1 e f, 2 d, 5 f, 17 f g, 18 b, 24 e, 25 d, 26 g, 27 b, 33 g.

J

Ji Chang, archer: Lie 5 n.
Ji Chi: Zhu 33b.
Ji Liang: Lie 4 i, 6 e.
Ji Tuo: Zhu 6 b, 26 j.
Ji Xian, seer: Lie 2 l. Zhu 7 e.
Ji Xing Zi, trainer: Lie 2 q. Zhu 19 h.
Ji Zhen: Zhu 25 j.
Ji Zi, prince: Lie 6 a. Zhu 6 b, 25 d, 26 a.
Jian Wu: Zhu 1 d, 6 d, 7 b, 21 j.
Jie Yu, the fool: Zhu 1 d, 4 h, 7 b.
Jie Zi: Zhu 25 j.
Jie, last Xia emperor, tyrant, dethroned in 1766 B.C. Lie 2 q, 7 c j, 8 a. Zhu 4 a b c, 11 a b, 17 a c, 22 e, 26 a, 28 i.
Jin, musician: Zhu 14 d.
Jiu Fang Yin: Zhu 24 j.
Ju Boyu: Zhu 4 c, 25 h.

K

Kan Pi: Zhu 6 d.
Kao Fu: Zhu 32 g.
Kong Qiu, Kong Zi, see Confucius.
Kong Zhou: Lie 5 p.
Ku Huo: Zhu 33 b.
Kuang Zhang: Zhu 29 b.
Kuang Zi, musician: Lie t j. Zhu 2 d, 8 a d.
Kui, known as Nan Bo: Zhu 6 e.

L

Lai Dan: Lie 5 p.
Lao Dan, Lao Zi: Lie 2 n p, 3 b g, 6 e, 7 i o. Zhu 3 c, 7 d, 11 b, 12 i, 13 e f g, 14 e f g h, 21 d, 22 e, 23 a c, 25 g, 27 f, 33 e. - Librarian: Zhu 13 e. - His departure for the West: Lie 3 b. - His death: Zhu 3 c.
Lao Lai Zi: Zhu 26 a.
Lao Shang: Lie 2 c, 4 f.
Li Ji: Zhu 2 f.
Li Zhu: Zhu 8 a d.
Lian Shu: Zhu 1 d.
Lie Zil, Lie Yukou: Lie 1 a n, 2 c e l m, 4 e f g, 8 a b c d. Zhu 7 e, 19 b, 21 i, 28 d, 32 a, 33 c.
Lin Hui: Zhu 20 e.
Lin Lei: Lie 1 i.
Lin of Hu Qiu: see Hu Zi.
Liu Xia Ji: Zhu 29 a.
Long Shu: Lie 4 h.

M

Man Gou De: Zhu 29 b.
Mao Qiang: Zhu 2 f.
Mao Qiu Yuan: Lie 2 g.
Men Wu Gui: Zhu 12 m.
Meng Sun Yang: Lie 7 h i, 8 t.
Meng Zi Fan: Zhu 6 g.
Mo Zi, Mo Di: Lie 2 r, 5 m, 7 i, 8 i. Zhu 2 c, 11 b, 8 a, 10 b, 12 o, 14 g, 29 b, 32 b, 33 b.
Mou of Zhong Shan: Lie 4 l. Zhu 28 g.
Mu, Duke of Zhu: Lie 2 q.
Mu, emperor, 1001-947 B.C.: Lie 3 a. 5 f m.

N

Nan Bo Zi Qi: Zhu 24 h.
Nan Guo Zi: Lie 4 e.
Nan Rong Zhu: Zhu 23 b c.
Nie Que: Zhu 2 f, 7 a, 12 e, 22 c, 24 k.
Niu Que: Lie 8 o.

Nu Yu: Zhu 6 e.
Nü Gua: Lie 2 q, 5 a.
Nü Shang: Zhu 24 a.

P

Pao Ba, musician: Lie 5 j.
Peng Meng: Zhu 33 d.
Peng Zai Yang: Zhu 25 a.
Peng Zu, lived eight centuries: Lie 6 a. Zhu 1 a, 6 d.
Pi Yi: Zhu 12 e, 22 c.
Pian Qiao, surgeon: Lie 5 i.
Pian, the wheelwright: Zhu 13 i.
Pu Yi Zi: Zhu 7 a.

Q

Qi Ying: Lie 5 i.
Qin Gu Li: Lie 7 g i.
Qin Huali: Zhu 33 b.
Qin Qing: Lie 5 k.
Qin Shi: Zhu 3 c.
Qin Zhang: Zhu 6 g.
Qing Ji: Zhu 20 c.
Qing, sculptor: Zhu 19 j.
Qiu Hu Fu, brigand: Lie 8 q.
Qiu: first name of Confucius.
Qu Bo Yu: Zhu 4 c, 25 h.
Qu Qiao: Zhu 2 g.

R

Ran Qiu: Zhu 22 k.
Ren Gongzi: Zhu 26 c.
Rong Cheng Zi: Zhu 25 c.
Rong Qi: Lie 1 h.

S

San Miao: Zhu 11 b.
Sang Hu: Zhu 6 g, 20 e.
Shan Bao: Zhu 19 e.
Shang Qiu Kai: Lie 2 f.
Shang Qiu Zi: Lie 4 k.
She, the collector: Zhu 20 c.

Shen Dao: Zhu 33 d.

Shen Nong, emperor, died in 3078 B.C. (?). Lie 2 q, 8 a. Zhu 10 c, 16 a, 18 e, 22 g, 28 j.

Shen Tu Di: Zhu 6 b, 26 j, 29 a.

Shen Tuo: Lie 5 p.

Shen Zi: Zhu 29 b.

Shi Cheng Qi: Zhu 13 f.

Shi Kuang, musician: Lie 5 j. Zhu 2 d, 8 a d.

Shi Qiu, lawyer: Zhu 8 a d, 10 b, 11 a b, 12 o, 25 i.

Shi Wen, musician: Lie 5 j.

Shi Xiang, musician: Lie 5 j.

Shu Shan: Zhu 5 c.

Shun, emperor, died in 2208 B.C. Lie 1 o, 7 a c j, 8 a. Zhu 2 e, 5 a, 7 a, 8 b c, 10 a, 11 b, 12 g j m, 13 a d, 14 b g, 16 a, 17 a c, 18 e, 20 e, 22 d 1, 23 a, 24 k, 25 d, 28 a i, 29 a b.

Song Xing: Zhu 33c.

Sun Shu Ao: Lie 8 n. Zhu 2 1 j, 24 i.

T

Tai Dou, coachman: Lie 5 o.

Tai Gong Diao: Zhu 2 5 j.

Tai Shi, legendary sovereign: Zhu 7 a.

Tang, emperor, overthrew the Xia, founded the Shang Yin dynasty, 1766-1754 B.C. Lie 5 a b, 8 a. Zhu 22 1, 23 g, 25 c, 28 i, 29 a b.

Tian Chang Zi: Zhu 10 a, 29 b.

Tian Gen: Zhu 7 c.

Tian Heng: Lie 6 a.

Tian Kai Zhi: Zhu 19 e.

Tian of Qi: Lie 7 a, 8 y.

Tian Pian: Zhu 33 d.

Tian Zifang: Zhu 21 a.

Tuo the Ugly: Zhu 5 d.

W

Wang Guo: Zhu 25 a.

Wang Ni: Zhu 2 f, 7 a, 12 e.

Wang Tai: Zhu 5 a.

Wei Sheng: Zhu 29 a b.

Wei Zi, prince: Lie 6 a.

Wen Zhi, doctor: Lie 4 h.

Wen, King Wen, father of Wu Wang and Zhou Gong: Zhu 1 4 g, 21 h, 29 a.

Wu Guang: Zhu 6 b, 26 j, 28 i.

Wu Ming Ren: Zhu 7 c.

Wu Xian Tiao: Zhu 14 a.

Wu Yuan: Zhu 26 a.

Wu Ze: Zhu 28 i.

Wu Zixu: Zhu 29 a b.

Wu, emperor, overthrew the Yin and founded the Zhou dynasty, 1122-1116 B.C. Lie 7 j, 8 a. Zhu 22 i, 28 j, 29 a b.

X

Xi Peng: Lie 5 f, 6 c.

Xi Shi: Zhu 14 d.

Xi Wang Mu, king or fairy: Lie 3 a. Zhu 6 d.

Xi Wei: Zhu 6 d, 22 l, 25 i, 26 h.

Xi Yong: Lie 5 f.

Xia Ji: Lie 5 a b f.

Xiao Yi: Zhu 26 a.

Xin Du Zi: Lie 8 t.

Xiong Yi Liao: Zhu 20 b.

Xu Wugui: Zhu 24 a b.

Xu You: Zhu 1 d, 6 i, 12 e, 24 k, 26 j, 28 a, 29 c.

Xuan, emperor, 827-782 B.C.: Lie 2 g q, 4 k. Zhu 19 h.

Xue Tan, singer: Lie 5 k.

Y

Yang Bu, brother of Yang Zhu: Lie 6 f, 8 u.

Yang Zhu, philosopher: Lie 2 n o, 4 i, 6 e f, 7 a b e d, 7 g-o, 8 s t u v. Zhu 7 d, 8 a, 1O b, 12 o, 17 c, 20 1, 27 f.

Yang Zi Ju: see Yang Zhu.

Yao, emperor, 2357-2286 B.C.: Lie 4 m, 7 a c. Zhu 1 d, 2 e, 4 a, 6 c, 10 a, 11 a b,

12 e f g j, 13 a d, 14 b g, 16 a, 17 a c, 18 e, 22 e, 23 a, 25 d, 28 a, 29 a b.

Yen Bu Yi: Zhu 24 g.

Yen Cheng Zi: Zhu 24 h, 27 d.

Yen He: Zhu 4 c, 19 e, 28 c, 32 e.

Yen Hui, the cherished disciple of Confucius: Lie 2 h, 3 f, 4 a d, 6 a. Zhu 4 a, 6 j, 14 d, 18 e, 19 d, 20 g, 21 c d, 22 1, 28 f h, 29 a, 31 f.

Yen Pingzhong: Lie 7 e.

Yen Shi, inventor of marionettes: Lie 5 m.

Yen Zi, philosopher: Lie 1 k, 6 h.

Yi Er Zi: Zhu 6 i.

Yi Ji: Zhu 25 a.

Yi Liao: Zhu 24 i.

Yi Yin, minister: Zhu 2 3 g, 28 i.

Yi, famous archer: Zhu 23 g.

Yin Sheng: Lie 2 c.

Yin Wen: Lie 2 d, 3 b, 4 n, 6 e, 7 i, 8 a b, 33 c.

Yin Xi, Guan Yin Zi: Zhu 19 b, 33 e.

Yong Cheng: Zhu 25 c.

Yu Ju, fisherman: Zhu 26 f.

Yu Qiang: Zhu 6 d.

Yu Xiong: Lie 1 m.

Yu, the Great, first Xia emperor, 2205-2198 B.C. Lie 2 q, 5 f, 7 i j. Zhu 2 b, 4 a, 12 g, 14 g, 20 e, 29 a, 33 b.

Yuan Feng: Zhu 1 2 1.

Yuan Xian: Zhu 28 f.

Yuan Xing Mu: Lie 8 q.

Yun Jiang: Zhu 11 d.

Z

Zao Fu, coachman: Lie 5 o.

Ze Yang, see Peng Zaiyang.

Zeng Shen, Zeng Zi: Zhu 8 a d, 10 b, 11 a b, 12 o, 26 a, 27 c, 28 f.

Zhan He: Lie 5 h, 8 m. Zhu 29 a.

Zhan Qin: Lie 7 c.

Zhan Zi: Zhu 28 g.

Zhang Yi: Zhu 19 e.

Zhao Wen Zi: Zhu 2 d.

Zhao Xiang Zi: Lie 2 k, 8 i.

Zheng: Lie 1 o.

Zhi Li: Zhu 18 c.

Zhi Liyi: Zhu 32 c.

Zhi, the brigand: Zhu 8 c d, 10 a, 11 a b, 12 o, 29 a.

Zhong Ni, see Confucius.

Zhong Zi Qi, musician: Lie 5 1.

Zhou Gong, brother of Wu Wang: Lie 7 j. Zhu 28 j, 29 b.

Zhou, last Shang Yin emperor, tyrant, dethroned in 1122 B.C.: Lie 2 q, 6 a, 7 c j, 8 a. Zhu 14 j, 17 c, 26 a.

Zhu Li Shu: Lie 8 r.

Zhu Ping Man: Zhu 32 c.

Zhu Xian: Zhu 19 e.

Zhuan Xu: Zhu 6 d.

Zhuang Zi: Zhu 1 f, 5 f, 14 b, 17 d e f g, 18 b d, 20 a f h, 21 e, 22 f, 24 e, 25 f, 26 b g h l, 27 a b, 30 a b, 32 d h f. - His wife's death: Zhu 18 b. - His death: Zhu 32 j. - His panegyric: Zhu 33 f.

Zhun Mang: Zhu 12 l.

Zi Chan: Lie 7 f. Zhu 5 b.

Zi Gao: Zhu 4 b.

Zi Gong: Lie 1 i, 3 f, 4 a d, 7 d.

Zi Hua Zi: Zhu 28 b.

Zi Hua: Lie 2 f.

Zi Lai: Zhu 6 f.

Zi Lao: Zhu 25 f.

Zi Li: Zhu 6 f.

Zi Lu: Lie 4 d. Zhu 13 e, 17 c, 21 b, 25 e, 28 h, 31 a f.

Zi Qi: Zhu 24 h j, 28 e.

Zi Sang: Zhu 6 k.

Zi Si: Zhu 6 f .

Zi Xia: Lie 2 k, 4 d.

Zi Xu: Zhu 10 a.

Zi Yang: Lie 8 d. Zhu 28 d.

Zi Yu: Zhu 6 f .

Zi Zhang: Lie 4 d. Zhu 29 b.

www.ingramcontent.com/pod-product-compliance
Lightning Source LLC
Chambersburg PA
CBHW061139120626
46546CB00005B/1860